The Se  Beloved

A CLINICAL

INVESTIGATION

OF THE

TRAUMA

OF BIRTH

AND PRE-NATAL

CONDITIONING

NANDOR FODOR

Hermitage Press, Inc.   New York   1949

MANUFACTURED IN THE UNITED STATES OF AMERICA
AMERICAN BOOK—STRATFORD PRESS, INC., NEW YORK

ACKNOWLEDGMENT

The following chapters appeared in print prior to the publication of this volume:

Chapter 3. *In* The Journal of Nervous and Mental Disease, *June, 1945.*

Chapter 5. *In* Journal of Clinical Psychopathology, *October, 1945.*

Chapter 6. *In* Samiksa, *Calcutta, January, 1949.*

Chapter 7. *In* American Imago, *July, 1948.*

Chapter 8. *In* The Psychiatric Quarterly, *April, 1946.*

Chapter 9. *In* The American Journal of Psychotherapy, *April, 1948.*

Chapter 10. *In* American Imago, *July, 1947.*

Chapter 11. *In* American Imago, *December, 1948.*

Chapter 14. *In* The Psychiatric Quarterly, *January, 1949.*

Chapter 15. *In* Archives of Neurology and Psychiatry, *November-December, 1945.*

Chapter 16. *In* The American Journal of Psychotherapy, *January, 1947.*

Chapter 22. *In* The Psychoanalytic Review, *October, 1945.*

Chapter 26. *In* The Psychiatric Quarterly, *October, 1946.*

Special acknowledgments are tendered to my wife, Amalia I. Fodor, for the inspiration she furnished for this book, and to Mrs. Nancy Roodenburg for her valuable editorial suggestions.

FOREWORD

LIFE is a continuity which does not begin at birth; it is split up by birth. The result of this splitting is pre-natal amnesia, but there is also an unconscious persistent effort to re-establish the lost continuity by annulling the trauma of birth.

The understanding of this continuity of life is of fundamental importance. It reveals a biological foundation behind many forms of neurotic behavior, and thereby lightens the individual's burden of social responsibility for immoral and anti-social drives.

Demonstration of the biological character of an abnormal urge cancels the patient's resistance to the therapeutic effort and permits a speedy integration of personality. Birth Therapy might be a convenient term to describe the process.

While Freud claimed that "all anxiety goes back originally to the anxiety of birth," he failed to accept birth as a distinct traumatic event. Otto Rank made the first attempt to biologize psychoanalysis. His approach was philosophical; mine is clinical and independent of his claims.

The argument here unfolded is based on case histories from my own practice and is addressed to the average psychologically minded public. Although it is advisable to keep to the continuity, the chapters permit independent reading when the fundamentals adduced in the first two chapters have been grasped.

NANDOR FODOR

New York, May, 1949.

CONTENTS

Contents

BOOK II.

Return into the Womb

BOOK III.

Traumata of the Unborn

BOOK I.

The Trauma of Birth

1.

BIRTH OR DEATH

Birth is a change-over from one life to another. After nine months of peaceful development, the human child is forced into a strange world by cataclysmic muscular convulsions which, like an earthquake, shake its abode to the very foundations. As if carried on the crest of a wave, the child is dashed not once or twice but without cessation for hours or days against the rock of the pubic arch. No adult could survive a similar ordeal, but Nature decreed that the child should. In its shattering effect, birth can only be paralleled by death.

Although the two events appear to be distinct and separate, an essential similarity exists between them. Birth and death are interchangeable symbols for the unconscious mind. Nature itself made them association pairs comparable to winter and spring, sundown and sunrise.

In Egypt when the Pharaoh died he became a little child again. Noticing the oval shape of the dying sun, the ancient Egyptians conceived the notion that the sun travels in the underworld and is hatched in the east as a young sun: the flame of a flame. This poetic image suffers from the illusion that the sun goes down at a fixed point in space; but there is no sundown at the end of the horizon because the end of the horizon is a subjective perception. What is sundown to us is sunrise to the opposite hemisphere. An instinctive appreciation of this truth may be gleaned from legends in which the heroes of antiquity find a new life on the western shores of a sea which they traverse in the belly of a monster. West is not a place of sundown but the beginning of a new life.

Such cosmic analogies no longer satisfy the modern scientific mind. The constant renewal of nature is not a guarantee of continued individual identity after the change of death. We cannot be certain of an individual life after death, but we know for a fact that there was an individual life before birth—the pre-natal state.

The change from pre-natal to post-natal life involves an ordeal as severe as dying. For nine months the child has developed and lived in a most peaceful, satisfying and ideal atmosphere; it knows no other world but the quiet warmth and comfort of its mother's womb. Many children are born dead for no medically known reasons. They die from the shock of the experience, though possibly it could be argued that in some cases the maternal organism fails to provide them with the necessities of life.

Disregarding this possibility, we may state that the fear of death begins at birth. We have no conception of what death is until we experience it; but we have all experienced birth, and if the fear of annihilation had not been overwhelming, the experience would not have been barred from our infantile consciousness. Nature has seen to it that the memory should be repressed. Locked up in the depths of the unconscious mind is the terrific impact of birth, the violent adventure that uprooted our pre-natal world. Instinct may warn the child that the end of its world is at hand, but cannot prepare it for the complications that may arise during the process of birth. The change-over from nourishment through the mother's umbilical cord to post-natal alimentation and pulmonary oxygenation, the shock of hunger and pain, the daze and whirl of the first sensory reactions, particularly of sound and light, represent a maelstrom of bewildering experiences. The memory of these stupendous sensations vanishes like a stone sinking to the bottom of a pond; but the emotional charge of the experience is too intense for the submergence to be complete. We do not know what sort of nightmares newborn infants may have, but the nightmares that often follow surgical operations performed in anaesthetic sleep clearly indicate that dreams of terror do not necessarily originate from consciously acquired experiences. The birth symbolism of some of our nightmares is all too evident. Phobias and symptoms of sickness may speak with similar eloquence of the trauma of birth, in an attempt on the part of the psychic system to dispose of a very inconvenient interloper whose continued presence seriously interferes with our poise and happiness.

The two principal ways for the disposal of this pressure are: projection into the future on to death, or displacement on to something in the present outside ourselves. If we can fear something distant in time or something avoidable, there is no immediate threat to our safety. Death may be far away; high places, tunnels, caves and compressions in crowds may be avoided; water we can keep away from; bridges we need not always cross. The trouble is that neither projection nor displacement offers release, or even relief. The future may crowd back on the present and the fear of distant death may turn into an ever-present dread of immediate extinction. Further, displacement might be too costly as some forms of it result in too much incapacitation or embarrassment. It is difficult to carry on daily activities if we have an abnormal fear of riding in elevators or if we cannot stay in a strange bathroom without leaving the door wide open. Yet such are very frequent manifestations of the trauma of birth.

Many of the birth fear symbols are so universal that they can be recognized immediately. The most general dream fantasies in which the trauma of birth may manifest itself are: creeping through narrow openings; being rooted to the ground or sinking into mud or sand; being crushed or compressed; drowning; being sucked down by whirlpools or dragged under by crabs, sharks or alligators; fear of being devoured by wild animals or monsters; nightmares of suffocation or being buried alive; phobias of mutilation or of falling to one's death.

There are other, more remote, forms. In many cases the fear of insanity, the fear of the supernatural, the fear of rape or the fear of pregnancy can be traced to birth. It is the intensity of such fears that justified our attempts to probe for their origin in the very beginnings of life.

Any fear which we cannot rationalize and which we dare not face because we do not know its source and nature can change into panic, and panic is a condition similar to insanity. We fear insanity if the pressure of forgotten panicky experiences becomes so strong that it threatens to emerge into consciousness.

The fear of the supernatural is based on a similar threat of recollecting something incomprehensible, that does not fit into the ordered scheme of science and is too frightful to contemplate.

The fear of rape or child-bearing may be due to the "translation" * of the trauma of birth from its source in the mother's body on to the daughter's own genitalia. Birth is a genital event and an impending confinement almost inevitably mobilizes the memories of that distant period when the prospective mother herself was in the position of the child within her womb. Not suspecting that such a translation of affect can take place, the prospective mother may respond with morbid fears because of the emotions connected with her own birth which tend to rise into her consciousness. The result is the delusion that her life is in extreme danger because of the impending birth. The truth is that her life had been in danger, but this occurred at the time when she first saw the light of day. If the confusion caused by fear reaches the stage of panic, what appears to be an accident may occur, bringing about miscarriage; or symptoms of sickness may arise that demand an abortion.

Many unborn children are deprived of life because of this unfortunate state of the mother's mind. Sometimes the pressure is controlled by the intensity of the prospective mother's yearning for a child; sometimes it is alleviated by wishful dreaming. A woman repeatedly dreamed of having given birth to a litter of kittens. Upon being closely questioned, it was discovered that the dream was a fantasy of easy birth—cats do not suffer much in delivering their kittens. The dreamer wished for an equally easy time, and

---

* "Translation" is a psychoanalytic term which I introduce as more descriptive than displacement when affect is shifted from another person on to one's own body.

6

chose cats for the further reason that she dreaded the responsibility of caring for a newly born infant. She had observed that cats discharge their young from their care at an early date. As every dream is a powerful auto-suggestion, continued dreams of easy birth are likely to have a cumulative action in relieving pressure, provided their message of consolation is understood and accepted by the conscious mind.

Many birth dreams are of the recurrent type, sometimes merely repeating themselves, at other times assuming a variety of forms, but essentially expressing the same content. As a rule, the recurrence of a dream is a reliable indication that a severe shock is hidden behind the manifest story which the contents unfold.

Typical Birth Dreams

Here are a number of short dreams that can be considered more or less typical of the trauma of birth:

1. I am going through a very big house in which there is a huge stove. Every time I go into the room containing the stove, the door shuts behind me and I cannot get out that way. To get to mother, I have to crawl through a tiny arch-like hole in the stove. It looks too small for me to wriggle through. It frightens me.

2. I am in a street. I turn around and see thousands and thousands of people. I cannot go back that way. An archway is in front of me. It is beautiful and big, but as I approach it, it becomes lower and lower. Finally only a small opening remains, and I have to squeeze through with a terrible effort.

Both these dreams come from the same woman and are recurrent. The arch symbolism is obvious.

3. I have to crawl through a high window and find difficulty in doing so.

4. We were trapped in a house. The door led to a railway track and was useless. We were all saved in the end, but how is not clear.

7

5. *I was being lowered into the sea through a hole in the ground, which was full to the brim of water. Two things had to be done: I had to descend and I had to be slapped on the body.*

6. *Below the house a big door shut off a cave full of alligators and crawling things. I wanted to get away, but even at a distance I felt strain, as if I had gone through an ordeal.*

7. *I dreamed of a cave, the walls and ceiling of which collapsed on top of me. I used to dream of dark roads, along which I crept on my stomach.*

8. *I was screaming in my sleep. I was submerged in the sea and was being choked by an octopus.*

9. *Sleeping in a haunted house, I dreamed that something shapeless and formless pounced upon me and began to devour me alive.*

10. *Many horses and cows rushed out of doors and passed over me. I lay flat, trampled underfoot, crushed.*

11. *I was in a buggy; an elephant was attached to it, always follow-ing, and I was frightened that as it came closer it would step on me. Then we passed through a building, in which the floor-boards gave way. The dream recurred throughout my childhood.*

12. *I was running on railroad tracks and could not move away when the train was coming. It was catching up with me.*

13. *For several years a recurrent dream caused me great anxiety. In it I find myself on a high railroad trestle, hanging from a tie by the tips of my fingers and in immediate danger of falling into a watery abyss below. No train is approaching, but I am conscious of the rail-road tracks alongside.*

14. *I am stealing a ride on a train, hiding in the machinery. The train stops at a station and I am hanging on to one end of a cylinder. When the engine starts, I shall be carried into its bowels by the cyl-inder's revolution. I am afraid, so I drop off the train, meaning to catch it when it starts again. I run into a tunnel because the train goes underground, and the trainman sees me and chases me away.*

15. *I was pursued by cowboys on horseback. I was a cowboy also, but I stuck in the mud and awoke in fear.*

16. *As a child I had recurrent dreams of walking through large feather beds and sinking in. These dreams always exhausted me.*

17. *Indians chased me on horseback over clear ground. I was plowing through deep snow with great difficulty, trying to get into the woods to hide for fear of being scalped.*

18. *I am on a flat boat like a barge, going down a narrow river. The progress of the dream is a transition from darkness to light.*

19. *I am trying to get off a boat. I jump to the dock and fall into the water. I am wearing my skunk coat. Somebody reaches down a hand and pulls me up with great difficulty.*

20. *I went boating. We got into a whirlpool. I was in despair. I could not save myself.*

21. *I am in the belly of a ship. It is like a house. I hear a gurgling sound outside. The thought comes to me that my brother has cut his throat with my razor. I rush out and see that lava is about to engulf the whole ship. I am saved, but everything I had in the house is lost.*

22. *I was going either through a long passage or up some stairs or through a door; maybe I was doing all three things. Every step of the way was a struggle. I fought and pushed. I don't know whether I was too fat or whether something was holding me back. Finally I reached the top of the stairs. People were there watching me. One of them reached out a hand and helped me to squeeze myself up. I felt free when I got into the open.*

23. *The time was night, and I was floating towards an open house and up to a horseshoe-shaped upper floor. My wife was with me. Other people were in the house. The lower floor looked like a restaurant arranged for a gay party. I started towards the stairway with the idea of going down. A woman who took care of the place began to ascend the stairs and I was gripped with terror. She also was frightened at finding me there.*

24. I threw a handball and started chasing it. A man tried to stop me and was killed. I crawled through the underbrush. An earthquake occurred. I got back safely to my friends with the ball.

25. I went up a mountain, through bushes, to meet my brother halfway across. He was bringing me an important message. I was on all fours and something stung me in the face. I was climbing through a window.

26. I was coming down with an avalanche. I kept grabbing at twigs, but they broke and I could not check my descent.

27. I was walking across the bridge over the Donau Canal and the wind was pressing me against the railing. This was a recurrent dream.

28. I have to pass an examination, a severe test. The last stage is in the synagogue. A door on the right side of the main entrance leads to a staircase. As we go higher the stairway flattens into a coffin, the top of which opens on hinges. We have to squeeze through this box from below. The clearance is barely ten inches. I say that I am too fat—I could never get through. I am ready to give up. The others urge me to go through. Now the coffin disappears. In its place is a small, narrow bridge, without handrails, curving downwards. I take off my jacket and inch my way forward. I lie on my back, stretch, because I am afraid of falling, and give myself a sudden push, feet forward. It is too great a push, and I am afraid I shall plunge over the curve and fall. The two men who are with me grab me and pull me through. I pass the test.

29. I dreamed of eggs which hatched real babies. The babies were tiny. I spanked one of them on the behind. It did not cry.

The choice of stove, archway, cave, water-hole, trap-door, coffin, bridge, house, window, stairs, ship, whirlpool, octopus, locomotive, railroad trestle, stampeding animals, dark roads, mud, snow, feathers, underbrush, mountain, avalanche, riverbanks, park, and streams of water as symbols; or of the dynamic element represented by falling, floating, descending, and the opposite of being rooted to the ground or pressed against an obstacle—all these are purely individual but definitely connected with birth fears. Obviously the dream often reverses the process of birth. The dreamer may go or come, fall in or fall out, but whatever he does the emotion expressed is fear and trembling, gloom or moody resignation, never cheerfulness. The heroic element is absent.

The associations of the dreamer usually throw light on his choice of symbols. The man who is lowered into a water-hole by a pulley was fascinated in childhood by the daring of his older brothers, who, if the bucket of the well fell into the water, climbed down the slippery stone walls, clinging precariously to the projections and crevices with extended arms and legs. The man who dreamed of alligators in the cave under the house had a cruel father who accidentally hit his child's finger with a knife and almost completely severed it. The dreamer who is stuck in the mud as a cowboy was warned by his mother that if he fell into a ditch he would be sucked under. The woman with the skunk coat hated her mother's body and despised herself for hating her. The man who is being devoured in the haunted house is swallowed by his mother's genitalia. The girl who is choked by an octopus is haunted by the same fear. The man who is nearly overcome by lava in the belly of a ship and the girl who is trapped in a house use the fear of being buried alive for the re-enactment of the drama of birth. The man who is fleeing from Indians in order to save his scalp equates the terror of birth with murder, because of the bruise which the pressure of the pubic arch left on his forehead.

The fear of railroad tracks, locomotives, stampeding animals or collapsing floor-boards emphasizes the crushing of the body as the principal fear memory of birth. The railroad tracks appear to meet in the distance in the shape of a "V," and this is apparently equated by the unconscious mind with the extended legs of the maternal body. Dreams of being lost in the bushes or in a park, swept away by an avalanche, pressed against the railing of a bridge, struggling in water, on stairs, through windows or other narrow openings, reveal the outstanding impression which the ordeal of birth leaves on the individual mind. In most cases the dreamer is alone. The presence of others is shadowy or uncertain. Mother is usually absent, as she is the environment and not a person.

Generally speaking, any event that threatens us with destruction of the self or of the organs of procreation may mobilize the fear of birth and cohere with it by a process of regression. At the moment when the pressure of fear becomes too intense, the dream breaks and the dreamer wakes in perspiration with fierce palpitations of the heart. When the pressure is so intense that the ego is unable to bear it, the dream may assume impersonal features, yet clearly reveal its origin in birth by the fatality with which the dreamer is faced. There is no escape in a traumatic birth dream, except by waking up. From the diagnostic point-of-view this is a feature of outstanding importance.

2.

GENESIS OF THE TRAUMA OF BIRTH

For NINE months the child lives and grows in the quiet contentment of its mother's womb. Without struggle or effort, all its wants are gratified. The sense of perpetuity with which its requirements are taken care of makes the child feel like a God in a universe of its own. Nothing comes to it in overwhelming abundance or in frustrating meagerness. Conditions for its development are ideal. The eternity of the fetal night knows of no breaks. The idea of change is beyond conception. Growth is a sensation giving strength and power. It not only leaves the child's environment unaltered, but enhances the feeling of omnipotence which the perfection of its environment inspires. The existence of an overshadowing, all-enveloping Supreme Being called Mother, the awe-inspiring reality of a vast outer universe peopled with incomprehensible giants are infinitely removed from the cosmos of the tiny God of the Womb.

Suddenly, in an apocalyptic upheaval, its instinctive awareness is trampled in the dust, its sensation of power is crushed; an abyss opens under the very foundations of its universe; and in the awful drama of birth the God that the child was discovers pain and fear. We cannot picture the bewilderment which these strange new sensations bring in their wake. We can only trace their origin from what we know about the physiology of birth.

Search for the Beloved

The rumblings of the approaching end of the fetal kingdom strike the child in the same way that primitive people are stricken by an earthquake or a tidal wave from the sea. The rock and the earth begin to move from under them; water bursts over their shore dwellings. They are confronted by a cataclysm presaging the end of their world.

Instead of a tidal wave, the ordeal of the child about to be born begins by the sudden ebbing away of the waters of birth. The amniotic fluid that cushions the child and safeguards it from the shocks caused by movements of the mother's body (or her falling accidents) begins to recede, whereupon contractions of the mother's ejectory muscles raise the curtain to the perilous journey to life. Compared to an unborn babe's power of resistance, this constitutes an earthquake. The breaking of the birth waters and the beginning of labor are not always closely linked. In cases of accident, the amniotic sac may burst days before, in which event the mother must be confined to her bed in order to avoid premature birth.

The loss of the waters is the first violent and unwelcome change in the pre-natal environment. It produces tactile reactions for which the child is not prepared. Of the five human senses, only the sense of touch operates in the pre-natal state. It is stimulated by a contact of the child's limbs with its own body, by the buoyancy of the amniotic fluid and by the feel, through the caul, of the fleshy folds of the walls of the uterus. An early loss of the waters deprives the child of the delightful sensation of floating (the memories of which we often recapture in swimming and flying dreams) and restricts the ease and comfort of its movements. The contact with the maternal environment becomes rough and irritating, and the mother's movements in bed may register as minor collisions.

In the course of birth the lower part of the uterus dilates under the constant pressure of muscles that contract on the body of the child, holding it in an iron grip. A hormone substance softens the mother's tissues and bones to permit necessary dilatation for the passing of the child. As a rule the child is in a head-first position. If not, birth cannot take place in the usual manner. The child may have to be pushed back and turned by instruments. Its skin, already

14

sorely tried by the ejectory shocks and the pressure against the pubic arch, is too delicate to be unaffected by the forceps, however skillfully handled. Severe bruising may result. After this kind of delivery, the child may scream for a day or two upon being touched. The bruises tell their own tale. Neurotics who have a morbid fear of being touched may suffer from the unreleased psychic pressure of the tactile shocks suffered in birth or prior to it from the loss of the amniotic fluid.

The beginning of the mother's labor is the second violent change in the pre-natal environment. Hitherto this environment was friendly and beneficent; now it appears hostile. When labor is prolonged, in the absence of consciousness of the purpose of the process, the child goes through an agony only comparable to the slow torture of death. There is no intellectual acceptance as in the case of the mother to mitigate the pain and terror of the experience. The mother knows she is not likely to die; the child does not. The mother may be helped by twilight sleep, which will also affect the child. The child may be born asleep. But the drug bars the pain and shock from consciousness only, and not from the organism itself. The unborn child is nothing but an organism. Unconscious as it may be, the pain and fear reactions will still register. It is possible, however, that sleep produced during the most critical period of delivery helps to develop the mechanism of repression. It is a moot question, though, whether such repression should be encouraged. It may make the release of the trauma of birth more difficult and thereby, in the long run, contribute to neurosis.

The third violent change in the pre-natal environment is the actual birth. During the pre-natal state the child is supplied with oxygen through the mother's blood, which reaches its system by way of the umbilical cord. The breathing apparatus is fully developed at seven months, but it does not begin to function until after birth. During the mother's labor, the child still receives its oxygen supply through the cord, but on leaving the maternal body the cord detaches itself from its mooring in the placenta and trails along attached to the navel of the child. As it no longer carries blood and oxygen, a time interval ensues before pulmonary activity begins.

Some babies cry lustily as soon as they are born. The cry means that the lungs have started functioning without external stimulation. Other babies, however, turn blue immediately after birth and are in danger of death from suffocation. When the doctor turns them upside down and slaps them on the buttocks, their lungs start working. These late breathers go through another shock—the sensation of air pressure on an uninflated chest. Morbid suffocation fears in later life may often be traced to such delayed breathing. Occasionally the delay is due to accidents. The umbilical cord may be wound around the child's neck and obstruct breathing until it is removed.

Reaction to the doctor's slap is sometimes shown in birth dreams. A young woman, in the course of dramatically re-living her birth on the analyst's couch, described the doctor's slap as "flames of light flaring up in my brain." ° The seat of pain is in the brain. Only by training do we learn to localize the sensation at the nerve endings from which the stimulus of pain started. Immediately after birth this training is absent. "Flames of light in the brain" is not only a vivid description of the nerve reactions of the new-born child but suggests that birth injuries veritably set the child's brain on fire.

The behaviorist school of psychology claims that there are two original fears, not acquired but born with us: the fear of loss of position and the fear of loud sounds. The behaviorists mean that both fears are part of our instinctual heritage because they are present from birth without any accounting for them. I am not in accord with this view. The fear of loss of position is acquired. It originates in the pushes the child experiences from the contractions of the ejectory muscles. The child is head-downward in the uterus and falls away from its post on being born. Most abnormal fears of falling can be traced to the fall from the uterine heaven into the terrestrial abyss. The legend of the Fall of Man is a record of our biological origin.

Trauma of Sound

The fear of loud sounds is distinctly post-natal. After the silence of the womb loud noises may strike with the reverberation of thun-

---

° See Chapter 8, Nightmares of the Supernatural.

der on the sensitive auditory nerves of a new-born child. Think of the shock we receive from a comparatively slight noise when on the verge of sleep! To be born during a thunderstorm is more than a calamity. One of my patients suffered from an abnormal fear of fire-crackers. The simplest cause of such fears might have been an injury which she suffered as a young child from an exploding fire-cracker. She remembered no such injury or shock, but she was born on the fourth of July and was exposed to a bedlam of explosive sounds before she was twenty-four hours old.

Another patient at the age of fifteen was abnormally afraid of a certain train whistle. His parents lived near the railroad tracks. Freight trains passed continually. One of them used to wake him every night between twelve and one. Other train whistles did not disturb him. As he was born in the same house in which the fear seized him, it was possible that the strident whistle stirred up, by regressive association, the fear memory of a very similar sound experienced soon after his birth. A shrill sound may produce an auditory sensation even through the bones of the skull.

We may logically expect that a sudden volume of sound of high pitch and intensity would produce a shock in the new-born even though it was experienced some days after birth. Owing to the fact that the second shock followed closely on the heels of the first, the trauma caused by loud sound would fuse with the trauma of birth. I know of a woman who was born on December 29th in a small town in the house of a bell-ringer. Two days later the New Year bells set up a clangor that lasted most of the day. She never connected birth and bells, but throughout her life she was exceedingly sensitive to loud sounds. The ringing of church bells used to give her a pain in the waist line. Other sudden and loud sounds affected other parts of her body. She jumped at the sound of telephone bells and she could not stand the ticking of a clock in her room at night. The first clues that her phonophobia originated at the beginning of her life came in a series of dreams plainly depicting birth. Before going to sleep she had a vision of the pendulum of a grandfather clock. At the moment of waking she heard a cannon discharged. In the midst of her dreams the analyst became a bell-ringer, and in her subsequent associations the church bells stood out as symbolizing death, through burials, and birth through Christmas. An unconscious attempt to abreact this trauma of sound manifested itself on the approach of the birthday of her brother. She suggested to her sister that she buy him chimes.

Trauma of Light

The eyes of a child may open soon after birth, but the child does not see. The effect of light is a bewildering experience to the newborn. The optic nerves need careful training. A harsh beam of light strikes the child like a dagger and causes a serious shock. Maternity wards protect infants from such shocks by subdued illumination. The same care is not always exercised after deliveries at home. I have on record a case of photophobia which caused a great deal of trouble to a thirty-six year old man. He had been delivered at home by a midwife in a room of indifferent illumination. As far as it was possible to reconstruct the story of his birth from a study of his dreams, some strong artificial light was used to assist the midwife and this light appeared to have been so directed that it hit the newborn child like a sledge-hammer between the eyes. In another case, the strong daylight of an early summer afternoon was responsible for the pains in the eye from which a thirty-one year old woman suffered on every awakening to daylight. She was born at two P.M. at home in a room with a southern exposure, and the light apparently was left undimmed by the midwife who delivered her. As we are re-born each morning on awakening, that moment is a propitious time to evoke the pains of our first arrival into the world.

The drop of silver nitrate with which the new-born's eyes are protected from infection may also produce an effect of shock. That may be as inevitable as the cutting of the umbilical cord, but we can guard against untoward effects. A thunderstorm may occur during a child's delivery, but the blinds can be drawn to prevent flashes of lightning from luridly illuminating the room.

A New York medical practitioner was born with a fracture in the occipital region of his skull. As a baby he suffered and cried constantly. Up to about nine years of age, he had very bad recurrent nightmares. One outstanding feature of the nightmares was the sensation of brilliant light over his forehead. He had no idea what the light signified. It is easy to guess that it was the light over the operating table on which he was placed after birth. It would be strong enough to affect the optic nerve of a newly born child even though his sight was not yet functioning. The fractured skull would have necessitated keeping him on the operating table for some time.

He suffered from chronic splitting headaches and frequently felt a swelling in his head for which there was no physical cause. From his youth, his ambition was to become a brain surgeon, a profession which would have permitted the release of his specific trauma of birth by sublimation. A vicarious re-living of an original ordeal by social service to others is sometimes the only psychological corrective we find at our disposal. Through the pressure of circumstances he became a general practitioner, but he had an instinctive urge to do surgery. No matter how tiring his day, an operation always seemed to put new life into him. The measure of his social service was lessening the limitations of his own personality. Unconsciously he understood the nature of his affliction. This was manifested in his habit of asking patients for their dreams and in venturing into psychoanalytic explanations. When the significance of his recurrent nightmare and of his attitudes was pointed out, he was speechless with astonishment—and promptly responded with a severe headache. Such symptomatic reaction during analysis is a good indication that the analyst is on the right track.

Trauma of Cold

Another source of shock to the new-born child may arise from the difference of temperature between the pre-natal and the post-natal environment. We do not bear 98 degrees of heat very well; yet this is the temperature of the maternal body and the pre-natal environment. That is why infants born even during a heat wave may get a chill. Modern hospitals are aware of this hazard and take precautions to prevent it, but a child born at home may be exposed to it. The midwife may not think the room needs warming, forgetting that for the newcomer the reception is a cold one. A woman once said of herself, "I was born cold and have never been able to get warm." There may be more truth than poetry in her statement, which illustrates the persistence of the first shocks which we experience.

"I used to have falling dreams of ice and snow," a woman stated. "I walked on large avenues of ice ending in free space. I was always afraid of falling off the edge into an abyss."

The memory of this recurrent nightmare returned during analysis, following a dream that pointed to an easing of the dreamer's trauma of birth. The dream was:

I am walking up a hill of snow with my little girl. Despite the hard crusty surface of the snowberg, I hold my little girl by the hand and keep warning her to be careful. Nevertheless, she falls through the snow's surface and is lying on her back in about one foot of snow. The hole in which she lies forms a sharp clear imprint of her body.

I pull her out and we continue to walk, this time downhill. At the foot of the snowberg she begins to slip—and slides into the clear blue water. She is almost covered by water up to her shoulders. She is in the same prostrate position as before, only she is buoyant and not immobile as she was in the snow. Again I reach for her and pull her out of the water.

The child in this dream stands for the dreamer herself. Her fall through the crust of thick snow and her second fall into the water surrounding the snowberg show an identification between snow and water with the apparent purpose of directing attention to extreme cold. Her attempt to pull the child out shows her own determination to deliver herself from the effects of both the fall of birth and the reaction to the change from pre-natal to post-natal temperature. Being surrounded by water, the snowberg is an island and is an outstanding symbol for the pre-natal state. The difference between her early recurrent nightmares about the avenues of ice and the present dream is striking. The anxiety of the former has disappeared, the fall is limited, and the sensation of danger is absent. The understanding achieved through analysis has helped her to release a good deal of her previous anxiety. She was born in Montreal on a warm July night. The precise conditions of her birth could not be determined, but she was delivered at home by a midwife; her parents were poor immigrant people, and it may be assumed that she did not receive the scientific care which she might have had in a modern hospital.

Here is a more dramatic story. The subject is the same woman who was born in the house of the church bell-ringer, and who suffered from a phobia of loud sounds. All her life she complained of a circulatory disturbance in her legs. They were weak from infancy and accidents were always happening to them. She had to wear woollen socks because of chilblains that would not heal for years. Her toes were constantly inflamed and painful. She dreamed continually of walking in slush and snow and of chunks of red, reeking, raw meat. Visions and dreams of a pair of legs came to her. Sometimes she saw a pair of pants, at other times babies' legs cut out of paper like a pattern, but ending at the waist-line; at still other times the hind legs of animals cut off above the thigh. The lower half of her body was constantly tense, and her inability to relax in this area was an important contributory factor in developing sexual frigidity.

It occurred to me that the symptoms and dreams referred to the trauma of podalic version: of being born feet first, that conceivably the frigidity of her legs was due to the shock of temperature difference from which she must have suffered with the upper part of her body at womb temperature of 98 degrees and the lower part exposed to the temperature of a country home on a cold late December day. However warm the room and however skillful the delivery, the midwife could hardly have saved her from the unevenness of temperature or from the pain of the grip she had to exert on the infant's legs in order to pull her out.

There was no one from whom exact data on the length and conditions of her birth could be secured, so I suggested that we wait for the reaction from her dream mind, which would in all probability either endorse my theory or reject it in unmistakable terms. After a night of headaches and exhausting dreams, the patient said,

"I think you are right regarding my being born legs first. I recalled after I left you an old dream in which I saw a barrel full of water and a baby's legs sticking out. The baby's head was completely under the water, together with the upper part of her body. I also remembered another dream in which I was coming down a hill and saw an animal on its back with its legs in the air and its belly cut open. Both dreams are understandable on the basis of your birth theory. My dreams last night seem to bear it out. I saw a little lamp turned upside down with its legs in the air. I also saw a filly upside down, then a baby carriage with a child's feet sticking out with braces on. I never wore braces but I certainly needed support for my legs. More important than the dreams is the fact that since yesterday I have had a totally different sensation in the lower part of my body. I can relax and feel an improvement in circulation. Moreover, last night, for the first time, I stated in a dream that I was not a frigid woman and proceeded to demonstrate the fact by my behavior."

No positive proof emerged during the later course of analysis that my solution of this patient's dream problems and symptoms was correct, but the improvement in her condition remained and the dreams which had haunted her for years ceased.

The Trauma of Smell

I now turn to the problem of whether the olfactory organs of the new-born infant begin to function immediately after birth. Georg Groddeck contends that they do, and that the pungent smell of genital blood, shed in the process of delivery, may leave a traumatic impact on the delicate olfactory apparatus of the child. It is to this impact that he traces the phobia of blood odor, and he postulates the existence behind it of a blood guilt relating to the mother, undoubtedly built on the fact that her blood is spilled on our arrival into the world.[*]

The possible validity of Groddeck's claim was suggested to me during the analysis of Birth Dream 28. After he had passed the

---

[*] Georg Groddeck, *The Book of the It*, C. W. Daniel Co., London, 1935, p. 76.

ordeal of the coffin and the bridge, the dreamer—a young man of thirty-one—found himself in a big hall surrounded by doctors and nurses. He was on a stretcher, just rolled out of the operating room, and was offered tomato juice by the nurse to restore his strength. He refused it as he felt strong and elated, no longer his old frightened self. He had passed the test and had a white band on his left arm, symbolizing that he was now a Commando.

In discussing the dream, he recognized the birth symbolism of the coffin and the bridge, but he objected to the delivery room at the hospital by saying, "I was born at home. I was delivered by a midwife . . . but wait, the medicine smell might be associated with hospitals . . . I can only smell a few things. People don't understand it. I usually tell them, just as some people are color blind, so am I smell blind."

Disinfectants were among the few things he could smell, and he liked the smell. I therefore shifted my query to blood. The answer was startling: "I don't smell blood. I never knew that blood had a smell. I did smell something though in the fencing room. I took it for the smell of perspiration. I am disgusted with it. If a workman sits next to me in the subway and smells of perspiration, I feel nauseated. My own perspiration does not bother me. . . . Perhaps I displaced my reaction to the smell of blood on to perspiration."

The chain of associations suggested that here was a case where Groddeck's claim might be put to the test. I explained to the patient what this claim was. Experience has taught me that the patient's reaction to an explanation frequently shows whether we are on the right trail or not. In this case the reaction seemed to be positive.

"I have an uneasy feeling in my stomach. It feels like a presentiment of something disastrous."

To soothe him, I suggested that there might be something more simple behind his olfactory inhibitions. The cutting of the umbilical cord, for instance, if it was followed by a haemorrhage, might account for olfactory inhibitions. This elicited an interesting memory:

"At the age of twenty-three I had my tonsils taken out. The doctor froze my throat, but the operation hurt horribly. I spat a handful of blood into the doctor's face. When he snipped my tonsils, an awful screeching sounded in my ear. The pain does not bother me now but the noise still makes me shudder."

The association is interesting. It rather suggests that an earlier trauma had reverberated in the patient's mind when the tonsils were snipped. The cutting of the umbilical cord could well have been this earlier event. The patient was so aware of this possibility that he immediately suggested that the white bandage on his left arm probably represented, by displacement, the bandaged umbilicus. The tomato juice (which he used to hate) was associated with blood. In turning it down he may have been rejecting, symbolically, the blood-spilling complex.

It remained for the patient's unconscious mind to show the choice between the two possible origins of blood traumata. The choice was made, and it settled the issue of birth. A few days later he dreamed:

I witnessed a murder committed by George, a friend of mine. He murdered a girl and I tried to cover him up before the investigators. One of them was my medical officer. He found my own bloodstained business card near the body, with a tiny red ribbon attached to it, the type of ribbon they use to tie business papers. He did not suspect me until I casually tore it up. I decided I would not give away my friend unless absolutely necessary.

Then I was on a train. The seats were of red plush and reminded me of the First Class compartments in the trains of my native country, but they were circular. There was a strange reason for this shape and it was this: When a woman gives birth to a child in a train, the breeze comes through the window and blows through the impregnated fabric of her nightgown and removes the vaginal odor.

Murder means bloodshed. It is a woman whose blood is shed and obviously he is the murderer. The friend is a cover for the unknown part of his personality which is responsible for the deed. The identity of the woman is not revealed, but the red ribbon may be a clue. It could well symbolize the umbilical tie, in which case the woman could only be his mother. If so, the murder still need not symbolize his injuring his mother in birth. The deed is too violent for that. The patient's mother is still alive and well. Though he was the first and only child, he never heard her complain about the difficulties of delivery. On the contrary, he always thought his birth was uneventful and normal. It may have been for his mother, but not for him. It is simple to assume that the dream reflects hatred of the ordeal to which he was subjected at birth; that instead of blood guilt concerning his mother, the dream portrays the impersonal aggressive reaction of his organism against the maternal environment that had suddenly turned hostile and destructive. It is also easy to conceive that his lust for blood may have evoked a defense reaction in the form of completely repressing the odor of blood. But there is the possibility too that the shock of the umbilical injury and copious bleeding could lead to the same result.

Fortunately, the second part of the dream helps to clarify some of our perplexities. First of all, it confirms that the dreamer is concerned with his birth. It speaks of a woman giving birth to a child. Secondly, the setting is intra-uterine. In a train we are carried as within the mother's body. The rhythmic movement of the train approximates the undulations of the body of the mother in walking. Red plush is a good substitute for flesh color, and it also indicates the comfort and luxury of the original native country: the womb to which the word "circular" symbolically alludes. When, therefore, the breeze that removes the vaginal odor is mentioned, we are left under no doubt that the inhibited function of the patient's olfactory apparatus is due to the trauma of his birth, regardless of the choice between the terms of blood guilt, birth hatred or umbilical separation. In trying to make a choice, we are more or less quibbling with terms. We must not forget that the impersonal aggressive reaction against the maternal environment would also generate guilt. As long as guilt feeling arises because blood is shed, it matters little whether we speak of the mother or of the maternal environment. I conclude, therefore, that the dream bears out Georg Groddeck's contention regarding the existence of a blood guilt relating to the mother and that, very probably, George was chosen for the murderer because of his name—a subtle allusion to the analyst whose theory was being corroborated by the case.

Search for the Beloved

Several weeks later a further fascinating feature of this patient's trauma of birth emerged. It was presented in this dream:

I am in a theater. On the stage is a grotesque dancer. She turns and I see that she is hunchbacked. Then, by the use of her arms, she gives the impression that she is holding a baby. After this I see a boy with her. I only notice his head. It is against her genitalia. The stage is now filled with water which reaches up to her waist and up to the boy's chin. On the stage is a huge wash basin and a piano of tremendous size. The actor (the dancer seems to be a man now) yells for the stage manager because he does not know how to open the piano. (Maybe it was a difficult birth.) The stage is now dry; the water has disappeared. Instead of the stage manager, the theater doctor appears, but he cannot open the piano. The stage manager (father) is there now, and tells the doctor that the actor is a fine amateur collector. That's why he is the director of the museum; he has at home a white Chinese floor inlaid with mosaic. Then I am on the stage eating dry salted Virginia ham (it should be sweet) but it is a musical instrument.

The comments in parentheses were volunteered by the patient in the course of narrating the dream. The symbolism of his arrival on the stage of life is transparently clear. With the fusion of the female and male (as shown by the change of the dancer into a man) we need not deal here, as that bears on the patient's bisexual attitude to his father and mother—a long and complicated story. The proportions of the wash basin and of the piano strongly suggest the perspective of a tiny infant as retrojected by the adult dreamer's mind. As a symbol of cleansing, the wash basin refers to the analytic effort. The piano is far more important. The patient called my attention to something I had failed to observe: that piano (barring one superfluous letter) is an anagram on the vulgar Hungarian word for vagina. He suggested that it stood for his mother's genitalia; that his, as well as the doctor's, inability to open it indicated the difficulties of his birth.

We can now see another reason for the fusion of the male and female. The actor is himself in the dual role of adult and infant.

Genesis of the Trauma of Birth

The museum, the patient thought, was a kind of "memorarium," and "director" described his unique position in the collecting of memories regarding his foundation. An oriental feature had appeared in a previous dream of this patient. He then suggested that "Orient" comes from the Latin "orior" and refers to birth. Now he added that Chinese means to him Chinese torture, and "inlaid" is laid in, while "mosaic" is a play on Moses, the child floating on the waters of the Nile.

The real problem to which this fascinating interpretation leads concerns the Virginia ham. A clue is hidden in the patient's feeling that the ham is also a musical instrument, which obviously identifies the ham with the piano. If the piano is the mother's genitalia, ham may be a covert reference to the thigh. The patient was quick to notice that "Virginia" has a female suggestion (virgin). What puzzled him was the oral contact and the salty sensation. All he could think of was cunnilingus—a sexual practice in which he does not like to indulge. He stated further:

"I don't like eating ham dry, and I don't like salty things . . . My lips are very dry. . . . My tongue gets parched too often. . . . All my life I have eaten almost everything without salt. The only thing I salt, and even over-salt, is soup . . . What nauseates me is not salt but perspiration."

Perspiration is salty. If we recall that he had recognized his aversion to perspiration as being a displaced reaction to the smell of blood and remember that the repression of the smell of blood had been traced back to birth, we are suddenly faced with the query: how close is the inter-action in this patient's case between smelling and tasting? He was not only unaware that blood had a smell, but equally unaware that it had a taste. Perhaps the ham, if moist, would have reminded him of blood. Perhaps its dryness is a hint as to why his lips are continually dry. It almost seems as if the salty and acid condition of the genital secretions with which the lips of the child (who is not born in a caul) may come into unpleasant contact were alluded to by the dream as an explanation.

It is hardly possible to secure proof of this; the dream revelation is recorded here because of its thought-provoking character and not as an argument for the traumatic impact of birth on the organ of taste.

The main argument in the preceding case might be criticized on the ground that the patient had heard about Groddeck's blood guilt theory from me and that his dream of confirmation may have been brought about more by a desire to please the analyst than to reveal his own emotional reactions. The objection deserves consideration, at least on theoretical grounds. The best answer to it is that there have been other cases which, although less interesting, are free from this criticism.

Sleep-walking

The cases thus far discussed do not represent the most severe birth conditions. Many children are born in street-cars, burning houses, during air-raids and earthquakes. They show remarkable tenacity for survival because the unconscious mind has an almost limitless capacity for absorbing psychic shocks. The pressure of such shocks may manifest itself throughout infancy, adolescence and adult life, seeking release. Pressure, like murder, will out. It is a law of the unconscious mind that one cannot keep pressure locked up indefinitely. Increasing age, sickness or shocks will offer an ever-growing opportunity for the pressure to burst forth from the subterranean domains of the mind.

Sleep-walking often represents an unconscious attempt to throw off the trauma of birth. The average sleep-walker makes a bee-line for a window and stops there. Sometimes he is discovered sitting on the window sill. At others he is actually found hanging from it by his hands in a rather dangerous re-enactment of the fall in birth. The window symbolizes for the unconscious mind the entrance into the mother's body. The desire to return to it is often advanced as an explanation of the sleep-walking act.* I believe the attempt to re-

---

* Popular belief holds that sleep-walking will cease when a girl becomes pregnant with her first child. Perhaps pregnancy acts as a substitute gratification for the desire to return. Dr. J. Sadger in "Sleep Walking and Moon Walking," *Nervous and Mental Disease Monograph Series*, No. 31, New York, 1920, fails to list the desire to return as a dominant motive.

lease the trauma of birth by pantomime might be considered a more important factor. A patient whose action suggested this thought used to pull a table away from the wall, wedge herself between it and the wall, and then wake up in panic. She was reproducing the conditions of her birth. She had been badly injured during delivery, and neither she nor her mother was expected to survive.

The window alludes not so much to the desire of the sleep-walker to return to the womb as to pre-natal life, to the trauma of birth, whatever its manifestations may be. The door is as much of a gate symbol as the window. Dream life, however, does not observe anatomic parallels strictly. Children in whose minds confusion exists between genital and anal birth may equally use the front and the back door in the sleep-walking act. In one case in my records, an eight-year-old girl used to walk out into the cold in her nightgown through the back door, go around the house, and then ring the front bell. When the door was opened, she usually awoke and started screaming because she did not know where she was.

Most sleep-walkers cannot be addressed without risking the shock of a sudden awakening, but some answer questions or even use gestures re-enacting an experience. A little girl who had been frightened at the age of four by the sight of a corpse and the burial ceremony began to walk in her sleep and was stopped by her father at the window with the question, "Where are you going?" She answered: "I go to bury the dead." A boy, at the age of nine, walked to the door in his sleep and took the brass latch in his mouth by bending his head as if under a water-tap. Asked what he was doing, he answered, "I am drinking." On another occasion he laid himself on the table and said he was on top of a haystack. In the first instance he used the latch as a substitute for the mother's breast, vaguely pointing, by the door symbolism, to fetal regression. In the second instance, he ignored the door but showed his yearning for the soft comfort of the womb by the haystack fantasy.

A man who was morbidly afraid of fire and always wanted to save somebody from a burning house tried to walk out of a third story window in his sleep because he dreamed that the house was on fire. In this case it was apparently the bruises of his own flesh in birth

29

translated into sensations of fire that led to this form of re-enactment of the drama of birth.

Sometimes the wanderings of sleep-walkers coincide with the hour of birth. I am unable to explain the process by which such evaluation in time can take place. For analogy I would point to the uncanny appreciation of important anniversaries which the unconscious mind displays in dreams. Personally there is no more important return date than birth, be it back to the day, the week or the year. I have cases on record in which the approach of the anniversary of birth cast a shadow of gloom over the patient's life for some weeks in advance. In another case a woman suffered for years from violent headaches and deep depression every Friday at two P.M. until it was found that this hour and day coincided with her birth. In a third case, two A.M. was the ghostly hour for a young man of twenty-eight. He could not bring himself to stay up until that hour, and felt unaccountably depressed at its approach. He remembered that even as a child he used to wake up at two A.M. and cry because he was afraid. On inquiry, the hour was found to correspond to the hour of his birth. It is not always possible to find out the precise hour of birth, but if fear symptoms, as for instance the unusual drying of the palate, recurrently set in at a certain hour and are conjoined with other clues of birth, the hour might be assumed to be the time of birth, however mysterious the mental arithmetic by which it is calculated may be.

Counter-Measures

Unfortunately the trauma of birth is not given sufficient recognition in child psychology and hygiene. A few modern thinkers have developed ingenious measures to counteract it or release it. The principle is simple. We have to re-create the conditions of birth and permit the child to re-live it with conscious appreciation. There should be tunnels in the nursery through which the child can crawl safely but with difficulty. By offering rewards, he should be encouraged to make the effort from which, at first, he will probably shrink. The fear of falling should be cured by making the sensation of dropping from a height—safely—a pleasurable one. If a child only responds with anxiety to being thrown up in the air, no matter how safely he is caught on coming down, such play activity must not be continued. Otherwise the child will remember with hatred the parent who exposed him to it and will show increasingly abnormal fear reactions to falling from a height. The fear of loud sound might be cancelled by making the child produce the very sound which most frightened him, if that is possible. The shock caused by the loss of the amniotic waters might be released by having the child float on air cushions from the time he reaches the swimming age, by encouraging him to dive or by techniques of sudden emergence from the bath tub. The fear of suffocation for want of air might be eliminated by breath-holding competitions in which the child is inveigled to participate by a promise of reward and is allowed to win.*

From a knowledge of the conditions of birth, a suitable technique of release should be worked out for each individual case. I know of a woman to whom twins were born in the cold season in Northern India in a hospital without a properly equipped maternity ward. Both children suffered from an abnormal fear of cold water, and she thought this fear originated in the lack of warmth which the children suffered after birth. Whether this was the cause or not, she succeeded in releasing their fear by dropping pennies in buckets of lukewarm and ice-cold water and letting the children keep the coins as a reward if they recovered them from the ice-cold bucket. After a good deal of hesitation they tackled the cold water and gradually got rid of their abnormal reactions to it.

The trauma of birth creates a predisposition to neurosis. If an actual physical injury or shock is coupled with the psychic shock, the child may set out in life with an actual neurosis. An Italian

---

* I have a case on record in which the door of the bedroom left open on a hot night to ensure free circulation of air acted on the unconscious mind of a girl of twenty-three, who slept in the same room with her mother, as a suggestion of freedom from suffocation fears originating in birth. There is a striking parallelism between this reaction and the response of the bladder to the flow of water from a tap.

woman came to me with nervous symptoms bordering on the psychotic, that had tormented her for years. She felt as if the nerves all over her body were being tied into knots. At the same time she felt a sharp pain in her navel. She insisted over and over again that her nerves were being tied in knots. After considerable inquiry, a significant fact was elicited about her birth. She was delivered at home, and her grandmother tied the umbilical cord, making a very bad job of it. The bleeding was unchecked, and by the time this was discovered the child was half dead from loss of blood. Here was a possible clue for the knotting sensation and the pain in the umbilical region. I explained the connection, with the result that the pain stopped and the knotting sensation vanished.

In premature birth the smallness of the child may ease the birth and decrease the physical trauma; but the psychic trauma is increased because the premature child is less able to endure the loss of warmth and security provided within the womb. My experience has been that those born at seven months look upon bed as their best friend and comforter. They are insatiable sleepers, as if trying to make up for the time lost within the womb. They are more helpless and dependent than those born at term, while those who have been carried beyond term seem to need far less sleep and show far greater self-reliance. As a symbol of the womb, the bed offers compensation for the ordeal of birth.

"Because I feel lost, lonely and unsheltered," states a woman patient, "I feel as if I had been premature, ripped off before my time. I was not ready for birth. I was torn away. That's my feeling. If left alone in the morning, I do not awake until I am ready to come out of death. Then I am satisfied. But having to go out early in the morning is like being torn away from something. I have the same sensation when I pull a leaf off a hedge, or a fruit from a tree when it is not quite ripe. I feel as if I were committing a terrible sacrilege, as if I should wait until it falls by itself. When a walnut is not sufficiently ripe and the green shell sticks to it, I have a feeling of suspense, as if I have done something wrong, an intense discomfort of having torn something away from where it properly belongs."

Genesis of the Trauma of Birth

Principles of Pre-Natal Psychology

I hold the following principles of pre-natal psychology to be basic:

1. In our present day life, birth is traumatic in almost every instance.

2. The longer the labor, the more serious the physical complications, the greater the trauma of birth.

3. The intensity of the trauma of birth is proportionate to the shocks or injuries which the child suffers during labor or immediately following delivery.

4. The love and care which the child receives immediately after birth is a decisive factor in the persistence and intensity of the traumatic pressure.

An actual injury converts a pure psychic trauma into hard reality and provides a point of fixation for its symptomatology. Caesarian birth would eliminate some of the trauma if the operation were not preceded by long labor.

Love and care are the only immediate compensation for the lost world and antidote to the instinctual desire to return into the state of pre-natal bliss. Puppies have been observed to turn around immediately after birth and try to climb back into their mother's body. Other pups make a bee-line for the teats and find in suckling the same comfort which a human child finds in its mother's arms. If for reasons of the mother's post-partum condition, the child cannot be comforted in her arms and lulled into the illusion that the lost paradise has nearly been regained, the foundations for later neurosis will be laid.* Furthermore, if the child becomes a victim of sickness shortly after birth, or if required medical treatment inflicts new injuries on its delicate system, the pain may prevent the birth ordeal from lapsing into the limbo of the unconscious mind, and we may

---

* On the effect of the child's isolation from the mother in hospital delivery see M. F. Ashley Montagu, "Some Factors in Family Cohesion," *Psychiatry*, Nov., 1944, p. 351.

have on our hands a morbid, complaining and frightened child. The greatest danger of injuries in early life is that they may mobilize and keep active the trauma of birth.

To explain the vast extent to which the trauma of birth may govern neurotic life, a detailed analysis of some of its manifestations will be undertaken in subsequent chapters.

3.

NIGHTMARES OF SUFFOCATION

AS I STATED previously, in the terrifying experience of being born from the protective maternal womb into this world, a fatal moment arrives when the blood supply of the fetus through the umbilical cord is arrested. As the function of the lungs may not begin until after the administration of a slap or two, for some time the child may be deprived of the life-sustaining oxygen conveyed by the mother's blood. If this interval is too prolonged, the baby will turn blue and suffocate. If the baby lives to breathe, it has tasted death by suffocation. We do not know of the agony that was compressed into this experience because we had as yet no consciousness to register it. The record, however, has been preserved in the unconscious mind and evidence of it can be found in morbid suffocation fears.* The victims of such fears usually remember an accident in early life in which they nearly died from loss of breath, and ascribe their extreme reaction to this event. Sometimes they know of it by hearsay; at other times they have no memory to offer. In the latter case, the recovery of the actual memory may put an end to the morbid fear, but not always. Then the analyst will search for other memories, buried still deeper, but may find nothing until it dawns on him that the most potent source of morbid suffocation

---

* For the five types of fetal asphyxia see Arnold Gesell, *Embryology of Behavior,* Harper & Brothers, New York, 1945, p. 68.

fears is the trauma of birth. My finding is that every experience in suffocation tends to mobilize the buried memory of birth and that, ultimately, the fear of dying from loss of breath is a re-enactment of the panic with which we drew our first lungful of air in this world.

This conclusion is based on the birth symbolism which suffocation nightmares so frequently disclose.

The following dream of a girl of twenty-four speaks of birth in unmistakable language:

I was near a railroad track. A little boy, or big man, the engineer of the railroad, was climbing down a manhole, head first. I remember thinking: "Good Heavens, it seems perfectly safe going down that way, but if I were he I would suffocate unless I came out quickly." Then I saw him backing out. The manhole was next to the railroad track.

The dreamer suffered from marked suffocation fears. Once she became panicky under the bedclothes because she could not find her way out. Occasionally she woke out of breath, gasping for air. The dream suggests that this fear originated at the time of her birth. The manhole is an eloquent genital symbol. The engineer going down head first re-enacts birth in reverse. Going in instead of coming out is a simple variation on the theme of birth. The confusion of "little boy or big man" prepares the dreamer for this interpretation. Backing out leg first raises the additional query whether the dreamer was not presented leg first in birth and had to be turned. It was not possible to find this out.

The reason why she represents herself by a male is complicated. Ordinarily, the use of the opposite would be sufficient to explain it, but this girl was a tomboy in childhood and suffered intensely from organ inferiority. She discovered the meaning of intercourse at a very early age and her dream life was replete with infantile sexual fantasies. The movement of the engineer in the manhole suggests the use of the whole body for the penis, in which case the head is a reference to the glans. She needs assurance that the penetration is safe because her own body, during her birth, was in penis relationship to her mother's genitalia. It is at this point of identification that the suffocation fear enters into the sexual fantasy.

At the age of seven she had a tonsillectomy. She fought against ether desperately. At the age of fifteen she took nitrous oxide for a tooth extraction. She went under in a rage, and then dreamed that she was tickled unmercifully. She laughed and laughed and wished that the dentist would stop, but he did not. She became terribly tired and thought she was going to die. "I have never taken gas since," she said. "I would rather bear pain than gas. I would much rather have my babies without anesthetic."

Tooth extraction may result in an unconscious fantasy of child-birth. People who lose a tooth often refer to it as a child. It is imbedded in the gum as a child is imbedded in the mother. A morbid fear of tooth extraction may be due to the fact that it tends to mobilize the memory of being drawn out of the mother's body in a similar manner. It is interesting that in this case the patient spontaneously associated tooth extraction with child-bearing.

Why was the manhole placed near a railway track? The patient revealed:

"I used to be terribly afraid of locomotives. I had recurrent dreams of crossing tracks, not knowing where I was and unable to get off in time to escape from the onrushing train. I often found myself rooted to the track and woke up before I was crushed."

To the mind of a child, the locomotive is an excellent symbol of overwhelming fear. As birth implies a good deal of crushing of the child's body, it is easy to displace it on an engine of destruction. Moreover, the railway tracks lend themselves to symbolize the mother's legs, between which the new-born infant is thrust forward or is immobilized prior to birth.

The air-hunger of many fresh air fiends may result from the fear of suffocating in a closed room. An illustrative dream follows:

I came home late and, contrary to my habit, failed to observe that the window of my bedroom was not open. I went to bed and dreamed of being buried alive. I found myself in a coffin and was struggling to lift the lid. Not being able to achieve this, I succeeded in waking myself. I was in a cold sweat. Then I discovered that the window was closed. I understood the dream, got up, opened the window and fell asleep in peace.

It is interesting to note how the understanding of a dream, even though superficial, can restore the dreamer's peace of mind. While the vitiated air may act as a somatic stimulant and lead to a suffocation dream, the affect shown by the dream is excessive. Sleeping in a closed room represents no threat to life, and only by dint of an earlier ordeal could the dwindling oxygen content of the room be interpreted in terms of being buried alive.

It is quite possible that the dreamer had noticed that her window was not open but repressed the observation with unconscious purpose, as thereby her dream mind was able to reveal that her air hunger was a symptom of a much deeper fear. The coffin in which we return to Mother Earth is a symbol of the womb, but because of its association with death and passing from the only known plane of life into the unknown, it also alludes to the transition from the pre-natal into the post-natal world. In the dream, she is fighting to force open the lid of the coffin lest she remain buried alive and suffocate in the womb or halfway between the womb and outside. The lesson of her birth was a lesson of suffocation for want of air. She disliked tunnels; she had a horror of rush hour crowds in the subway and felt out of breath in any closed room. She learned the lesson, but her interpretation was not quite correct. However, the waking anxiety of keeping her window open, the symbolic gate to life, served the purpose of incessantly protecting herself against the recurrence of the ordeal of birth. The case is a good example of repetition compulsion, and the need of self-defense could not be done away with until full realization descended on her that she was trying to protect herself against a peril that had been successfully overcome at the beginning of life.

Fetal Distress

Air-hunger may have a still deeper motivation in fetal distress. Besides protecting the dreamer against the recurrence of the ordeal of birth, the struggle of getting out of a coffin or tightly enclosed space may also represent an escape from the womb into life when the conditions of the pre-natal abode undergo a vital change and prove no longer favorable for supporting the life of the unborn. The dream which first taught me this lesson is my own:

A ship is under the water and I am in its belly. The air is becoming poisoned. I must get out. There are only two possibilities—diving out of the boat on one or the other side, and coming up to the surface of the water. I feel anxious regarding the left side as the way to the surface is obstructed by machinery all the way up; the vault may be completely blocked. To be caught there would mean death by suffocation. Then I discover that it is quite easy to get out on the right side where there is no machinery, only water. The discovery of this route of escape is somewhat due to my friend, Wishner.

The uterine symbolism of the dream is clear. Under the water in the belly of a ship is within the body of the mother. The poisoning of the air suggests deterioration for lack of sufficient supply of oxygen. Nature may contrive birth to take place precisely at the time when the mother's body is no longer capable of providing fully for the needs of the unborn child. The load on the maternal organism in supplying the system of a fully grown infant with food and oxygen, and in removing the waste products of the child's body is tremendous, and a saturation point must exist at which the provision begins to fail. The failing of the child's oxygen supply might become a factor impelling the child to be born and thus counteract, to some extent, the ordeal by which birth is accomplished.

The two-way escape in the dream suggested to me the oral and the vaginal (or substitute anal) outlet. The first probably originates in infantile notions that the child is born of a seed which the mother swallows, in which case a way out above must exist through the machinery of the body. There is, however, no such way out. The vault is blocked. The choice is made in favor of the relatively simple way below. I believe that I introduced the name Wishner to indicate the wish to be born. It adds a deliberateness on my part to the process of birth which fits in well with the designs of nature.

4.

FEAR is an emotional reaction to a threat to security. In this reaction the relationship between cause and effect is clear. When the relationship is disturbed and the effect becomes disproportionate to the cause, we have a morbid fear or phobia. Claustrophobia is a widespread morbid dread of confined spaces, small rooms, caves, tunnels, elevators or pressing crowds.

Suffocation fears do not always lead to claustrophobia, but one of the primary symptoms that accompany claustrophobia is the sensation of a sudden loss of breath and the panic which develops from this sensation. The secondary fear of being crushed is not as easily recognizable as the first. Wherever he is, the afflicted person has to get out instantly or he feels he will die. Claustrophobia is a very crippling condition. Its attack is equivalent to a nightmare in the waking state. It is followed by a complete prostration.

All victims of claustrophobia have a very vivid dream life and may pack almost incredible horrors into their dreams. In almost every instance that has come to my analytic attention, the trauma of birth was the fundamental event to which claustrophobia could be traced. My most outstanding case was that of a forty-four year old London woman who, for many years, was unable to travel on buses, in elevators, on subways, through tunnels or over bridges. She lived in a ground-floor apartment and could move about only in her own car. One of her worst nightmares gave the clue to her condition, and it also revealed a projection of her invalidism on to her husband as a scapegoat.

It was night, and I was looking for my husband who was supposed to be on top of a bus. I passed three gibbets from which three figures were hanging. One of them, with knees drawn up and back hunched, was my husband. I woke with an awful shock and could not get over the horror of the dream for a long time.

Then, falling asleep, I was again on a bus, strap-hanging. My husband was next to me, but he was now a little boy and suffered dreadfully from pain. To put him out of his misery, I took a silver hammer and knocked him under the jaw. I heard a click, similar to a shot, and awoke again in fear and trembling.

The two dreams are plainly connected. In the first, the husband is strangled by rope; in the second, he is put out of his misery and presumably dies. Ordinarily, one would immediately diagnose such dreams as revealing murder fantasies. It was this very construction which frightened the patient out of her wits. She told the dream very reluctantly, obviously afraid that I would charge her with sinister designs. I hastened to allay this fear by pointing out the clue of strap-hanging. When the second dream begins, her husband is alive and it is she who hangs. Moreover, her husband is a little boy and she did not know him when he was little. Thus it seemed that the central theme of the dream was not an aggression against her husband, but against herself. As hanging causes death by suffocation, the dream concerned some event in which the loss of breath had threatened her with the loss of life.

The first indication of the nature of this event came in associations with the silver hammer. It reminded the patient of her mother's tool box. Then, because of the brightness of the hammer, she thought of a surgical instrument of delivery. Putting her husband (the little boy) out of his misery was a kind of delivery—a delivery from pain. Attention was thus immediately directed to the patient's own birth, and she had a good deal to say on this score. Her mother nearly died in giving birth to her and she herself was so severely hurt by instruments that her life was despaired of. For two days she was not allowed to go to her mother and had no comfort to make up for the ordeal through which she passed. In knocking the child under the chin with a surgical instrument while strap-hanging in the bus, she was intent on delivering herself from the terror of suffocation in the course of her birth. With the three bodies hanging from the gibbets she associated Christ between the two thieves, crucifixion of an innocent man. The innocent man was herself, and now the significant question arose why she should represent herself by her husband, putting herself in a masculine role.

The story was not difficult to piece together. The patient's father died shortly after she was born. Her mother did not marry again and she grew up fatherless. As is usual in such cases, she developed a very dominating personality. There being no man in the household on whom to rely, she had to rely on herself. For this reason, it is logical to assume that the boy represents her masculinity, which, in its erotic aspect, was repressed at great cost. If the partial foundation of a woman's masculinity is that in birth the body of the child is in a phallic relationship to the mother, she was symbolically delivering herself both from the trauma of birth and of her masculine sexuality in putting the boy out of his misery. The bus in which she was travelling at night was her mother's body. She was travelling within the bus, but expected to find her husband outside, on top. She did find her masculine regret outside her mother's body, after birth, and passing into the post-natal world she experienced the strangulation which the peculiar position of her husband's body on the gibbet reveals. Disregarding the fact that in England hanging is done by dropping the victim from a trap, no corpse could hang from a gibbet with knees drawn up and body hunched. The position reminds one of the fetus within the womb.

Here emerges another, highly curious fact. The patient's husband was slightly hunched and her daughter inherited this bad carriage. This was a grievance against her husband which she could not give up and by it she rationalized her sexual hostility toward him. The secret root of this hostility was her own masculinity, which protested against her playing the feminine role. The husband was a wonderful peg on which to hang her own invalidism on every score. When he is pulled up on a gibbet, she represents herself being pulled out of her mother's womb, strangled and suffocated, hunched as a fetus and hunched as her husband carried himself. When she sets out to look for her husband on top of the bus, she is also looking for the child that she was, lost in the darkness of the night of her birth. For twenty-five years she woke up every night at 2 A.M., with her palate parched and her tongue sticking out. I strongly suspected that this was the hour of her birth, but unfortunately no living relative could furnish verification.

Indications that this analysis of the patient's claustrophobia hit home came in sensations of relief. In her first separation dream from the previous acute distress, her husband was still a scapegoat but more detached, a strange man about to depart. This was the dream:

A ship at a pier and many strangers sitting around a long table eating. My husband was a complete stranger and told me he was going to leave. I was overjoyed, but he did not believe me. I said: "I have less feeling for you than I have for a louse; in fact you are more trouble to me than a louse has ever been." The man was short, waspy and horrible looking.

A horrible condition is about to end. There is a farewell party and a boat is about to pull out. On the boat, the hated husband is leaving but being a stranger, his image suggests the Hyde element behind Dr. Jekyll. It seems as if the revolting appearance of the stranger stood for the patient's claustrophobia personified, and the man is compared to a louse because this parasite is a good symbol for something dirty and infectious that is "eating us." As the ship is also a symbol of the boat of life and the mother's body, it appears that the separation equally covers the trauma of birth. The latter element was more explicitly shown in a later dream:

I was driving to my cousin's big house. On entering the drive, the road turned and I found myself going backwards and falling into a crevice on the road. The crevice was bottomless and it seemed that this was the end; but I only fell in waist high and succeeded in crawling out.

The big house is the mother's body and the crevice is the vaginal door. The dream re-enacts her fall in birth. The dream shows both the fall and the fear, but the horror is no longer unbearable. The dreamer is able to crawl out and convinces herself that she is not threatened by death. The pressure in the dreamer's unconscious mind is easing. The crucial point has been passed when she was able to face death. From then on recovery was only a matter of time.

What would happen to a victim of claustrophobia if he were sent to jail? Very likely, he would have to be sent to a prison hospital as he would behave like a maniac and might go insane if kept locked up in a cell. For this very reason, victims of claustrophobia are not likely to commit an act that would land them in jail. They have great respect for the law; the instinct of self-preservation helps to keep them on the straight and narrow path. Nevertheless, the fear of being jailed might become part of the claustrophobia complex because of repressed aggressive fantasies. Such was the case of a patient who, though engaged for over two years, resisted marriage because he could not persuade himself to leave his mother. Here is a hypnagogic vision which he reported: "My fiancée, at my home, takes some tablets and commits suicide. Thoughts of my claustrophobia rush into my mind."

The vision shows a death wish against the fiancée. If she would take poison, he would not have to leave his mother. One cannot have such fantasies with impunity. If she did die, he would be her murderer and would have to go to jail. The very thought of that was sufficient to make him shiver. He had a morbid dread of prisons and his thoughts of claustrophobia often centered on a prison cell.

The reason was the strange equation which existed in his mind between a prison cell and his parents' bedroom. As an infant, he was cooped up in the parental double bed between his mother and the wall. His father was a drunkard and a brute. He always came home late and started fighting. His mother was sadistic and used to feed her children on horror stories about people locked up in cupboards. The room in which he slept was like a prison. It had only one door. Recently, at his brother-in-law's house, he had to go down into the cellar to fetch something. He became violently afraid that he would be locked in. "All my life it was an ordeal for me to go to bed. The very thought would keep me awake. I could sleep anywhere but in a bed. I don't like beds. I would rather sleep in a chair."

It would be desirable to possess statistical data as to the incidence of mental disorder in penitentiaries following claustrophobic reactions in prisoners who committed crimes without premeditation. The treatment of claustrophobia by Birth Therapy might become a valuable asset to criminology.

5.

FROM CLAUSTROPHOBIA TO INSOMNIA

THE psychological structure behind chronic insomnia may show considerable complexity. It is not an isolated form of neurotic behavior; hence it cannot be cured without unravelling a good part of the patient's psychic life.

The subject of this case is a forty-six year old man who suffered from insomnia of a particularly severe character. He used to go to bed in fear that he would not fall asleep. When he did sleep, he awoke two or three times a week within an hour in such panic that he had to get up and walk until he was exhausted. His wife could not let him pace the streets alone in his panicky condition, and the strain of lost sleep began to tell on both. Medical measures were of little help. He took luminal pills and he drank beer before going to bed; neither of them guaranteed sound sleep. However, he did experience some relief from enemas, which he began to take regularly.

This patient was the youngest in a family of four sons and three daughters. He was bullied by his older brother and sisters, suffered from a strong feeling of inferiority, and was very shy and apologetic in his manner. At the age of nineteen, for no reason he could explain, he attempted suicide by taking an overdose of luminal. He was frightened of the future and of his superiors and could never stand up for his rights. Nevertheless, his character was rigid, duplicating a very pedantic father's strict habits. In his home everything

46

had its habitual place and he went into tantrums if anything was moved. Yet, politically, he used to participate in revolutionary activities. He was brought up as a strict Catholic, but he resented saying his prayers because, in childhood, this meant going to bed; and he had very unhappy memories about his confirmation because, in a white tie and ribbon, he looked like a girl and was mercilessly teased by the other boys. At the age of twenty-two he became impotent for a year and a half. Occasionally he still had pains on ejaculation as though he had been stabbed by a knife.

The first discovery bearing on his insomnia was that it began after his mother died in Budapest a year and a half previously. The news prostrated him, and for two and a half months he was in bed for what were thought to be "spots on his lungs." The doctor later admitted that he was not sure of his ground but felt advised to make an impression on the patient because he was very run down and needed rest. With this diagnosis, a new dread of being tubercular was added to his life, and he insisted on repeated examinations to assure himself that there was nothing wrong with his lungs.

The second discovery was that symptoms of claustrophobia were hidden behind his insomnia. Going to sleep felt like running out of breath, a sensation which frightened him. The same feeling of breathlessness overcame him in subway crowds. He felt suffocating; he had to tear his shirt open and run out of the train. He had recurrent dreams of the subway tracks running up to the point of a "V," and these dreams were always accompanied by a feeling of constriction and anxiety. Years ago, in Munich, he climbed an 1800 meter high mountain. He became very upset on the plateau without being able to understand his feelings. He had to cross a suspension bridge, which made him exceedingly nervous.

I asked him to observe himself more closely and report the thoughts that came to his mind if he had another attack of fear. The attack came on a Sunday night and he remembered thinking just previous to it: the Sunday is gone, another week is beginning, I am getting older, my organs are getting worn out, I cannot stand the pace of other men, I am afraid of going to bed.

Here was the germ of a third discovery: the fear of death disguised as the fear of the future. "Sleeping is but a-dying." He was afraid he might never wake again.

Years ago he had a tonsillectomy and fought madly against the anaesthetic. He suddenly realized that his breathing difficulties before going to sleep were localized in his nose. His shortness of breath produced agitation; he had to get up and do something.

This threw light on his nightly perambulations. Dead men do not move. As long as he moved, he answered his death fears, he could convince himself that his legs and organs were functioning, that he was not about to die. Was he so frightened of death even at an early age that he flew to it by suicide? He was conscious that the luminal tablets he took merely acted as a sedative and not as a sleep-inducing drug. He admitted that he was badly frightened of the future, that he would not be able to make a living, that he would starve. The current situation supported such fears. His earning power was very slight and constantly reduced by sickness. He was kept by a hard-working wife, and he was mortified because of it.

In searching for death fears in his past that he could have projected into the future, he recalled that at the age of eight to ten a grocer's pushcart hit him from behind and threw him over. He picked himself up, ran home and there promptly fainted. Later the memory of a much earlier accident returned. A janitress pushed him off the top of a first-floor staircase, and he fell down backwards, bruising himself badly. He thought he was picked up unconscious in the street. In 1918 he participated in the national revolution in Hungary. The police shot at the crowd in which he was, but he escaped injury. Later, during the reign of White Terror, he was stopped in the street by a Jew-baiting group which demanded proof that he was not a Jew. Though he could have easily proved that he was not circumcised, he was so frightened that he gave up and resigned himself to death.

After another attack of fear at night, he noticed that he had a very "crowded feeling" * and recognized that he was frightened of going

---

* This "crowded feeling" deserves the name of mental claustrophobia. It is a pressure of affairs, with a feeling of panic, in view of the inadequacy of normal means of discharge.

insane. The grip of this feeling was so strong that he was in a daze throughout the day that followed and could neither see nor hear. Then he recalled having heard that those who had once poisoned themselves with luminal went insane sooner or later. Some time after this he remembered his fears of being caught at masturbation, his feelings of shame when night losses left their trace on the bedsheet, and the stories which he heard of masturbation leading to madness.

The query now arose whether insomnia was a defense mechanism against night losses and whether he had associated the state of sleep with insanity. In a sense, going to sleep does stand for the extinction of reason and the surrender of the most precious attribute of conscious existence. Getting up and demonstrating physical mobility proves that this extinction and surrender are not permanent. The motive of the patient's nightly perambulations was probably rooted in the frantic need to convince himself that both his body and his mind were alive.

During the first two weeks of his analysis, in which he had only four interviews, the patient had but one vague dream. In that dream he was moving out of his apartment or improving it; he could not tell which. Such confusion in recollection is usually the sign of ambivalence; both versions of the dream are intended. Looking for a new apartment is a usual symbol of the search for a new personality, while improving it indicates the re-shaping of the old personality; both constructions amount to the same thing. The acceptance of the analytic process is well indicated by such dreams.

In his second dream, he was pushing furniture around the whole night. He was in his present apartment. His oldest brother, John (who lives in Budapest and is the head of the family since the father's death), was present and stacks of wood were piled against the wall. His wife pushed the pile around as if it were on wheels. For a moment it looked as if the wood pile would smash into his ten gallon fish tank, but he snatched the tank away in time.

This dream has a number of linguistic keys to which an understanding of the Hungarian language is necessary. The technical term in which he described the stack· of wood is "öl fa." "Fa" means wood and "öl" is a cubic measurement, but it also means lap (of a woman) and, as a verb, to kill. Further it conceals the root of another verb "olel," which means to embrace. Fish is "hal" in Hungarian, but the same word, as a verb, means to die. The fear of the smashing of the fish tank thus may simply refer to the patient's fear of dying. The linguistic ambivalence, special to the Hungarian language, serves to illustrate how the phallic symbol of the fish may mean, instead of life, its opposite, death—in which we need not see any evidence of confusion from the moment we accept the essential identity of birth and death as transitions similar to the change of the seasons.

There is no fear dream, I claim, which does not contain a hidden clue to the origin of the fear. The very ambivalence in the meaning of the word "hal" (fish) reveals symbolic values. On superficial considerations the dream conveys the impression that the idea of changing (represented by the shifted furniture) gives the patient the feeling of dying; also that the dream probably prepares him for the death of his old personality, which, of course, he is reluctant to give up as it is the only one he knows. An interpretation on a deeper level becomes incumbent the moment we add to the death value of fish (dying), which equates with "öl" (to kill), the ambivalent life value of "ol," which means lap. As the patient's wife enters into it by a kind of carrying along the pile of wood (the chopped up, lifeless remains of what was once a living tree, a tree of life), we cannot help thinking of the mother's lap and of the fish in the tank as fitting symbols of the child within the womb. The fear of the tank's being crushed thus appears to be a displacement of the fear of birth from the contained onto the container, while the symbolism of the chopped wood shows an additional identification between the fear of life and the fear of death. One is also tempted to add that the same ambivalence which brings killing and the mother's lap together can be found in the tank, which is a container for the fish but also an instrument of killing in war.

For all these reasons it seemed as if the patient needed a shift regarding the organismic memories of his birth, the basic shock underlying many neurotic manifestations of personality. This view is in full agreement with Freud's claim that "all anxiety goes back originally to the anxiety of birth." It seemed possible that the compression suffered in birth was the anchor of the patient's claustrophobia. If we recall the "V" shaped subway track in his constriction nightmares, we may well query if "V" stood for vagina, on linguistic grounds, or was just a pictorial reference to the maternal body with extended legs preparatory to giving birth.

The same night that the fish tank dream occurred, the patient also dreamed that he would have to fight Joe Louis, and he was frightened. The interpretation which he offered was that Joe Louis stood for pressure because he felt a mental pressure from the moment he woke from the dream.

The association was interesting. It hinted at claustrophobia. Why should he personify it? I knew by this time that the patient was on bad terms with his oldest brother, John, now the head of the family. John was in his dream when the fish tank was nearly smashed. As the head of the family, he undoubtedly stood for the patient's father. Was it possible that Joe Louis combined John's image with that of the ogre father? All authorities are father symbols and Joe Louis as a colored boxing champion could well represent the black father who takes away the mother from the child and whom one learns to fear as soon as a mother fixation develops. If both Joe Louis and John stood for the father, the smashing of the fish tank indicated strong castration fears—which explains the patient's collapse when attacked by the Jew-baiters. He had to expose his penis to show that he was not circumcised, and this exhibitionistic act was well calculated to mobilize the secondary component of his claustrophobia: the fear of genital crushing or castration. But birth is also a genital event and a form of genital crushing (by the mother's genitalia), which opens up vistas of identification between birth, incest (fundamentally the desire to return, at least partially, into the "fish tank") and castration. The latter must have played the principal part in the patient's psychic impotence.

He now recalled that at the time of the Jew-baiting incident, he was frightened on the sun roof of a public bath by a stranger who sat beside him and touched his penis. His eyes were closed and he thought the touch was his friend's. When he opened his eyes and saw the stranger, he received a shock. An altercation ensued, in the course of which his friend slapped the stranger and they both escaped from him by jumping into a "Pater Noster," the name for an open elevator in constant motion with cars on top of each other.

The name was a new one for me. It seemed to precipitate the patient's father into the midst of a homosexual situation. I pursued my inquiries along this line and found that this friend with whom the patient lived, had an enormous penis and that whenever he suffered cuts from female pubic hair, the patient used to prepare tampons for him. He also remembered seeing his friend's penis in erection and hearing the groans of the woman with whom the friend had intercourse; but he always avoided being in the same room when he had intercourse because the scene filled him with disgust. Suddenly, the patient realized that his period of impotence coincided with the time when he lived with his friend. It now seemed distinctly possible that an unconscious identification existed between the friend and the patient's father and that the cause of the psychic impotence may have been twofold: the fear of the father and the desire for the father, the latter as a repressed homosexual attraction producing temporary loss of virility in punishment of the very desire.

One revelation now followed another. Before the patient's insomnia began, he used to think a lot about a sweetheart who had the habit of putting her finger in his anus during intercourse. This excited him sexually. The woman also liked to be on top of him, thus placing him in the feminine position. As a small boy, the patient was often called a "sissy" and he intensely resented it—because the description was not quite unwarranted. His features were rather feminine, his skin very white and almost hairless. On reflection, he admitted that his fear attacks were rather suggestive of feminine hysteria. If we recall that he was in the habit of curing his insomnia by enemas, the homosexual evaluation of which is apparent, and if we consider further that he had suffered from piles, bled from the anus and took injections to cure them, we face the additional query as to what extent insomnia was useful as a defense mechanism against homosexual dreams and fantasies, and as to what extent castration was a punishment.

The next component of insomnia emerged from an examination of the patient's alarm clock anxiety. He was always afraid that the alarm would not ring and that he would over-sleep. This fear seemed slightly paradoxical in a patient suffering from insomnia. Its origin was soon traced to the patient's childhood. He used to go to bed at 10 P.M. Before doing so, he always went to the lavatory, but five minutes later he always had to get up and pass water again. The reason for this compulsion was that an older brother, next to him in age, was often beaten for habitual bed wetting. This recollection argued for the possibility that the infantile fear of wetting the bed while asleep might be another factor preventing him from going to sleep and urging him to get up for his nightly wanderings. This possibility was strengthened by the discovery of some marked infantile traits. The patient always carried an extra handkerchief in his pocket which he called the suckling rag. Keeping it in his trouser pocket, he used to rub his finger on it, trying to find a cool spot. He knew how this curious habit originated. He used to suck his two middle fingers until a late age; also, he used to hang his mother's blouse over the same two fingers and smell it. Some women appealed to him because of the smell of their sweat, others did not for the same reason. It seemed that he was still unweaned from his mother and that in unconscious fantasy he kept up that delightful sensation of oneness with the maternal organism on which all mother-body fantasies are based.

Presently came the clear revelation that his claustrophobia originated in the trauma of his birth. Again on a Sunday night, after his fifth session, he woke from a dream in panic and with very bitter feelings. He dreamed:

I was running on housetops and was enjoying it. We wanted to sneak into a sport arena and found ourselves between two fences which formed the entrance. A dense crowd was there and I was compressed. I became frightened and woke up gasping.

Further indication that the story of his claustrophobia was breaking could be found in his dream of the night before:

I was in a car with Joe, a fellow worker, who often takes me as far as the tram. We reached a place where a truck was stuck in the mud. Its back was open. We were asked to help pull it out of the mud. I don't know what we did, but presently we saw it moving, and we jumped into the back of the truck. There was plenty of room.

The first dream immediately recalled to the patient his subway compression nightmares. These, in turn, brought back two other memories. As a young boy, his head stuck between the bars of a chair. He could not pull it out and became badly frightened. The second such fright occurred in a Catholic procession to which he was taken by his brother Joe. He was very small and could not see the crowd. Presently he felt that he was getting no air. He wore a round cap with a wire in it to keep the brim stiff. The hat was crushed and the wire came out. He could not bear the situation any longer and began to scream.

The crushed hat as a covering for the head suggests an injury to the head. The memory of such an injury must have been the cause of his panic when his head stuck between the bars of a chair. The cap described is called "tányér sapka" (dish cap) in Hungarian. If the associations given with a dream are part of the material from which the unconscious mind builds the dream by a process of condensation, we cannot fail to notice a certain similarity of representation between the shape of the cap (dish cap, plate) and the bowl of the arena. The arena, because of the linguistic phrase "arena of life" and because of its hollow shape, is frequently used for symbolizing the womb. The two fences, which form the entrance to the arena, clearly suggest the mother's legs, while the compression within refers to the tribulation of birth. The choice of the symbol was due to parallel memories. He used to sneak into a sport arena through a private garden at the end of which there was a fence. Between this fence and the fence of the arena was a narrow passage in which a dangerous dog was kept. He could jump from one fence to the other and escape the dog; but there was always the danger that he might slip and fall, in which case the dog would get him.

The truck stuck in the mud symbolizes the difficulties of birth. Joe, the fellow worker, stands for his brother, whom he mentioned in the incident of panic in the church crowd. The request to pull the truck out of the mud is an unconscious bid for freedom. The open back of the truck suggests the infantile notion of birth through the anus. Jumping into the back of the truck is a reversal of the process of birth. Brother Joe joins him because he is dead. He who is dead has returned to Mother Earth. Birth and death represent the same concept for the unconscious mind. Thus the dream also teaches the lesson that the fear of death is the fear of birth. The recognition of this simple but fundamental fact may stop us from converting the fear of birth into an abnormal fear of death and may deliver us from the worst spectre of our earthly existence.

A further important revelation came from another dream fragment in which he was at home and stayed with his mother while the other members of the family went on a picnic. His mother had a glass of chocolate with two wires running into it, and these wires were attached to a piece of metal at the bottom of the glass. It was supposed to be a kind of electric warmer, but it did more in the dream; it evaporated the chocolate, leaving but a little brown sediment at the bottom of the glass. His mother said, "Don't mind it, we shall make another."

Chocolate—a milk product—was always a delicacy in the patient's home. He exposes it to the catalyzing effect of an electric current and, judging by the sediment, dissolves it into its component elements. It seems as if the dream expressed the desire to resolve the patient's attachment to the breast, a desire which met with some resistance as his mother promised to replace the vanishing chocolate with a fresh supply.

The dream proved to be important because it led to the recollection that his mother had suffered from insomnia in the same way as he did. She, too, took luminal. (By trying to commit suicide with luminal, was he obeying an obscure desire to return into the peace of his mother's womb?) She, too, got up in the night and walked about. She used to come into his room and say, "Oh, my dear boy, I don't want to wake you up, but again I cannot sleep." Together with this came the memory that in 1937 he was cabled to return to Budapest because his mother was sick and her death was feared. She recovered, however, and wanted to keep him at home. He would have liked to stay. But he decided to play the tough boy; also, his wife was in America, so he returned.

When his mother died, the thought began to haunt him that this would not have happened if he had stayed at home. The reason he returned to America was his wife. If he were guilty of his mother's death, so was his wife. Hence, while punishing himself with his mother's insomnia, he saw to it that his wife shared the punishment and dragged her along on his nightly perambulations.

While I pointed this out, the patient was silently ruminating, then confessed that during his insomnia attacks he felt a strange hostility to his wife which he could not understand.

He had one more fear attack, which finally convinced him that the root of his claustrophobia had been hit. The attack came after a dream in which he was a cowboy and was pursued by other cowboys on horseback and got stuck in the mud somewhere. He woke with panicky feelings, but instead of turning against his wife, he turned against her dog, and kicked it because it whined, declaring that it must go.

The cowboy is the cow's boy, and the cow, because of its life-giving milk, is one of the most ancient mother symbols, dating back to Isis, the cow-headed Goddess of remote Egyptian days. Of mud the patient had always been afraid. Once in a new suit, he fell into a ditch which was full of sticky mud. His mother frightened him by telling him that it was the type of mud that could have sucked him under. At another time, in a rye barn, he was afraid he would sink into the rye. On the seashore he could not tolerate being covered with sand. He could not sleep in a very soft bed for fear he would sink into it and suffocate. His father used to cover his face with a handkerchief when he went to sleep. The patient always became panicky if anything covered his face. When his nose became clogged, his impulse was to jump into the air, as he used to do at night when the sensation of loss of air assailed him in bed. Pitch darkness impressed him as a dark cover which one must throw off. He could not suffer a plaster cast on his face, or hot towels in a barber shop. Mud also suggested feces to him (and anal birth— a hint at an additional value in the brown sediment left from the chocolate). He remembered throwing fire-crackers between the legs of prostitutes in the street and their swearing at him, "Why did your mother defecate you into this world?" His mother used to say that dreaming about mud or dirty water meant illness. She suffered from the fear of being buried alive, and this thought gave the patient acute discomfort, too. In bed he always pulled the covers right up to his neck. At one time he worked in a hothouse. He always wore a shawl around his neck, but had no idea from what he was protecting himself.

Presently the patient reported that he was able to travel in the crowded subway without discomfort. He was now sleeping well, but he still took his beer and luminal as he dared not trust himself without it. Slowly his confidence grew, and the tension in his dream life relaxed. He reported:

I dreamed that the bathroom was flooded by water. I don't know whether it came from the tap or the toilet but it was clean. It ran into the living room. I jumped up with the same quickness with which I used to wake from nightmares and ran for the mop. My wife was asleep. All this was part of the dream.

The breaking of the water of the womb (bathroom), an event that heralds birth is indicated. The cleanness of the water alludes to the patient's deliverance from the pressure memories of birth or, at least, it initiates the process of liberation. The significant link with his previous nightmares is the quickness of his movement; but the dream woke him without tension and he was able to go back to sleep.

A few days later he dreamed:

Somebody handed me a cigar. As I bit off its end, I found it saturated with sugar. I saw tiny red sweets in the tobacco and it was wet. I said to myself: I am not chewing tobacco, and I threw it away.

The patient did not see the man who handed him the cigar, but he guessed it could have been the director in his old job who used to offer him cigars. The tiny red sweets were the kind he used to make with menthol in the pharmacy where he worked. Suddenly he realized that he always smoked mentholated cigarettes and was unable to break himself of the habit in spite of the doctor's warning. I asked him what the sweet thing symbolized by the cigar could be. He thought it could be the bottle. I pointed out that the bottle is a substitute for the breast. Then came an important memory. At home, when he used to smoke, his mother always chided him, "Must you have the bottle in your mouth again?" He could now see the meaning of the cigar dream. Like a puppy which suckles in its sleep, he "dreamed" while smoking that his mother's nipple was in his mouth, thereby assuring himself that he had not really lost his mother by weaning, that his mother was still alive and looking after him, that he had not really been born at all, and reality was a dream. When he threw away the cigar, he showed a determination to separate himself from his mother and to become as much the adult as his director was.

Proof of the patient's growing up was forthcoming fast. With some trepidation, he tried to see if he could stand the steam of the bathroom. He could. Then he tried the hot towel in the barber shop. He felt no panic. He gave up mentholated cigarettes. He cut down on his luminal tablets and showed the consolidation of his unconscious position by a beautiful dream of re-birth.

In front of our shop somebody dropped flowers into the gutter. I picked them up and found them to be lilacs and gardenias, both of them fastened to the end of long metal sticks as if growing from them, the type of stick which, with a loop on it, dogcatchers use.

He associated lilacs with Spring. The Hungarian word for lilac is "orgona," which also means organ, the musical instrument. As soon as the patient's attention was directed to this ambivalence, he recalled his first experience in claustrophobia. He was taken to a midnight mass. He was small and sleepy. People around him smelt of wine. He could not see and could not get enough air. He felt ill with the same sensations he later associated with claustrophobia. He remembered the organ played a song about Jesus and the manger in which He was born.

This may have been the first event that mobilized the patient's trauma of birth and brought forth a fear reaction to compression and loss of breath. In the dream we see the symbol of death (the dog-catcher's loop) replaced by lilacs, the symbol of Spring and new awakening. The patient never liked gardenias; their smell reminded him of funerals. So we have two flowers, one standing for life, the other for death. The shop before which he finds them is his wife's shop and the two sticks, in phallic evaluation, represent his emotional attitude to the mother and the wife. His morbid attachment to his mother was the death of him by neurosis. To his wife he had unconsciously assigned the place of a mother substitute. If he could detach the mother pattern from his wife, and make her a successor instead of a substitute, he would be free and adjusted right down to the basic levels of his personality, as the symbol of which he chose the gutter.

The patient balked at this second important task of his analytic labors. He was a fractional patient, coming twice a week, finding it very difficult to pay his way. Believing that the immense relief he gained from all his symptoms in twenty-two sessions was permanent, he broke away, heedless of my warning. How much share his wife (who seemed to resent his analytic treatments) had in it I could never fully ascertain. Perhaps, unwisely, he discussed with her this problem of mother identification and detachment of libido and she became frightened that in case of complete analytic success she would lose him. Whosoever was responsible, the price which the patient paid was heavy. Presently he lost the ground he gained and came back, four months later, in a pitiable condition. I saw him a few times, and succeeded in pouring new life into him, but again he used his strength against himself and broke away before his analysis could have been finished. However, the last news I had of him several months later was encouraging. He had control of his claustrophobia, was able to sleep and travel back and forth between his house and his place of employment, a far more remunerative one than he had had for years. Though the cure was not completed, the main purpose of his analysis had been accomplished, in spite of the resistance with which it had to contend.

6.

NIGHTMARES OF FALLING

FALLING headlong from heights is a typical dream the occurrence of which has been noted since ancient days because of its frequency and the anguish which accompanies it.* Yet remarkably little progress has been made towards understanding the motives that inspire such dreams. Barring cardiac conditions, no general circulatory or nervous disturbance has been found responsible for them, in view of which it is reasonable to assume that a psychological condition of universal application may hold the key.

The temptation to draw an immediate parallel between falling and flying dreams has proved irresistible to most psychologists. Like a schoolboy switches from the subject of his lesson to another which he knows better, they change from falling to flying. The transition is easy, as falling is a form of downward flight and the victim of falling dreams seldom hits the ground. But the analogy ends right there. Flying dreams do not inspire anxiety; on the contrary, they are accompanied by a great sense of exhilaration.

Books on dream interpretation devote little space to falling dreams. The subject is exhausted before it is begun. Freud's *The Interpretation of Dreams* is still a classic, but all he suggests is that childhood experiences of falling out of bed might be the cause of such dreams. Then he continues:

---

* "*De montibus altis se quasi praecipitent ad terram corpore toto*" (Lucretius, Book IV, 1014-15).

61

"Their interpretation when they occur in women is subject to no difficulty because women always accept the symbolic sense of falling, which is a circumlocution for the indulgence of an erotic temptation." °

While moral fall may cause great anguish to women of rigid religious education, the prevalence of falling dreams is far too widespread to be accounted for on this basis. The idea that sex may have a bearing on the occurrence of such dreams is due to the original Freudian tendency to find erotic motives behind most dream manifestations. As a universal motive, the fear of death is much more promising, as it requires no sexual distinction. Meeting death by falling into an abyss must have been one of the most elementary experiences of the race. In cases of extreme fatigue, the very process of falling asleep gives the sensation of falling down a deep shaft. From the study of cases of severe insomnia, I am satisfied that loss of consciousness in going to sleep, together with changes in heartbeat, respiration and other metabolic functions, does convey the suggestion of dying. I also find it very probable that not understanding the restorative function of sleep, primitive man considered it his worst enemy because sleepiness robbed him of his strength and exposed him to wild animals and human enemies in a condition of complete helplessness. Our archaic heritage, stimulated by collapse and fainting experiences in the waking state, can well be the basis for the dramatization of the fear of death in dreams of falling; yet clinical experience has led me to adopt a much simpler generic view which, though I do not claim it to be of universal application, not only helps to understand nightmares of falling but also enables us to release them.

The essential discovery was made by the behaviorist school of psychology, but they stopped short of its exploitation. According to their claim, the fear of falling or loss of position is one of the original fears with which a child is born—original because there is no experience to account for it; the reflex movement of the hands thrown up in the air in self-protection is not conditioned.

° Sigmund Freud, *The Interpretation of Dreams,* rev. edition, Macmillan Co., New York, 1915, p. 239.

Nightmares of Falling

I accept that the fear of falling is with us at birth, but I claim that it is conditioned because birth is an experience in loss of position; it is a falling away from the mother's body under the influence of an irresistible driving force.

The reaction of the arms changes later in life as a result of falling accidents. The child learns that its body will not be protected if the hands go up in the air and that bruising is less likely to occur if the hands are used for a landing on all fours.

Fiction writers like to exploit the child's first curious protective reaction. They see in it an archaic reflex, a reversion to the simian stage. They say that the child acts like a monkey, that it is trying to save itself by catching a tree branch above. They also point out that in falling nightmares we do not hit the ground. Only the fear of hitting it has been handed down, because the monkey that actually hit the ground died and could not pass on the ancestral memory.

This pleasant fiction has nothing to do with facts. Gravity is almost non-existent for the child within the womb. Its arms are bent at the elbows and folded over the chest. After birth they are free to explore the space all around. In falling, they do not snatch at the branch of a tree above. Slightly modified by the acquired flexibility of the arms in the new environment, the protective movement appears rather to be conditioned by fetal memories. It is a regressive phenomenon, a dynamic manifestation of the desire to resume a position of security. Nor is it true that we never hit the ground in falling dreams. We do. Actual falling experiences provide the pattern. People sometimes wake up on the floor, having fallen out of bed at night. Then they do remember hitting the ground. The actual impact is carried into the dream.

It is true, however, that in the typical falling nightmare we wake up before we reach the ground. In the present chapter we are mainly concerned with this type of dream. It is accompanied by great anxiety. The emotional charge is far heavier than experiences in falling justify. We would never survive falling into such bottomless abysses as the nightmares portray. The dream seldom stops at the fear of falling. We are actually plunging down into the deep and the dream has to break or we would die of the anxiety. The dream breathes the unknown. Those who are recurrently afflicted by it often suffer from the twin affliction of claustrophobia. In such instances it is wise to keep in mind that the fear of falling might originate in birth.

A doctor's wife tells me that when she was a small child her father would not leave her alone on the swing. He would toss her up so high that she was seized with dread as soon as she saw him coming. She still shrinks from her father because of these emotions. She used to have a recurrent dream in which she fell out of a high window and flew up on an arc to an opposite high point.

As falling out of a window is a typical birth memory, the recurrent dream shows how the fear of falling from the swing succeeded in mobilizing her trauma of birth. Claustrophobia developed. For a long time she could not use elevators. Getting out of them was a dreadful moment because she always expected them to fall.

Here again the emphasis is on getting out, which corresponds to leaving the mother's body. She was unable to use elevators because, to her unconscious mind, they suggested her mother's womb; at the moment when the elevator stopped the threat of the flooding of the conscious mind with the memory of an unbearable ordeal became acute. Not knowing what this ordeal was, she protected herself against the rising memory by avoiding elevators as far as possible. The arc symbolism is worth noting because of its correspondence with the pubic arch.

The varieties of such experiences are endless. A pregnant woman fell down the stairs and had a miscarriage. Ever since she has had an abnormal fear of descending stairs. She is no longer pregnant and consequently cannot lose a child; she is sure on her legs and she remembers the fall; therefore, she is frightened of something else, to which falling down stairs is a symbolic clue. My conclusion is that the miscarriage revived the ordeal of her own birth. It is as if she gave birth to herself in losing the child, as if she were going to her death on the stairs. To save herself from a recurrence of the harrowing experience of her first fall from the womb, she has to avoid stairs as far as it is humanly possible.

Nightmares of Falling

Another woman cannot sit on the balcony in a theater because once she lost her balance, rolled from the balcony to the bottom of the stairs and hurt herself badly. She cannot travel in subways because as a child she saw dead, burnt bodies being brought out of the tunnel of the Metro in Paris after a dreadful accident. When anybody has a conscious memory of such horrors and yet suffers from morbid fear, we may safely assume that another deeper, forgotten experience lies behind the remembered one, and that this is the principal determinant of the reaction. My experience in the interpretation of dream symbols encourages me to assume that the subway tunnel, with the dead, burnt bodies, concealed memories of the journey from the womb into this life and that the injury caused by the fall from the stairs of the balcony could not be forgotten because it set aglow the long buried pain and fear of being crushed to death by the contracting walls of the uterine passage.

Heart patients complain of anxiety dreams of falling. Such dreams are believed to result from the irregularity of their heartbeats. Any break in the regular functioning of the heart carries with it the suggestion of death. The missing beat is converted into a sensation of falling and into dread of an abyss. To our unconscious imagination the heart is more alive than any other organ. It moves within our body as a child stirs within its mother's womb after the quickening, and the parallelism is further strengthened by maternal statements about childbirth: "I carried you within (or under) my heart." If the heart is a child within our "maternal" organism, the falling sensation caused by the missing heartbeat would, of necessity, associate with the fall in birth. A lady dreams:

I was in a room, with my back to the door. The door opened and I suddenly became aware of danger. I turned and saw an awful abyss behind me. I was terrified. On awakening, I recalled a close call which I had in the subway recently. The door of a speeding express train opened right behind me and a sudden lurch almost threw me out on the tracks.

Some weeks before the dream this patient underwent a thyroid operation; it was rendered urgent by the constant over-secretion of thyroxin into her blood stream. Her heart muscles were affected and an erratic cardiac activity ensued. The subway association is a valuable clue to the meaning of the dream. It suggests that the dream is a birth nightmare. All immediate associations are part of the dream. We may, therefore, treat the accident as if it were a dream. The tunnel is a symbol of the uterine passage and the tracks on which she almost fell are suggestive of the mother's legs extended in birth. The probability is that the shock of the near-accident set up very distant reverberations in the lady's unconscious mind and was responsible for the dream. The memory of cardiac irregularity helped in the choice of symbols. The room in the real dream is her body and the awful depth behind the door is a dramatization of the intensity of the fear which her real heart condition had mobilized.

The fear of pursuit and the fear of falling are dramatically represented in the following dream of a 36-year-old attorney; it was one of many similar dreams that occurred again and again over a number of years:

I am chased and get to the end of a cliff. There is a ladder going down. I climb down to the last rung, below which is an abyss which seems to be thousands of feet deep. The people who are chasing me descend the ladder after me and I am cornered. I can move neither up nor down. I wake up in a cold sweat.

The ladder symbolism deserves special notice. In this case the ladder suggests an inverted tunnel: instead of compression by the two banks of the tunnel, there is a lateral limitation within narrow bounds. It is a substitute for immobilization by compression. The intensity of the fear is represented by the bottomless abyss and the pursuit, which renders the escape hopeless. It is this touch of hopelessness in birth dreams which causes such agony of mind that the dreamer simply must wake up or he would die of horror.

Jacob's ladder is perhaps the oldest ladder dream we have on record. It symbolizes man's descent from Heaven to Earth and illustrates the loss of our spiritual estate by incarnation and birth.

Nightmares of Falling

For contact between Heaven and Earth, a better symbol would be difficult to find. Swedenborg gives us a good illustration how ladder, stairs and the fear of falling can be correlated with aspirations to reach the spiritual world:

"Quite freely and boldly, I stepped down a large stairway; by and by there was a ladder, below it there was a hole which went down to quite a great depth; it was difficult to get to the other side without falling into the hole. On the other side there were persons to whom I reached out my hand to help get over. I awoke. It is the danger in which I am of falling into the abyss, unless I receive help." *

From his interpretation of the dream as shown in the last sentence, we see that Swedenborg was unaware of the birth symbolism of the abyss. The only certain way in which we can return to the spiritual world is the way we came. It is "difficult to get to the other side without falling into the hole." The choice of the way via the uterus is instinctual, but Swedenborg, having found another way in his trances and visions, had to struggle against it because he was unable to assess the fears which it inspired at their true significance.

---

* Emanuel Swedenborg, *Journal of Dreams and Spiritual Experiences in the Year 1744*, Academy Book Room, Bryn Athyn, Pa., 1918, p. 15.

7.

NIGHTMARES OF WATER

LIFE on this planet began in the tepid primeval sea of countless ages past. Then it was that, according to the Genesis story, the creative "Spirit of God moved upon the face of the waters." Many millions of years later, the most stupendous step in evolution was accomplished: the adaptation of aquatic life to existence on solid ground. Not since has evolution taken a comparable stride. Yet, in our short lifetimes, we may witness often—every time a child is born—what is at least a symbolic re-enactment of this epochal event.

Human life begins in the tepid, amniotic (primeval) waters. In nine months, the embryo passes through the principal stages—from that comparable to the amoeba to that of the "highest" vertebrate—which it took eons for the race to achieve. In birth, the child is thrown from the waters to the land, as its first land-ancestors were stranded on the shore by the ebb of the ocean's warm tides. It is hardly surprising therefore that, in the study of neurotic personalities, so much morbid fear is found centering on water.

The fear is very widespread and its manifestations show exceeding variety. It may be linked to oceans, rivers, lakes or a common bathtub. The victim of the displacement may dread looking down from the railing of a ship into the water below. He may be afraid of drowning, never having learned or being able to learn to swim.

68

Nightmares of Water

He may explain his actions by a number of ingenious reasons; but all this is rationalization. He is simply afraid, so it appears to this writer, of drowning in, or being engulfed by, the flood of waters that once upon a time was his reassuring, shock-absorbing, life-supporting element. The fear may be disclosed in dreams or in waking inhibitions. In dreams whirlpools, tidal waves or cloudbursts may threaten his life. Awake, he may be unable to cross bridges or stand the sound of rushing water from the tap.

It is not easy to understand the mental process by which the unconscious identifies water with the amniotic fluid and impending birth. It appears that it does so and, according to my findings, it bases this identification on obscure organismic memories and not on a philosophical acceptance of the waters as the source of all life.

It matters little on what ground the ordeal of birth is displaced on water as long as it is so displaced. The issue involved is a practical one. I contend that if the displacement is successfully demonstrated to the victim of water phobia, if he is able to see intellectually and feel emotionally his mental error, he will learn to conquer it, thereby annulling the trauma of his birth.

The following cases will serve for illustration:

A woman going home from her place of business avoids a certain street because it leads to a bridge which she would have to cross. She is afraid that the bridge would be the first object that enemy raiders would choose to bomb. This is rationalization, which rests on very poor grounds. The bridge in question is just a crossing over a gap in the ground in Brooklyn, not even by the wildest stretch of imagination a military objective. When her attention is directed to this point, she admits the thinness of her reasoning and recalls something that really matters:

"My mother used to say that if a cart drives across a bridge at night, the horses become panicky because they can see the spirits of the dead frisking in the water."

She heard many other stupid stories in her childhood. The supernatural filled her with dread and she could not participate in any discussion about God. While it is a far cry from ghosts in the river to the Spirit of God upon the face of the waters, she did connect the two and feared both because she had transgressed against the laws of her religion.

However, it soon became clear that she was not only frightened but also fascinated by water. If she looked down from a bridge, she felt the water calling to her, and she dared not stay on the bridge for fear that she would jump. Near the house in which she was brought up was a brook, and across it was a plank. From this plank she fell into the brook again and again. Once she rolled down from the top of an adjacent hill into the brook, and was pulled out covered with blood. So many accidents in her life were connected with water that it seemed as if she had suffered from a repetition compulsion. The origin of this compulsion was revealed during the analysis of an old dream which she vividly remembered after the lapse of years.

In this dream she saw a girl of her childhood fishing on the further bank of the brook. The girl was putting the catch into a small sack, but first she took out a knife and cut off the heads and "legs" of the fish. The dreamer saw the blood on the knife, then asked somebody to take her across the plank.

In narrating the dream, the patient did not notice that she spoke of the "legs" of the fish. As fish have no legs, we are justified in assuming that she speaks of a human creature who is being killed and that, instead of castration fantasies directed at the male sex in general or in particular, she dreams of birth-castration and offers a clue to the water fears from which she has been suffering. I suspected that, being a native of Hungary, she made use of a linguistic ambivalence peculiar to the Hungarian language with which I had had previous experience. As explained in Chapter 5, in Hungarian "hal" (fish) is both a noun and a verb; as a verb it means to die. As fish also relate to a remote stage of our embryonic development, pulling a fish out of water and mutilating it strongly suggests that the ordeal of birth is hidden behind the water fears. Crossing the brook is a birth symbol in itself, standing for the transition from pre-natal to post-natal life.

Curiously, after she came to America, the land of re-birth, this patient could not eat fish without getting eczema. In discussing this, she suddenly recalled that she had suffered from the same complaint once before—during a pregnancy which ended in miscarriage. I concluded that the child in her womb was unconsciously accepted as an equivalent to herself within her mother's body before birth. The memory of the bruises which she had suffered during delivery from the maternal waters was repressed. As it related to the skin, she converted it into eczema, a skin irritation.

The interpretation had a startling effect. The allergy to fish disappeared; the patient was able to eat it without breaking out in a rash.

Another woman combined claustrophobia with fear of waters. Shut by a barn worker into a cornbin as a small child, she nearly died through suffocation. When her voice was almost gone from shouting for help, her last whimpering was heard by a brother and she was rescued. The experience left her with a fear of closed rooms. Once she was asked to work in a place where the door was papered like the wall and almost indistinguishable from it. A trap-door above added to the suggestion of a prison cell. She broke out in profuse perspiration and was unable to stay in the room. She had no idea how to deal with the situation. She thought the story of her claustrophobia began with the cornbin, but her dream life plainly revealed the presence of a much deeper trauma. She had recurrent birth dreams in which she had to climb through a narrow hole in a rocky cavity to reach the beach, and was badly frightened.

The story of her water fears revealed the same structure. She was always fearful of the Trent, the Derwent and the Mattock, all three being rivers near her parental home in England. She was afraid of crossing stone bridges, even London Bridge, and could not bear heights. As a young girl she had to fetch the doctor for her mother. The Trent was flooded and water lay on part of the bridge which she had to cross on her bicycle. She was afraid that the waves would sweep her away and suck her under, and became convinced that bodies of water contained treacherous holes. She took the whirlpools of the Trent as evidence of the existence of such holes.

A short time before her first analytic session, she dreamed that she was in an orchard, which was surrounded by a hedge. Both the orchard and the hedge were "unkempt." She passed through a hole in the hedge and fell into a canal. There she was sucked into a hole under the water where everything was peaceful. She knew that water was above her and that someone was calling her name but she experienced no distress.

The birth symbolism of this dream is so obvious that we can no longer doubt the connection between the patient's water fears and her arrival into the world. The dream reflects it in the fashion of a mirror. An orchard is a place where fruit grows from seed. It is a symbol of the Garden of Life into which she has been ushered through the "hedge," a thicket with a corporeal significance. Her fear of whirlpools was the fear of being "swallowed back" into the mother's body. The bridge was a substitute for the pubic arch; as a link between the ante-natal and post-natal state, it fits well into this fear complex. The canal is the uterine passage and the peace is that of the womb before birth. The calling of her name is the first indication of her new destiny, but it inspires no distress as the ordeal of passing into another life is as yet unsuspected.

She recalled another dream in which she fell into the water from a weir and was saved by her mother. Then her mother fell in and she saved her. The latter act reveals the typical childish fantasy of reversal of generation. It is best described by the statement of a small girl: "When I grow up, Mummy, I will be so big and you will be so little and I will carry you." By the patient's dream, her infantile mind was crying for release from her water fears.

One of her water nightmares was particularly frightening. She was looking across a river and saw a hedge on the further side. Dark and threatening shadows spread over the water. Suddenly a wooden beam shot into the water on which, in a crucified position, was a big man with an evil grin on his face. He pulled after himself another beam on which, tied in a similar position, the frail body of her doctor was pathetically spread. The evil man stood higher up in the water on his beam, swayed it with his body and submerged the doctor.

The pathetic little doctor turned out to be a father substitute.

Nightmares of Water

The patient's father was the underdog at home, completely dominated by a financially independent wife. Her heart went out to him with motherly affection, and she showed many signs of an identification with her father. In the dream, she appears to be displacing on him the trauma of her own birth, which she symbolizes by crucifixion. The big man with an evil grin is a personification of fear.

Her falls in water were paralleled by other falls. As a child, she used to tumble off her swing. Her father used to throw her up high and catch her, but she was always afraid that he would miss. She fell from horseback several times. Once she jumped over a wall and her foot caught on the top. She landed on her head and remained mentally affected for a few days. She never could look down cliffs without a feeling of compulsion to jump. Once she slipped and fell off a cliff with a tea tray in her hand. She did not lose her grip on it and had a strange and delightful fantasy of floating in empty space, holding her sister's baby in her arms. With this baby she associated a bad fright. The child was asleep on her cot in front of the medicine cupboard, to which she wanted to gain access without being noticed by her mother. The latter was addicted to taking laudanum; the patient resented this and, unknown to her mother, she used to dilute her drug potions with water. Somebody warned her to be very careful because, if she were caught, her mother might turn on her with the fury of a beast. She lifted up the baby very gingerly, but the child awoke and began to cry. She was terribly frightened, feeling sure that her mother would find her out.

With the help of this memory we may conjecture what happened when she fell off the cliff. The shock of the fall must have broken the last fetters keeping the trauma of birth locked up in her unconscious. The laudanum incident had already filled her mind with fear of death at the hand of her mother. The fury of a drug addict and the panicky emotions of birth together were too much to bear. She would not have been able to survive the psychic pressure. To save herself, she slipped back into the ante-natal state. Her sister's baby in her arms represented herself peacefully floating in the amniotic waters.

She was found unconscious at the foot of the cliff, but she was not injured seriously. Perhaps her extreme state of relaxation had something to do with her lucky escape.

Occasionally, anatomic symbolism is combined with the fall into water, thereby revealing birth as the origin of the fear:

"When I was a little girl, we used to have a Y bridge across the river. The floor was of solid wood, but occasionally a piece of board would be torn up and then one could see the river below. I used to have frequent dreams of falling through that hole."

It is hardly possible to escape the inference that the Y is the human body with outstretched legs. It is from the security of her mother's body that the dreamer was falling away, the water being symbolic of the waters of life.

The bridge and island symbolism in birth dreams is very frequent. The fetus is an island in the amniotic fluid, and the first threat to its security is the draining of these waters. The fear of floods and drowning or the fear of bridges develops as a measure of self-protection against the recurrence of an event that proved fatal to pre-natal security. The threat is unreal, because fetal security, once left behind, is only a will-o'-the-wisp, but this is kept out of consciousness and the fear endures as if it had no relationship to time. The reason for this deathlessness of pre-natal fears is that time stands still for the unborn child, who knows of no periodicity outside the rhythmic pulsation of the mother's blood and is unaware of the existence of any fixed point in outer space to which its rhythmic functions could be related; it lives in a timeless continuum, and has no standards by which its own growth could be measured and compared.

A fascinating objectification of the fear of water and the fear of falling in an amphibian creature is exemplified by the following dream:

A lake in mountainous woods and a girl in a car. Renaissance architecture is suggested by pilasters which form a semi-circle around a bay. Cut in the rock are winding steps. The girl is descending. She is afraid that somebody is after her with a knife. A gigantic crab comes out of the water and grabs something, but this is hidden from her view by the turn of the steps. When she rounds the corner, the crab speaks: "All right, lady?"—and attempts to seize her. It seems that the crab wanted to know if she was ready. She was not. Presently the crab comes back; in its claws is a big turtle, on the back of which seaweed seems to be growing.

The same night she saw a newly born baby floating over the floor. It was transparent like an alabaster statuette of the Virgin Mary. She also saw a Zodiacal circle in which people had to stand under the sign of their birthday.

The birth element in her dreams is over-determined. Birthday is expressly mentioned. A new baby is shown. The pre-natal state is referred to by floating. The fear of death is displayed in the flight from the knife and in the crab's invitation to drowning. What does it all mean? Let us trace how this dream was worked through analytically with the help of the patient's associations.

The dreamer's first association with crab was Cancer, a sign of the Zodiac. Then she discovered that the crab must stand for her mother because Cancer is her mother's astrological sign. But her mother does not speak in a deep voice; Popeye the Sailor does—she heard him in the movie.

The patient's father is a naval commander. The gigantic crab seems to represent both her father and her mother; it is the symbol of the destroying parents, the witch mother and the ogre father.

She never liked crabs. In France she was badly frightened by a large spider crab. It had pincers that cut through the flesh like a knife. She liked to "pop" seaweed, but was always afraid there might be crabs in it. Turtles she did not mind. They walk slowly and retire into their shells at the sight of danger. "Shell" recalled a peculiar birth fantasy of her own. They had a picture at home of Botticelli's Venus on Shell. She fancied she was born in a shell because her birth place was New Rochelle.

Let us now examine the scenery. The lake in the mountainous woods can well represent the fetal waters. The woods that surround it may symbolize the anatomic setting by nature symbolism as in Joyce Kilmer's poem:

75

Search for the Beloved

"A tree that may in summer wear
A nest of robins in her hair."

In continuation of this symbolism, the semi-circle suggests the pubic arch; the rock is a graphic representation of the mother's hard labor; the winding steps are a variation on the spiral, which is an ancient symbol of birth and creative energies; it unfolds like life and its windings suggest the shape of a snake. Renaissance, the term by which she describes the style of architecture, means re-birth. Primitive men knew but one way to re-birth: through the uterus. The perplexity of Nicodemus: how can a grown man re-enter his mother's womb, was answered by Jesus, who said that the Kingdom of Heaven can only be reached through the water and the spirit. He who aspires to find it through his mother is doomed. He will be dragged under by the crab, gored by the knife-like pincers, lose the breath of life by drowning.

Yet this is but part of the story. As an amphibian creature, the crab also symbolizes resurrection, life on two planes. The girl was not prepared for the appearance of the crab. The question: "All right, lady?" would not have been posed if she had been ready for the Kingdom of Heaven. She was not ready because she knew no other way but the limbo of the womb, where death bars the path. The Way is Immaculate Reconception; she must emerge pure and transparent like the alabaster statuette of the Virgin Mary. The teacher of Alice in Wonderland was a tortoise, "because she taught us." She, too, must learn from a tortoise or a turtle. She has to grow, slowly but surely. Evolution is as slow and as sure as the turtle. The seaweed growing on the back of the turtle represents this growth. As the turtle is swallowed by the crab, so must she pass through the womb of resurrection to gain a new life.

The cosmic note which the dream strikes is an excellent illustration why we are afraid of the unconscious. Water is the symbol of life but also of death. A symbolic death is the price we have to pay for a new life and, as nightmares of water testify, we are as afraid of paying it as we were at the time of our first arrival into this world.

8.

NIGHTMARES OF THE SUPERNATURAL

CHILDREN love wonders and mystery. The critical faculty is a comparatively late development, and to exercise it costs considerable effort. To accept things at face value, to side with old wives' tales and superstitious beliefs is so much easier. Fairy tales have to be discarded at a certain age, but the realm of the supernatural provides an excellent substitute. We can never prove that ghosts do not exist, because negatives cannot be proven. We know that the fear of ghosts or the delicious shivers which ghost stories send down our spines refuse to be argued away. The real problem is not the belief in ghosts but that of why some people should be fascinated and others frightened by it. Referring such an attitude to childhood experiences is not facing the complexities of the situation.

The possibility demands consideration that the fear or fascination of another world arises from a basic biological experience. We all have lived in another world—before we were born. All utopian visions reveal a nostalgia for the bliss which we lost on leaving the maternal womb. The intensity of the ordeal of birth may have a determining influence on the fear and fascination of another plane of life.

It happens very seldom that a patient is able to relive the cataclysmic event of birth on the analytic couch. A good deal of corroborative evidence must be obtained before an apparent re-enactment of an experience so highly charged with emotion as birth can be accepted as a presentation of the actual event and not of a fantasy concerning it. However, such fantasies in themselves are of absorbing interest. For this reason, I shall reproduce the copious association material of a young London actress, a sado-masochist, the study of whose suicidal compulsions and anxiety states first presented this problem to me.

On the fourth consecutive day of her analysis, "Yvette" reported:

I dreamed that I was a little baby and somebody hit me on the bare back, which gave me an awful shock. I was on my "tummy," not much bigger than a doll, and the shock was like flames of light flaring up in my brain. It mingled with surprise. I had no sensation of pain and did not cry. Then I heard my mother say, "Your father would go and have an affair with the nurse in the next room while I was lying-in."

Did Yvette recall in this dream the doctor's slap after birth, which started her breathing? The description of the shock as flames of light flaring up in her brain, the astonishment with which the experience is received and the reference to her mother's labor point strongly in this direction. On further questioning, however, a detail emerged which argued equally strongly against this interpretation. She added that she was wearing a long "nightie," which was pushed up to her neck. Obviously, she was not born in a "nightie." We are faced with the following alternatives: (1) that the first impression given by the dream is wrong; and (2) that a recollection from a higher level has been combined with the birth experience. The latter view is supported by the story of her father's affair with the nurse. Yvette used to spy on her father and report to her mother his visits to the nurse. She also remembered her mother's complaints about her father's faithlessness. She understood that her father had an affair with the nurse while she was being born.

This admixture of intercourse with a birth-dream calls attention to an interesting fact: that in retrospect birth appears to us as a genital event; that the passing of a child's body through the uterine passage in birth can be evaluated in terms of intercourse.

Nightmares of the Supernatural

I kept these reflections to myself. Before analyzing the dream, I asked the patient for free associations with words of my selection. The first was "milk." She answered: "Water, rice, bread, tea . . . knife." There was a pause before she uttered knife, she grew emotional, felt weak in the knees, but continued: "Cook, supper, water." At this point she began to sink into a mental state in which she appeared to re-live her own birth. Without the slightest prompting, and much to my surprise, she reported her sensations as follows:

"A funny sensation in my legs. I feel faint. I am falling. A sinking sensation, a nasty feeling. I feel floating as if I were going under an anesthetic. My head is downward. I am going downward. I feel being born. It is a bit difficult. I make an effort with my legs. It is an extraordinary position. My head is on one side. I shoot down. I feel frightened. Now I feel nothing."

Her head dropped sideways and she was half hanging from the sofa. She shook herself and sighed:

"It is an awful bother—this business of getting born."

She opened her eyes, apologized for all she had said, and assured me she was not making things up.

"There was trouble about my head," she continued.

Suddenly, she remembered a statement by her mother regarding her birth; that she was delivered by instruments; that her head was in the wrong position and was injured. As evidence, Yvette pointed to a faint scar on her forehead. Then she added a supplement to the account of her sensations:

"I was lying against something hard. Do you know, I think I saw my mother's body, the lower part. The legs were huge like the Colossus of Rhodes."

This was followed by a second supplement, this time to the dream with which our discussion began: A man with a nasty face was leaning over her crib and frightened her. Then she saw him washing his hands. A nurse, with hard, hawk-like features, handed him a towel. The man picked up a little bag and closed it. She thought he was the doctor.

This second supplement raises a curious problem. We can take it as evidence against the original memory of birth, as no newborn child could register such distinct pictures on an untrained retina even if sight began to function immediately after birth. On the other hand, we may be acting on limited knowledge; sense perceptions need not necessarily represent the only channel of awareness that might be open to the child at the time of birth. Its unconscious mind, not yet flooded with impressions through the sensory organs, may function in the same archaic way which we encounter in the study of telepathic and clairvoyant phenomena. If such mental powers exist at all, we may safely postulate that their cognitory function, for reasons of self-preservation, would turn towards this new and bewildering life. Before self-consciousness forces these functions back into the twilight realms, they may register events with that photographic quality which is peculiar to the unconscious mind. Whether this registration takes place through the mind of the mother, to whom the child remains tied by a psychic umbilicus, or independently makes little difference. As long as experiences of this kind exist, there is no reason why the dream mind should not draw upon them. Practically, however, we need not become lost in such speculations. The picture about the doctor and the nurse may have been registered at a much later date; it may have been fused into the dream in the same way as was the mother's statement about her father. As we are dealing with the dream of an adult looking back at her past, a regression of association would necessarily combine wayside memories with the original reactions to birth.

In her next statement, the patient pictured herself in her mother's bed:

"I am a little doll, lying on my back. I have dark hair, more than I should have for a baby. My mother is covered. I am covered, over her body, near her arm. The bed seems to be gigantic."

This was followed by a vision about feeding. She saw her mother's breast bared and was conscious of the feel of it. Then she felt tired and sleepy, and remembered nothing more.

Falling and Suffocating Fears

Let us now return to the fear of falling which is revealed in her association fantasy by the words: "I shoot down. I feel frightened."

Nightmares of the Supernatural

In her first year, the patient had had a very unfortunate accident. The bell rang; and the nurse, forgetting that the baby was in her lap, suddenly got up. The baby fell on her head and developed cerebral meningitis, which almost cost her her life. In talking about it, Yvette seemed to slip back to the time of the accident and gave a dramatic description of the coming and fading of consciousness—a description which again appeared to be fused with that of birth:

"I feel reaching to light, vivid light, the kind of light which I experienced when I went into the silence of mystic meditation. The light grows stronger. It is very bright. My legs are going funny. I feel as if I was being born. I want to get nearer to that light. I don't want to leave it. I feel it is something beyond earth. I feel I am going back to my real home. The desire is now fading. My legs still feel funny. My head is swimming. I am frightened a bit. Now I am going back to that light again. I keep going and coming. I can feel the urge of my mother to make me come back. I am gone again. Somebody moves my head. I am on my mother's arm."

This feeling of "beyond earth" was the starting point of the development of a reincarnation fantasy. It was bound up with suffocation fears, fears of the supernatural and fears of "insanity." The suffocation fears were introduced by the following memories:

"A Chinese mask we had at home . . . An evil mask and a Chinese suit of armor of which I was very afraid . . . A Chinese dummy on a special stand in our dining hall. It had knives in its belt. Lots of knives and a double mask. I used to be afraid to go past that thing . . . Oh, I remember something . . . Daddy taking the sword out. I was scared. He was playing with it. He was a fine fencer . . . Something about Mummy and Daddy. They were fooling about in the dining room. I don't know if there was a sword around, but I know that mother lost her temper and said he was hurting her. He was only playing . . . I keep on seeing a shadowy figure in one of those fencing helmets. I nearly passed out yesterday in my dancing act. They put an octopus mask on me. I had to make a great effort to stop myself from screaming. I cannot bear masks on my face. I cannot bear those masks one dances in. I nearly fainted when I had to wear one for the dressmaker. They had to cut holes in it. I can see now from where it comes.

81

I can see it at home, and it gives me a very uncomfortable feeling; a red mask, with nasty, beady eyes and an evil grin."

I asked Yvette to put the mask mentally over her face.

"I cannot. The best I can do is to hold it before me."

I suggested she should make a mental effort.

"It is all gone. Shall I try again? It fades out every time I get it near my face. I cannot put it on. I can put it on a little girl over there who is me, but I cannot put it over my face. She is bouncing up and down with it."

"What else do you remember about masks?"

"I am reminded of the chest trouble I had when I was eight to ten years old. They put an inhaler over my face, a cage-like affair, because I could not breathe. I had to have it over my mouth for a quarter of an hour every day.

"When I first had an anesthetic, and the mask was clamped over my face, I fought against it because it frightened me. I had anesthetic again at fifteen, and took it well because the anesthetist just held the mask near my face. When I had an abortion it was bad again because it was given roughly.

"I have a vague idea that something used to be tied around my mouth . . . a scarf, a white scarf. Those beastly white mufflers! I was always getting bronchitis. They used to holler at me. The doctor worried about my chest. I could not breathe when I had that illness. I used to fight for breath. I had pneumonia or something. They used to give me a kettle of steam and hot poultices which burned my chest. I was never out of bed; I was always ill."

Haunted House Horrors

Fear of the supernatural and fear of "insanity" were disclosed in the following recollections:

"I seem to recall something about a lighthouse at Beachy Head on the cliffs . . . Oh . . . Where is Stonehenge? I don't know why it has come to my mind. Maybe it is the shape of the stones. Stonehenge . . . I went there as a very little girl. They took me to a haunted house where all sorts of tortures had taken place. Thumbscrews. They tickled the feet of the victims until they went mad. The father of my Ger-

man playmates used to tell these gruesome stories. I was so frightened. The governess of the same boys told tales about screaming
skulls. That reminds me of my own head. I could imagine, until
eighteen months ago, my own head without flesh on it. Sometimes I
heard noises in my head and was never quite sure whether they came
from there or whether a dog was howling outside. I never heard them
when somebody was with me in the house, only when I was alone. I
could hear that screaming sound inside me now. It reminds me of
another story that woman told me when I was seven years old. Two
sisters in a haunted room saw something so horrible in the night that
one went raving mad. I also remember something about a bride buried
in a box in her wedding dress. She played hide and seek: the lid
shut on her and she was not found until years later. I used to hate to
go for a walk with that German governess as she was always telling
these stories and I expected something similarly awful to happen.

"I can still hear the cuckoo clock on the night that Daddy died. I
cannot bear cuckoo clocks since. I was in the theater. When I came
home, I found a note from my mother. I knew immediately that my
father had committed suicide. Earlier in the day, over lunch, I heard
a loud report and exclaimed: 'Oh, somebody has shot himself.' Then
I dismissed the subject, thinking I was getting morbid; but I was not.
It was the hour when Daddy killed himself. When I saw my mother's
note I knew what had happened, though she did not tell me. I stayed
with my mother all night. The cuckoo clock kept on striking every
hour. It was horrible.

"The doctor said Daddy was temporarily unbalanced. I have been
awfully afraid of insanity ever since. My grandfather went peculiar
at the age of eighty-three. My God, I thought, am I going to end in
the same way? When I hear an automobile backfire in the street, I
cannot control myself. I get so frightened that I shake all over. It is
not normal. Anything I read about madness frightens me. I cannot
bear books on haunted houses and ghosts. I saw a film, 'The Student
of Prague.' He goes mad, looks into a mirror and wonders if he is real.
That picture had a terrible effect on me. I moaned and groaned, I
could not bear it, I had to shut my eyes and get out. Afterwards I
found myself looking into the mirror in the same way as he did.

83

Search for the Beloved

"I vaguely recall another ghost story; somebody's throat was getting cut. I can see that throat gaping open. I wonder who that was. Oh, nonsense. But I remember, Mummy said Daddy was sure to try to cut his throat because she found all the razors spread out in his room and he was fingering them in a peculiar way. She took them and hid them.

"Now I remember another fear. If I see a knife or a pair of scissors, I am afraid I might stab myself with them in my sleep. Until recently, I dared not have them in my bedroom. I am still afraid of razors when I shave myself for the stage. I sweat, for fear it might slip.

"Another thought which haunted me: supposing I jumped out of the window in my sleep. I think I walked in my sleep before I heard ghost stories.

"I seem to remember Hans Andersen's fairy tales. I was afraid of some of them. There was one . . . All I can think of at the moment is Macbeth. Lady Macbeth killed Macbeth * in his sleep; but I would not have read that story so early . . . I know: the 'Babes in the Wood' and being suffocated in bed. I believe I was taken to Madame Tussaud's and saw them; and I was also taken to the Tower where the little princes were strangled. I was frightened by the 'Sleeping Beauty.' I saw her chest rising and falling at Madame Tussaud's. I still hate wax figures. Occasionally, the sheet gets across my mouth when I sleep. Then I fight like a madman until I wake up."

A Reincarnation Fantasy

That the monstrous fears of murder, death and "insanity" which have haunted Yvette, originated in an earlier, forgotten experience emerged from a strange story about an Egyptian mummy—a story bound up with reincarnation fantasies and with fears of being buried alive.

She drew a curved knife, with a cross-shaped handle, and wrote in her diary:

"This knife, the emblem between the two of us for which we search, still eludes us. The deepest meaning of it all from some past life I feel we could recall in the destiny."

---

* Yvette's own error.

Nightmares of the Supernatural

The quotation is verbatim. It was followed by a burst of lyrics which revealed a strong transference to the analyst:

"In Egypt's fair land where first we met wandering in fields on which the grass was soft and dewy, yet the trees and flowers blossomed forth and in the corner was a tiny pool of tristram (?) plants. I feel the breath of breezes on my cheeks, turning, wondering at your voice which speaks the words I long to hear. I long to hear again those words which cost us suffering and pain. Again I say, 'I love you. It is nothing new, it is true. But as then, so now, what can we do? It is nothing but the end, until the end, a happiness greater still.' "

At the bottom of the page, the following note appeared:

"Remembered fright I got when I saw the mummy. Had the strong urge to go at once to the British Museum to find the knife and see the mummy again."

Then followed the words:

"Singer of Amon. Mut-em-Mennu."

I asked her for associations with the word "mummy," and this is what she gave:

"Blankness, black, stifle, red mist, knife, afraid of being buried alive. I am going to be cremated instead. The young man that talked to me in the museum said that he was looking for a mummy whose face changes expression. I said: 'I know that one.' 'Oh, you are a student of Egyptology,' he said. I said, 'I am not. The mummy is again downstairs.' The keeper spoke up: 'Yes, it was taken downstairs; are you interested in these sculptures, too?' I said, 'I am more interested in the type of knives they used.' I stopped at a case which contained a more or less unwrapped mummy. Then the man said: 'It is most extraordinary, she was found with the Singer of Amon. It is extraordinary, because the Singer of Amon died 1,200 years before that woman did, yet the body was in the same sarcophagus!'

"There was an inscription: See Case G. No. 10 in first Egyptian room. I said, 'They got the wrong case there.' There was an argument. It was discovered I was right." •

It was now apparent that Yvette was developing a reincarnation fantasy with an unusual motivation. If she could not have her analyst as a lover in this life, she would have him as her lover in a previous life. The foundation on which the fantasy was built was an incident of strong affective value. At the age of four, on a rainy day, she was taken by her mother to the British Museum. There, for some reason, she was badly frightened by the sight of a mummy. In trying to recall what happened, the following associations came:

"I can vaguely see the kind of clothes I had on, a funny little fluffy velour hat and I see long black curls. My mother's umbrella was causing us a lot of trouble. Daddy said: 'Take the child's hand.' I remember clutching my mother's arm. I see one of those painted mummy cases. Now a picture flashes to my mind: a bony, shrivelled arm, lifted up all by itself. One minute the mummy seems to be wrapped up, the other minute it is not. I feel as if my own legs were wrapped up. It seems as if one of my arms were wrapped up."

Homosexual Revelations

We see the patient identifying herself with the mummy and we have a hint that her fright must have been caused by the hallucination that the mummy moved. Her fear of the supernatural, therefore, did not originate in the ghost stories she heard at the age of 7; that memory was important but did not go deep enough. Further light was vouchsafed four days later in a long and complicated nightmare:

I was in a hotel with Gilbert, my producer. He was annoyed with me for having done something that he did not like—at least, he reproved me in public. I remember taking the elevator to a higher floor and seeing Gilbert beckon mysteriously from a telephone booth where he was talking to his wife. I tried to listen to what was going on between them, but Peggy came up and would not give me a chance. Then I was saying goodbye to Gilbert at the front door of our house. He was clearly silhouetted against the dusk. As I shook hands with him, he turned into Peter, grew into a terrific shadowy shape against the sky, and I became very frightened. Invisible hands seized me and I fainted from fear.

The next thing I remember was being in a bedroom, in a dressing gown of sorts and looking out of the window. The Germans had arrived. I rushed into the sitting room. I heard the Germans mounting the stairs and they came in wearing uniforms with red bands around their hats. The man at the right had a fearful looking sabre. I remember sending my twin brother into the next room to tidy himself. I defiantly faced the man with the sabre, although I was very frightened. I edged towards the older man on the left who had no sabre. The one on the right threatened to kill me and the sword nearly got me. The left-hand man was protecting me and said to the other, "What about seducing her?" I said, "Oh, anything, I am at your mercy." The older man was surprised. I was in an awful panic. Beads of sweat were on my face. I corrected myself, "I'd rather do anything than be killed."

Just then my twin brother appeared and the attention of the two men was turned to him. He was dressed in an Eastern garb which made him look effeminate. He was "cheeky" with the officers. I begged him not to be rude and to take in a manly fashion whatever they would do to him. The officers then began to hit him on the hand and face with their fists, and he bled. I found that the blows were really falling on my head. They were hot, searing, hurting blows.

Then I was near a window and a nurse pointed to the woodwork where my head hit the window and dented it. Another nurse spoke up. I said, "I was dropped." The first nurse said, "Oh dear, on which chart shall I make a note of that, the good one or the bad one?" I did not quite know. Then it dawned on me what she meant and I said firmly and smilingly, "Oh the good one, of course." She smiled happily, too, and made the note.

To understand this long and complicated dream, one must first marshal up some of the patient's associations with the *dramatis personae.*

Gilbert, the producer, was married. At first he took no interest in Yvette, but later showed signs of infatuation. She refused to listen to his wooing. He was "queer" and associated a good deal with homosexuals. Yvette herself had been addicted to sadistic and masochistic perversions, but through psychoanalytic re-education she was growing out of them. The pressure of her old practices manifested itself in this apparently incongruous association:

"How ridiculous! I see again the Carter girl, one of my nurses. She had a rather loose face. I can see her in the nursery, lying on the bed, leaning half against the wall, very flushed in the face. Whether she had just beaten me or was still doing it, I don't know. I must have had an orgasm from it. I remember a hotel near Notting Hill Gate before the war. There was a little girl there; in the drawing room, we discussed these funny feelings. I told her how nice it was. She was most interested but uninformed. I was seven years old then. Lots of German officers and spies were staying in that hotel. One of them turned King's evidence, another one was shot.

"Peter was shell shocked. He used to go into awful jitters. I used to take him out of the room and hold his head. He was seeing things, his dead friends that were blown up. He was altogether queer.

"The twin brother was like me but also like a little boy who had a homosexual affair with Peter. (I am not a twin and have no brother.) He was a nice boy and had similar emotional experiences to my own. I saw him in a nightclub after my own affair with Peter was finished. Peter infected me with gonorrhea. I went up to the boy and said to him, 'Hello, you are a friend of Peter's, aren't you?' He said 'Yes.' I was fascinated and repelled by this homosexual business; fancy me, competing with boys! There were several such boys in love with me who never loved a woman in their life before. I liked them because they had a lot of understanding which other men did not have. They made me one of them. I always felt there was something wrong with me to be accepted like that. Just before I broke up with Peter, he gave himself away blatantly. He took me to a swimming club on the Thames which was run by these men. About a dozen of them were there. I am convinced that the club was a cover for homosexual practices. They let me listen to their conversation. It was fascinating. They talked to each other: 'Don't you be a silly girl; don't be such a cat, etc.!' "

It should be added to these revelations that Yvette had a strong incestuous attachment to her father, and remembered fantasies in which she had given him a baby. The dream which we are about to discuss reveals a curious twist of this fixation.

In the opening phase of the dream, she is moving away from parental involvement to a higher level. This she indicates by taking the elevator to a higher floor. There she sees Gilbert in the telephone booth talking to his wife. Gilbert, being her employer, stands for her father. His infatuation with her was as one-sided as Yvette's infatuation was with her father. The telephone talk between Gilbert and his wife hints at the "connection" between her parents on which she used to spy. She vividly remembered how she used to look through the key hole and saw her father exposed and ready for intercourse. The booth is a genital symbol. Telephone contact is a symbolic substitute for sexual contact. The public reproof is a form of self-condemnation, the basis of which is her spying guilt. The affair between her father and the nurse was just one of the determinants of this guilt. The identification between Gilbert and her father is well established when she says goodbye to him at the front door of her parents' country home, which Gilbert never visited. The goodbye reveals the constructive aspect of the dream, which is father-separation. Then Gilbert changes into Peter, who was "queer" and gave her venereal disease. As a love disease, gonorrhea or syphilis is often used in dreams to symbolize incestuous feelings. Her father was also "rather queer." Why should the figure grow into the sky and be so frightening? Her answer was:

"It was a big, empty kind of silhouette, just like a large, empty mummy case."

It seems that Peter is used as an adjective to describe Yvette's father in some frightening respect. I recalled the fear caused by the moving hand of the mummy and asked her to picture that hand, and relax.

"They were thin, bony hands, mummy's hands," she said. "I wonder if that mummy had a distorted face and looked like Peter when he had his dithers? I don't like Peter any more because he is always grabbing me . . . I feel a bit peculiar. My head is swimming. Something funny is happening to me. I feel awfully cold. I am going to faint . . ."

As she had fainted in the dream when Peter ascended into the sky, this promised a revelation regarding the invisible hands that seized her.

"I cannot see the mummy case now. It seems high up. I must have

89

looked over the top. I remember clutching my mother's arm afterwards; I don't know what happened . . . I keep on seeing eyes, a painted face, and slit eyes. I have a feeling that the mummy has no wrapping on. I am sure it was nasty, blackened . . . I cannot see anything now. I have a violent urge to go to the lavatory. I always do that when I get scared . . . I think the mummy had one arm across the breast. I feel a bit like a mummy myself. It is ridiculous. I feel as if my legs were swathed around. You know the mummy's face, the original face? I was just thinking that it opened its eyes. It is a funny position. I am half it, half looking at it. I cannot explain it. It is a stifling feeling, awfully cold. It is as if someone were putting little bandages right over my mouth and were going to wrap them around my face next. A kind of rocky, earthy place. I suppose it is like a tomb, a cave. What ridiculous nonsense . . . People are round with implements. Something like a pick-axe. It is a very sunny day. I am outside. It is gone. My legs feel like lead. I want to move them but cannot . . . I see someone with black hair, nice hairdress, three rubies in front, the eyes closed, a bracelet on the left arm with turquoise blue stones, nice hands, jewels around the neck; the face reminds me of my own face but I don't think the features are as small as mine. The cheekbones are rounder, the nose broader. The skin looks like my own. It is just dead. She half opened her eyes as if she were not quite dead. It gives you a fright to see a dead person open her eyes like that. She has very long black eyelashes and dark brown eyes, heavy-lidded like Peter's. That look from under the closed lids is a horrid, sensual look. I am back in the museum again. It was in the museum that I saw the mummy's eyes opening. There was a look of evil in them . . . Until today I thought the mummy was a man. Again I feel just like it. How awful it is to be wrapped up like that when you are still alive. I was always afraid of being buried alive. I am still afraid. I want to be cremated."

Yvette calls her mother, "Mummy." In this unusually interesting set of visions, she vacillates in identifying, now herself, now her mother, and now Peter, with the mummy. The only situation in which she herself could be the mummy, wrapped tight, speechless and buried alive is the pre-natal one. The unborn child, from the post-natal point of view, is half-dead, half-alive; it is bound by spatial restrictions as a mummy is swathed. The rocky, earthy place, looking like a tomb or a cave is the womb. The horrid, sensual look is not difficult to understand if we remember that the patient could not separate the idea of intercourse from the genital aspect of birth. Her father entered into it in her very first birth dream. Now the fear of her father's penis, which she saw through the keyhole, is dramatized into an assault by German invaders. She had mentioned the sabre before. Father had it when he was fooling with mother in the dining room. The phallic significance of that sabre is now quite clear. A supplementary recollection furnished the last confirmation:

"The man with the sabre got so close to me that the sword almost touched me on my genitalia. I wriggled away to the other man. In a sense, he was even worse than the other. He looked like Uncle Jack, who tried to have intercourse with me."

She also felt that the red bands on the hats of the Germans somehow tied up with blood and sex. She could not explain the reason of the feeling. The Freudian claim that the hat is a symbol of the female genitalia fits well with her feeling.

The appearance of the non-existent twin brother raises the problem of bi-sexuality. Rather picturesquely, it calls attention to the patient's homosexual (Lesbian) component, which was already indicated in the mummy fantasy; for the mummy, while being herself, also had Peter's eyes and his sensuous look. "Peter," in vulgar language, stands for the penis, therefore for the masculine self. This is apparent when the blows suffered by the twin brother (who reminds her of the boy who had a homosexual affair with Peter) hit the patient's own head. They are hot, searing and hurting blows and recall the injury to her head which the surgical instruments caused in her delivery. The shadowy shape in the sky into which Peter's figure grows is a graphic representation of the ghostly, other worldly character of the attack against the unborn—an attack tearing its universe apart.

The final phase of the dream refers to the patient's accident at the age of one. The memory of this accident was fused with birth in her associations. We see it fused again. Instead of the floor, her head hits the window and dents it. This injury to her head redetermines the birth reference. It is the genital window of which she dreams.

"I wanted to be put down on the progression chart. I got over the fright of the bang on my head."

She could not have gotten over it, unless she were getting over her trauma of birth at the same time. That is why two charts are mentioned. "I was dropped" refers to falling in birth. That should be registered on the good chart. It had to happen. It is a racial inevitability.

It seems as if the main purpose of this long and complicated dream is to show the inter-relationship between birth and post-natal sexual traumata for the purpose of adjusting the problems raised by bisexuality, her sado-masochism, her reincarnation fantasies and her fears of being buried alive.

My conclusions may be wrong but their plausibility did the work. A marked change took place in the patient's sexual disposition after she assimilated the contents of this dream. It was revealed ten days later. She dreamed of walking down a narrow, muddy lane. A gate was at the end, and a naked man looking like Pan was waiting for her. She felt scared because she became conscious of her nudity. Then she discovered that she was not quite nude. She was dressed like a nymph, and she covered her breast with her hands.

"The meaning of this dream dawned on me right in the dream," she volunteered. "I realize now that sex is a different thing from what I thought it was, that I had not quite understood it before. At the moment when I lifted up my hands to my breasts, I felt a great change come over me. I always looked upon sex from the sadistic angle. All of a sudden I knew that I had it all wrong, that sex means perfect love and understanding, and lots of other things I never connected with it before. Last night, in the theater, I was a new person. I feel as if the past had dropped away from me, with everything that was nasty and beastly in it. I feel almost ready for my first affair."

Heretofore, the supernatural was evil. Now the ghosts have yielded their place to the God Pan. Judging by her emotions in the dream, he represents pure and protective love—a magnificent succession to the destruction which a series of sexual traumata had wrought in Yvette's life.

9.

T HE symbolism of fire is exceedingly widespread in linguistic usage. We speak of creative fire, flaming passion, red-hot anger, consuming desire, burning zeal, smouldering hatred, glowing heart, embers of love, and searing pain. Accordingly, a corresponding use of fire might be expected in dreams. The associations of the dreamer can be relied upon as a guide to the specific meaning of the symbol in each individual case. The emphasis is necessarily always on the individual, yet since fire is an elemental force of nature, an archaic impress of the race on the psyche must also manifest itself in dreams. Civilization and the moral evolution of humanity owe perhaps their greatest impetus to the discovery of fire. The gods may have had a monopoly of the Promethean Fire; the church may have taken possession of the Holy Flame; but neither would have much meaning had not the race been dreaming of begetting and birth in terms of fire.

Struck by Lightning

An ancient instance in which fire is linked to human generation is in Plutarch's writings about the dream of Olympias, the mother of Alexander the Great: [*]

---

[*] William Bolitho, *Twelve Against the Gods,* Harper & Brothers, New York, 1929, p. 17.

"The night before the consummation of her marriage, Olympias dreamed that *a thunderbolt fell on her belly, which kindled a great fire,* and that *the flame extended itself far and wide before it disappeared."*

By the seers of the court, the dream was interpreted as an announcement of the conception of a son who would conquer the world.

In our modern days we rarely dream of the descent of the spirit in terms of fire, but we have some evidence of the survival of this Promethean thought in dreams that use stoves, ovens and fireplaces to symbolize the womb. To be shoved back and baked again is a term which I heard a mother use pityingly in talking to her ailing daughter. The story of the witch who threatens to put the babes lost in the wood into the oven is a fire fantasy that may conceal similar motives. The actual issue out of the womb is a cosmic catastrophe in the world of the unborn. In this life, the commonest and most awe-inspiring manifestation of cosmic power is lightning. Plutarch tells us how it was used for the symbol of conception in the dream of Olympias. The following modern instance shows it associated with birth:

I was going to the door when a terrible streak of lightning struck the house across the street. The bottom part of the house came out and the road seemed to be full of water. It looked like a lake. On the lake was a rug and on it two children. I just reached out, rescued the two children and brought them into the house.

The dreamer, a woman, had two children, of the same size as in the dream. The house is a symbol of the personality and often of the body. If the house is used in the latter sense in the dream the cataclysmic event that thrusts the two children out is an obvious allusion to the ordeal of their birth: lightning destroying the pre-natal world, threatening the children with drowning in the bursting of the waters.

However, we are not in the habit of dreaming of the troubles of others. Nightmares are always personal. We are concerned in them with our own problems. Bearing a child, being a personal event, is more likely to be the subject matter of a mother's dream than the ordeal to her children. As a matter of fact, this mother was not affected by the labor of delivery in any unusual manner. This was brought out in a supplementary recollection:

"The children were playing on a small rug in the house when the lightning struck and the bottom of the house slid out. The color of the rug was blue. I have a rug like that at home. They kept on playing unconcernedly, even when they were floating."

The unconcern of the children describes the dreamer's own state of mind. It corroborates that as far as the mother is concerned, the delivery was no earth-shaking event. We may, therefore, rule out the idea that the dream depicts the trauma of bearing. This mother feared neither death nor drowning when she gave birth to her children. Lightning, however, fills her with morbid fear. She pulls down the shades in her house and hides her head in the pillows when she hears thunder. She explained the origin of the fear by a terrible experience at the age of fifteen.

At Savin Rock, Connecticut, where she spent her summer holiday, she was swimming in the ocean when a storm broke. There came a blue flash, and a man a few yards away from her was struck. He screamed and grabbed at his hair; then he turned blue and went under. He was dead when he was pulled out. She swam ashore in panic, and for a long time could not get the experience out of her mind.

In the dream she experienced no fear when the lightning struck; but we know from her story that death in the waters is associated with it. The affect is detached because the traumatic memory is used as a cover situation. Accordingly, it is a house across the street which is struck, not the house where she is. Yet her own children are in that house, playing on her "lightning-blue" rug, showing that the condition is of personal significance, though spatially removed.

The truth is that she is concerned with her own rescue from the trauma of her own birth—an event which in its shattering effect compares with a thunderbolt. "Across the street" is a useful symbol of another state of life, a good allusion to a radically different condition. Giving birth to a child differs radically from being born oneself. The lightning and flood refer to the long repressed birth relationship of the dreamer to her own mother. In the last reduction, one's own child in a dream always represents the dreamer as a child. Nothing is as likely to mobilize the impacts left in the organism by birth as the bearing of a child. The trauma of bearing, whenever it is found to exist, is an echo of the trauma of the mother's birth. The two children of the dreamer lend themselves well to the representation of this duality.

The rescue was effected with ease, and by the dreamer's own efforts, which was an excellent augury for analytic progress. The dream was the first which this patient reported. Her smooth progress on the analytic path bore out the augury very well.

Morbid reactions to fire are very common. The first determinants are usually found in specific events occurring in the patient's life. My experience, however, is that if the investigation is pushed to deeper levels of the mind it may be found that fire traumata are utilized for the representation of the drama of birth. Here is an illustration from the associations of a girl on the analytic couch:

"I see a fireplace in the hallway, downstairs. . . . I used to have a rag doll; it was called Raggedy Anne and had red rope hair. It was filled with sawdust and I loved it. Grandmother, in a fit of anger, threw it into the fireplace. I still feel exceedingly angry at grandmother because of this."

The patient who recalled this scene was called Anne and had flaming red hair. Children very frequently identify a doll with themselves. In this case the name and the red hair helped the identification. Her further associations proved the point:

"Fire fascinates me and yet, at the same time, frightens me. . . . Now I can see the closet under the stairs where they kept coats. . . . Something about a furnace is associated with this closet. . . . That my grandmother would put me in the furnace. . . . I have a feeling of suffocation. I guess I am in the clothes closet. I can smell rubber overshoes."

We see how the patient associates the closet (a very common symbol for the womb) with the fireplace and how she hints, by her feelings of suffocation, at the trauma of birth. She was brought up by her grandmother. The burning of Raggedy Anne in the fireplace was likely to stir up the fiery sensation of bruised flesh as a memory of her birth. She was not nursed by her mother, and as it was her grandmother who attended to her every need she could not tell, as a small child, who gave birth to her. Many times she had nightmares of fire and would wake up violently sick at the stomach.

"I always hated red hair. Raggedy Anne had red hair. Yet I loved that doll and I have used the expression 'raggedy' all my life for describing myself. They called my hair flaming red. How I hated it!"

These reactions are so strong and so contradictory that we may rightly suspect that the emotional charge of Raggedy Anne's fiery death has been regressively fused with the memories of birth, and that the foundation of her nightmares of fire at night and of her morbid fear of flames in the waking state was laid at the time of her arrival into this world.

Immolation by fire in a particularly gruesome form is illustrated by this dream of a lady:

I was going through a place like a museum, looking for something. I first approached a deep chasm. Somebody jumped in. Then I got into a room which was covered with royal blue velvet, including the floor. As I stepped on the velvet of the floor, I was seized with horror because it was heaving and somehow I felt that all sorts of corruption and rotten bones were underneath. As I went further, I saw a man lying in bed. He was burnt coal black like a mummy but he was alive. I had to pass him to get to the door. He begged me to take him back with me to civilization; there he would be all right.

The museum is a place where things of the past are preserved. Here it is used as a symbol of the womb. The patient is looking for something that antedates consciousness. The chasm into which somebody jumps brings in the fear of falling. The origin of this fear, on the deepest level, is in the falling away from the mother's body in birth. The heaving of the floor well describes the muscular upheaval which leads to the cataclysm of birth. The folds of the womb are almost invariably represented in dreams by red or blue velvet draperies. This dreamer's favorite color from early childhood was royal blue. Her room at home is decorated in blue, walls, curtains, and even the bindings of her books are blue. The royal reference is befitting to the state of the unborn, because we associate royal with the acme of happiness, a condition which we have once enjoyed within the womb. Our utopia is cruelly destroyed by the ordeal of birth. This ordeal is sometimes represented by murder, or by corruption and decomposition. The man who is burnt black as a mummy dramatizes in terms of fire the pain sensations which result from the bruising of the child's body. "Returning to civilization" reveals that this museum is an isolated place. The womb is an isolated place. If she took the man back when she passed through the door (into life), she would understand the trauma of her birth and would become free and well.

That the burning describes, indeed, the trauma of birth, was further indicated in another dream with an interesting variation:

I was walking in a huge, triangular bathtub, as big as a swimming pool, all alone. The water only reached up to my calf. I let more water in. One minute the water was burning hot, then very cold.

To this dream the patient added the recollection of an older one, in which she saw two tiny, new-born babies, not twins but of the same age, with hot steam issuing out of them.

The bathtub is one of the commonest symbols for the womb. Its very hugeness suggests pre-natal perspective as retrojected from the adult level. What interests us most in this and in the next dream is that the element of fire is replaced by hot water and steam, and that we find new-born babies associated with the latter. Because hot water or steam may cause as severe injuries as burning by fire, they lend themselves to the symbolic representation of the trauma of birth equally well. This point is further borne out in the case of a young woman suffering from frigidity. She dreamed:

I was in a room. In front of the window there was water reaching up to the sill. As I looked out, a man was wading in the water towards me, and I handed him something through the window. I asked: how can you stand that hot water? I could not even put my hand in it. He said: that is nothing, and ducked under and came up. I had the feeling that his whole body must burn.

The dream reveals some typical birth symbols. There was reason to suspect that it had reference to the dreamer's frigidity. She establishes contact with a man through the window. As the window is a genital symbol, she might speak of sexual contact. She is afraid the water will burn her. There was evidence that her passion was repressed because she feared it. The man in the dream was just a casual acquaintance who played no part in her life; but she knew that he had forged a check and got into "hot water." Forging a check is a "false situation." Was this a reference to her frigidity? Clinical experience has convinced me that frigidity sometimes arises from the trauma of birth which, by an odd mental confusion, is given a genital evaluation. In such instances every genital contact threatens to recall the ordeal of birth. If so, she had to avoid, in self-defense, becoming "hot." Yet the hot water was all there, and the man, by ducking, proved that it did not burn—a lesson of no mean importance, as the hot water reaching up to the window sill was on the point of inundating her own room. Indeed, another dream which occurred during the same night proved that the critical stage in her frigidity problem had been reached. The prognosis proved to be true. A few days later, for the first time in seventeen years, she thrilled to a man's touch.

People born in the South or West of the United States know of the manifestation of elemental power in the form of tornadoes. In their dreams the fear of annihilation is often symbolized by exposure to the fury of this cataclysmic force. Occasionally the wind is combined with fire. As a rule, the tornado does not hit the dreamer, but I know of a case in which it did, and nearly caused heart failure.

This dreamer had a recurrent nightmare for many years. A terrible windstorm was about to break and she always had to save some people, getting them into a house or cave. The windstorm passed without hurting them. There was another variation in which she found herself riding in a train. The sky darkened, the storm broke, but before the gigantic funnel of the tornado reached her, the train went into a tunnel where it was safe. When it came out on the other side, the danger was over; the air-spout had passed.

I suspected that the dream was a dramatized version of the dreamer's birth. It was she herself who needed saving from the memory of a terrible experience. The house, the cave or the train in which she was riding was a symbol of her mother's body, the tunnel a reference to the uterine canal, and the tornado to the upheaval of birth. The apocalyptic feeling symbolized the extremity of terror which some children experience in birth.

The dreamer did not receive the explanation with much sympathy, as she was prejudiced against the pre-natal element in psychoanalytic inquiries. Nevertheless, it made an impression on her mind, which may have had something to do with two later nightmares in which the world seemed to crash and she perished under its ruins.

I was in a medium-sized building in a room several stories above ground. I suddenly noticed that wind clouds had partly darkened the skies and the roar of wind was quite loud in the distance. I knew we were in the middle of the vortex this time. My husband tried to close the windows against the terrific gusts of wind, which seemed to me a futile enterprise, like sweeping back the waves of an angry ocean with a whisk-broom, but I tried to help him in spite of my terror and a feeling of certain doom.

At this point we moved into an inner room . . . and I felt a tremendous energy being exerted so that my whole body was being at one and the same time compressed by the terrible weight and density, and torn apart by some gigantic flux. I felt every cell, every atom quiver and gasp as though being pounded to bits and smothered in this angry sea of energy. I murmured to my husband: this is it, and prepared to give up the struggle of resistance. Things were growing heavier, it was getting black, I let go . . . and woke up.

It was in the dead of night, no sound or light, except the pounding of my heart, a loud shooshing sound in my ears like an engine puffing with steam as it leaves a station, the sound of a heart murmur many times magnified through a stethoscope. My whole body was quivering as though the nerves had given way, like in times of near or actual physical accident of a violent nature. I got up at last to try to get rid of the noise in my ears, and after a few minutes went back to sleep.

My reaction in the morning was that in the dream I had a heart attack and died, that at last the "thing" had caught up with me. I told my husband so as I described my dream. I even shed a tear or two over my own demise, but the greatest feeling of relief was present. At last the worst had happened—it was over.

Perhaps a week later I dreamed of being in a burning city. The fire was quite out of control, coming nearer every minute to the building we lived in. All efforts to stop it had failed, even flight might be impossible. I was trying to persuade a group to leave the building. They persisted in risking their lives to carry out furnishings and belongings, which caught fire as soon as they were set in the street. The walls of the building were aflame. I tried to lead the people to safety, but doubted myself that we could get through. A high wind was fanning the flaming embers around us. A thin stream of water just seemed to feed the creeping flames. Just as I began to realize that escape was practically impossible, a huge wave of wind . . . tornado if you like, swept down and in one cosmic gush extinguished every bit of fire. Just like blowing out a candle flame. At last the terrible wind justified its existence. I stood entranced at the miracle and woke up.

The dreamer's description of the terrible compression by the energy of the tornado confirms the explanation already advanced: that she was dying from the ordeal of birth. In previous dreams she awoke before the worst had happened; this time she went through; she was actually born.

The dream about the burning city expresses the same message: the ordeal is real, but there is no death, only birth. The tornado extinguishes the flames; the trauma of birth is resolved.

The dream illustrates one of those rare cases in which exceptional spiritual development promises to solve an almost insoluble problem at a considerable psychic cost but without recourse to trained psychological help. I predicted that her tornado dream would not return. Over a year passed, then—as fate would have it—her nightmare materialized in real life.

She was driving alone in Montana. Coming out of the mountains, she found herself in the midst of a tornado. The windspout caught her and hurled her car into a ravine where, in the flooded waters of a creek, it came to rest upside down, with herself locked within. With remarkable presence of mind, she wound down the window and crawled out to safety before the air was forced out by the inrushing water.

The shock of the experience produced a renewed series of nightmares, but without tornadoes. Instead, the birth symbolism stood out so well that at last she saw that the unconscious mind equates birth with death, particularly if waters or the fury of the elements are involved.

In one of her nightmares there was a pool, and as she approached it she saw that it was completely filled by the body of a monstrous wolf. Frightened she tried to withdraw before the wolf noticed her, but it saw her and sprang after her. She found a chair in her hand and tried to ward off the attack of the monster, then awoke in terror.

The dream shows the waters of birth yielding their place to fear personified in the shape of a monstrous wolf against which human power cannot prevail. The fear is on the same elemental scale which her previous tornado dream had shown; yet the very size of the wolf reveals a new and reassuring element: the fear is down to earth and is objectified in one single representation; the lake is left empty after the wolf emerges. It is easier to face something so concrete as a wolf, no matter how monstrous it is, than the intangible elements of Nature. The fear had shown its face, which is the first step towards finding ways and means of combating it.

A devouring animal in dreams often symbolizes the fear of uterine reabsorption by the mother. The fear is well exemplified in Little Red Riding Hood. In this fairy tale, the grandmother is a substitute for the mother, but being one generation removed is also a cover symbol for a previous life. The wolf is a personification of the fear of birth and re-enacts the drama of birth by reversal, it swallows the child instead of disgorging it. However, poetic justice demands that the innocent go free and the guilty should be punished. Hence the wolf gobbles up grandmother, and Little Red Riding Hood is saved by the woodsman who chops off the head of the wolf. She had to be saved because she was successfully born. The fairy tale illustrates the racial need of release from the shock of birth which haunts our unconscious mind as the wolf haunted the woods of Little Red Riding Hood or filled monstrously the lake of living waters in the tornado victim's dream. As Little Red Riding Hood needed the woodsman to be saved from the wolf, so would the other lady need trained help against the monster which proves too much for her un-aided strength. The chair, being a symbol of a presiding influence, expressed this need in that weird manner in which the unconscious mind sends up its mysterious messages.

To return to fire, a birth dream is not necessarily a re-enactment of our arrival into this world. It may present a symbolic situation to indicate rebirth or a vital change in life. The elemental power of fire lends itself excellently for such dramatic representation. We see it portrayed in the legend of the Phoenix, the bird which every 500 years consumes itself in fire and is reborn from its own ashes. We must not dismiss such legends as silly tales. They fill psychic needs or can be used for such portrayal, as shown by this dream of a sol-dier, occurring shortly after enlistment, to which he looked forward with manly pride:

There was a big brush fire; autumn leaves and smoke drifting in the air. A huge eagle flew right through the fire and its wings caught the flame. I saw it go on fire. It uttered a piercing scream and fell in a blaze unto the ground.

The dreamer recognized the Phoenix touch. He had a life insur-ance policy with the Phoenix Life Insurance Company and, on en-tering the army, had exchanged it for an army insurance policy. By this act he had surrendered the security of his old life and accepted a new one. We may now take it for granted that the autumn leaves symbolize the dying of the old order and hint at the arrival of a new one. For this he was prepared by psychoanalysis, which he under-went just prior to enlisting. The pain with which the eagle dies in the fire shows that the surrender of our old life is not without suf-fering and fear even when willingly undertaken, and that consider-able unconscious readjustments are necessary before we can rise out of the ashes of the past.

10.

T HE term castration is used rather loosely in psychoanalytic literature. Originally it meant the operation whereby a man's testicles were removed for the purpose of rendering him impotent. Practically, it is used for all genital injuries in the male. This enlargement of the original concept is based on the discovery that the unconscious mind reacts with equal gravity to all threats to the organs of reproduction.

There are other more questionable uses of the term. Many writers speak of injuries to the female genitalia as the castration of women. Others say that a woman is born castrated and that the desire of a young girl to be a tomboy is a compensation fantasy. Perhaps the notion is not as preposterous as it appears at first sight. The cutting of the umbilical cord might be the foundation of a castration fantasy, as in dreams the trailing umbilical cord sometimes assumes the significance of the penis.

Some psychoanalysts describe the trauma of weaning as breast castration. Once we accept the term castration as equivalent to libidinal injury, we may speak, with equal justification, of anal and capital castration (subdividing the latter according to cranial, oral, aural, ocular, nasal and dental localizations); we may describe the loss of a finger or leg as digital or pedal castration; or use the same language for appendectomy, tonsillectomy, thyroidectomy or hysterectomy. We can go even further and consider birth as a form of castration because it involves a violent tearing away from the maternal body and because the cutting of the umbilical cord results in actual wounding and shedding of blood.

Little is gained by such looseness of terms. We effect no unification by placing all bodily injuries under the heading of castration, but rather lose the original content of the word, which expressed a distinct and strictly localized damage to the organism. Yet, owing to the existence of the curious unconscious mechanism called transposition from below to above or further below, it would be an equal mistake to be too restricted in the definition of our terms. In dreams, we do not limit castration to the genital area. Moreover, the dream mind is mainly concerned with it subjectively. The castrator is not an outside agent, but an inside one: our own conscience meting out draconian punishment for reasons of sexual guilt. Hence I define castration as a self-imposed injuring, or impairing of function, of parts of the body that lend themselves to sexual representation. The term "self-imposed" excludes accidental or operative injury in which guilt feeling (conscious or unconscious) plays no part. We are interested in internal factors, and the purpose of this chapter is to show how the trauma of birth can be traced in varieties of self-castration.

Regressive Association

In the last reduction, the psychological motive behind the attempts to make castration a comprehensive term is that all bodily injuries threaten life itself. Castration, in that sense, is *pars pro toto*, and it mobilizes the same defense mechanism which a threat to life would set in motion. In fact, it may very well be that all bodily injuries mobilize the memories of previous dangers to life and make our unconscious reactions totalitarian. On this basis we can understand the hysterical behavior which some people exhibit over slight wounds or at the very sight of blood. In such cases the forces of repression fail and the totalitarian effect emerges into the conscious mind. In others, the repression is sufficiently strong for the victim to ignore a light or even a severe injury.

The mechanism which permits such totalitarian reactions is regressive association. It means that we put two and two together not only consciously, but also unconsciously, not by reasoning but by an automatic feeling process. As blobs of mercury flow together to form a bigger blob, so does the pressure of an unreleased, repressed anxiety over a past threat to life increase with each renewed attack against the integrity of the body. This is, in my opinion, the main reason why the forces of repression eventually fail, and we become aware of the anxiety or convert it into local symptoms.

When we say that a present shock mobilizes a forgotten injury, we express the same idea, except that the word "forgotten" has no real meaning. Whatever enters the conscious mind is, *ipso facto,* the property of the unconscious mind. The moment we forget it, it becomes exclusive to the unconscious mind. As the natural state of the unconscious mind is one of dissociation from the conscious mind, everything which is in it is "forgotten." Paradoxically, only that which is so buried does really and permanently exist, regardless of ease or difficulty of recall. Assuming a principality and power over our unconscious processes, we must grant it control over the total content of the unconscious, otherwise the concept of this mind is meaningless as mind is meaningless without a power of comprehension and organization. The comprehension which the unconscious mind exhibits is not the understanding with which we are endowed by the logical faculty. The evidence is abundant that unconscious mental processes differ fundamentally from conscious ones. We have as yet but scant knowledge of their nature. Psychoanalysts are satisfied that the integration of personality is more dependent on unconscious than on conscious co-operation. Something in the patient's mind desires "wholeing" and sees to it that at the proper time the right material is brought forth in dreams and associations. We may call this principality the integrative design, the soul or the higher self; the name does not matter. It matters that it exists, that it weaves strange patterns on the loom of dreams, giving us hints of depth within depth until, as a result of our educational efforts, a partnership develops between the patient's conscious and unconscious mind, serving the mysterious purposes of the latter without full comprehension on the part of the former.

Of Cats and Castration

One often hears the old cliché that a dream is like a spool of cotton. If you go on winding it long enough, you can unwind the whole life of the patient from it. This simile also argues for the totalitarian reactions of the unconscious mind. We can find examples of this in dreams which, while apparently revealing castration injuries, present a cover situation for the much more deeply seated trauma of birth. Here is the dream of a man whose new-born son had a hernia operation:

> *A cat ran up my leg under my trousers and was clawing me severely. I called to Mrs. L., and she was holding the cat by its tail while I hastily took off my trousers to get rid of it.*

The word castration can be written in large letters over the face of this dream. That cat in the trousers is obviously clawing at the dreamer's genitalia. Such dreams may reproduce the memory of an actual injury or represent a fantasy. As trousers are not wide enough to permit a cat to run up a man's legs—and the patient had no memory of an even remotely similar event—we may assume that a hidden danger to his genitals is indicated by "under the trousers."

From a dream which I had obtained from the patient a short time previously, I was able to conclude that he did suffer from castration fears; that these fears were centered on his father and that fantasies of incest with his mother were responsible for them. Mrs. L., to whom he called for help in the present dream, was his fellow passenger on a journey from England to Canada. Boats are universal symbols of the maternal body in which we cross the waters of life. The joint trip qualifies Mrs. L. for the role of the dreamer's mother. Could the cat, by any chance, stand for the father? Could it be that the patient appeals for help against castration by his father?

At first sight, the question seems preposterous. Cats are mainly identified with women. In our unconscious reactions we seem to gloss over the fact that there are male and female cats. The probable reason is that to the infantile mind the cat is often the wife of the dog, as the cow is the wife of the horse. The cat then should primarily stand for the mother. Yet it can well stand for the castrating father, because the unconscious mind also associates the cat with the mouse as its mortal enemy, and the mouse is a penis symbol. In devouring the mouse, the cat eminently fulfils the role of the castrator. Women who grow hysterical at the sight of a mouse and jump on a chair, disclose the phallic association with the mouse. They are really frightened of a sexual attack: of the mouse running up under the skirt into the genitalia. I have seen the same hysterical fear manifest itself in a medical man who suffered from strong homosexual repression; only he was frightened that the mouse would run up into his anus.

Standing for both father and mother, the cat exemplifies the bisexual value of all sexual symbols. On the castration level, it is father; on a deeper level, it is mother. An allusion to the existence of this deeper level is shown when Mrs. L. holds the cat by the tail. The physical contact has a phallic aspect, which the dreamer's state of undress attempts to conceal by justified anxiety. At the same time, the tail end points to something way back, at the end, further than incestuous fantasies carry. Considering that the dream came to the patient after a hernia operation on his infant son, the question immediately arises whether he speaks of his own trauma of birth in castration terms, displacing the crushing of his body in the uterine passage on the clawing cat and on his own genitalia on the basis that birth is accepted as a genital event.

Before the question rose to my lips, the patient himself began to speak of his birth. Without any apparent association link, he stated that he was born with the left side of his face paralyzed by the instruments used in delivery. He still had a trace of it in a tic-like movement which appeared under his left eye when he closed it.

Now we can see new light on his appeal to Mrs. L. It is not against his father that the dreamer needs assistance. It is his trauma of birth which he wishes to see released. As the trauma was caused by his mother, she is the logical person to help. She does so by pulling the cat out of the dark passage formed by the trouser leg. The cat is not only a father and mother symbol but also represents the patient himself. Mrs. L. re-enacts the drama of uterine delivery.

Anal Castration

Let us now see an instance of the so-called anal castration and see whether it is also possible to carry our research to a deeper level. It comes from the medical patient who was afraid that a mouse would run up into his anus. He reported the following hypnagogic vision:

A girl standing on her head on a springboard. She is about to dive. I picture myself as falling and feel afraid.

The community of feeling identifies the patient with the diver. The diver is a girl and as such represents his femininity. That this was a profoundly disturbing aspect of his character, which manifested itself in fears of homosexual aggression, was revealed some time before in this awful nightmare:

A man in the dark played the piano, then took a leap from a diving board and landed on top of me as I was lying on my face in my bed at home, and he attacked me sexually in the anus. I felt small, helpless and terrified.

Bedrooms are not equipped with diving boards; but if the bedroom also represents a pool of water, the feature is not incongruous; it is part of a telescopic picture in which the water has been suppressed. The feeling that he is a woman is similarly suppressed, yet this is what the anal aggression, or—to use Freudian language—anal castration indicates. He is raped as if he were a woman, but it took another vision and another diving board to show himself upside down as a girl.

The nightmare and the hypnagogic vision are obviously linked, and our first task was to find out the identity of the aggressor. This was not difficult. The patient immediately identified him with his own father, because his father had the habit of playing the piano at night in the dark and because he had committed an awful act of aggression against him when he was still on the breast. Enraged over the delay in weaning a troublesome child of a year and a half, he tore him off his mother's breast and, to intimidate the mother, pushed him out of a third story window by the seat of his pants, threatening to drop him. The patient vaguely remembered the incident, but not the shock. The latter was partly displaced on an abnormal fear of high windows. The rest of the shock was absorbed by his anus. His father's grip on the seat of his pants was, perhaps, the principal reason why he became overconscious of his anal region. Evacuation guilt was another factor. He was often told how his father used to rage about the smell in the parental bedroom.

But why is his father's assault of a sexual nature? The explanation of this vital question was found in the patient's fantasies of identification with his own mother. This identification assumed a corporeal significance. In a compulsive fear fantasy, he had been trying to re-enact—according to the anatomic facilities of his male body—the conjugal act which he had witnessed in the parental bedroom. In his vague and confused memories the act appeared as a vicious aggression against the mother.

Nor was this all. In another strange flower of fantasy he equated the window (from which his father threatened to drop him) with the genital door to life. Having been held out of the window after a violent emotional scene, his organismic memories of falling away from his mother's body in birth were stirred up by the sight of the abyss below. As in his early youth he had reached the conclusion that the place of issue from the maternal body was the anus, he automatically invested that part of his anatomy with the fear which the peril of the window elicited. The fear manifested itself in chronic spasms of his anal sphincter, preventing him from passing flatus and causing him hours of agony in each attack. The call of the bowels never produced such constriction, only flatus. The reason proved to be rather startling: the flatus tension was a symptom of his mother's pregnancy with himself and, owing to his corporeal identification with the mother, passing flatus was equivalent to being born. Some gods of Hindu mythology are credited with the amazing feat of giving birth to themselves. The unconscious mind of modern man is archaic enough to harbor strange survivals of such racial thinking.

The conscious mind will struggle to keep them out. In this case, the spasm of the anal sphincter served a similar purpose: it aimed at preventing the memory of birth from rising into the patient's consciousness.

The means of defense is puerile; but this holds true of most unconscious defense mechanisms. That is why, on finding their origin, the victim is able to throw them off—as the patient of this case succeeded in doing. How could he maintain such reactions when they related to a fantasy of giving birth to himself through his own anus? He could only laugh at it; and laugh he did—with a complete cessation of the trouble.

The fear which he experienced at the sight of the girl diver's impending fall into the water is a comparatively simple representation of birth by the reverse. The upside down position of the girl is a reversal symbol and alludes to a falling out of the waters of life instead of a falling into them. The position, as the patient suggested, also invited attention to the anus and was exciting; in exhibiting the legs and the buttocks, it was an emphasis on the part of the human anatomy which matters most in birth. The face of the girl being away from him was a further indication that the dream did not move on the intellectual plane represented by the head, but on an emotional one represented by the sexual region.

In dreaming of himself as a girl, the patient gave a clue to a novel understanding of how defense reactions of an apparent homosexual character may develop from distorted notions of the trauma of birth.

Oral Castration

Let us now illustrate so-called oral castration by the first dream under analysis of a widow of forty-eight. Weeks passed before the full significance of the dream was revealed.

I was a waitress, and this filled me with a good deal of surprise and pain. I had to get up very early and could not find my corset. Then I went into the bathroom; to do so, I had to descend two or three steps. I wanted to wash my mouth. Lifting the glass to my lips, I must have bitten into it and ground the bit to pieces. I was

111

trying to spit out the glass and woke up, facing the steps leading out of the bathroom, with a finger in my mouth.

The dream reveals an oral injury and shows the desire to get rid of it by washing the mouth, spitting out the glass and coming out of the bathroom. As the act of descending steps often symbolizes a descent into the past, the sunken bathroom immediately called for searching attention. The patient had no sunken bathroom, so I wondered if the two or three steps could have referred to the date of the dream. It is my contention that most dreams have a hidden date. They reveal the period of life into which the events of the dream fit. If I was right, it was possible that between the ages of two and three something very serious had happened to this patient, causing pains as severe as ground glass would produce within the digestive system.

The patient responded with the statement that she had weak intestinal walls because a tumor had been excised from one of her ovaries, and she wore a corset for support. She liked the erect bearing which the corset helped her to have. It meant dignity and an ability to hold a stiff upper lip.

When I asked what the psychological weakness was from which she was defending herself by a stiff upper lip, she confessed that she was trying hard to conceal her financial insecurity and fear of the future from the members of her social set. In her social position, to be a waitress was the last degradation; that was why she felt so pained at being one in the dream.

As the fear of the future is a projection of fears from the past, I made the mental note that the oral injury must hold the clue to her feeling of insecurity.

It took twenty analytic sessions for the memory of the oral injury to rise into her consciousness. It came in the wake of a nightmare.

She dreamed that somebody was getting married. She was about to receive a legacy, as if the marriage had been a funeral and she had come into an inheritance; but she only received two dollars. Then a group of gangsters came into the kitchen, together with two women. They demanded the key, in order to seize the money which she had inherited. She had no key to give them, whereupon the two women pounced on her and held her down, while a man made an injection in her right arm. Then she lost consciousness, and woke up, badly frightened, feeling as if somebody had slapped her in the face.

Later in the night she dreamed of sitting in a room, doing embroidery. The door opened and a cat brought in a mouse. It was a terrible sight. Only the tail of the mouse was visible, feebly moving; the rest of the body was within the cat's mouth.

This dream is an excellent illustration of oral castration in its ultimate equation with death. It is not the tail which is bitten off, the picture is not of plain mutilation; the whole of the body is about to be severed from the tail and swallowed.

The mouse as a helpless little creature suggests the patient as a child, while the cat symbolizes the destructive parent. This is an assumption made on general symbolic grounds and it cannot be considered valid until confirmatory material is obtained. That material is hidden in the dream of assault. Unquestionably, the injection and the loss of consciousness after an attack by two women shows her in a situation which equals being put to death. Mention is made of a key, which, taken symbolically, must mean the key to her psychological condition.

At this point, the veil of memory was suddenly rent and the memory of an awful experience came back:

"I was three years old when an epidemic of diphtheria broke out in our town. It was a small town, having two doctors only who had to attend to dozens of families. I fell sick and ran a high fever. My father could not get a doctor, but he obtained instructions what to do. The doctor's wife gave him swabs and iodine. He began to treat me. He needed the assistance of my mother and the maid to hold me. They grabbed my hands, my father held up my chin with one hand, ready to swab with the other. I would not open my mouth and he shouted at me. Then, when I opened it, he jabbed at me with the swab, which was dripping with iodine. He wanted to be sure. The iodine burned me like fire and I felt awfully frightened and hurt. The performance was repeated every hour throughout the night. My life was saved, but father knew he had been very clumsy and had

113

injured me, because afterwards I heard him cry and tell my mother, 'Oh, I am ashamed of myself.'"

One has to place oneself in the position of the small child to understand the horror of this experience. We see the reaction in the patient's dream forty-five years after the event. Her father and mother figure in it as gangsters; but while the women only immobilize her, it is the father who, in the role of the doctor, robs her of consciousness by injection. All her life she bore a hatred to her father which she could not understand. Yet she married a much older man who was an obvious father substitute. She married him against her mother's will, and in another dream she depicted her mother as a dragon over which she became victorious by tearing its jaws apart. She paid a price for her victory on her wedding night. She fainted after defloration and had vomiting fits when consciousness returned. It looks as if the wedding night mobilized the memories of her oral castration, which may explain why in the dream marriage is confused with a funeral. Her father and her husband— as identical to her unconscious mind as two dollar bills—left her a very bad legacy, the key to which was buried in her diphtheria memories; the injection in her right arm apparently refers to the application of the iodine coated swab by her father and to the defloration by her husband. The injury was displaced on her right arm because she was receiving menopause injections in that arm, the genital evaluation of which is obvious.

If we now return to the patient's first dream, we shall find a deeper mystery behind the fact that the oral injury is caused by ground glass and the scene is laid in the sunken bathroom from which she is about to emerge. She is spitting glass and wakes up with a finger in her mouth. Further, she pictures herself as a waitress with no suggestion of any waiting to be done on others. The oral injury reveals a glimpse of an earlier ordeal of life: the trauma of birth, hidden behind an equation of the mouth with the genitalia, an equation which the calling of the labia lips always facilitates. The bathroom is a widely used symbol for the womb because we float in the tub as a child floats in the amniotic fluid. The ground glass that would crush her intestines alludes to the crushing of her own body within her mother. She is facing the steps to show the coming out into this world, and she has her finger in her mouth to demonstrate the relationship between the small child (finger) and the uterus (mouth). As the finger leaves the mouth by being pulled out, so does the child leave the body of the mother in delivery. The cat swallowing the mouse shows the same relationship reversed. This reversal is an excellent mechanism to illustrate the fear with which we are ushered into this world. The confusion between marriage and funeral also bears on the shock of birth. Marriage is a separation from home, from the mother, and it is an ushering into a new life. The genital injuries of the wedding night are apt to mobilize the trauma of birth; the result is an equation of the latter with defloration. In this identification lies the key to a trauma with which so many women are stricken; a key which explains the breakdown that so often follows the bridal night.

Now we can guess why the patient is a waitress in the bathroom. A waitress is somebody who waits. The suspense of birth is mainly due to the waiting for its full accomplishment. No one gives the child support in its tribulation. No corset holds it up. Further, being a waitress also helps to illustrate the unconscious device of transposition from below to above. The uterus is replaced by the mouth, the needs of the mouth are satisfied by waiters and waitresses. Having a job as a waitress is, therefore, an appeal for help; it is an indication of the acceptance of analysis. It shows that the patient has entered on the analytic path actively by calling attention, in her very first dream, to a fundamental injury, the implications of which were too far reaching for immediate understanding.

Vaginal Castration

Mention has been made at the beginning that injury to the female genitalia is sometimes also described in terms of castration. The psychic repercussion of such injuries does not depend on the actual harm done but on the victim's evaluation of chastity, or on the fear associations which surround defloration. We have seen this fear

115

operating in the previous case as part of an oral trauma. Now we shall have a clearer illustration of its mysterious workings in a genital setting:

I dreamed about Violet, a Polish girl who used to work with me when I began my business career. I looked in through the window of her husband's office and saw five or six clerks busy at desks and Violet in their midst, very large with pregnancy and too busy to talk to me. She returned my greeting but indicated that she would talk to me at her convenience, not at mine.

Something in Violet's appearance reminded the patient of Anna, the wife of an undertaker, who had given birth to a baby a few weeks before. She had met Anna the previous day. Violet's pregnancy thus called attention to birth on two accounts, but also brought in allusions to death through the undertaker. The dream hinted at something important, and resistance to the revelation was indicated by the fact that Violet was too busy, or not yet ready, to talk to her.

From Violet, the girl, the train of the patient's associations led to violets in a country walk near a cemetery for colored people. She recalled that a colored boy of sixteen had murdered a little girl there, with an axe. The scene of the murder was a few feet from the house of Irma, a friend who recently appeared in her dream—also pregnant.

Violet's pregnancy now seemed to be linked with murder. Presently came another important memory. During the first world war, the patient went on a vacation with Violet. On the train to Cape May, they made the acquaintance of a soldier who was stationed at a hospital for the insane; he invited them to visit the hospital. Violet did not accept, but she did—to her grief. The man showed her into a room, locked the door and raped her.

We now see Violet directly associated with violation—a probable motive also behind the murder of the little girl by the colored boy, though the patient could not recall it. With a slight change of spelling, the name Violet turns into "violate." However, the patient was not sure what happened to her on that occasion in the hospital. She was definite that she did not become pregnant as a result of the assault.

The following day another dream gave further information:

I thought someone had received a postcard from the war zone and that it had a flower on it. The flower was of wool or cotton. When closely examined, it appeared to have fresh blood on it. It seemed to be from a young man in our purchasing department, and I said, "It is Paul's blood"—although the man in my mind was another boy called Bob. It looked as though he had tried to get a secret message through.

A woman's flowers symbolize virginity. The word defloration originates in this notion. The freshly spilt blood on the dream flower may stand for defloration or menstruation. The cotton points towards the latter; it suggests a menstrual pad. But menstruation in itself is a symbol for genital injury. The war, as a substitute for internal conflict, accentuates the gravity of this injury. The patient speaks of Paul's blood, but she has somebody else in mind. If Paul can take the place of another boy, he may also take the place of a girl, of the patient herself, as the flower points in the direction of the feminine and she had a strong masculine disposition. Bob, the name of the other boy, has a feminine connotation. To bob means cutting hair—of a woman; and hair cutting might symbolize castration; in which case the secret message refers to a genital crime and the dream links up with the one about Violet, violation and pregnancy.

The choice of Paul, as a substitute for Bob, must have a motivation of its own. Violet is a Polish girl. Paul and Polish have a distorted phonetic equation. The unconscious mind is not ruled by logic. Logic demands precision; the unconscious mind is satisfied with approximations. I have studied dozens of dreams in which Polish was related to pole, the big male organ, and dozens of others in which the name Paul was used in the same sense. Paul's blood simply stands for blood on the pole; it is the blood of Violet, it refers to the patient's genital injury caused by the big pole. Paradoxically, men often describe it as their little one, the child. That

117

thought may hold a clue to Violet's pregnancy. The child, in the course of birth, is in the same relationship to the mother's genitalia as the penis is; it inflicts injury on her, it sheds her blood. It is on this basis that Georg Groddeck conceived the existence of blood guilt to the mother. Does the patient's dream bear this out, or does she refer to her own injuries in the process of delivery, the memories of which had been mobilized by her own violation?

A few days before the dream about Violet's pregnancy, the patient dreamed about the Christmas rush in the post office and saw Elsie, a young girl, behind one of the windows. Violet was also there. Elsie's eyes looked red as if she were very tired, but she kept smiling.

Christmas has a birthday significance. It celebrates the birth of the Babe of Bethlehem, and the window anatomically equates with the vagina. Elsie had red eyes and the patient's first association was: windows of the soul. If the eye is a window, it has depth and it can be penetrated like any ordinary window or its genital equivalent. The realization of this gave the clue to the patient that the red referred to the color of the vaginal membrane. At the same instant she recalled something very important:

"As a child, I used to have a great desire to look inside the lips of my vagina. I held up a mirror, but I became scared. I don't know why. I had the feeling it was forbidden to look."

It is not difficult to guess what the forbidden thing was: to see the meaning of the mother's big stomach, to find the child within, to find herself. On a deeper level, Violet, Anna and Elsie are so many substitutes for the patient's own mother. Her curiosity is directed at the mystery of pre-natal life, and the genital crime (of which the rape memory and the Paul dream speak) is her own violation in birth and in assault. Blood is shed in birth in the cutting of the umbilical cord. Whether Groddeck is right or not about the shedding of the mother's blood, there may be a registration in the organism of this personal event. The internal crushing in rape and the external crushing in birth are the two poles of a long chain of biological and emotional development. They are repetitive events for the unconscious mind, but along this chain no libido can travel freely until a correlation is established by conscious understanding.

Birth and Castration

In the patient's case, this lack of correlation was also shown by thyroid symptoms. She reported on the analytic couch a sudden pressure in her thyroid glands, and pains in the nape of her neck; and complained of extreme exhaustion. Periodically, she suffered from such symptoms and could not account for their onset now. When I related them to the trauma of rape and the trauma of birth, the symptoms vanished, and stayed away subsequently. It is tempting to assume that they were due to after-pains of birth. As the throat is often equated with the genital passage in dreams and waking fantasies, it is possible that the swelling of the thyroid gland was a conversion symptom for pregnancy and birth.

As this patient revealed abundant traumata forming a solid structure on a high level, it may be queried: is it necessary to relate them to birth? The answer is in that new principle of dream interpretation which I have already claimed: all sexual traumata tend to mobilize the trauma of birth. Just as all fears ultimately nest in the fear of death, so do all sexual injuries trail back, through symptoms, associations and impressions registered on the deepest strata of our unconscious mind, to birth, an event which in its stupendous significance can only be matched by the great drama of evolution when life emerged from the tepid waters of the primeval ocean and took its first root on land.

11.

IT IS NO more unnatural for a woman to be afraid of rape than for a man to be afraid of castration, or of any other injury that threatens the integrity of the body. Only when the fear of rape is excessive and morbid are we justified in assuming that it is conditioned by traumatic events.

Usually, such traumata are discovered in layers upon layers, going back as far as the primal scene in the parental bedroom which was inadvertently observed and misconstrued. Sometimes, however, sexual traumata well up from still greater depth and are of a more biological than personal nature.

A beautiful girl, twice unhappily married and about to make a hit-or-miss attempt at happiness for the third time, was discussing with a friend her mother's hysterectomy, which was necessitated by a tumor. That night she had a terrible dream:

I was with my mother at a party in the country. I had to go to the bathroom very badly. I went up a long, narrow staircase and found myself in a peculiar room. It was round and had two small high windows, at one of which I saw a small dummy man, with a moustache, pointing a gun at the other window. The toilet was very white, but it had no seat. That did not bother me as I always stand over the toilet in a strange bathroom. I passed water very slowly and painfully. All of a sudden, I looked down and saw a white mass looking like discharge on the floor. It had come from me.

Birth and Rape

Then I saw a tank full of water and floating in it was a tumor, as big as a coconut. The blood vessels stood out vividly. Suddenly, the tumor was sucked down to the bottom of the tank and I felt that something had been pulled out of me. It was very painful and frightening. I heard a voice: Let it come out; it is all over now, it is a tumor.

Compulsive Urination

On waking from the dream, an urgent need to pass water drove the patient to the bathroom. For three days afterwards, she felt sore in the genital passage as if she had passed something. This is an excellent illustration of the suggestive influence of nightmares over waking life. In this case, it exemplified the urgency of psychological therapy.

The dream is very rich in analytic material. One of the first impressions it conveyed was that the patient suffered from compulsive urination. There was the feeling in the dream and after the dream that she had to go to the bathroom very badly and there was the absence of the lavatory seat which elicited the confession that she is compelled to stand over the lavatory in strange bathrooms. She admitted, indeed, that compulsive urination was with her a serious complaint. Not only did she have to get up every night, sometimes twice, to go to the bathroom, but the need to pass water was particularly strong in the pre-menstrual period, and sometimes during intercourse; she had to interrupt the coital act and go to the bathroom even though she had urinated just before. On resuming intercourse, the pressure usually returned. She had to urinate whenever she put her foot into a tub of water, touched water with her hand or heard it running. Sometimes she had to get out of the tub and urinate a second time, though she had taken precautions before beginning to bathe. The same compulsion manifested itself on the beach.

As usual, no medical treatment availed against this frequency of urination. Her medical history revealed the following data: scarlet fever at the age of seven (for which her mother blamed her father as she caught the infection from a little girl with whose mother her own father kept company); pains in the kidney several years ago, but a recent examination showed her kidneys functioning normally; chronic bladder inflammation for the previous three years.

In the dream, urination is very slow and painful. This was often the case in reality. The pattern may have been her mother's, who had a bladder inflammation after hysterectomy. For neurotic purposes the bladder is a good substitute for the womb because it is near the genital area and it is expendable. Sexual guilt is frequently converted into bladder affliction. As the patient had an abortion after her first marriage and later underwent ovariotomy, it seemed likely that sexual guilt was a factor in this specific complaint. Tumors, in the fantasy life of neurotics, often take the place of a dead child or represent pregnancy fantasies.

That in this patient's unconscious a link, indeed, existed between childbirth and the bladder, was presently shown. She dreamed that she had to go to the toilet several times. To reach it, she had to creep on all fours along a narrow passage and had to duck under an arch. The place was in darkness but light came in from the passage through which she crept. She sat on her dog's saucepan (which her mother used to give her when she was sick) and the water came slowly.

The uterine element in this dream stands out clearly. Ducking under an arch is a picturesque illustration of birth; but it does not follow that painful urination is due to an after-pain of birth. The birth picture may only point out the relationship between inflamed bladder and pregnancy. Abortion or other injuries and fantasies may be more likely responsible for the pain because the element of fatality that characterizes birth dreams is absent. As a matter of fact, any emotional injury could be converted into a bladder complaint. People can cry with their bladders; and she seemed to do so. If she quarrelled with her fiancé, she had to rush to the bathroom again and again until the quarrel was smoothed over.

Jack the Ripper Fears

To return to the strange bathroom: the patient's comment on her habit of standing over the toilet reveals that she also suffered from infection fears. Her mother used to warn her never to sit on the seat in a public toilet. The seat was a threat of contracting venereal disease from which intercourse and pregnancy anxieties developed to an unusual degree. She refused her first husband the consummation of marriage, and sewed up his borrowed pajamas (in which she used to sleep) in order to protect herself. After a month, her husband raped her, and she suffered excruciating pains. The only way she could find sexual gratification was by masturbation. She tried to help the situation and had herself surgically stretched; but it made little difference. During the year and a half her first marriage lasted, she derived no pleasure from conjugal life, yet felt compelled to complete the act of intercourse by secret masturbation in the bathroom.

Her first husband habitually practiced cunnilingus and forced her to practice fellatio on him. Both practices filled her with disgust. She never could kiss a man with a moustache. Recently, she had seen an old photograph of her present fiancé, which showed him with a beard. In a flash, she knew the reason of her odd aversion. The moustache reminded her of pubic hair, her own in cunnilingus and, on a deeper level, of her father's "moustache" below. At a picnic, when she was six years old, she saw her father urinating behind the bushes and was frightened by the size of his organ. Later a man who was sitting next to her on a bench exhibited his erect penis and gave her a shock. She was again scared some years past on seeing her brother asleep on a bed, with his genitals exposed.

The reason for her fright went back to Jack the Ripper, stories of whose crimes were in the newspapers when she was very small. She failed to understand what it was all about, and believed that Jack the Ripper was killing children with a knife. Perhaps, unconsciously, she had placed herself in the position of the attacked women whose bellies were ripped open by a knife. Her mother made the situation worse by constantly warning her against strangers. The result was that she became very timid in the company of men whom she had not met before. This timidity was very much in evidence at the time that her analysis began.

Search for the Beloved

Rectal Traumata

The patient's association of moustache with pubic hair calls immediate attention to the dummy man in the bathroom. He had a moustache and was armed with a gun. The patient's father wore a moustache, but the dummy man was of small stature and resembled Jack, the patient's young brother. As the gun has the same symbolic value as the knife of Jack the Ripper, an investigation of the patient's relationship to her brother became incumbent.

She recalled incidents highly charged with emotion. Jack's anatomy used to excite her imagination and she remembered playing doctor and nurse with him, during the course of which mutual exploration of the genitals and of the anus took place. Once they were caught by their mother, and she was considered the initiator of the game as she was the older one. The feeling of humiliation and guilt stayed with her and, at the time when she came to analysis, she was shy about looking her brother in the face, wondering if he remembered.

Other memories were wrapped in a haze of mental confusion. They concerned Jack's circumcision. Having been caught by the nurse in masturbation, she was threatened with the cutting off of something. This recalled a mysterious remark which the doctor made when he circumcised Jack. It was to the effect that she, too, would need circumcision. The meaning of this remark was never cleared up. Perhaps she had an over-developed or overgrown clitoris, perhaps the doctor was misunderstood both by her mother and herself; the fact is that she had been so frightened by the doctor's words that when the memory of the incident returned she hardly could resist the desire to take a mirror and look for some abnormality or traces of operation.

In the dream, Jack's gun pointed at the other window. The round shape of the bathroom and the long, narrow staircase leading up to it seem to symbolize the womb. The two small high windows suggest entrances. Anatomically, we only know of one entrance, through the vagina, but in childish fantasy the anus is often substituted. The "other window," therefore, we may assume, is the anal one; it was further back, as it is in reality. It must have some importance in the dream if the gun is pointing at it.

We have already established that the dummy man, through the moustache, is a telescopic representation of the patient's father and brother. When she was very small, she witnessed intercourse between her parents. Having seen her father behind her mother, she assumed that he was urinating into her mother's rectum. A large part of this patient's incestuous fantasies with her father was built on this memory, and this became an important component of her urination compulsion. Her chronic bladder inflammation may well have been caused by the guilty passion which the scene inspired. The excitation was probably also responsible for her involvement in sexual situations with her young brother, who appears to have been responsible for her rape fears, both genital and anal, to a considerable degree. She dreamed, for instance, of foxes biting her on the leg and arm, and of being in bed with her mother in a barn, together with a Mr. and Mrs. Lynch, whose presence, for some reason, was frightening. With the name she associated lynching, and the barn recalled memories of digital exploration by Jack in the barn-like garage. This, in turn, reminded her of a man who had tried to rape her in his car in the garage-way while she was still a virgin.

When her father died, she fell victim to a severe attack of rectal pains. Seven years before analysis, she slipped on a dance floor; a big man crashed on top of her and she injured her coccyx. This injury had caused pains ever since. She was in the habit of constantly falling on her back. It is possible that such an accident could be contrived on unconscious purpose for self-punishment. On medical examination, her uterus was discovered tipped, and she underwent an operation.

She suffered from chronic constipation and from haemorrhoids. As a small child she passed a tapeworm. Menstruation and intercourse gave her pains in the rectum. Chiropractors found it impossible to adjust her coccyx because the tightening of her anal sphincter prevented the entry of the finger. The attempt at examination hurt her for weeks. The summer before she began her analysis, she contracted an infection by poison oak in the woods. In the course of evacuation, the leaves must have touched her buttocks, and she was laid up for a week. Twice she had anal fissures. The last time she thought she had cancer in the rectum. Nobody in her family ever had cancer, but she had caught "crabs" (an odd equation with cancer) from her first husband, who had also tried anal intercourse unsuccessfully. Between these various anal traumata and genital complaints, she was lost in mental confusion. After the last fissure operation, as she came out of the anesthetic, she wanted to embrace her doctor. She thought that the doctor was her analyst, about whom during the operation she had had an erotic dream.

As a mechanism to lessen the surgical shock, the dream served her well, but it also reveals that she both feared and desired anal intercourse. The desire was not permitted to rise into her consciousness as it was heavily invested with the fear of death. In place of the usual small-vagina complex, she suffered from small-anus fantasies because the infantile measuring up of her own anatomy against her father's had survived the passing of time without change. The legitimate nature of the operation which she was undergoing must have had a share in persuading the censor to permit the dream, but the very operation is exploited for the purpose of demonstrating the equation, from the viewpoint of the unconscious, between rectal enlargement and anal defloration. The pains that had led to the discovery of the fissure were first noticed in her fiancé's apartment. They were in bed when a loud knock sounded on the door. Her heart suddenly stood still; she could not help thinking that her mother had found her out and was at the door in one of her old furies. The rectal pains appeared during the next intercourse. But strangely, the operation did her more good by enlarging the rectal passage than by the actual repair of the fissure as, for her fantasy life, it replaced the small anus with a big one and permitted her to grow up.

That the analyst in this rectal intercourse fantasy stood for her father appeared probable from the study of another dream. In this, she saw her father in a coffin, dead. Then he came to life and grabbed her by the arm. After this the scene shifted. She was on her back, naked, and a man pounced on her and touched her coccyx with his penis. She does not say in the dream that, in order to do that, the man had turned her, at least into a sideways position, and she only admitted after considerable hesitation that the man looked like her analyst. Her father came to life because the analytic relationship permitted the objectification of her fears and desires for a father in the person of the analyst. When her arm is grabbed by her father, she speaks of the grip in which she is held by her feelings for her father. The coffin looked like a box couch into which she was shut once by her brother and like a hope chest they had. Apparently, the hope chest was her rectum. She hoped that her father would take notice of her or would drop dead.

Plenty of evidence came to light to show that her love was inseparable from her hatred of her father. As a very young girl, she was shocked by catching him with a woman in his lap. She felt that she had lost her father to a stranger. The feeling was aggravated by her mother, who used to take her along to trail the father and this woman to a movie. She discovered, too, that she was an unwanted child. Her father had opposed her coming, and only married her mother because she became pregnant. When finally he deserted his wife and child, the mother developed an attitude of excessive morality, trying to live down her own guilt and dreading that her daughter would go her way. It made things very difficult. She had dreams in which her mother was killed or burned to death at home. At the age of four to five, she enacted a perfect fantasy of matricide by shutting up a cat with a bulldog in a large garbage can. The bulldog killed the cat, and she could never forgive herself for the cruel deed.

It is significant that the bathroom nightmare should follow a discussion of her mother's hysterectomy. At one time she believed that when a child is ready to be born, the mother's body is cut open by a knife. Thus the conversation about tumors and operations naturally re-animated her early feelings about childbirth and Jack the Ripper fears. It is more than likely that the tumor floating on the top of the tank—something unwanted and sickening—represents herself as a fetus. The simultaneous sensation of the tumor being sucked down to the bottom of the tank and its coming out of her appears to be a symbolic re-enactment of her mother's pregnancy and her own birth.

When she heard from her mother authoritatively how babies were born, she was filled with horror. Until she was freed of this horror by analysis, her mother's body was repulsive both to her touch and sight. She hated herself for this revulsion. She could not even stand being kissed by her mother and her birth shame was so acute that if her mother entered the bathroom when she was there naked, she experienced acute embarrassment. If she found curly hairs in the bathtub or on the soap, she was filled with disgust.

A Garden of Eden Fantasy

The night of the tumor dream the patient also had a Garden of Eden fantasy, the pre-natal coloring of which is a strong indication that the tumor dream is concerned with birth, as it is generally accepted that all dreams occurring the same night express the same fundamental thought:

I have been so unhappy at home with my mother that we went into another house at the seashore. I was cleaning strawberries in the kitchen. My favorite movie actor was outside. I saw him and followed him down to the edge of the water. There we turned to the left, and right in front of me was a big, gorgeous garden. I followed him through the gate. Outside, I felt unhappy. As soon as the gate closed behind me, I lost the man and had the most wonderful and peaceful feeling. I never felt so happy in my life. I dashed around right and left. There were tiny little houses, caverns, nicely furnished. I walked way down to the end, the distance of a couple of blocks. Beautiful trees were growing everywhere. I walked out of the garden at the other end, and immediately an awful feeling of desolation came over me. I went back, the depression lifted and I was divinely happy once again. I visited all the little houses and walked back to the front entrance of the garden. In a booth, sitting, I saw an elderly man with grey hair. He was trying to advise me as I passed through the gate.

At first reading, this dream of happiness and the bathroom dream of horror have little in common. Yet, we may note, that the garden has two gates in opposite directions which agrees with the two windows of the bathroom that suggested the vaginal and the fantasied anal entrance into the womb. The garden of happiness is a romantic reference to pre-natal life; the bathroom is a functional one. She is given helpful advice as she leaves the garden through the front gate, and she is similarly encouraged when the tumor leaves the vaginal door: "Let it come out; it is all over now; it is a tumor." If the seashore symbolizes the waters of life, the bathtub embodies the same idea. A motion picture actor is a dummy man, in a sense; yet, as a hero ideal, he may also be the early image of the father. He disappears as soon as she enters the Garden of Happiness, which is understandable as the father was not known in the womb; possibly, this is another reason for the *lifeless* dummy in the tumor dream. The little houses could suggest the comfort and all-sufficiency of pre-natal life. The elderly man at the gate giving wise counsel may be the analyst or the Mysterious Helper which Jung describes as an archetype, representing the wisdom of the unconscious. The dream seems to teach a lesson: you must not seek happiness in the past, only in the future; the horror of birth stands between you and memories of pre-natal bliss; discharge this horror as the tumor was discharged; prepare yourself for a second birth and your happiness will be assured.

Children who do not have a happy infancy seem to retain the anxiety of birth at a higher pressure than others. This patient was a cry-baby, always very nervous. After eleven months, she was weaned because her mother became pregnant again. The weaning was done in a brutal manner. To make nursing disgusting to the child, the mother covered her nipples with alum. The disgust reaction duly took place, but it was directed both at the breasts and at the mother. All her life, the patient was filled with revulsion at the sight of her mother's breasts. The bottle used to give her constant colic, and to this day she is indifferent to milk. She is irritated if she sees her fiancé suck at his pipe and she cannot bear the sight of a suckling child; but she bites her thumb and smokes thirty cigarettes a day. She starts as soon as she wakes up, smokes in the lavatory and smokes in bed. Yet she does not like the taste, puffs once or twice and then throws the cigarette away.

Curiously, the development of her own breasts has been arrested. They are almost completely flat. She had a promising voice but lost it during the first year of her second marriage, after her husband, in a fit of rage, tried to strangle her. This was a cover memory for having seen her father seize her mother by the throat. She remembered going to her rescue and having tried to beat off her father with her tiny fists. She used to suffer from swollen thyroids and had dreams that showed an equation between her oesophagus and uterus in which the uvula took the place of the clitoris. The clearing up of these fantasies was indicated in a dream in which the analyst was killing a German police dog by forcing a hose down its throat and turning on the water in full force.

At the time of the strangling attack by her husband, the patient was hit on the nose, and since then she had a feeling of fullness in it. As the nasal passage contains dirt (in the form of dry mucosa), it may equate in dreams with the rectal passage, once it has been invested with a traumatic charge. The following dream shows how this transposition from below to above had taken place in the patient's case:

I looked into my nose and the passage looked as large as my rectum when distended, even larger. There was a hard mass in it which, by the color, looked like No. 2. It was brown and it would not come through whole. I was picking at it, probably with my finger in the left nostril. The nose did not seem to be mine, yet I knew it was mine.

This dream came to the patient after a serious quarrel with her fiancé. Now that she came to think of it, her fiancé reminded her a good deal of the strangling husband. On this occasion, he used cruel words and raked her over the coals by pointing out her faults and declaring that he would postpone marrying her until her analysis was finished. In the dream, her left nostril is blocked, preventing her from breathing freely and thus interfering with her vital air circulation. This is an admission of her inhibited emotional state, as air circulation has a close symbolic equation with the flow of libido. The essential element of the dream is that she attempts to clean out her nose or rectum, but she is not very successful in getting out the obstructing mass because she wants to get it out whole instead of slowly breaking it up in the analytic process.

The impasse in which she found herself was the result of slow accumulation from many sources. The masturbation problem contributed to it considerably. When her menstruation came, she was unprepared and had a shock. She thought she had injured herself during masturbation. Curiously, she later did this very thing. In the course of digital exploration of the vaginal passage, her nail must have torn her hymen. She bled for a day and apparently lost her virginity. She felt so guilty about it that when her husband looked for traces of blood on the sheet after their first intercourse, she was unable to confess and rather put up with the accusation that she had had an affair before him with another man.

Thinking about her first menstruation, she wondered now how she could have been so ignorant. She recalled that as a small child she looked through the keyhole and saw her mother take off a sanitary napkin which was covered with blood. Once she found another one in the garbage can, and knew that it came from her mother. She could not quite figure out its meaning then. While living with her first husband, she had unusually severe menstrual attacks. Each was similar to child labor. The pains were knife-like thrusts. She stayed in bed and took injections, though the injection needle always frightened her; apparently, it was another symbolic reminder of rape. Yet, in spite of her suffering, she welcomed her menstrual pains because they protected her from her husband's attention.

The Trauma of Being Born Asleep

Darkness was always full of terrors. She had an aunt who used to take care of her. By way of discipine, the aunt locked her in the cellar and in the cupboard. At other times she threatened her with the bogey man and the washerwoman who would wash her to death. Ever since, the patient had a morbid fear of cellars or other dark places, such as the roof of the house at night. She fancied burglars and gangsters lurking in dark corners and expected them to pounce on her. On entering tunnels, she felt uncomfortable; being in crowds always gave her an uneasy feeling. A mild form of claustrophobia was indicated, justifying an investigation of her birth, an event which is ideally suited to leave the organism with symptoms befitting the syndrome of claustrophobia.

The first indication of something unusual came with the discovery that loss of consciousness was a source of special dread for the patient. Experiences in adolescent life appeared to furnish ample ground for the existence of such fears. Her mother's moral strictures drove her into bad company, and so she took to heavy drinking. Once, waking from a drunken sleep in the apartment of a girl friend of loose morals, she found an old man lying on top of her making coitus movements between her legs. The shock was so great that every time she passes the house where this happened she still feels sick. Thereafter she had dreams in which her voice was small like a child's and she felt as if she had been assaulted. The time was always 2 A.M. According to her mother, this was the hour of her birth. Then came a big dream which seemed to indicate that her rape fears were due to a conversion into the vaginal passage of the compression of her whole body in birth:

I was in my place of business. Long, heavy, cream colored draperies separated one room from another. The rooms were in a roadhouse or country club. I was sitting at the dressing table, reading Groddeck's Book of the It. *Suddenly, I felt very sick and started getting weaker and weaker. Feeling I was going to faint, I stood up and held on to the drapery for support. The forelady came in saying, "Come on, girls, we got to get going." At seeing me ill, she became excited and called the boss, whom we call Papa.*

I became still weaker, and started across the room to the other side where the door was. As I reached the middle of the room, my face and mouth became paralyzed. I became panicky as I could hardly talk. Before I got to the other side of the room, I lost my sight. The light went dimmer and dimmer, then the fuse burnt out and the room was in complete darkness. I reached the telephone table on the other side, got hold of it and told the girls to get me a glass of spirits of ammonia, as I was going to faint. With that, I dropped on my knees and became unconscious.

Then I remember coming out of the faint, still dreaming. As I got on my feet, I became conscious of a terrible headache. A girl handed me a glass of spirits of ammonia. I did not drink it then. I figured I needed some air. I walked out to the balcony and from there went down the stairs and sat down on the grass. My boss came out on the balcony and was very annoyed. (He always is when anybody stops working.) I walked inside a great lobby like a hotel's and there were some girls standing at the desk talking. I sat down, still very weak, and drank the spirits of ammonia.

The patient used to drink spirits of ammonia after hangovers, and often gave it to people who felt faint. Speaking of hangovers, she recalled a party at the house of Vivienne, a friend. Heavy drinking was going on. She wanted to go into the bathroom, but a boy beat her to it and jammed the door on her two fingers. An X-ray examination showed a fracture in both fingers. The nails came off and she wore a splint for weeks. When the door slammed on her fingers, she screamed with pain. They gave her three glasses of neat whiskey and in a short time she fell asleep on the bed. When she woke up, it was quite dark but she could see necking couples in the room.

"As I sat up on the bed, the awful fear came over me that I had been raped while asleep and that I might have caught some disease."

We speak of conversion when some forgotten psychic injury or guilt materializes in a chronic physical complaint. In the present instance, the reverse is the case. A physical injury to the patient's fingers was translated into the fear of rape and disease. We learn, at the same time, that darkness and unconsciousness are invested with the same fear. The situation is somewhat similar to the patient's adventure with the old man after a drunken bout. She had pains in her vagina after that incident, though he did not penetrate her. Now her pains were associated with the bathroom—which has more than vaginal significance, as the dream mind often uses it as a symbol for the mother's uterus.

The spirits of ammonia offered a promising line of inquiry. Ammonia has strong associations with urine. In *The Book of the It,* which the patient is reading in the dream, Groddeck describes his own method of curing certain aversions. People who were unable to eat eggs were forced to eat them until they could retain them. As this procedure made a deep impression on the patient, we may query if she was drinking ammonia in her dream with the object of curing her urinary complaint. In other words, was she attempting sublimation by the "spirit" of ammonia?

Significantly, the patient did not have to go to the bathroom after the dream. She slept through the night and was entirely free of pelvic pains on awakening.

But the IT must have some deep significance. IT means that the nail was hit on the head, that an answer to a great problem has been found. The girls in her place of business work in slips which they remove when they go behind the drapery to put on evening clothes. In a previous dream, the patient was in Chicago, her birth town, and wore an evening dress which was slit in the front and showed her vagina without any pubic hair. Was the IT a hint at the source of her first rape fears?

The scene is laid in a country club, which is combined with her place of business. It looked like the W— Country Club, where once she had to throw a man out of her room because he wanted to sleep with her. As the patient is a stunning beauty, the uninvited attention of one man more would not make much difference and justify the use of the Club. I recalled that in her tumor nightmare she was also driving to a house in the country. She loves the country; and country means beautiful landscapes. Pre-natal feelings are often expressed in the beauty of the land. It seemed possible that the country, the position on the balcony and the big hotel lobby were so many references to the womb. The child is housed in the mother's body as in a hotel. The balcony could well be the snug position in the upper regions of the reproductive system, and the lobby the vaginal entrance. The spirits of ammonia which she drinks in the lobby is suitably placed there if it also refers to urine. The fainting, the paralysis of face and mouth, the loss of sight and the blowing of the fuse (lights out) may be considered so many features of a dramatic re-enactment of birth by the process of reversal. The communication between the two worlds (symbolized by the telephone and the crossing of the room) is severed, light is being snuffed out, she loses speech, becomes helpless as an infant and is in the throes of the fear of death.

The paralysis and the terrible headache necessitate the inquiry whether the dreamer had been injured on the head during delivery. The annoyance of Papa in finding her in the open air is understandable if we remember that she was an unwanted child.

The day before the dream, the patient had a talk-out with her mother on this very subject. Again she was told that her father did not want children and went into a fit when her mother became pregnant. They had violent arguments about her while she was being carried. Further, she proved to be a large baby and her birth was very difficult.

I encouraged the patient to find out more precise details from her mother. She was then told that she weighed eight-and-a-half pounds and was delivered, after fifteen hours of labor, with forceps that left two bad bruises on each side of her forehead. Before birth, her mother was taking sulphur baths. During labor, towards the end, the mother was put to sleep by gas.

These findings suggest an explanation of the patient's bad headache and loss of consciousness in the dream. The gas given to the mother apparently put the child also to sleep.

"When my mother recovered consciousness, she was waiting anxiously for the cry. They had taken me into the kitchen and she did not hear it at first."

It may have taken the doctor a little time to wake the newly born child. Perhaps the spirits of ammonia, with which she wakes herself in the dream, refers to this artificial revival.

The data are sufficient to warrant the conclusion that the fainting dream re-enacts birth and that the patient's rape fears were cover symptoms for the greater fear of birth, by a displacement of the all-over pressure on her body into a pressure within her own genitalia. The memory of the ordeal of birth laid the bedrock for her neurosis, and also seriously interfered with her sexual gratification, as intercourse always tended to mobilize the forgotten injury. To escape it, she preferred a man with a small penis, as that permitted her unconscious mind to be less alarmed. In her sexual behavior, she was still the little girl who, with a frighteningly small anus-vagina, fantasied herself in her mother's place with her father and also re-experienced anal-vaginal birth in each intercourse.

It took forty analytic sessions to uncover this identification between rape fears and birth. Many problems remained for future sessions to deal with, but the findings as presented have made a great difference in the patient's emotional life and in her health. She lost her urination compulsion, her constipation and her nightmares. The rectal and vaginal pains rarely returned and she was able to reach a sexual peak which she had not known before.

12.

SUPERSTRUCTURES ON BIRTH

THE elements of which birth dreams are constructed are simple and easy to recognize. Eggs, seeds, germs, fruits or things that grow or move underground represent the fetus; gardens, parks, landscapes, islands, boats, trains, carriages, houses, rooms, cellars, lofts describe the uterus; seas, lakes, rivers, waterfalls, symbolize the amniotic fluid; falling, compression, suffocation, burial alive and various forms of slow and painful death at the hands of humans, ghosts, animals or machinery represent the ordeal of birth; tunnels, caves, stoves, archways, windows, doors describe the uterine passage; river banks, rails and "V" shaped structures refer to the mother's legs; grass, bushes, forests, fur and hair allude to the pubic region.

These symbols have no exclusive content and their content is subject to individual choice and modification. In themselves they no more produce a birth dream than a jumble of words makes a sentence. Moreover, every single birth symbol can lend itself to a variety of interpretations other than birth. Even when the manner in which they are presented indicates that they allude to birth, the dream may not be concerned with the trauma of birth. The dream picture may be symbolic and serve the purpose of releasing some pressure other than the physical pain of birth and the attendant psychic shock. The birth situation may be but a convenient foundation on which the structures of other traumata rest. In such dreams the emotional pressure which normally accompanies birth dreams is absent. When no nightmarish effect is present, when no direct or displaced "catastrophic reaction"* is felt in such dreams, we may safely assume that the uterine setting is used for symbolic purposes.

To such exploitation of birth symbolism only the dreamer's fantasy can set limits. A few applications might be considered more or less general. The origin of sex shame, for instance, might be explained by dreaming about birth. Children who receive their enlightenment comparatively late, when they have forgotten their early burning curiosity about how babies come and the fantastic solutions they had conceived, often give expression to their feelings in such words as: "My father and mother could not have done such a dirty thing." In our culture, for the juvenile mind, birth is a shameful event because the excretory function of the female and male genitalia overshadows and also sexualizes the event. To overcome sexual shame, it may be necessary to clear the mind of the conflicts which arise about this situation; hence, the picture of birth will be woven into the dreams that aim at solving this problem.

In almost all mother fixation dreams there is a rich display of birth symbolism, without which the fixation cannot be understood. Resistance to marriage is often motivated by the umbilical situation, which psychically may persist throughout a lifetime. A general feeling of insecurity in life might be explained by the harrowing experience of birth which endures in the unconscious mind.

Birth dreams may be used for consolation purposes, like examination dreams. The man who is frightened in a dream of an examination that he has successfully passed, usually stands before an important test or decision and is encouraging himself with the thought that as he passed the examination in the subject of which he dreams, so will he pass again in a test of reality. The uterine state can be described as a school of life. Birth is the greatest examination of physical fitness that life imposes on us. It is only natural that by the use of birth dreams the dreamer should tell himself: "As you have passed the ordeal of birth, so will you pass through this new trial which you are dreading just now." The impending decision or trial may give a new

---

* Kurt Goldstein's term in *The Organism*, American Book Co., 1939, p. 36.

departure to our life. We are in the habit of describing great changes as a new life, a re-birth. As a result, whenever such a great change, particularly of a spiritual character, impends, we may expect a birth dream, preparing us for the forthcoming event or revealing the existence of anything that blocks and delays its arrival.

As long as morbid attitudes to life are built as a superstructure on the trauma of birth, dreams that present problems for analytic release are likely to be saturated with the symbolism of birth. There are many phobias, suicidal compulsions, mystical inclinations, frigidity and potency problems, dispositions to unhappiness or pessimistic philosophy which cannot be understood without such presentation.°

Origin of Sexual Shame

The reason why birth lends itself so well to symbolic exploitation is that birth is a genital event. Any allusion to birth may serve as a cover to the dreamer's genital problems. Here is an illustration from the dream life of an unmarried girl:

There is a beautiful garden. It is landscaped and has everything. It seems to be an ideal place. I am standing indoors, looking through a window. There is a square body of water in the garden which is frozen. A little later I see it thawed, very green and limpid.

I had similar dreams to this before about swimming. I am not sure if there was not something about swimming in last night's dream too; swimming and the fear of drowning in a not-too-deep pond. I survive swimming. I walk up the landscaped grounds and see long canals running through.

The beautiful garden with its lake and canals, viewed through a window, is an easily recognizable description of the uterine state. The swimming and the danger of drowning are equally plain indications of birth. Yet the frozen water suggests a problem of different character; it points to sexual frigidity. The subsequent thawing of the ice and

---

° For an unusual manifestation of the trauma of birth, attention is called to Dr. Grace W. Pailthorpe's "Deflection of Energy as a Result of Birth Trauma, and Its Bearing Upon Character Formation," *The Psychoanalytic Review*, July, 1941.

the square shape of the lake may anticipate the analytic resolution ("squaring") of the trouble. Such anticipations are frequently found in the dreams of patients under analysis. In this case, the antecedents of the dream furnished actual proof, by the dreamer's own recognition, that the clue was correctly read. She dreamed:

I am walking through the street naked. I manage to cover my breasts with one hand, the pubic hair with the other. Some hair still shows, but I am indifferent to people who walk in the street. I enter an office building (I think of my new job). People gape and look at me, but I don't care outwardly. Inside I am embarrassed. Upstairs I talk with two people. They are supposed to do something for me, but they are unfriendly. A woman is particularly gruff. She wishes me to wait for the service to be performed. I don't wait, but go outside in a coat and warm clothing which I have stolen, and I climb a steep, icy hill and feel I must hurry as I am being pursued.

The covering of the breasts and the pubic hair indicates that the dream deals with sexual shame. The conflict between the patient's conscious and unconscious attitude to sexual life is clearly revealed. Outwardly she defies the world, inwardly she feels embarrassed; she is not free. The new job is the analytic job, the adjustment of the sexual conflict. She had two analysts before, both of whom failed her; hence they are represented by the two unfriendly men. The woman who is gruff, she supposed, was her mother. But the dreamer failed to understand her statement about waiting for the service to be performed. It is plain enough that the marriage service is meant. She did not wait for it. She gave herself to her friend and now had qualms that he would not marry her. Her sexual life is not legitimate. It conflicts with the moral law. Hence she is a thief in the dream. By the theft of a coat and warm clothing she shows that she is frigid. She feels the cold. The icy hill confirms this representation. She finds climbing difficult. She cannot reach culmination because of the moral conflict. She is pursued by her conscience.

The moral conflict is so plainly described that there is no need to search further, at least on the basis of this dream, for the cause of her frigidity. The uterine picture, the swimming and the fear of drowning in the shallow pond should be considered symbols of her fear of genital indulgence.

Origin of Incestuous Emotions

Because through regressive associations we inevitably picture birth ,as a genital event, intercourse fantasies, particularly those of an incestuous character concerning the mother, may point to this remote adventure as their foundation. Here is the nightmare of an adolescent girl which helps one to appreciate this important notion:

Mummy took me to a hospital for an operation. It had something to do with plaster, also with a bamboo ladder which had to be applied somehow. It is a bit confused. The doctor who was to operate on me was an insane man. There were many nice doctors around, but this man had rolling eyes, and he threw himself on me, tearing and biting me in a sensuous embrace. He did it four times, until I finally convinced Mummy that the man was insane. Then mother agreed to take me home. She said the man who "fixed up" Ronald Colman would attend to me. I remember also that the insane doctor kept his thumb pressed on one of my ribs and I thought he would break it, it hurt so much. Then I saw compartments of lockers. I was standing there covered with a towel, and I was conscious of the presence of boys. The girl lost the key to the locker. I said, "I have one in my bag."

During the day preceding the dream, the dreamer was asked by a girl friend where she was in 1922. She answered that she was nowhere. One of the girls amplified it: she was just happening. In the dream, she shows herself happening. The attack of the insane man and the pressure on the rib which hurt so much speak of panic caused by birth. The plaster obviously symbolizes the fixing of something dislocated or broken. A ladder implies climbing or falling. Birth is the first fall we experience; we fall away from our mother. As bamboo ladders are made of hollow tubes, they may additionally symbolize the uterine passage. The dreamer associated Ronald Colman with fatherliness and love. The man who "fixed him up" should be able to resolve her fears analytically. The key in her bag indicates the trans-

141

lation of the ordeal of birth to her own genitalia, hence the association of insanity with incestuous eroticism. The doctor is a father symbol and the patient's own father was a doctor and a psychotherapist. As the body in birth is in masculine relationship to the mother, there is also a vague hint conveyed by the presence of boys that we may perhaps look to birth for the root of masculine aspirations in girls.

13.

THE curiosity of children as to how they came into the world is closely paralleled by the grown man's restless search for an answer to the meaning of life. We have learned how we came, but we don't know what we came here to do. The latter mystery is no less absorbing to us than the former is for the child. It is a riddle too great to trifle with, and when we are preoccupied with it, we resent levity or insipid response. If we had the same respect for our children's eagerness for knowledge that we demand for ourselves, we would hesitate to feed them with the traditional stories that insult their intelligence.

"When I was a child I thought children dropped down from the sky, were picked up and brought home," says an anthropologist, and he remembers his mother telling him that she saw somebody's baby rolling down over the roof of the barn and being picked up.

"Mother told me that I was found under the stoop of our house," says a lawyer. "It was a current joke in the family that I used to crawl under the stoop and investigate the spot."

"There was a picture of Botticelli's Venus on Shell in our house. I was born in New Rochelle and I always fancied that I came in on a shell from the sea." This is the statement of a teacher. Her mother encouraged her in her belief, but she discovered later that the story was not true, "because babies were born through the mother's navel."

"I am ashamed to tell you, but at the age of twenty-two, two years after I was married, I still believed that babies were born through the navel. My mother made some remark and I gave myself away by calling out in surprise: 'What is the belly button for?' My mother went into a fit of laughter and said something, to which I answered: 'Where you go to the bathroom?' I thought of the rectum and felt a wave of disgust sweep over me. Luckily my mother did not know what went through my mind." This is the confession of a poet and a writer, a woman of exceptional intellect but of an orthodox family background and education.

"In Central Park in New York, where it was quite common to see women nursing their children, I discussed with other youngsters whether children were born from the breast. We used to watch these women to see if we could get some clue." This is the recollection of a woman journalist following a dream in which a round pebble, which seemed to have been reposing in the nipple of her left breast, fell out and she felt relieved. She added another memory: "When I was ten years old, I saw a pregnant woman at my cousin's house. Mother used to tell me: 'If you don't stop walking on your heels, you are going to have a stomach like Jenny's.'"

Such stupid threats serve no educational purpose and they may do a great deal of harm. The burning curiosity of children cannot long be satisfied with tales about the stork, the cabbage in the garden, the doctor's or the postman's bag. Modern parents acknowledge the child's right to an answer which is at least near to the truth. Some say they prayed to God and the child came; others are more precise and explain that the child grows from a seed in the mother's heart or stomach like a fruit—only to shut off the child when the fateful question comes: "But how does it come out?"

No child can long be deceived by preposterous answers. Instinct will tell them that they are misled. The pressure which the ordeal of their own birth leaves in their unconscious mind will drive them on until they find an acceptable formula to cover a deeply buried organismic knowledge. Sensible answers would help to release the unconscious pressure through understanding; stupid stories achieve the opposite result.

Varieties of Birth

Left to themselves, children develop theories of their own in a manner which is often reminiscent of tales of mythology. The girl who thought she came in from the sea on a shell might have adopted the birth of Venus as her own. The anthropologist who thought that babies dropped from the sky had a key to the legend of the Fall of Man. The lawyer who was looking for his tracks under the stoop could have been stimulated by the legend of Proserpine's capture and return from the underworld. Similar motives could have been ascribed to the anxious search of a young woman for new-born calves in crevices of the earth; she was told by her father that calves were found that way. Most astonishing, however, is the duplication of the legend of Cadmus and the sowing of dragon's teeth which I found in the masturbation fantasies of a young man. Having splashed his seed on the bare earth, he expected that in due time armored knights, about a foot tall, with spears pointing upward, would spring forth from the soil. He could not remember the legend of Cadmus, but whether he knew it or not, the fantasy reveals an original interpretation of the myth.

The birth fantasies of mythology are no stranger than those uncovered by psychoanalysts today. Pallas Athene springing fully clad and armored from the head of Zeus is an excellent illustration of the fantasy of cranial birth. The brain has a certain analogy to the fetus in the mother's womb, and we give unconscious recognition to this notion in speaking of a brain-child or of being pregnant with ideas. Karna, the human son of the Hindu god Surya (who is one of the heroes of the Mahábhárata) emerged from the ears of the Princess Pritha, who set him adrift in a basket on the river Aswa. This example of aural birth is paralleled in our world by mediaeval paintings of Jesus Christ in which the Holy Ghost enters his mother at her ear in the shape of a dove. The idea of navel birth is suggested by a picture by Fra Filippo Lippi, now in the National Gallery in London, in which a dove, directed from the sky by a hand, is making for the Virgin's navel. The Shinto sacred work, the Ko-ji-ki, gives an example of ocular birth when the creator Izanagi washes the filth of Hades from his left eye, whereupon the sun goddess Ama-terasu comes into existence. Our Golem, Frankenstein and homunculus stories reveal attempts at similar escapes from the genital concept of birth. The failure of all these fantasy attempts is demonstrated by the evil which these artificial beings wreak and by the fears which they inspire. Immaculate conception, as the other extreme, at least delivers from "sin" if not from the actual ordeal.

Anal Birth

The most simple, most natural and most satisfying theory which a child can reach without the aid of grown-ups, is the theory of anal birth. It is rarely remembered in later years but it manifests itself in dream life, in waking fantasies and in popular vulgarities.

If the child is informed that the mother's body plays a part in birth, it will inevitably reach the conclusion that the place of issue must be the anus, because it is the only orifice through which something solid can leave the body. Children brought up on a farm may tumble by themselves to the significance of the mother's internal anatomy in the coming of babies. Observation of the intimacies between the cock and the hen will naturally direct their attention towards the anal passage.

Further, every child learns that it is food which turns into feces. When they discover that the child is in the mother's "stomach," they not only expect it to pass through the anus but also identify it with feces. In cases that border on psychosis this identification may manifest itself in odd forms. A woman, for instance, wraps up her feces, writes her name on the cover paper and throws it out of the window. By so doing, she acts out her conception of birth, seeking—presumably—release of the pressure of birth through a symptomatic act.

A male child may remain unaware for quite some time that there is another orifice through which birth can take place. As he urinates in a standing position, while his mother always sits down, he naturally assumes that she passes water through the anus. Even if he sees his mother's naked body, he will only notice the absence of the penis and is likely to identify the vagina with the anus because of its proximity.

Strangely, the true notion is the last one at which the child may arrive. Vaginal birth is received, when first heard, with the greatest incredulity. The child is often incapable of accepting the notion that

the vaginal orifice may permit the passing of the body. In relationship to the anus, the incredulity is less, as all children have some
ideas of its extensibility. Any parental explanation that the child grows
from a seed invariably feeds this fantasy solution. I myself heard a
little girl ask instantly on hearing the seed theory, "Did you swallow
it, mother?"

The content of the stomach must enter through the mouth and
leave through the anus. It is through such notions that neurotics invest the whole of the alimentary canal with a genital significance and
cause themselves endless disturbances in eating, digesting and elim-
inating. Hysterical vomiting in women is not so much due to the in-
gested food as to the secret desire to safeguard against pregnancy or
to rid the body of one incurred or imagined. This is a clue to the
morning sickness of pregnant women. Unconsciously, it would appear
that they are trying to rid the system of the toxic influence of the
child by expelling it from the stomach through the mouth.

In some cases of constipation I found the sufferer protecting himself against re-living an extremely traumatic birth by refusing, within
possible limits, to let fecal matter pass out of his body. In one curious instance a girl, unenlightened at the age of thirteen, felt badly
frightened of becoming pregnant because a step-brother touched her
on the vagina. Thereafter she used to sit for hours on the toilet in
the hope that she would pass the baby. Her morbid fantasies of body
odor and hypersensitivity to vitiated air were successfully traced to
the concept of anal birth. Whatever comes out of the rectum smells.
Her smell complex arose from the disgust over the infantile notion
of anal birth.

Many surrealistic paintings and automatic products of the medium's art disclose unconscious fantasies of anal birth. Sometimes they
place the breasts in close proximity to the buttocks or right on top;
in other cases the rectal region is depicted so big as to suggest pregnancy and birth through the anus. A patient of mine remembered
that as a little boy he drew a picture of a woman walking and a child
looking out of her rectum. When he was asked what it was, he explained: "The child is impatient to be born and is looking out . . . I
only discovered when I was thirteen that children were born through

147

the vagina. It was a tremendous surprise to me. Until then I thought they were born from the rectum. I discovered the truth on reading Boccaccio. A man is told that he is pregnant and he laments: 'God, what am I to do, women have a natural orifice to bring a child into the world, but what about myself?' Then I knew that my previous notions were wrong."

A girl of twenty-four was speaking of her hatred of rain. All her life she associated rain with dark things. It made her feel as though she were dying. She queried whether her morbid reactions to rain could have had something to do with her birth. The question was quite unexpected, and suggested that the breaking of the heavenly waters may become associated with the bursting of the amniotic fluid; that the repressed memory of this pre-natal event may manifest itself, through the mechanism of projection, as a foreboding of the future. As she relaxed on the analytic couch, a remarkable vision came to her:

I can see an elephant's trunk. It seems to be trying to suck up a child and the child is in terror. The trunk appears to close on the child's body. . . . It is horrible. . . . I see the same child in a white coat. . . . I cannot. . . . This is awful. . . . The talk we had. . . . Maybe I thought babies come out of the back. . . . That's what this little child. . . . The elephant's trunk suddenly became the back of a woman. This child came out of the back of this woman.

The patient gave this exactly as quoted. That the fear of rain may have something to do with the breaking of the amniotic waters was news to me, and I certainly did not suggest it. The vision leaves but little doubt that both this fear and her fear of water in general is connected with birth, of which, as a child, she fantasied in anal terms.

Another anal mechanism that serves the purpose of keeping a grown-up unborn manifests itself in thrombotic haemorrhoids. It is a pregnancy condition in miniature, the clot within the swollen vein taking the place of the child. It is my experience that by releasing anal birth fantasies and by overcoming fetal inertia the re-formation of thrombotic haemorrhoids can be prevented.

The inability to pass flatus is also well adapted to conceal the pressure of birth memories. Those who suffer chronically from flatus may aim at keeping themselves in a blown-up condition. All abdominal swellings are instinctively and immediately associated with pregnancy, and fantasies of self-impregnation by gases or by air-swallowing (aerophagia) may result from a translation of the mother's condition into our own bodies.

Flatus and breath are close identifications, and breath is the most ancient symbol of life and spirit. Even the problem of claustrophobia may enter into the condition, because of the obvious analogy between suffocation and internal compression by gas tension. Suffocation means an inability to take in breath; gas tension is an inability to pass it out. When, in linguistic vulgarism, we find the flatus identified with a sigh, we have further evidence of the closeness of these correspondences. Another relationship is created by consonance between fetus and flatus or between flatus and afflatus. The latter significance was pointed out to me by a poet who brought the following dream:

I had two rooms, similar perhaps to my own, one having lots of books like mine, but the rooms were in a boarding school. A small child was somewhere in the background. There was a toilet near the bed. In the bed the child must have soiled itself. It was as if a blanket, similar to my own, had been taken off with fecal matter and stuffed into the lavatory. The blanket was coming out all over. There was also a face towel which seemed to show fecal stains. The smell in the room was awful. I thought it was a terrible thing to have this happen in my home. I went down to the basement to ask the laundry woman to come up and take the blanket and towel.

By over-cleanliness, by keeping her apartment and her own person compulsively clean, this patient had been fighting all her life against the "terrible thing" which happened in the dream in her home. The very wording of the dream bears out the analytic finding that excessive cleanliness is an over-compensation for repressed uncleanliness, a guilt feeling probably incurred in the course of anal discipline at the hand of an over-severe parent. The patient had an over-severe mother. At the time of analysis she was fifty-six years old, and all her life she had been badly constipated, suffering mainly from excruciating gas pressure, to relieve which she was in the habit of taking high irrigations almost every night.

The most important part of the dream is the blocking of the toilet. This corresponds to a blocking in the patient's own psyche. The blanket is a cover. The question is, for what?

The obvious answer is, it is a cover for the patient's bed. The bed itself is a symbol for the womb. The patient used to curl up in it as she did in the embryonic position. The boarding school bears out this interpretation. The patient defined it as a place where one is prepared for life. As the boarding school was telescoped into her own rooms, the patient suddenly realized how well it describes the womb, where for nine months one is prepared for life. She volunteered that in German, a language which she speaks, "Bildung" stands equally for building and education. The disposition of her two rooms in the dream also had a reference to two levels of existence. They formed a duplex apartment, a stairway with banisters connecting them. In reality, her rooms were on the same level. As she is both a child and a grown-up in the dream, the two rooms well correspond to the higher and lower level of her own personality or, in a larger sense, to the pre-natal and post-natal life.

The purpose of the dream is self-cleansing. There is no laundry in the basement of the patient's house. In descending into the depths to find an agent of cleansing, she appeals to a power within, she tries to rouse her own higher self into activity. The inference is that she had not been able to deliver herself from her chronic constipation and turn a really clean face towards life for reasons peculiar to the mother situation.

Into the patient's mind floated the picture of a tube which in hospitals is inserted in the anus to help pass flatus. This, in turn, recalled a thinner tube which her mother used, pushing it through the cervix, into the womb, letting air in to produce abortion.

Here was a direct association between fetus and flatus (air) and also birth (abortion). As birth is an ordeal and loss of security for the child, resistance to it, within the limited means of the unborn, must be expected. Physically, this resistance does not amount to much. Psychically, it is likely to be very strong. The question thus arose:

was the patient's refusal to pass flatus equivalent to her refusal to be born? All her life she had resisted her mother. The relationship between them was exceedingly bad, not through her fault. Did she retroject this bad relationship into the more remote biological past, thereby justifying her resistance to being born, and converting this resistance to holding herself as flatus within her own body, which has taken on the maternal role?

It was at this point that the patient made the remark: "I am mentally constipated, too. The divine afflatus is blocked up. Only under great emotional stress does it break forth."

The real meaning of the dream now begins to unfold. Through the linguistic link between flatus and afflatus, constipation appears as a symbol of the patient's frustrated creative self-expression. Both flatus and afflatus demand expression (pressing out). Because this expression was confused with expulsion from the womb and threatened to recall the awful memories of being born in agony into a life of unhappiness, she protected herself against it by withholding both. The result was that she carried herself within herself—a strange psychological condition, of which one odd manifestation was a weird yearning to creep into the body of the men she loved. She rationalized the yearning by saying that she would know all their thoughts if she were within. In reality, she was indulging in fetal fantasies, totally missing the only important point that mattered—that psychologically she was less than a child, she was a fetus, still unborn and not wanting to be born.

The case could be more fittingly described as a bowel-birth fantasy than as an anal one. Such fantasies are most frequently seen in big-bellied men who look, to all appearances, as if they were pregnant. It was Groddeck, the great Viennese psychologist, who first suggested that the condition hides pregnancy fantasies. Yet he failed to go deeper and missed the point that the child within is the big-bellied man himself, that the fantasy behind such abdominal monstrosities is one of self-begetting, and that the body is in a maternal relationship to the fetal self, on which the person's unconscious mind is obsessively fixated.

Oral Birth

Proceeding higher along the alimentary canal, we reach the throat. An obstruction in the throat (whether real or fancied) as, for instance, a globus hystericus, tonsil, adenoid or thyroid swelling, can serve the same fantasy purpose as constipation. It prevents birth through the mouth or the nose, and it also prevents fantasied stomach pregnancy by not permitting the seed to be swallowed.

The unconscious mind may also associate tooth-pulling with childbirth. When a patient gave me an account of the birth of her daughter, I felt prompted to ask her an unusual question: "Did you have an erotic experience in giving birth?" She was puzzled by the query but suddenly recalled a very odd experience. She was skating, and a man locked his skate into hers and pulled. She did not fall, but a thrill ran through her body. It was similar to the sensation of a tooth being pulled, of the sucking effect felt when the tooth leaves the gum, and it vaguely reminded her of the feeling she experienced when her child was pulled out of her body. The feeling was strange and it created a bond between her and the man.

In spite of the obvious implication, this patient remained sceptical about tooth-pulling as a symbol for childbirth. She gave up her opposition after a dream in which her new personality was visualized in dental imagery:

I was losing a very corroded tooth. Still, I felt bad about it. It finally fell away. Much to my surprise, a baby tooth was pushing through under it. "Gosh," I thought, "that's why I am losing it, I am getting a new one." I touched it and it came out. It was a tooth that had been filled. I pushed it back and could feel the root slipping into place.

The corroded tooth is the old personality; the baby tooth is the new one which she is achieving through analysis. But the tooth-child is not quite there yet. For the time being repair only is being done. Nevertheless, the goal of a new birth is set and improvement is indicated regarding her own trauma of birth. She felt bad about the loss of the old tooth because of a superstition in her family that dreaming of tooth-pulling is prophetic of death. Further, she had lost three teeth through abscesses. Each time she felt that a great injustice had been done to her, as if the loss of a tooth were equivalent to murder.

The prophetic interpretation current in the patient's family is highly interesting. As the unconscious mind tries to dispose of the trauma of birth by projecting it into the future in the form of the fear of death, the origin of the superstition becomes clear as soon as we think of the tooth-child. Being born must feel like being murdered. The superstition should be reworded: dreaming of tooth-pulling is admonitive of how we came into the world. The new tooth is filled because pregnancy is a form of filling and birth and pregnancy are association pairs.

Emotionally, the patient was now ready to accept her tooth dream as a dream of approaching analytic re-birth—and her associations pointed in this direction. While proof that would satisfy the scientific mind as to the meaning of the dream is absent, she did obtain a new point of view and an orientation which seemed to align unconscious strivings with the realities her consciousness could accept.

14.

T HE difficulties with which a child is delivered vary considerably, but on one point agreement is universal: bearing a child imposes a great strain on the maternal body and sometimes results in serious injury.

Bad as the trial of the flesh is, the psychic injury accompanying it may prove even more damaging. It is my contention that bearing a child becomes traumatic whenever the similarity between giving birth to a child and being born approaches close to the threshold of awareness.

No sexual injury is more likely to raise the ghost of our own arrival into this world than bearing a child. It cannot be disputed that bearing a child is a sexual injury. It is also agreed that while time heals the worst wounds as far as consciousness is concerned, for the unconscious the passing of years has no meaning. This part of our personality does not know of oblivion, and the dynamic tension of the memories stored up in its hidden recesses is apt to cause disturbance as soon as a parallel psychic state arises in the conscious mind. This phenomenon is analogous to electric induction where a current in a closed circuit produces a similar current in a parallel circuit without generating source. The relationship between the two momentous events of one's own birth and bringing a child into life is very close, and it raises problems of considerable importance.

The Trauma of Bearing

The number of women who become panic-stricken at the prospect of bearing a child is larger than is generally thought. The fear is often repressed; the victims know that they are not likely to die, yet they feel as if they were confronting death. It is a common experience that many women so afflicted lose their children by miscarriage or abortion. The yearning for the child is there; their conscious intention of carrying through term cannot be doubted; but an accident, shock or illness will bring about premature labor or necessitate surgical intervention. The prospective mother may not even suspect that she had set an unconscious protective mechanism in motion. The alibi is always excellent. Without it, the unconscious purpose of losing the child could not easily be accomplished.

Imperative as the breaking up of the maternal condition on the organismic levels of the prospective mother's mind may be, the purpose is by no means always accomplished. The will to keep the child may triumph over the unconscious urge to destroy it. I know of a mother who kept herself on her back for two months after an accidental loss of the amniotic fluid in order to save the life of the child. She won. The vitality of the fetus also plays a part in such victories. In the face of attacks directed against it, the fetus may show amazing tenacity. That tenacity is a great asset at the time of birth, when the panic of the mother is likely to aggravate the difficulties of delivery.

The mother may pay a price for this panic even after her confinement. Where delivery was dreaded, after-pains of bearing are more likely to develop than if the mother was comparatively fearless. The menstrual flow may become excessive and painful, tears may refuse to heal, the breasts may prove troublesome, and the kidneys or the bladder may show weakness, all testifying to the psychic storm through which the mother has passed and of which, in her unconscious, she is still in the throes.

Through the study of the dreams of mothers before childbirth and after, I have reached the conclusion that the morbid fear of bearing arises from the prospective mother's identification of herself with the child in her womb. Way back in the past, the mother was in the same position: she, too, was a child about to be born, and she is as frightened now as though she were about to re-live her own birth. It is as if she had lost the distinction between being a mother and an unborn child; it is as if she were giving birth to herself.

The life of many a child is lost because of this confusion in the mother's mind. The psychological education of pregnant mothers is sadly lacking. Of the relationship between their own birth and the birth of their child they know nothing. They do not even suspect that the child feels as if it were dying during a difficult labor, because they have forgotten their own birth experiences. Nature saw to it that the awful memory should be repressed. How, then, can they suspect that unconsciously they are dreading the recurrence of this terrifying event?

The study of dreams that precede and follow delivery should be very instructive. The expectation and the actual delivery of the child tend to mobilize falling fears, nightmares of water, fire and suffocation, and may even produce symptoms of claustrophobia. The dilatation of the uterine passage in delivery is often reflected in dreams of large and gaping cavities opening in the body, sometimes in the nipples, or even in the baby's mouth. In some dreams the nipple opens and assumes the semblance of the vagina.

One woman who gave dry birth to a son had a recurrent dream for many years in which her son was always under water, drowning. The dream filled her with foreboding as she automatically projected it into the future and placed a prophetic construction on it. One day she herself conceived the thought that an early loss of the amniotic fluid might have been the origin of the dream. She recalled how frightened she was that her child would be born crippled or dead; suddenly she realized that she had kept this fear alive and played it again and again as one plays a phonograph record. From the day of this realization, the recurrent nightmare stopped.

Nightmares of mothers fleeing from pursuit (to escape the ordeal of childbirth) may alternate with erotic dreams in which a newborn son figures as a lover. Such dreams indicate that the child is in the same relationship to the genitalia in the process of birth as the male organ is in intercourse. In slang, the male organ is often called the little man, the child. This may help to explain how the birth of a child can liberate fantasies of intercourse or rape. There is no reason why the young mother should be ashamed of such dreams. By repressing them she may sow the seeds of future trouble. By understanding and frankly discussing them, she may free herself from their recurrence.

My experience is that any event which is capable of mobilizing the memory of birth produces fear. The trauma of bearing is particularly apt to merge into the mother's birth trauma. On understanding the part which the trauma of one's own birth plays in childbearing, an almost miraculous relief may be obtained from complaints resulting from a difficult delivery. Without such release, the neurotic condition—now a double-barrelled affair—will persist unchanged. Successive deliveries may be easier but psychically still very trying. As the years pass, more and more of the pressure will be converted into symptoms necessitating internal operations or causing some other physical debility.

A mother dreams that she is in a bear cage and is torn to shreds by a polar bear. She wakes in terror. She cannot imagine what could have given her such a nightmare. Those who have closely followed my reasoning in the preceding chapters will have little difficulty in interpreting the dream. "Polar" suggests ice, frigidity, fear. "Bear" stands for bearing, giving birth and the fear of one's own birth. The cage is an excellent symbol for confinement and pressure from which there is no escape.

The dreamer is well past the childbearing age, but she has been a frigid woman all her life and has suffered for many years from extremely high blood pressure. The birth of her first child was a very difficult affair, an instrumental delivery, resulting in a breech birth. Further, the child was not wanted, and the mother had to go through a good deal of hardship on its account.

The dream suggests that much light could be shed on the dreamer's chronic hypertension by an investigation of the trauma of her bearing and its foundation, the trauma of her own birth.

Proper psychological education as a preventive maternal therapy could bestow immense benefit of health on the female population of the nation.*

Bearing and Abortion

Moral considerations might be as important as physical ones in producing a trauma of bearing. The stigma of having an illegitimate child or the conflict with the criminal code because of an abortion obviously increases the psychic burden. Guilt reactions appear in dreams even when the loss of the child was unintentional or was demanded for medical reasons. The harrowing experiences of illegitimate operations do not settle the moral score. How soon the unconscious tribunal of justice, which the Freudians call the superego, converts the guilt into sickness depends on the sensitivity of our conscience. The dead child is usually replaced by a cyst or tumor in the ovaries, the uterus, or the breast. While these punitive substitutes do not produce malignant growth, I do not hold it impossible that, other factors being favorable, cancerous development should also arise from excessive psychic pressure.

The extent of self-destruction by successive operations to which miscarriage and abortion guilt may lead knows almost no limit. Life is inexorable in its demands for the perpetuation of the species. It seems almost as if the woman who loses a child through her own fault sins against the race, and as if the retribution which follows would be an archaic evolutionary safeguard. Yet too much importance should not be attached to this appearance, in view of the relative ease with which the guilt is resolved. Basically, it seems to originate in the trauma of one's own birth.

The reason why an understanding of this trauma produces relief and an almost instantaneous change in neurotic behavior is that it lifts from the psyche the burden of personal responsibility. It is a marvellous relief to find that our conscience does not demand punishment for past transgressions and that we are victims of a universal calamity. Guilt ceases to be guilt if it is universally shared. We cannot be beyond the pale if everybody else is similarly afflicted. It

---

* The work of Dr Grantly Dick Read is notable in this connection. See *Childbirth Without Fear*, Harper & Brothers, New York, 1944.

is not our fault that we were born. However, this high road out of neurosis is destroyed when self-inflicted abortion merges with the trauma of birth. It not only raises the dynamic tension of birth but invests it with guilt; hence the intensity of punitive reactions and the persistence of the demand for self-destruction.

Some dreams so openly reveal the psychic pressure of abortion that to tell them amounts to a public confession. Here is an illustration:

I was lying on my back naked, with my legs apart in the shape of a V. A shadowy person seemed to be repeating whatever I did. I felt her but I could not see her. I had a hatchet in my hand and was hacking away at something that was between my legs. It was not part of me. In doing so I scratched my thigh, and I could see a long, thin, red line. Whoever the person was with me said, "You cut your leg." I said, "That's nothing, a little iodine will fix it," and I went on hacking. Then I had a baby in my arms and the baby's head was cleft from the forehead to the back. I could see the pulse beating under the cerebral membrane.

No explanation is necessary. The shadowy person is the dreamer's conscience. Its representation as a split-off part of her personality explains why she should be so unconcerned regarding the injury which she had inflicted on herself by abortion.

Curiously, she was not quite aware of the meaning of the dream. I believe she deliberately shut her eyes to the implications; but the airing of her guilt had a very salutary effect. A few days later she dreamed of a court scene; it was the dramatization of her self-trial for abortion. A sequel, leading to another important revelation, came in the following dream:

I went to the bottom of our garden at home and crept into a thicket of wild roses. Then I saw that the rose bushes were suspended in the air, one on each side of me, a tremendous growth of roots hanging from them as if they had been violently torn from the earth. As I was standing there, I saw a meat safe to the left of me, the old-fashioned wire affair which we hung on trees in Australia to

159

let the wind blow through it and keep the meat cool. A lot of rotten meat was in the safe. The bottom of it was torn away and the whole safe was hanging in the air.

On awakening, the patient's immediate association was a butcher bird which she had once seen in their garden sitting on the bough from which the safe was suspended. The butcher bird is a beautiful but very cruel bird; it kills other little birds. The wild roses reminded her of a song in which a boy wants to pluck roses and they threaten to stick him with their thorns.

These two associations explain the dream fantasy. A child may well be called a rose. The torn-up roots suggest the violence of the separation from Mother Earth or the maternal body, also revealing the strength of unconscious ties. The meat safe is the womb. The bottom which has dropped out alludes to the opened cervix. The fact that she is not hurt by the thorns when she creeps into the thicket indicates that her burden of guilt is becoming less heavy.

However, so far the patient only confessed to one abortion. The dream hints at two—by the two rose bushes. Was there one which she only suspected to be an abortion but of which she was not quite certain?

"There may have been another," she stated. "I had a queer menstruation once, previous to my abortion. A lot of white fluid came out and I had fever. I had the suspicion that I might have been pregnant and that for some reason the pregnancy was naturally broken up."

This fits in well with the intimation of the dream. If we accept the two wild rose bushes as referring to two illegitimate children, we have an impressive indication that abortion guilt may arise even when the conscious mind is unaware of the loss of the child and that the superego, from its residence in the unconscious mind, may sit in judgment over the organism itself for failing to fulfil its destined role.

Here is another eloquent illustration of the unfailing record kept by the organism as regards reproductive activities:

"I cannot eat beets, red beets," states a patient. "The other night

I dreamed of walking in a field with my husband and seeing two horrible large purple beets and I had to scrape them."

The scraping suggests curettage. The two beets indicate two abortions. She is with her husband; she committed no adultery. The patient admitted that she had had one abortion. She took injections to prevent a second pregnancy when her menstruation was delayed. It is quite possible that her unconscious mind looked upon these injections as a form of curettage, whether she was actually pregnant or not. She had injections a third time also, but subsequently thought there was no need for them. The dream seems to confirm that she was pregnant on two occasions only.

"I used to dream a lot about pocket-books, open and closed. There was a black one which I had to get through a window. It was hard to get it. I had to scratch it off with my hand when I reached for it."

This is another dream of curettage. The black pocketbook is her womb. The window is the vaginal entrance. The scratching stands for scraping.

Projection, Displacement, Transposition and Translation

The two principal ways in which the pressure of birth may be disposed were described in Chapter 1 as projection into the future on death and displacement on something outside ourselves. A variation of displacement is the transposition from below to above or further below. For the unconscious mind all bodily orifices equate with each other. We have seen this exemplified in the discussion of anal and oral birth. A fourth way of disposing of the trauma of birth is translation. In its most common form a woman's own genitalia are substituted for the mother's, and the trauma of birth is converted into frigidity, pregnancy anxieties and a morbid fear of bearing children. In other instances the translation takes place in accordance with ideas of anal birth and produces chronic constipation. Of other organs which can substitute for the mother's womb, the stomach should be singled out because we feed our infants with stories that the child is carried in the mother's "tummy." In the course of conversion, the trauma of birth may manifest itself in chronic attacks of nausea and other digestive disturbances. The total result may be a morbid expectation of operations, an inability to contemplate marriage, or fainting spells or epileptic seizures.

The following case should be of unusual interest because the trauma of bearing caused by an illegal operation was converted into a painful growth, called verruca, on the patient's right foot just under the arch. From the viewpoint of the trauma of bearing, this was a case of transposition from above (the genitalia) to below (the foot). From the viewpoint of its remoter determinant, the trauma of the patient's own birth, it was a case of translation. The growth must have taken considerable time to develop, but the patient only began to feel pains when her analysis started. She thought she had a corn with a very deep root. Eventually, she was delivered from her discomfort and pain through the services of a chiropodist, but not until some curious association and dream material illuminated the psychological background of her complaint.

The first revelation came in recalling that for six months after her arrival from Germany she was very reluctant to pronounce the word "foot." The reason was the similarity of the sound to "Futt," an extremely vulgar German term for the vulva. The association permitted the assumption that the foot had been invested with a genital significance. The position of the verruca right under the arch now appeared in a new light. The arch suggested an equation with the pubic arch, and in that case we had the right to query whether the growth represented a child lost by abortion or miscarriage. Indeed, at the age of twenty-one, the patient had had a curettage performed on herself after three months of pregnancy. The revelation was made with considerable reluctance. Two weeks later, she had a dream in which the curettage and the verruca in her foot were linked in a fascinating manner.

There was a new-born baby and I put it very secretly into a zipper bag. I did not want anybody to find out about it.

Then I was in the woods and moss was on the ground. I shoved it aside with the instep of my right foot and it started to glow like coal and burned my shoe. It swelled up too, and the moss was a small spot of green on top of the glowing thing.

The Trauma of Bearing

Then I find a zipper bag and take it home. There is a dead baby in it. I put it behind the stove and am trying to figure out the best way of disposing of the body without anybody knowing. Perhaps I could put it in the incinerator or throw it from the Empire State Building. Then I open the bag. It is full of water and the dead baby is in it.

The zipper bag figures twice in the dream. It is a symbol for the womb. Putting the baby secretly into the bag suggests conception, while finding it dead in the waters indicates the opening of the womb for curetting and the destruction of the child in the amniotic waters. No doubt was left as to the last interpretation when the patient recalled, in connection with the stove, that the doctor had put the scrapings into the fire of the stove, which made a horrible impression on her. The curettage took place in Germany and there was no incinerator in the patient's house. Therefore, the incinerator, as well as the Empire State Building, infuses into the dream the current level of experience. As incineration is a means of disposal of waste, its introduction reveals the purpose of the dream, which is to deliver the patient from her abortion guilt. The Empire State Building is a confirmatory reference. "Dropping a baby" is a common expression for miscarriage. Dropping from the "empire state" has a certain reference to the fetal dominion. The patient's only association with the building was that it was empty. We may say that the emptiness of her womb produced by the dropping of the child was the foundation of her bearing trauma.

All this is almost self-evident but only part of the story. The really startling element centers in the moss. The normal way to scrape it off the earth is with the point of the toe. In the dream she does it the hard way, with the instep of her right foot, thereby pointing to the very spot where a growth was within her flesh. Moreover, her own name begins with the letters "MOS." As the moss is a very slight growth on the body of Mother Earth, we cannot fail to note the allusion to curettage. The glowing coal and the burning of her shoe are excellent references to the injury inflicted on herself. Any further doubt as to the representation of pregnancy guilt is dispelled when a ball-shaped swelling with green moss on top is formed. Generally, it is unusual to find such a clear-cut example of transposition and conversion of abortion guilt into an actual growth. While the revelation of the psychological mechanism by no means disposed of the need for operative intervention, it prevented the continuation of the game of hide and seek which the guilt complex imposed before it was bared to consciousness.

15.

THE TRAUMA OF ILLEGITIMATE BIRTH

FOR the normal development of a child, the presence of each parent is equally necessary. No man searches more passionately for a dream woman than the child who grows up motherless. The mother is the foundation stone of the world for the infant. A stepmother, nurse or orphanage care never fills the gap which the absence of the mother leaves. However exemplary the manner in which the child's needs are cared for, foster parents and institutions cannot enter into the same psychic bond which the pre-natal community of life and immediate post-natal maternal care establish.

While the need for the mother is peremptory and immediate, the father does not enter the child's life until consciousness develops sufficiently for the meaning of home and family to be grasped. When this stage is reached, the absence of the father or suitable father substitutes leaves the child without an important balancing influence. The male parent should be a pillar of strength and a hero ideal for children of both sexes. He should be a god in the infant's universe. His twilight will assuredly come; it is right that it should. But if by brutality the eidolon is shattered prematurely by the father himself, the child's character development may be warped by hatred and fear of the strong parent, and seeds of neurosis may be sown, with the promise of an unwholesome harvest. A boy whose father is cruel may run away from home too soon and vent his hatred on the social order by becoming a criminal or a revolutionary. A girl may develop a masculine character because she has to lean on herself; she may not marry for fear of finding the father duplicated in her husband, and she may be driven to her own sex for the satisfaction of her love needs.

A similar situation to that created by the absence or failure of the parents results from the feeling of not being wanted. The parent who inspires this feeling in the child is guilty of nothing short of a crime. In the world of grown-ups the child is at a natural disadvantage and far too open to adverse suggestions. Because life can be overwhelming, every child needs constant assurance of its own goodness and welcome, or self rejection will follow. The child who has failed to accept himself will grow up with a crippling feeling of inadequacy or, if the environment is conducive to the development of an aggressive character, in open rebellion against society.

In the case of illegitimate birth the child's reactions to life are bound to be completely abnormal. It happens but very seldom that children are left unaware of the stain on the family escutcheon which their very life represents. To be fatherless is hard enough, but to be fatherless with the stigma of illegitimate birth is a psychic catastrophe. It is one of the iniquities of our Western culture that a man may morally fail his child with impunity and that instead of the father we punish the child. It would be far more logical to make the father a social outcast than the child, if we must have a conception of illegitimacy.

For an abnormal development it is not necessary that the child should be actually illegitimate. The imputation of such illegitimacy produces equally severe psychic scars. I shall illustrate it with leaves from the life of a forty-year-old man who came to me for help seven and a half months after a violent attack of schizophrenia.

Ever since the attack he had heard subjective voices from various isolated compartments of his unconscious mind. These voices produced much mental confusion but also answered questions and told surprising stories of their relationship to the total personality.

The patient's dream life appeared to be more or less independent of their influence. The voices developed so much interest in psychoanalysis that the effect often was as if there were several patients on the analytic couch instead of one. They listened with avid interest to the dream revelations and to the interpretation of the symbols used, often trying their own hand at the art.

One day the voices reported that an important message had come through in the patient's dream. This is how they worded it:

Your mother says you were not wanted. You were brought into this world because she could not help it. You were more trouble to your father and to your mother than you were worth. It is not alone that you were sick at birth and thereafter. Your father thought that some one else had been with your mother. He used to scream at her, "I would like to kill that s—— of a b—— who slept with you while I was working in the fields to keep the house going."

Later, the voices quoted another statement of his father:

"That d—— bastard should have died before he was born. . . . I will kill that bastard yet."

The accusation was untrue. The patient grew up in his father's likeness and with many of his character traits. From the age of four he was accepted by the father as his legitimate son.

However, the damage was done. Added to it was the fact that because of the father's hostility, and perhaps for many other reasons, the mother's resentment against him was even more serious. The voices claimed that they were aware of her hostility from earliest childhood and that the patient's suicidal compulsion developed under the effect of the mother's constant death wishes against him.

Whether the voices quoted from forgotten memory, telepathic perception or fantasy makes little difference. Their statement was evidence that great harm was done to the patient by the failure of both parents, and this harm had the lion's share in his final psychotic outbreak. According to his own account:

"I went out of my head and wrote to my sister that I was crazy. The voices told me that I was and that they were going to kill me. The Devil offered me unlimited power if I would do his bidding. He said he would give me half of hell to rule over when I died. He would under no conditions let me go to heaven because I knew too

167

much about him and would put him out of business. I was supposed to rule the world and wipe out civilization. There was a new force by which the mind of man could be controlled. It came from another planet, and it manifested itself through me."

Being a bastard (as it was impressed on his infantile mind), he was locked out of the family circle, as Lucifer was cast out of heaven. As Lucifer raged against God and man, so did he, never fully realizing that he wanted to destroy his own father and mother and that God and the world were substitutes on a stupendous scale for the family into which he was born.

The strength of his moral streak kept him from committing homicide, and by a miracle he escaped being locked up. The voices raved and cursed, impelling him to kill his father and mother and his younger brother, Al. He resisted them. By the time he came to me for help, his homicidal mania had died down, but amazing light was shown on it in retrospect by the dialogue that took place between him and the voices when he was on the analytic couch.

"We did not kill father, did we?" the voice said.

"No, he is still alive," he answered.

"But, Fred, you swore you would kill him!"

"Of course I did, but I was angry then."

I interrupted: "Did you swear to kill Al, too?"

"Did I?" he asked, and the voice answered:

"Yes, you did, once."

"I did not swear that, but I did swear to kill my mother."

"When you swore that, we knew it would not be done. But how could you forgive your father? Can't you remember those things? We have it all here. We hated him."

"I did, too."

"But, Fred, don't you want to kill him now?"

"No."

"We can't understand that. We must give up and realize that those childish things are gone. Fred, we hated him awfully much."

"Yes, we did; but that does not matter now."

"Fred, we don't understand. We hate him here because we have

not been told how to stop it. Because we hated father, hatred of Al still stays. We transfer it back and forth. When you worked on Al, we transferred it back to father. How could we but keep it alive? Why don't we kill father? We hate him here. We have never given that up. It is only your conscious mind that has forgiven him. Now what do we do? We told you our fantasies, as you call them. They are real here. We hate him, and we swore we would kill him. Why didn't you shoot him when you had a chance? When you were home at Christmas and saw his gun? Why didn't you do it? Don't you see, Fred, we hate him; God damn it, we hate him! When we cannot hate him, we hate you."

Here was the startling revelation by the inner voice that the hatred of his father, not being allowed a release in a criminal act, turned on him and was destroying the peace of his mind. Now he realized it himself and worded it this way:

"The voices made me my own father. They turned on me to keep the hatred alive."

"Yes, Fred," the voice answered. "We kept up this hatred against you because you would not kill father. We were killing you instead. We wanted him to die in pain. We wanted to chop his head off. We wanted to have his guts out. We wanted to burn him, as he burned Al's hands with a match. Do you remember how he screamed? Fred, would not fire have been a good way to kill him?"

The statement explained a lot of fire fantasies that came out in the patient's dreams.

"We wanted to kill father for beating mother. She was fighting him. We wanted to help her, but you were afraid. He kicked her and hit her, and she kicked him back in the crotch. We did what your mother tried, kicked him there. We do that, don't we?"

Here was the explanation of a persistent pain in the testes from which the patient had suffered ever since his psychotic dissociation began. He always ascribed it to the voices, explaining that he was tortured by them. For the first time, the story was out. He suffered the way he wanted his father to suffer. But he suffered on a double score, not only because he had criminal fantasies against his father, but because he refused to yield to them—a truly amazing psychic state.

Political Conversion

Another case illustrates the impact of illegitimate birth on the dream life of an English woman who, on her mother's side, came from a noble line. She dreamed:

A Nazi general was walking down the street. I had just read that all our ships were destroyed in the Channel. It was simply terrible. I called to him and asked him if his name was Nègre. He turned round politely and came back to where I was reading the newspaper. "Is this you?" I asked, pointing to an article in the London Times. *I put my right hand on his left sleeve and said: "Curse you; curse you; curse you!"*

Then he walked away and two women, strangers, came to find out my name. They seemed to belong to this German. They did not believe me when I told my name and looked inside my dress where it was sewn under the left shoulder. They left, and I walked fearfully down the street. I entered an inn and went to the upper floor, looking down from there into the lobby, watching people come and go. Then I came downstairs and went into a room where a venerable bishop was sitting. "I am afraid the invasion is on," I said. "God will protect us," the bishop replied. A woman sitting near him kissed the ring on his hand.

I woke up from the dream with the thought: "I have been disobedient; I ought to have shot the German." I recalled a statement in the English newspapers that all German soldiers appearing in England must be shot on sight. I thought at the time what a terrible responsibility that was.

I asked the patient for the most emotional element of the dream. She said it was the cursing of the Nazi general. She cursed him three times because everything happened to her in threes. When she was in South America, a man took her for a Nazi sympathizer and proposed a toast to Hitler. She lifted her glass and cursed: "To Hitler; may he rot in Hell!"

Dreams are not influenced by one's political views. Rather are one's political views the result of one's feeling attitude toward people who were in authority over one in childhood. The patient did not know her father, and the stigma of illegitimate birth was rendered heavier by her mother's noble blood and loss of caste on account of her love attachment. It is to be expected that to the unconscious mind of a patient so afflicted, Hitler or a Nazi general or Nazis in general should symbolize the devil father.

In the dream, the patient's concern with names stands out conspicuously. She asked the Nazi general if his name was Nègre, which is "Negro" in French. She obviously was intent on abusing him. By reading the *Times,* she hinted at past times as the source of her hostility. She associated with Negroes blackness and fear, and with French sexual abnormality. Illegitimacy, by a stretch of imagination, could be considered a sexual abnormality. One can never quite divest one's mind from the notion that birth is a sexual event, and the patient observed that the *Times* is prominently used for birth notices.

I asked her to define cursing. She said it was the refuge of one who is absolutely helpless to do anything else. Cursing thus may well represent an infantile form of self defense.

She discovered in the same breath that the Channel may refer to the uterine passage and that the destruction of ships could represent the danger to her particular ship of life and could stand for the fear of death during the process of birth.

The inn and the upper floor appear to be picturesque allusions to the womb. While she was writing down the dream, the sentence tumbled into the patient's mind: "Jesus entered an inn and went to the upper floor." The association gives this part of the dream a transcendental touch; but as "transcendental" simply means another life, it may as well apply to the Great Before as to the Great Hereafter. The venerable bishop as a symbol of spiritual protection is a good representation of Providence, the good father in heaven, in opposition to the bad father on earth, who forgets to look after his child. No inn can better minister to the needs of its guests than the maternal body to the needs of the child. The invasion was on, and there was death in the Channel; but God's protection did not fail, or the dream would never have been dreamed. However, the Nazi general should have been shot on sight. As the associations on awakening are considered part of the dream, the guise of wartime legality openly reveals the dreamer's death wishes against her father, who rendered her illegitimate.

The aggressive emotions revealed by the dream have been stored up in this patient's unconscious mind for half a century. She knew no way of releasing them and was not aware of their destructive character. They redounded on her as they redounded on the psychotic patient, but in a different and very odd form. She fell into her mother's pattern and punished herself for hating her by becoming the mother of an illegitimate child herself.

It is said that the daughters of drunkards almost invariably marry drunkards, even though they had been exposed to a great deal of suffering on their father's account. It would be rather interesting to know what is the percentage of illegitimate motherhood among those who were born illegitimate.

16.

BIRTH AND WEANING

IN THE womb, the child is the center of a universe. The sole reason for the existence of this universe appears to be to minister to the needs of the unborn; it is subservient to, and part of, the child. This feeling persists for some time after birth, as the discovery of a world apart from the maternal universe is too tremendous for easy assimilation.

Savages never lose the feeling of mystic participation in the universe around them. Woods, lakes, trees, and animals become endowed with part of their souls because they failed to learn to dissociate the pre-natal from the post-natal world. If the bush soul is freed by the killing of the corresponding animal, they believe they have to die.

Because this psychobiological tendency to ensoul the world is rooted in pre-natal reactions, the first great shock in the life of the unborn or the born must arise at the time when the universe not only refuses to minister automatically to the needs of which it had been taking care with unfailing precision, but actually reveals a hostile intent, as in cases of fetal distress, birth, or in hunger attacks after birth. The mother's enfolding womb, arms, or the comfort of her breasts is the only means by which the illusion of being at the center of the world can be maintained. As long as the mother is at the beck and call of the child, it can persuade itself that the separation from her body has not taken place and that the universe is still submissive to its demands.

At first, the child is unable to realize that the mother's breasts are not part of its own physical and psychic organism, that the mother is a being apart. The rage into which tiny infants fly when they are in pain, is similar to the anger of the Gods at a rebellious world. The mother is expected to be a subject and not a ruler. The child is unwilling to court the mother's favor by good behavior. When it finally does, it is because a psychic revolution has occurred and turned its whole world upside down. This revolution is brought about by the discovery of sacrifice. The child learns to recognize the reality of pain and finds compensation for the surrender of its imperious demands as each sacrifice brings its own reward by unfolding new horizons and securing social advantages.

Life can be described as a succession of weanings from previously established and dearly cherished conditions. Weaning from the maternal body in birth is followed by weaning from the breast. Then comes weaning from the parental bedroom. Going to school is the beginning of weaning from the family. Going out into life to earn a living, getting married, and losing the mother by death complete the cycle.

Psychically, each of these steps is a fateful one. Those whom their mothers continue to keep on the umbilical leash just cannot make the grade. They fail at school, they refuse to work for a living, they cannot marry or, if they do, they bankrupt their marriage in a short time, and they collapse both physically and mentally when the mother dies. They find themselves suddenly "born" into a world of which they had persistently refused to take notice, and are as panicky at the thought of standing up against it alone as an infant is at birth. Such cases tragically display the damage which overlove by the mother and for the mother can do to a human being. The world is full of psychic cripples who still want to be carried in their mother's arms as a baby, or within her body unborn. The mother has no control over the weaning of the child from her body; Nature times and regulates the process. Over the weaning from the breast she has control, but unfortunately she does not realize how great a responsibility it is. Because the suddenness of this separation may reactivate the dim organismic imprint of the violence with which the child's body was wrenched out of its mother's, the time of weaning from the breast often proves to be the critical period at which the psychic and nervous future of the child is determined. If the weaning is too cruel, too abrupt, the child will suffer a shock and may develop a traumatic condition which, having mobilized the panicky, inarticulate emotions of birth, can lay the foundation for a neurotic life. Also, the hunger for the breast may persist into mature age and lead to strange fantasies and afflictions.

Cancer and Kleptomania

The latter point will be well illustrated by the recurrent dream of a New York chemist:

An old man led me to a field overgrown with milkweed. The old man broke a stem, pointed to the milky fluid and said, "If you collect this when the sap is rising, you will have a cure for cancer."

The dreamer woke up in a state of great excitement, and believed that he had had a supernormal visitation. When the dream recurred again and again, he was certain that he had a revelation. As a result, he spent many months in trying to persuade people to experiment with the sap of milkweed in order to develop a certain cancer cure. He had no other basis for his belief than the dream. A few questions were sufficient to lay bare the foundations of his interesting fantasy.

First, he was a spiritualist. That is why the wise old man (whom Jung would describe as the archetype of the Mysterious Fellow Traveller) was taken for a spirit guide who could not possibly fail. Then he admitted that he often uses the word cancer to describe something that "eats" him within. Finally, he added an important supplement to the dream; that when he saw the sap of the milkweed, it made his mouth water for milk. He could never have his fill of milk.

I put to him the straight question: what did he know about his weaning? He knew that he was weaned too suddenly and always had a pang of envy when he saw babies feeding at the breast.

The meaning of the dream is now clear. Instead of a remedy for cancer, it reveals the trauma of his weaning. He suffered from an unfulfilled yearning, a hunger for the breast. The dream states no more than: had you had your fill, you would not be hungry; you are sick because you were taken off the breast too soon, and you had better do something about it.

The dream is valuable from the sociological viewpoint, too. The dreamer's enthusiasm for a cancer cure is an illustration of the manner in which dreams may direct our energies into socially useful channels. It was not his fault that the milkweed revealed no medicinal virtues. If by chance it had revealed any, the discovery would have sublimated his persistent unconscious yearning, and the service performed for mankind would have released him from a false pursuit by offering a constructive channel for the use of his energies.

The failure of sublimation of the trauma of weaning may manifest itself in breast fetishism, in masturbation with breast fantasies, in compulsive smoking without pleasure and even in kleptomania. To illustrate the latter:

"I began to steal because I was hungry," confessed a young girl, the daughter of a millionaire. "Then I began to enjoy the thrill of getting the best of somebody else, and turned to stealing precious stones. I stole them from shops in Egypt, and lied at home that I found them in the sand. . . . I used to have fantasies, one of which was that I was born with a pearl in my navel. I remember trying to put one of mother's real pearls into my navel to show it to my girl friends."

She was only fed on the breast for a week. Then her mother's milk "went wrong," it made her sick and starving. Such was the impact of this starvation that at the age of twenty-four when her analysis began, her greatest delight was to buy a baby bottle at Woolworth's and suck milk from it. The primary motive behind her kleptomania was the desire to still this hunger by an equally precious substitute that afforded a direct association (through the pearl) with her mother's body, for at some time in her early life she believed that children were born through the navel.

Birth and Weaning

The Bottle-fed

The failure to sublimate the hunger for the breast may lead to illness and serious incapacitation for life. For the unconscious mind,
love and food are synonymous and interchangeable terms. The
breast-starved child can be recognized late in life by the tremendous food fantasies which may fill his dreams. An overabundance of
such dreams unfortunately sets up a corresponding physiological
mechanism: an overflow of digestive juices will occur to dispose of
the fantasy food, with the result that the surplus acid will attack the
walls of the stomach or the duodenum, producing serious gastric
disturbances and possibly eventual ulcers. Experiments have shown
that the secretion of digestive juices is at the maximum during the
state of sleep when unconscious fantasy activities are at their high
point.

Those who are fortunate enough to find a positive social outlet
escape serious trouble. Love of the culinary arts, "cooking with
love" as one of my patients described it, playing hostess, becoming
a restaurateur, manager, dietician, editor or contributor to maga-
zines on feeding, offer a tolerable sublimation of a passionate yearning for the mother's breasts.

The bottle-fed are not exempt from the same frustration. Psychoanalytic experience suggests that the comfort of the maternal breasts
cannot be replaced by the bottle. Holding the child against the
breasts while feeding from the bottle helps, but the comfort of
suckling on the breasts makes it easier to live down the ordeal of
birth. Either for biological reasons (because of instincts handed
down through thousands of years) or through the sight of other
children feeding on the breast, the yearning for something unattained, something missing will be present in the psyche of the bottle-
fed child.

Here is a strange dream from an anthropologist who was never on
the breast, yet suffered from an unconscious yearning for it:

I was in a reference library looking up matters in Mexican arche-
ology. An elderly woman wanted to see a picture of the God
Quetzalcoatl, and asked the librarian to show it to her. I wanted to

177

see the God Maya Teotl (Teotl means God, but in the dream I took
the whole as the name of God). The librarian said that the two Gods
were the same and proposed to show their identity by taking off her
blouse and exposing her breasts. My reaction was one of revulsion,
as it seemed such a stupid thing to do. The breasts were pendulous
like those of an old woman.

Waking from the dream, the anthropologist had the feeling that
the librarian looked like his mother, and he immediately put himself
on the defense by saying that he had never seen his mother's breasts
exposed. Whether he did or not, I recalled distinctly his earlier admission that as a young man he used to dream of his mother's
breasts. The memory of these dreams had now faded; he could no
longer recall them, and this failure to remember revealed an unconscious blocking.

The patient explained that Quetzalcoatl is the Supreme Being of
the Aztecs and that the name means Feathered Serpent. He is the
God who brought civilization and culture to his people and is interchangeable with all the other Gods who stand for his different aspects. He is, for instance, the White Tezcatlipocl, the God of Illusion, and he is also the Black Tezcatlipocl. Tezcatlipocl means
Smoking Mirror—which is a picturesque description of illusion.

"I happen to know, too," he continued, "that Maya means illusion
in oriental philosophy. 'Ma' means mother (that is how my grandmother was called) and 'ya' in Aztec means 'already,' 'now.' The
Mexican God of Illusion was a magician playing tricks on human
beings."

Here is an indication of the purpose of the dream. It is to show
that the patient has been the victim of a tremendous illusion regarding the maternal breasts. The dream shows him waking from this
illusion by the rejection of the breasts to which, in his fantasies, he
was so much attached. The elderly woman was somebody he had
met ten years before. She was obsessed with a scheme that would
solve every problem of society. As a savior of society, by aspiration,
she filled the same role as Quetzalcoatl. Both Quetzalcoatl and
Maya Teotl are represented by the maternal breasts. That is why the

librarian says they are the same and demonstrates it by exposing her two breasts. The librarian, by the dreamer's recognition, is his mother and the archeological setting of the dream is an excellent reference to the forgotten and buried age in which the unattained breast had a magic value and played on his imagination with the fascination of a magician playing his tricks.

17.

AFTER-PAINS OF BIRTH AND BEARING

THE agony of birth is both of body and mind. It is easier to believe in the former than in the latter. The maternal body does not stretch sufficiently to save the child from the crushing pressure of the uterine walls and the pubic arch and from the vise-like grip of the ejectory muscles. The mental ordeal is not so apparent as the physical one. The unborn child is not credited with a mind. It is very disconcerting to be reminded of the outstanding fact that while we can trace the beginnings of the conscious mind, we know nothing of the beginnings of the unconscious mind; for if the unconscious mind exists in the pre-natal state and we admit its existence, we might have to face questions as to its function. Mind cannot exist without functioning. The least reason for its existence must be to keep its house in order after that house has been built, and to register pleasure or pain. It is hardly conceivable that without mental registration any traumatic condition could exist.

If there is a mental registration in the organism of the unborn, we have to clarify and broaden some of our notions. The term "after-pains of birth" should be reserved exclusively for the child; the mother's pains should be called "after-pains of bearing." While the mother's after-pains are acknowledged and properly treated shortly after delivery, no similar therapy exists for the child, nor is the necessity of such recognized. The mother's after-pains are in evidence,

180

the child's are not unless its body is injured in birth. The mother can communicate with the doctor; the child cannot. No means exist by which its unconscious mind can be tapped at an early age, and in pediatrics pre-natal considerations are not yet given sufficient hearing.

Nevertheless, it would be a mistake to believe that the repression of such after-pains is exclusive to the child. In the mother's unconscious mind such pains may also exist, buried for many years because of the trauma of bearing which for lack of psychological education remained unreleased.

Nightmares of Amputation

The following case reveals the presence of such pain after a lapse of twenty years. It manifested itself in a nightmare which considerably alarmed the dreamer:

I dreamed that both my legs had to be cut off from the middle of my thigh. Dr. W. implored my husband to let him do it. I deliberated whether I should poison myself or not. All this took place in a dentist's office or in a dental hospital. My husband remembered that my tooth had to come out.

Dr. W. had not been in medical attendance on the dreamer for over fifteen years. He had delivered the dreamer's child twenty years before. Thus he was linked up with her anatomy precisely in the region described. The dental references confirm the assumption that the operation refers to childbirth. A tooth is imbedded in the gum as a child is imbedded in the mother. The tooth that had to come out is symbolic of the delivery of the patient's child, which had taken place in a hospital.

It occurred to me that the patient's dream panic over losing both legs could have arisen from the memory of nerves benumbed by the pressure of the child's head against the pelvis. Such benumbing may give the mother a shock. Legs that cannot be felt can easily stir up fears of amputation. It seemed possible that the dream attempted to release the after-pain of bearing.

The patient's association confirmed this interpretation. Before she told me of the dream, a photograph of her mother floated into her mind. In the photograph her mother had a bulging waist-line, and the thought came to her that it would be a good idea to cut the picture off at the waist. So she herself had linked up the amputation with a maternal condition. Then she recalled a conversation the day before about somebody's blown-up stomach and about the legs of her daughter's bed, which she had sawed off to make the bed lower. A friend of her daughter's, who was "all legs," made the remark, "Perhaps you will saw off my legs next." She resented this as an evil remark.

It looks as if these day remnants had stirred up the latent memory of her own legs benumbed in childbirth. A good deal of pain and fear must have been associated with the event. The repression now failed and the forgotten shock succeeded in getting through in an awful nightmare, the depressing effect of which was happily dissipated by timely analysis.

After-pains of the Child

As far as the child is concerned, the most common afterpain of birth appears to be a compressive headache, usually described as steel bands around the skull. I have succeeded in tracing such headaches to the pressure of the pubic arch or of the instruments of delivery on the head in the course of birth. Such conclusions must remain a matter of opinion. There is no way of proving them except by the result. If the release of the trauma of birth banishes these pains after they have resisted previous therapeutic measures, we may claim that the diagnosis is correct.

In other instances I have traced severe pains in the navel to the cutting of the umbilical cord. Chronic pains in the shoulder with a feeling of warm currents of blood rushing up and circulatory disturbances in the legs due to the grip of the obstetrician in feet-first births have yielded to the same analytic therapy. I have reason to think that epileptoid fainting spells without any apparent cause may also echo the trauma of birth. Catatonic phenomena often seem to re-enact the child's ordeal during the mother's labor. The tension of the new-born baby's fists (which as a muscular habit often persists

in grown-ups) reflects the enduring character of the grip in which
we are unconsciously held by the experience of birth.

Easy bruising, a morbid fear of being touched, oversensitivity to
blood-letting, to the smell of blood, to anaesthetics, to colds and to
fever, together with anxieties over falling, drowning, fire, suffocation, etc., may also fall under the heading of after-pains of birth,
provided they can be traced to this event. We cannot speak of the
trauma of birth without after-pains in one form or another. Sometimes the after-pains are purely physical; sometimes they are entirely mental. Every birth nightmare is an after-pain. Today we call
all fear dreams nightmares. Originally the word was meant to describe an oppressive dream in which pressure on the chest threatened the dreamer with suffocation and he woke in fear and gasping
for air. I believe that such nightmares originated in the atmospheric
pressure on the uninflated chest of the new-born child.

The mechanism of transposition from below to above and further
below and also the mechanism of translation from the mother's genitalia to the dreamer's own here again afford opportunity for fascinating studies. Menstrual disturbances frequently represent a complaint
against the trauma of birth, the pain and disorder representing
an unconscious attempt to release this pressure through the corresponding part of the feminine anatomy. To achieve this end, the
hidden birth fantasy must be exposed and acknowledged by the
conscious mind. Few people can reach this understanding by their
own unaided effort. In the male sex, the re-enactment of birth is
more complicated than in the female. Some men are seized with
anxieties during and after intercourse, because their unconscious
mind equates the penetration of a woman's genitalia with their own
passing through the mother's uterus. If the anxiety is too severe, impotency or *ejaculatio praecox* develops in defense. In other instances,
nocturnal priapism may manifest itself. I do not share the prevailing
opinion that unconscious sexual fantasies are responsible for constant and painful night erection or that the pressure of water in the
bladder causes it. Sexual fantasies would come to light in the patient's dreams, the emptying of the bladder would stop the erection
for the rest of the night, or pressure of water would provoke it in

the daytime as well. None of these factors accounts for this disturbance. The absence of erotic dreams and the persistence of erection, even though the sexual appetite has been satisfied, suggest that the penis stands for the child stiff with fear because of memories of birth.

Air-Hunger of the Unborn

In one instance, a young man's refusal to marry his fiancée turned out to be due to a fear of vaginism. He could not face marriage because of an unconscious belief that in intercourse his wife's genitalia would clamp tight on his penis and then he would be lost. He had been born after five days of labor, with the help' of instruments. It appeared that he had accepted the little man (the penis) as a substitute for himself, that he had dreaded marital intimacy because his wife would give birth to him during the act.

This case was unusual because the patient also translated the trauma of birth on to his own body and transposed it from the genital to the abdominal region. He complained of a chronic blown-up sensation in his abdomen after evacuation, and he had an odd feeling that something remained sticking in his anus. From a study of his dreams the conclusion emerged that he was suffering from unconscious air-swallowing (aerophagia). Of this he was entirely unaware, but he revealed that he always smoked when sitting on the toilet and that he belched more than he thought was normal.

His dreams, however, went further than diagnosing this condition; they also revealed its origin. It appeared that, during her pregnancy with him, his mother suffered a double shock from the death of her mother and the suicide of her sister. She fell very ill and her metabolism was considerably upset. As far as it is possible, from the dream of the child dramatizing pre-natal conditions, to infer the condition of the pregnant mother, her oxygen consumption fell below par, owing to which a condition of air-hunger developed for the unborn. This air-hunger seems to have remained with him as an after-pain of birth and was seeking release by the compensatory mechanism of unconscious air-swallowing.

For reasons of anal theories of birth, the sensation in the rectum may have been an additional determinant of this psychic block. The first indication in this direction came in a dream in which he bought an oblong cardboard box with unknown contents. When he opened it, he found it had a false bottom which contained lots of ties and shirts. I inferred that the dream indicated false views about his bottom, and that these views had kept him tied to neurosis.

Confirmation came in other dreams the same night. He dreamed it was Saturday and his mother asked him to clean the windows. He was annoyed at her and said Saturday was his day of rest and he would not do anything for anybody on that day. As the patient came from an orthodox Jewish family and his mother would not ask him to do work on Saturdays, the window-cleaning must be symbolic of something tabooed. This something is linked up with his mother because he resists her. Windows in dreams often symbolize the entrances into the body. Front windows have a genital, back windows an anal significance. The patient lived in a corner house. The corner did not quite correspond to the back, but it pointed in that direction. The patient recalled that his mother used to wipe his behind with a soft rag until a very late age and that he had very pleasurable sensations from this practice. A significant part of his mother dependence and anal eroticism appeared to originate in these memories. Here was a valuable hint as to how the anal block came into being.

Continuing the dream, he found himself in a church and opened a few windows to air the place. The paint was peeling from the walls and he was conscious of the need of repairs. Then he saw his analyst and spoke to him about the "rectum of the church." Immediately he corrected himself in the dream to "rector," and heard me answering, "They are spelled the same way but are different."

This dream confirms that the false bottom was correctly interpreted, but it also identifies the box with the church, and the church windows with his mother's house. In vulgar language, "box" is a woman, while to the unconscious mind the church is symbolic of the womb. It is difficult to escape the conclusion that something has to be corrected regarding his pre-natal situation. When he opens the windows of the church, we do not yet know what he means, as airing need not symbolize more than bringing something to light or creating a better atmosphere. The following night, however, he continued the theme (there was no analytic session in between) and had a revelatory dream:

I leave my goldfish tank outside on the sidewalk all night. It catches rain water, which will refresh it. In the morning I go down to get it and it is not there. The street is not where I live now, but where I was brought up as a child. I see another fellow with a goldfish tank and big fish. He puts one in my tank. (It seems I have found it now.) Then I take the goldfish tank to the place where I work. I believe I am late and I am under the impression that I have forgotten to punch my time card. I go back to punch it, to find that I had punched it. Then Buddy H. puts most of my fish into a pool. He puts one on the edge of the pool and the fish seems to jump or walk over by itself into the pool.

The most important element in this dream is the reason why the patient left the goldfish tank out in the night in the rain. Refreshing the water means oxygenating it. During the day, one of his goldfish looked sick. He is always worried about them; he tends them as if they were babies. The wording of the dream reveals the human symbolism, which embryonic correspondences render particularly appropriate. The big goldfish "jumps or walks" into the pool. Fish do not walk; human beings do. The gradual increase of proportions is another hint that he is concerned with something much more important than the welfare of the fish. His small fish is replaced by a bigger one, then the fish tank is changed into a pool, which is a suitable representation for the amniotic waters. Buddy is suggestive of "body." Buddy's parents had a pool and Buddy gave all sorts of advice to the patient on how to take care of his fish. The patient was particularly impressed by Buddy's statement that in winter the fish often freeze into the ice, but that does not interfere with their oxygen supply; they revive when the ice melts.

We can now understand his anxiety over the welfare of the fish. He is trying to save them from air starvation. The windows of his mother's apartment could not be cleaned without opening them. The church windows he actually opens to let air in. The sickly fish must represent himself as the unborn child hungry for more oxygen, which his mother's system could not supply as amply as his twelve-pound bulk required. The meaning of the anal block is now completely clear. As long as the anus is the speculative place of issue from the mother's body, this orifice lends itself admirably for the release of the abdominal pressure which the substitute satisfaction of air-hunger had created in him. This release, however, cannot take place unless the message of the symptom is understood. The proof of the correctness of an interpretation is its effect on the symptoms. In this case, the effect was a salutary one; the obstruction in the anus vanished immediately, and after a short period of re-training in his toilet habits, the unconscious air-swallowing also petered out.*

Water-Hunger of the Unborn

Another case impressed upon me for the first time that after-pains of birth may also manifest themselves on account of a water-hunger in the unborn. Again the difficulties in proving such an appearance are tremendous. The mother's medical history is usually not available, and the patient's hearsay story is too unreliable for any conclusions to be based on it. Palaeontologists may restore from a single bone the skeleton of a prehistoric animal. The task is a light one in comparison with diagnosing from the child's complaints the sickness from which the mother suffered before delivery took place.

The patient had suffered from an insatiable thirst for water as far back as he could remember. He dreamed of eating a stolen apple by the side of a pool. The apple was dry and the pool was shallow. The people who dived in it seemed to hit the side of the pool and bounce from there into the water, but they did not get hurt. Nobody paid attention to the fact that the water was too low for diving.

The dissociated parts of this patient's personality always had their own try at the symbolism of the dream as discussed in Chapter 14. He just grew quiet, listened inwardly, and heard a voice say:

"This is a dream about the beginnings of your life . . ."
Then he changed into the first person:
"The apple stands for my birthright. I always craved water. I won-

---

* For progressive oxygen privation of the pre-natal baby see Margaret A. Ribble, *The Rights of Infants,* Columbia University Press, New York, 1943, p. 16.

*der if that has anything to do with there not being enough water in
the birth sac?"*

The query was entirely spontaneous. It never occurred to me to
link up his water-hunger with the amniotic condition. But now I remembered a previous statement through the voices: that something
had happened to the patient before he was born. I began to wonder if
hitting the sides of the pool and bouncing into the water stood for the
insufficient cushioning from shocks which the absence of the protective fluid would bring about. One of this patient's neurotic symptoms
was a constant swaying of his body; another manifested itself in occasional explosive jerks that resembled an electric shock. He connected
the swaying with his mother's walking, but he had no explanation to
offer for the jerks. Further, I wondered if his insatiable thirst for water
was a compensation mechanism.

The voices said:
*"We always wanted something we could never get. The mother was
too thin. She would not drink enough water. We always liked water.
We were always crying for water."*

*Could it not have been, I asked, that the mother did not have enough
water in her system and that the supply of water to the organismic
needs of the unborn child was insufficient?*

*There was an excited affirmative response from the voices. Such
responses did not always follow; the voices often differed. Now they
said:*

*"You hit it. The mother was a New England woman, thin, bony,
drawn in the face, dried out, a bag of bones."*

Then the patient added in the first person:
*"I told you I had a faint feeling this morning. I think I had it within
my mother's body. It came from lack of water. My mother's blood
was bad. She was always taking pills. I have to drink two to three
glasses of water as soon as I get up."*

Then he changed back to the voices again:
*"We did not have enough nourishment. After birth, we could never
get water, only milk. We protested and protested. It was hot. We
were out of doors, we needed water, but we never got it."*

After-Pains of Birth and Bearing

The protest refers to a strange sickness from which the patient suffered for six weeks. He had to be rocked day and night, as his body was constantly shaking. In his family, it was not customary to give water to a small baby. Perhaps he was shaking for water. What a simple cure it would have been!

It is, of course, impossible to prove that the diagnosis is correct or that the cure would have been effective. One consideration alone militates in its favor. It is that the discussion on water starvation had done something to the patient's unconscious mind. Several weeks passed without any reference to hunger for water. Then I asked him if he still suffered from the compulsion of drinking water. He said:

"No. I still have to drink at night, but the mad desire for water which possessed me, as a drunkard is possessed with the craving for 'booze,' has vanished. The same thing has happened to the constant craving for sweets. I used to hear a childish voice hammering at my brain: 'We want candy, we want candy,' and whether I wanted it or not, I had to stuff myself with cookies and sweets. While my will power is still weak, I am no longer obsessed by either of these desires."

18.

RELEASE OF THE TRAUMA OF BIRTH

WHEN we hear of dissociated personalities, we seldom reflect how little this term is understood. Fundamentally, we all suffer from dissociation, beginning from our birth. Our mind splits when we arrive into this world.[*] To the degree that the conscious mind develops, the unconscious mind recedes, and finally it assumes a naturally dissociated state. At a considerable cost, we adapt ourselves to this baffling world. Whether or not we pay with neurosis for this adaptation depends on our ability to withstand shocks before the crust between the conscious and the unconscious mind becomes sufficiently hard to keep the stormy emotions of birth out of echoing range.

Birth is a test of fitness for survival. Nature had an eye on the future of the race when it rendered the child's entrance into this world difficult. This test of fitness is not a matter of physical stamina alone; it has a psychic counterpart. But for the impact of the ordeal suffered in being born, we would shrink from the struggle for existence and concentrate on finding a way of regaining the lost pre-natal peace and happiness.

Physically, return is a manifest impossibility; psychically it is not so. Ample proof exists in the fantasy life of humanity of the persistent

---

[*] "Man's first experience, birth, is schizophrenic"—Harry Stack Sullivan before the American Psychiatric Association, May 12, 1939, at Chicago, Ill., quoted by J. S. Kasanin in *Language and Thought in Schizophrenia*, University of California Press, 1944, p. 4.

belief in an attainable Utopia and of the powerful influence which this Shangri-La wields over our imaginative life. Not even the worst ordeal of birth can banish the haunting memory of pre-natal bliss. Were it not for the Flaming Sword of the Angel of the Lord at the gates of the Garden of Eden, we would yield to the yearning to return to the womb—with fateful consequences for the future of mankind. For if the psychic energies of the race were universally focussed on the past, no evolution, no human progress would be possible. Because we quail at the thought of the ordeal once experienced, we refuse to yield to the regressive urge. Because the memory of pre-natal bliss is poisoned by the ordeal of birth, we choose to go forward and, cherishing the vision sublime, attempt to create a state of Utopia in the here and now. In so doing we become reformers and are paid tribute for being inspired by high ideals. If we fail to go forward, we become neurotics; and if we succumb to the regressive desire without restraint, we end as inmates of mental institutions.

The ordeal of birth, in this light, is not a senseless affliction. From the racial point of view, it is evidence of wise planning. If the conditions of our civilization contrive to make the burden unnecessarily heavy, let us blame our way of life instead of Nature, and devote ourselves to the task of finding special correctives. As it is difficult to do away with prolonged labor and prevent complications of childbirth, we should attack the problem from the therapeutic end, build up a body of knowledge regarding the devastating effects of the trauma of birth and work out methods for its release.

The trauma of birth is not a new discovery. Dr. Otto Rank was the first psychoanalyst to call attention to it. The Freudian school, of which he was a prominent member, did not receive his claims with much sympathy. Perhaps they felt it was too big a thing to have been missed by Freud, or perhaps it disturbed their omnific conception of Freud and psychoanalysis. Freud himself acknowledged it but minimized its importance. The Oedipus complex was too much in the forefront of his attention. It seemed to be the axis on which all neuroses turned. The discovery of the trauma of birth threatened a shift of attention too soon. The desirability of the shift was not apparent to Freud, as he failed to perceive that the trauma of birth would actually clarify the Oedipus situation and present it in a simpler and more acceptable form.

Nevertheless, the pre-natal state did not escape psychoanalytic attention. The dreams revealing it were called mother-body fantasies, and they were fitted to the Oedipus complex as covers for incestuous thoughts. That they could call attention to actual situations was too preposterous to contemplate. It was more in line with prevailing Freudian ideas that the child was back in the womb for the purpose of spying on intercourse between the parents. Falling fears were symbolic of moral fall, water dreams referred to sexual passion, dreams of crushing stood for castration, and dental dreams for masturbation. The fantasy life of the patient was fatally revolving around the sexual possession of the mother's body.

Much of the resistance to psychoanalysis is still due to the crudity of these early notions. The Freudian claims could have been stated in a more acceptable and less humiliating form. They were formulated by adults to fit the adult view, which is too one-sided. Because no one challenges it, we accept it as a fundamental proposition that the unborn child is part of the mother's body. We forget that in the psychic universe of the unborn the exact reverse holds true: the mother is part of the child's body because the mother is an environment only. What if the aim of incestuous fantasies is a re-establishing of the pre-natal *status quo* by reversing the process of birth and entering the mother's body by the part instead of the whole? It is a simple thought, which automatically follows from adopting the viewpoint of the child, but what an enormous difference it makes! On this basis, incest becomes a universal biological issue instead of an individual moral one, and we need have no feeling of guilt for trying to express an instinctual urge in the only available, though sexual, form.

The same simplification can be achieved regarding homosexual repression. If babies are born from the rectum—an instinctual conclusion to which the observation of bowel functions impels the child— early sexual fantasies will concentrate on this part of the body. By a process of identification with the mother or by a translation of the memories of our own birth, the anus of a man assumes the role of the female genitalia. Because of this distortion, we are visited by dreams

192

and fantasies that bear the stamp of homosexuality, yet have no homosexual content. They may not reveal more than the fusion of sexual ideas with the trauma of birth. To call them evidence of homosexual repression may be just as mistaken as to interpret the return into the womb as an incestuous fantasy.

Problem of Catharsis

Another reason for resistance to acceptance of the trauma of birth as a matrix of neurosis may have sprung from the unconscious fear that the Freudian technique is not adequate to meet the situation. Catharsis (abreaction) is the cornerstone of Freudian psychology. It is said that unless the patient recovers the memory of the repressed, and in recovering it re-lives the original event, he cannot become free.[*] It is claimed that emotions can only be released through consciousness. Catharsis is the process of releasing disturbing buried memories; therefore, without catharsis the patient cannot be cured.

Note that the emphasis is on memories, which—strictly speaking—postulate something that at one time was in the possession of the conscious mind but faded out, was suppressed or repressed. To talk of unconscious memory (in an exclusive sense) is paradoxical. Whatever is purely unconscious (and not simply forgotten) cannot be memory; if it is not memory, it cannot be brought "back" into the conscious mind; it will not be accepted as such. Memory begins with sensory functions, consciousness is built on perceptions and sensations that begin after birth; there is no consciousness before birth or while we are asleep. How then can we re-live something that never entered consciousness or antedates its very existence?

On the basis of such reasoning, it is impossible to abreact the drama of birth. No technique exists to meet the situation. Yet some patients can be led back to birth and do appear to re-live this remote event. Are they enacting a fantasy only? If so, why should the enactment of such fantasy produce a feeling of utter prostration, and afterwards a tremendous feeling of release?

---

[*] It was later conceded by Freud that the early memories may only appear in the form of fantasies from which the original situation could be reconstructed.

The position will not be clarified until we review our notions regarding memory and the real nature of catharsis. There is no reason why memory as a process of mental recording should be considered the exclusive attribute of the conscious mind. In dreams we can remember dreams we had years before and have forgotten. It is true that it would be extremely difficult to prove such remembrance to be something else than a dream, yet most people are satisfied that these recollections do refer to previous unconscious experience. We know that the unconscious mind records many impressions which the conscious mind is not able or too preoccupied to notice. When the impression emerges, we may or may not remember its actual moment of impingement. If we don't, we may consider the memory purely unconscious. All repetitive acts give evidence of memory. The very function of our vegetative system is inconceivable without postulating unconscious memory. How could replacement of destroyed tissue take place without a memory in the organism of the original pattern? But if there is an organismic memory, there must be a registration within the same organism not only of the process of growth but also of the reaction to dangers that threatened the whole of the organism with destruction. We need not be conscious to experience fear and pain. Our nightmares of injuries suffered while asleep prove the point. If a dream is an urgent message speaking of pressure in the unconscious mind and demanding its release, there must be a way of releasing that which the conscious mind has never experienced, or dreams could not possibly serve any psychological purpose.

It should therefore be possible to release that which we never experienced consciously by building up the corresponding knowledge in the conscious mind, by verbalizing emotional experiences of a prelingual period of life. This is the first important deviation from the orthodox concept of catharsis. A second deviation can be found in the fact that we often find emotional release without recovering the memory of the precise event that oppresses us. A crying fit will relieve a woman even though she does not know why she cries. We can get rid of delayed shock effects by locomotor disturbances weeks after the original event. We work off the pressure of nightmares by screaming, gesticulating and jumping out of bed. We release surgical shocks through repeated nightmares of being murdered.

If all this is true, in analytic practice we should not complacently sit back and wait until the patient remembers something that he cannot remember. If truth makes us free, knowledge is just as likely to bring about emotional release as emotional release is likely to bring back forgotten knowledge. By the power of his intuition or by the evidence he has gathered, the analyst may present the truth to the patient with the effect of a shock, producing instantaneous catharsis and the cessation of annoying symptoms. If a man is shot in his sleep but recovers, he will have no conscious memory of what happened to him. He would know it from being told, but the knowledge would not rest on experience. His nightmares, however, would reveal the impact of the shock on his unconscious mind. Being told that he was shot in his sleep would not stop him from dreaming about it; but an intelligent explanation showing how his dreams were related to the aggression to which he fell victim would be appreciated and accepted by his unconscious mind, producing an adjustment and a cessation of his nightmares.

The analogy holds good for the shock of birth. Very few patients are capable of re-living it on the analytic couch. Even when it so happens, the patient is conscious of a feeling of unreality despite the emotional release which follows. The patient invariably apologizes and assures the analyst that he was not making up a story. This is the very reaction we should expect. As his birth emotions have never been verbalized, in putting them into words the patient *is* making up a story. It is a true story, in spite of the fact that it is not based on memories registered by consciousness but rests on organismic impressions. The imprints of the latter may be just as real and vivid as the rings in the cross-section of a tree showing its physical growth.

Another complicating factor is that birth memories do not appear isolated from other similar events. The shock effect combines with other shocks and forms a kind of emotional alloy in which we may see signs and symbols pointing to birth without being able to state with conviction that the patient has gone back to the primal event of his life.

195

Search for the Beloved

Earthquakes and Birth

A fascinating illustration of the difficulties of pigeon-holing dream revelations is shown in the dream of a theatrical producer:

I was standing on the seashore with Aunt Dot and my cousin Derek, her son. The sea was rough and came in in high rollers. I was very worried about certain rowboats. I saw them coming across the bay from left to right. Every moment I expected them to capsize because the rollers were sweeping over them, but each time they were submerged I was relieved to see them come up again safely. One boat contained three women; another, much larger than the rest, contained two or three boys as well as men, and I was certain this boat had overturned. I waited to see the heads of the swimmers bob up after the wave passed, but they seemed to have righted the boat and proceeded, rowing hard. I thought I noticed one head in the water, but expected the boat would pick the man up.

The dream is quoted from the patient's own notes. My impression is that it illustrates the stormy passage of the boat of life. A cousin, in the unconscious appreciation of family ties, is a brother once removed. The patient, after arriving from India as a young boy, was brought up in Aunt Dot's house. She was a good mother to him and Derek, as a "brother," can stand for himself. So we have mother and child standing on the shores of life and watching, in a retrospective fantasy, the drama of landing. Only one boat capsizes and only one man (the dreamer himself) falls into the water, but the dream ends with the expectation that he will be rescued.

Immediately after reading the dream, the patient revealed an anxiety symptom of which until then he had made no mention:

"I still have a fear that the ground might move from under me. It comes to me while I work. Sometimes I feel hopeless in attacking subjects; I just don't know what it is. I feel as if the ground will be taken from under me."

This feeling seems to be dramatically portrayed by the pitching boat; but the patient had no memory of ever having been at sea in a

similar situation. I made him relax and asked him to tell me whatever came to his mind. He began immediately:

"A Black Book is being opened for me. I read the words: 'Fear,
fear.' The leaves are turned over in a bunch, then shut again.

"Another book with Shuck Headed Pete on it, with long hair and
nails. I feel a sudden fear that his fingers have been cut off. I remember the nurse pouring mustard on my hands and standing me in the
corner for licking my fingers.

"I see a blue glass bowl spinning around; it draws near, spins fast;
it is the shape of a cone; it is right past me, my head goes right into
it. Tremendous depth. I am looking down the pointed end. Lava.
Grey like a cloud, heavy like mud. . . . The whole thing seemed to
envelop me. It made me afraid. I forced it back. Then grey mistiness.

"Now this glass cone is spinning away like a syphon . . . no, cyclone,
over the map of India. I am . . . oh, I know where I am . . . that's where
it is! I am in the Central Provinces, not in Darjeeling where I was
brought up. It is spinning away towards Bengal. It goes up to Darjeeling. I was born in the Central Provinces. I could not make out
why I was that side of the map. The map cracked open with a shock.
It has just cracked open again. I am frightened of falling through it.
. . . I am falling to the right. . . . (He shows signs of shock and cries:
'Oh, I feel sick.') The rock came over to the left again. Rocking like
this. (He is nauseated, distressed and breathes heavily.) Pins and
needles in my forehead. . . .

"It was not spinning towards Darjeeling until I realized that I was
in the Central Provinces. It would not have hit Darjeeling if I had
not thought about it.

"I am picked up sick. Oh . . . pins and needles down my legs and
arms (signs of nausea and extreme distress).

"I have only been sick three times in my life. Once eating chicken,
once on account of everybody being sick on a boat because of the
smell, and once crossing from France. Though I can stand the rough-
est weather, though I want to be sick, I cannot be sick from eating
food. I always get diarrhoea instead of nausea.

"I see myself being held in a nurse's arms. I am frightened. Somebody is taking my bedclothes off the cot (nausea again and distress).

Still standing over the cot. Now my mother is ill. I am still frightened of that tipping from side to side. . . .

"I know why I am so frightened. Because I cannot go to my mother. A dark nurse is holding me. She seems quite kind, but I am not getting comfort. I cannot get that comfort. Mother is lying flat on her back, her legs apart. I want to get to her and I cannot. (He squirms on the sofa, turns his toes and legs, kicks and breathes heavily.) No satisfaction, lying like this in a nurse's arms. Mother is in bed. She is ill. Perhaps of the illness from which she died. She is quite still. I want comfort. I cannot get it from the nurse. I am at the far end of the room. I cannot walk. I am too small to walk. I am only a child in arms. How old would I be?"

"Is anything in the room overturned?"

"No; the cot is nearly upset. That was what I found wobbling. I nearly fell out of the cot. I did not realize I was in the cot for some time. When I was being sick, I realized I was in the cot. There was an earthquake. The nurse came along and took me. She turned me over to let me be sick. The earthquake upset me, gave me a fright, made me sick. I still get pins and needles. I wanted my mother to comfort me. I could not go to her. In that sense the ground was cut underneath me. Nothing could comfort me. Nothing could comfort me. That's why it is all wrong. Yes, that's why it is all wrong. I feel, oh, if I could only go to her, it would be all right. If I could just lie for a few minutes in her arms, I would be all right. That makes me nervy, makes me have pins and needles, wanting to go to her.

"I was very ill here a little while ago from smoking that pipe after the taste of chlorine in my mouth from the swimming pool. It made me feel terribly ill. I could not vomit. I got a terrible attack of diarrhoea. Imagine sickness going through the intestines like that! It gave my whole system a shock. The awful taste of smoking after chlorine in the mouth. . . ."

The patient was weak and exhausted when the above recital was over. It appeared that his strong reaction to the chlorine of the swimming pool and the desire to vomit had some subtle connection with the dream about the storm in the bay. At any rate, the event pushed into the forefront of his mind the anxiety problem of the ground slipping from under him, and through the visions which spontaneously came, he reached an understanding and achieved catharsis successfully. The anxiety returned no more.

As to the facts: the patient vaguely remembered being told that he was in an earthquake as a tiny child. He thought, however, that the earthquake took place in Darjeeling. The vision placed it in the Central Provinces, which he left when he was a year old. His mother died about that time from complications arising from childbirth.

The description of the effect of the earthquake on him as a suckling is plausible and dramatic. In his misery and panic, he would want to go to his mother for comfort. Inability to do so would produce tremendous distress. But the fantasy of the spinning cone, the cyclone that sucks him down and makes him fall, suggests birth memories. The two events were separate. He was not born during an earthquake; but birth is an earthquake. It stands to reason that a real earthquake at such an immature age would mobilize the far greater fear of birth, with the result of extreme distress.

The catharsis of the earthquake is also a catharsis of his trauma of birth. It is quite possible that the heaving sea stands for the dramatization of his buried earthquake memories. I believe, however, that the storm is a symbol of an independent event, and alludes to the real source of his anxiety. The ground slipped from under him when he was born. The complications which subsequently cost the mother her life were hardly likely to permit him a smooth passage into this world.

Jacob's Ladder

Where the trauma of birth manifests itself as falling fears, freedom to climb heights may be the form in which liberation is expressed by the unconscious mind. Consider this example:

My father was in front of me and we were climbing a steel ladder which reached higher than the tallest skyscrapers in the vicinity. He was ahead of me and we were way up in the air. I happened to look down and then my hand slipped. I was frightened that I would fall and cried for help. My father did not help me, so I got a grip on the rungs again and started going up.

199

Search for the Beloved

The first association which the patient volunteered was that she was ascending Jacob's Ladder heavenward. Her father did not help her because she had to help herself; she did so and regained the lost grip.

The dream reveals a deep spiritual symbolism. Jacob's Ladder served for a two-way traffic. The first time we lose a grip on its rungs is in descending. The descent of the spirit, the Fall of Man or falling in birth, refers to this remote event in the racial and individual mind. Climbing upward means more than spiritual progress. It illustrates liberation from a definite condition which represents weakness as the steel ladder represents strength. A skyscraper is a link between heaven and earth. As such it is an excellent symbol for the mother's body. Note that the ladder reaches higher than the tallest skyscraper in the vicinity. It rises above them. The maternal situation, the fear of birth, is being left behind; no more will it dominate the patient's life; she is free to follow her father and her spiritual destiny.

It may be objected that the symbolism of this dream is too general and liable to other interpretations. Let us, therefore, examine another dream in which we meet the same elements in a more definite form:

I went into a place where a skating rink was supposed to be on the first floor, and there I found a friend, a stout woman. The skating rink was only a room, large and sparsely furnished, and I was told they had altered the rink to a swimming pool. All I had to do was to climb through a window, arched on top, square at the bottom, and dive from the springboard on which I should find myself. It was the only way into the pool. I did climb through the hole and found myself at a great height. The pool was far below and the springboard frightfully narrow. I sat on it astride and waited. The woman friend saw my hesitation, climbed out in front of me with two children, and said she was going to show me. She handed me one of the children, a boy, to dive with. I did not want her to see what a coward I was. Moreover, the child was in danger of slipping from my arms. I lifted my leg over the board and jumped from a sitting position. I found myself falling very slowly, as if from a skyscraper. The pool might have been that of the Capitol Hotel in New York.

We need not go into the patient's associations on the dream any deeper than is necessary to appreciate the relief which she shows from the trauma of birth. She was a good skater. Gliding over the smooth surface of the ice is a variation of floating fantasies, the pre-natal roots of which we discussed in Chapter 6. Skates assure ease and speed in movement, the attainment of which seems to be the purpose of the dream. However, the firm foundation of the ice is missing, the rink is changed into a pool, revealing that the ice is just a cover symbol for the waters underneath and that, regarding these waters, an important change of attitude has occurred on the unconscious levels of the dreamer's mind. The curtain lifts and we see the story of the change unfolding in eloquent and dramatic pictures.

The pool represents the amniotic waters or waters of life. The skyscraper or Capitol Hotel is an allusion to the maternal body; the straight and narrow springboard is the uterine canal, and the arched window is the pubic arch. Diving off is the only choice. The drama of birth is re-enacted by its reverse: going back into the waters instead of coming out. As the father had set an example in the previous case in climbing up the ladder, so does the mother inspire this patient with courage. She is represented by a stout lady.

The conquest of the fear of birth is shown by several references. The dreamer is out to prove that she is not a coward. She exhibits no fear in passing through the arched window and but little hesitation in diving off the board. The hopeless resignation to fate which we find so often associated with birth dreams is absent; instead a note of heroism is imparted to the dream. It is probably for this reason that the dreamer represents her childhood by a little boy and not a girl. She was a tomboy and always wanted to do things which others could do. The only two references to inevitability are found in the statements that the only way into the pool is through diving and that the child is in danger of slipping from the dreamer's arms, which additionally determined her to take the leap. The inevitability is the fall, which is symbolic of falling away from the maternal body in birth; and the slowness of the descent is the final indication that the fear of falling (the most common symptom of the trauma of birth) is cancelled.

Search for the Beloved

Plowing Up the Cemetery

The patient whose phonophobia was discussed in Chapter 2 (church bells associated with funerals and coffins) showed release from her trauma of birth in her eighty-first session in a picturesque manner. I shall quote from my notes and comments in her case history:

The patient had some trouble with constipation. She was not quite sure where she stood, but recognized, for the first time, that she might produce mild neurotic symptoms for the purpose of delaying the analytic separation. She herself suggested that from the next week we should cut down the analytic hours to every second day and test her reaction. Then she narrated the following dream, which shows considerable progress in analytic separation:

I dreamed of the number 44. Two fours. I took them for chairs and put them together, the seat of one on top of the other, forming two squares. That, I thought, made the figure 8, the number of pre-natal and post-natal integration.

You were sitting at a counter like a telephone operator and looked at everybody to see what they were doing. I saw several other counters. I was looking at you, and recited an Ady poem teasingly:

> *We have until the midnight tarried,*
> *To see a passing coffin carried.*
>
> *Whom bury they? Neither ask nor tell:*
> *But join the train and toll the bell.* °

Then I plowed up a long, narrow piece of land. It was a cemetery. Then I formed graves and put seeds in them to bring forth green grass.

The beginning of this extraordinary fantasy of integration suggests that the patient's constipation is rooted in an anal conception of birth. She began her account with a reference to constipation. Chairs are symbolic of stools, squaring means integrating. While the symbolism

---

° Translation by William N. Loew, *Modern Magyar Lyrics*, Wodianer F. És Fiai, Budapest, 1926, pp. 13-14.

of the figure 8 is not original but based on previous analytic discussions, its representation by two chairs combined into squares is entirely novel. Whether original or not, the use to which the symbol is turned in the dream is unmistakable.

As a telephone operator, I am making connections. It seems as if the patient were representing me as the supreme authority over the nervous system, of which the house exchange is an excellent symbol. The counter, this time, stands for organization and not conflict (countering). Her teasing attitude is particularly interesting. It indicates release of tension, growing ease. No doubt can exist that this tension was caused by her death fears, which originated in her birth. The coffin and the bell (with their rich association material previously discussed) prove it. Midnight is 12 o'clock. When it strikes, the hands of the clock have described a complete circle on the dial. That the emphasis is on completion is very simply and dramatically revealed by the plowing up of the cemetery and by the sowing of grass seed into the graves. Life replaces death; growth and fertility replace destruction.

To these notes I soon had the good fortune to add another: fertility had a precise personal meaning. The patient became pregnant, and approaching motherhood, for the first time, filled her with joy. She had been pregnant twice in the past but had broken the pregnancy for reasons of psychic complications. Now her mind was at peace; she no longer associated death with birth and bearing.

The Life to Come

"I dreamed of a pair of new black socks which I received for my birthday," reports another man. "As I took off my shoes, I noticed that the socks had no sole at all, the shoes seemed to have worn them away completely."

Here the birthday association is the clue to the dream. It is not the socks that are completely worn away but the dreamer's trauma of birth. Black is the color of death, and the sole of the socks represents the lowest level on which we stand. This black level is gone. The fear of death which originated in the fear of birth is banished.

Indeed, this dreamer's outlook on life was remarkably serene and composed. Death held no horrors for him. He looked forward to it as to a glorious new adventure, a birth into a new and exciting life.

Humanity has been fighting the specter of death ever since life was found good and worth living. Religion obtained its hold because it taught the science of a life to come. However, we have failed to realize two things: that our desperate struggle against extinction is the echo of our actual arrival into this world from the Kingdom of the Great Before, and that the fear of this experience might be the principal conditioning factor of a disbelief in a future life, as the acceptance of such a belief commits us to facing in death the ordeal of birth and brings the agony of the lost pre-natal bliss too distressingly near to conscious realization. As the atheist denies the existence of God because he is afraid of Him, so may we deny the possibility of a future life because the trauma of birth saps our courage to pass into it.

If this could be established, the release of the trauma of birth would exercise as profound an influence on our philosophy as it did in the case just discussed. We would no more need to defend ourselves against a Hereafter on the basis that we are projecting the certainty of a pre-natal life into the Great Beyond. The change in unconscious attitude would eliminate our resistance to a claim which has been upheld by all the great spiritual teachers of the race and is supported by the deepest archaic instinct within us.

Pre-natal psychology may shatter the last fetters with which scientific materialism has bound our minds.

BOOK II.

Return into the Womb

19.

FANTASIES OF PRE-NATAL BLISS

THE vision of a faraway fairyland, where all strife ceases and life rolls smoothly in a state of perfection and bliss, holds man as spellbound today as it held him two thousand years ago when the first Utopian book, Plato's "Republic," was written. Though the word "Utopia" means "no such place," the search for the El Dorado of the Incas, for Samuel Butler's "Erewhon" ("nowhere" backwards) or James Hilton's "Shangri-La" will never cease because of the whisper of a still, small voice that a distant, inaccessible country where happiness reigns supreme does exist and that we lived in it once in a dim and glorious past.

Whether we yearn to return to a desert island washed by waves of the sea, or to a lonely mountain top with an unbroken horizon bathed in oceans of air; whether we are spellbound by stories of sunken Atlantis, cities under the sea, in the bowels of the earth, in the moon, or on other planets floating in the vast interplanetary void; whether we search for the Garden of Eden or the City of Gold of apocalyptic prophecies, we are yielding to a mysterious assurance that such visions are not idle dreams and that we once knew the reality on which they are based.

Our very belief in a future life may spring from the certainty of a past existence, the haunting glamor of which forever escapes clear recollection. Some project this certainty backwards and become firm believers in reincarnation; others project it forward and become spiritualists or theosophists. The instinctual acceptance of either direction rests on the simple foundation of having lived before birth within the mother's womb.

Memories of such an existence, in the strict sense of the word, we have none. We may curl up in bed and sleep with arms folded across the chest without ever thinking of the position of the embryo within the womb. We may love being rocked by cars, trains or boats like a child in the cradle without realizing that the soothing effect is due to the unconscious identification of the gentle movement with the undulation of the mother's body in walking while we were sheltered and protected within her. We hardly devote a thought to the strange passion of children to be cooped up in tiny places which they call houses, because so many of us have contrived to twist such childish delights into claustrophobia. We pass without comment the water fantasies of friends, whether they spend many hours a day floating in a tub of hot water or swimming under the water in warm seas, face up and eyes open watching the wonders of submarine life or the sunshine above. We have little curiosity for the psychological motives that impelled a William Beebe to construct diving bells for the exploration of the bottom of tropical seas; or a Williamson to build a submarine post-office to which one has to descend through a vertical hollow tube from the belly of a ship; or a Hubert Wilkins to reach the North Pole by submarine under the Arctic icefields; or a Houdini to have himself buried underground, or shut in boilers and safes and packed in boxes, to be thrown into the sea. It never occurs to us to seek an explanation for a morbid love of hot-houses and an obsessive interest in things growing in flower pots, because we have forgotten that we were tropical creatures once upon a time and that one of the first shocks on our arrival was the coldness of the post-natal world, for which the delicate human plant was not prepared.

"Déjà Vue" and Pre-natal Nostalgia

To some people the haunting memory of the pre-natal Garden of Eden is just a dream of a Never-Never Land. Others are more conscious of its psychological reality and experience strange stirrings and disturbances. Here is how an anthropologist describes his sensations:

A strange feeling of remembrance used to come to me until I was eighteen to nineteen, often years apart and more frequently in childhood. Looking out of a window towards the North or the East when the sun was in the West, I would vaguely remember a place that was extremely beautiful, with a kind of violet or amethyst coloring, and I would have a most intense longing to be there. I used to think it was the memory of a previous life, that it argued for reincarnation.

I had a similar mystic feeling in a dream in which I wandered through a large number of rooms and finally got out into the open and saw a beautiful, white city in the distance. I felt I belonged there, that it was a city of my own.

Experiences of this type are classified by psychologists under the heading of "déjà vue" (already seen), to explain the strange familiarity which unexpected landscapes sometimes inspire. A curious depersonalization may accompany the experience; reality becomes vague and undefined and a feeling of historicity, of living somewhere else, in a past and distant epoch, takes its place. Probably no single explanation is sufficient to account for all such experiences. My own view is that pre-natal emotions, which the unconscious mind often clothes in scenic pictures of a fairyland, play an important part in the genesis of such sensations. A beautiful landscape in dreams may represent a beautiful feeling. Idyllic life is rarely represented without a sylvan setting. Poets have always known how to translate into pictures the mysterious emotions of the heart. The poems that depict these strange yearnings live. Göthe's "Kennst du das Land wo die Citronen bluhen" stirs us today as it stirred his generation. Yet the lines are almost too simple to hold so much magic. In a rough translation of my own they read:

> Knowest thou the land where the lemon blossoms into flower,
> Oranges glow like gold in a dark and leafy bower?
> Where marble statues stand and at thee silently gaze?
> Why, poor child, tears are streaming down thy face!

And there is "Faust" and the mother's kingdom. As Georg Groddeck explains:

Search for the Beloved

"Man seeks the depths of the body of Mother Earth, strives after them all his life long, until at length death puts him to rest in her. How absorbed the soul of man is with this likeness, which brings love, night and death, the mother's womb, and the bowels of the earth into mysterious association, we may see in the prophetic reference to the mother's kingdom which we find in 'Faust,' that untrodden, unattainable kingdom where there is neither time, nor space: everyone is thrilled by these words who hears them uttered from the stage. The miner, like Faust, is driven into the kingdom of the mother; his calling is this eternal, never-ceasing longing for the body of the mother, into whose depths the shaft leads him with unholy magic, in whose depths rest all the joy and the delight of life and all love, whose blessedness is dimly and unconsciously remembered in the idea of a lost Paradise and the hope of a heavenly kingdom and eternal happiness, as well as in the fear of the unceasing fires of hell." *

A prose quotation from the unpublished autobiography of a well known American poet, which I quote with her permission, will further illustrate the problem of "déjà vue":

"But there was another land—where had I known it? A land of idyllic meadows and fair skies, a land of satisfying symmetries, of melting music, where loving and beautiful companions greeted one with reassuring gestures and harmonious speech, a land where one's sweetest impulses broke spontaneously into dancing and singing, a land where nothing was forbidden because everything was good, and where young and old met and mingled in pleasure and in vibrant peace. A land that, however clearly I could see it in my mind's eye, lay deeper in my consciousness than anything that the eye could see or hear. Truly a land of wholeness—a land of the heart.

"What is the source of such preoccupations? Can it be, as Robert Chambers suggests in that moving poem, 'The Trial by Existence,' that life upon Earth is the

> 'sacrifice
> Of those who for some good discerned
> Will gladly give up Paradise?'

---

* Georg Groddeck, *The Unknown Self*, C. W. Daniel Co., London, 1937, pp. 150-51.

Fantasies of Pre-Natal Bliss

"I cannot say. Nothing has answered that question. I only know that this vision is bound up with my earliest memories and that I cannot connect it with any earthly experience, that a recurring nostalgia troubled me with the conviction that it was something I had left rather than somewhere I was going—or could hope to go—and that over and over again, in the face of disappointment and failure, I have been teased and seduced by the dream that the perfection I seemed to remember could be approximated on this rich, exciting, baffling but still imperfect earth. This desire for perfection was so strong and so unreasonable that I projected it like a garment fabricated out of the stuff of my yearning over one or another of the beings I loved—a Jean's, not a Joseph's coat of many colors. Discomfited were they who had to wear it, and the unwanted garment was returned to me again and again, often in shreds, but like the magic robe it was, it made itself whole again for the next idol—or was it victim?"

The poet who wrote this fascinating confession was completely unconscious of its pre-natal significance, even after the fantasy assumed more precise shape in musings over the soap bubbles that her mother blew for her:

"Before it rounded itself into the bubble, for all its fragility, it swayed heavily and pear-shaped, and reminded me for a startled instant of my mother's breast. Then it settled roundly for a moment, and in that moment the red brick high school, separated from our backyard by an alley, the locust and maple trees, the bright blue sky with its floating island clouds, were reflected sharply and upside down, glazed over with the mother-of-pearl shimmer of the bubble. I saw an enchanted world. I must cast myself into it and dwell in that clean place of lovely colors. 'What is it, oh what is it, Mamma?' I questioned, carried out of myself, breathless. 'Germany, that's Germany,' said my mother, smiling down at me as the bubble burst.

"Germany was the place Mamma had come from when she was three. Germany was the country where the Rhine River flowed at the base of the castles, where Die Lorelei and the horrible Master of Ringen who was eaten by his own rats, the Black Forest and the horse market of Elberfeld, and all the best musicians, mingled together in a fairy-tale-like picture that had no beginning and no end."

Having confessed to her haunting vision of Utopia, our poet all but yields to the desire to throw herself within that fairyland, now associated with her mother's pear-shaped breasts. Her mother was caught by the same spell. She, too, had known a fairyland, a far-away country, the mother land, the womb. Lorelei, who enchants the swimmers and drags them under the waters, is a beautiful representation of the fear and fascination of the pre-natal return.

In many poetic confessions the place of the mother is taken by the Beloved. Here is how Louis K. Anspacher describes the same deep nostalgia in "The Pilgrim":

> "It's somewhere hereabouts that she was born.
>> She told me once and I have not forgot.
>> Her eyes, when they first opened, saw this spot
> That now is sacred to me. Here the morn
> Was sunnier and the night was less forlorn
>> Because of her. I pondered: Is there not
>> Some music clinging, or I know not what
> Of footfalls somewhere on some pavement worn
> Ever so lightly by her passing? So
>> I wandered through the clangour of the street,—
>> I was so still. I listened, walked so slow,
> Looked everywhere among the hurrying feet
> For some dim traces of the long ago.
>> An ache came on me, but an ache so sweet
>> I would not change for many a joy I know." *

More inchoate but still recognizable are the pre-natal elements in this make-believe fantasy of a child:

"Underneath grandfather's house was another world, inhabited by mice or rats rather like grown-up people, hoarding treasures of gold and diamonds, and a little railway full of trucks running in the middle transporting the treasure. Secret doors permitted these people to come into the upper world."

The fascination of secret doors for the imagination of a child is

---

* Louis K. Anspacher, *Slow Harvest*, Brentano, New York, 1943.

identical with the mystery of its arrival into this world. We do arrive through a secret door, and the high valuation we set on pre-natal happiness could hardly find more fitting description than in terms of diamonds and gold in making the womb an Aladdin's cave. The mice or rats that are like grown-up people approximate the parasitical underground existence of the human embryo.

The appeal and success of Tarzan novels is chiefly due to a response from the pre-natal levels of our minds. The jungle, to the Western mind, is a place of darkness and of mysterious life. Tarzan's ape-like prowess, his solitude and his tremendous strength, meet with an echo of recognition from the depths of our being. Remotely, we feel identified with him because we all had Tarzan dreams when we were young and may still have them. The essential elements of such dreams are very simple; climbing big trees, swinging about in the branches with ease, being friends with wild animals, gamboling, laughing, being happy together with other children. The presence of other children is the usual indication that the dream is to be interpreted on the infantile levels of life.

Varieties of Nostalgia

Nostalgia is a yearning for our country or home town. The definition is superficial. It is our childhood for which we yearn in a nostalgic mood. On a still deeper level, as we have seen, the yearning for the pre-natal home is concealed behind it. The forms of fetal nostalgia vary considerably. It may appear as a fascination for mysteries in general or as a specific passion for cave exploration, submarine research, voyages of discovery, the lure of faraway islands or the desire to climb unconquered mountain peaks.

Sometimes it manifests itself in childish forms, in an excessive fondness for sweets, as suggested by the following statement of a young married woman:

"When I wake up dazed from a heavy sleep, I have to rush into the kitchen and eat any sweets I can find in the ice box or elsewhere. It is a hunger which I find impossible to control. It only comes when my sleep was very heavy."

It seems as if sweets had been accepted as a compensation for the loss of uterine sleep.

"I always wanted to go to Rio de Janeiro," confesses a girl. "The place fascinated me and the thought of going there was a kind of obsession. I had no idea why. I knew nobody there and I could not think of any reason why it should mean so much to me, until I discovered that Janeiro means January and that the complete translation of the name of the place is River of January, so called because the river was discovered in January. January happens to be my month of birth and my middle name is *Jean*nette. From the moment I made this connection, the obsession disappeared."

"Where would you like to live best?" I asked one of my patients of Germanic stock. She answered unhesitatingly:

"On a mountain, in pure air. All great things were given on mountains: the Ten Commandments and the Sermon on the Mount. When I dream of my dead husband, I always meet him on a mountain top. He used to call me Carpathian Princess because I was born there. I used to love to climb mountains. I don't like sea-level. Down in the valley means to me to be on a low level, being unable to reach upward. I was fascinated by Thomas Mann's 'Magic Mountain.'"

In this case the fresh air was an antidote to a slight claustrophobia. The mountain meant freedom of body and mind, the valley the reverse. The legends of the race invest mountains and high places with a feminine significance. Venusberg is a symbol that could not have failed to impress the unconscious mind of a woman of German education. To her husband, she was a mountain princess. Never had anybody appreciated her so much before, nor since. So, befittingly, she meets him in her dream land, the place of that fulfilment which she last knew in her mother's womb.

The neonate's resentment against being expelled from the womb is revealed in the following dream of a professional life guard:

I was in a small boat by a pier as a life guard. Two fellows were swimming. One dived and stayed under the water too long. At first I paid no attention, as I thought he was only playing. Then it occurred to me that perhaps he had drowned. Next I saw him being

214

*pulled out. He was wading in shallow water in a rage and shame
over what happened.*

The patient commented on the dream in this fashion:

"Drowning people always swear and curse at life guards after
they are rescued. Nobody knows why. A fellow guard saved three
hundred men. Only one of them gave him a gift, a box of cigars, and
he did not smoke. . . . I was saved by a life guard when I was four
years old."

The association is exceedingly interesting. As dreams deal with
personal concerns, the inference is plain that he himself was mad
and ashamed at being pulled out of the waters. That he was once
pulled out, is shown by his recollection from the age of four. At the
time when this dream occurred, the analytic problem under discussion was why he suffered from unreasoning attacks of rage throughout his life. The dream seemed to provide an answer: he had resented being born, he had hated being pulled out of the uterus and
this hatred had survived in him throughout the years without any
knowledge of its preposterous foundation.

Royalty Fantasies

Behind the fascination that royalty holds for the youthful mind,
one may frequently trace the vague memory of an ante-natal royal
estate. The general assumption is that such fantasies indicate unhappiness in the boy, that he is dissatisfied with his lot and dreams
of being a foundling in the parental home. If he were a foundling,
he would have real parents somewhere. They would be of high
lineage and one day they would come and help him regain his lost
heritage. While it is quite true that unhappiness is the first cause
leading the child's mind away from reality, we need not see an escape in royalty fantasies. Obscure organismic memories of a truly
royal estate account well for the pattern which their fantasy takes.
Here is an example from the confessions of the anthropologist whom
we quoted before:

"For a long time, I was crazy about royalty. I would read everything about the doings of royal personages in Europe and would
imagine myself partaking in their activities. When I was eleven to

twelve years old, I pretended to be the King of England and my three aunts and sisters would enter with me into these imaginative games. Royal blood was something very special in my eyes. The fantasy was gradually transferred upon teachers and professors who became a special caste to me."

This is the usual form of royalty fantasies and it is generally ascribed to the child's fondness for make-believe. Occasionally the regressive element appears with sufficient clarity to show the inadequacy of this view:

"I often think there must have been an imperial side to my family. The feeling is strong when I see royal palaces and elegant furniture. When I was young I had the idea that I was a foundling, and not a child of my parents. A few days ago I dreamed that I was in a tall, dome-like place and saw there very rich red furniture and draperies. The place was very quiet and luxurious in atmosphere, something I never saw before. The architecture was renaissance."

The rich red furniture and draperies are a typical reference to the gentle folds of the womb. Of this the dreamer was not aware. But he succeeded in putting in the word renaissance, which, as a birth reference, is a covert pointer to the pre-natal state.

Ecstasy of Floating

The search for pre-natal happiness emerges from many floating fantasies. Those that have a uterine setting are marked by curious exhilaration. The dreamer remembers little else than the delightful sensation. He may fly as a bird or swim in the air as if it were water or combine both:

In my flying dreams I used to make motions with my hands as if I were swimming. I could sustain myself in the air that way. At first, I was sitting in a box. Later the box disappeared.

Here the box is a reference to the womb.

My flying dreams would always start from somewhere, a roof, a porch or a tree, not from the ground. When I become conscious of flying, I am already elevated, making motions like swimming and having the most wonderful sensation. In one instance, however, I started to fly up from the ground. I flew up, then down a ravine, following its configuration, to the other side and up, where my whole family was standing. When I landed, nobody took the least notice that I had done something out of the ordinary. But I felt that I had done something mankind had always yearned to do but was never able to accomplish.

This is the dream of the poet whose autobiography we have quoted. Note that in flying from a roof, porch or tree, she would describe the same downward swing as she does in flying down the ravine. She follows the outline of a semi-circle, the obverse of an arch. The "most wonderful sensation" suggests pre-natal exhilaration, in which connection the arch is descriptive of the pubic arch. The feeling of having done something that mankind always yearned for is characteristic of the omnipotent emotions of the unborn. The appearance of the family on the other side of the ravine is a reference to birth which, from the point of view of the family, is nothing much to get excited about.

The bird gods of Egypt probably originated in pre-natal floating fantasies. The ancient Mexicans frequently identified themselves with birds. The medicine men wore bird masks and they used whistles in bird form. The bird to them was a symbol of power; some birds, like the eagle, of supernatural power.

Prophets of the Bible were caught up by the Lord. In Scotland fairies were responsible for mysterious aerial transportations. Witches of the Middle Ages were carried to the Sabbath by the Devil. Spiritualist mediums who figure in vanishing mysteries ascribe the feat to the spirits of the dead, while lesser miracle worshippers report experiences in astral projection.

Modern man no longer has to dream of flying by becoming a bird or by invoking mysterious powers. Technical progress has placed the aeroplane at his disposal. Man flies like a bird, even more so. The accomplishment may satisfy the hunger for uterine bliss in ace pilots and in those who cannot stay off a plane. Theirs is the example how inventors can harness the desire to return to the womb constructively, for the good of mankind.

The connection between flying dreams and aeroplanes is clearly revealed in the astral projection fantasies of the life guard previously mentioned. He had recurrent floating, flying and gliding dreams which alternated with apparent self-projection.

I was conscious of being in my body, yet at the same time I had a sensation of floating as if I was two separate beings, yet in my body all the time. I heard a voice tell me that if I went out I would not be able to come back.

I always had a desire to fly and I particularly wanted to learn to fly a glider. I figured I was a born flyer because my hand is steady, even though I am scared to death. I have made up my mind that I shall buy a glider as soon as I can afford it.

The suicide element in the astral projection fantasy was significant. I had plenty of reason to be satisfied that the patient's floating dreams were of uterine origin. In that case, his astral projection fantasy contained a warning that by returning into his mother's body he would die. Indeed, the patient was haunted by strong suicidal impulsions. He fought them off, but he said if he had to die, he would rather die in the course of astral projection than in any other manner.

The silver cord which is said to tie the astral body to the physical during life time is an excellent substitute for the umbilical cord. I find it quite possible that people who are obsessed with the idea of astral projection are trying to satisfy an unconscious yearning to return into the womb. Occultists and spiritualists who spend half their lives on the astral plane will not be thrilled by this solution of their preoccupation. On ripe reflection, however, they will find little ground for militating against it. We cannot be certain what happens to us when we die, but we may safely say that at one point we have been in definite contact with the Infinite: at the time of conception, within the womb.

20.

THE outstanding motive behind the desire to return into the womb is the attainment of happiness in the only perfect form we have known it.

The Biblical concept of heaven is a projection of organismic memories of a Canaan flowing with milk and honey, where wants were satisfied without wanting, and where we reigned as kings and were the absolute center of the universe because nothing else seemed to exist, the post-natal world being as yet beyond comprehension. None of us ever succeeds in completely forgetting this royal state. The measure of organismically remembered perfection is the very drive behind our restless search for happiness and our ceaseless struggle for betterment.

In normal circumstances the memory of this happiness is an ideal and inspiration. With faith in our strength and worth, we turn towards the future and pursue happiness in a forward march. Only when we lose courage, when we grow weak or ill, when continued failure casts a pall of gloom over us, do we veer around and seek solace, safety and refuge in the glory of the past as in a beautiful dream.

For the average dreamer, such visions serve the same purpose as consolation dreams. They adduce argument against a pessimistic philosophy, against loss of faith in the quest for happiness, and they

219

imbue him with new courage to go forth and resume the struggle. In that form the desire to return and the splendor of the vision that unleashes it are assets to humanity.

Unfortunately, we do not always find the vision turned to such constructive use. The neurotic personality sees in it the promise of an easy escape from unhappiness. Because of the grandeur of the dream the persuasion develops that its attainment is a positive goal and that in the very safety of the womb lies the guarantee of ultimate happiness.

Colloquial language well expresses this delusion: we want to crawl into a hole when we are deeply hurt and feel unwell; we sink into the earth in humiliation and shame, vanish from the face of the earth or feel so small that we almost shrink out of sight. On close examination all our escape fantasies from the trials and tribulations of life reveal the spell which pre-natal security and happiness cast over our unconscious imagination.

The simplest of such escape fantasies manifests itself in retirement into bed in our misery. Bed enfolds and consoles, it lulls us into sleep and gives us oblivion from all earthly cares. It makes us feel safe and secure as if we were back in the womb. It entices with the promise of a new life, of a magical transformation. When "The Sleeper Awakes" (in H. G. Wells' fantasy), he finds himself the owner of the world. When Snow White opens her eyes after her long death sleep, she finds the Prince. As a faithful friend, the bed has few rivals. Closest in the race is the home itself, in which we can dream of the past and work for the future.

While love of the home is the rock on which family life is built and is the basis of the social structure, it is also a medium of escape for those who cannot face reality. Neurotics who closet themselves in their homes and deny admittance to others attempt to lock out the world in the manner of the unborn whose happiness depended on complete isolation. Not realizing that the land of enchantment beckoning in dreams and visions is as unattainable as the Fata Morgana of the desert sky, they persist in playing the victim of this ancient sorcery and fight for their dreams with tooth and claw. To convince them that once we have been admitted into this world we can no longer keep away from it, that the healing balm for frustration cannot be found by regression into the womb, is an important and difficult educational task. The proper function of the home is the reverse: to change reverie into constructive activity, to transmute the power of our yearning into the creation of an ideal unit in a network of homes all over the land, thereby substituting social orientation for self-seeking.

Those who are not blind to reason can discover a jarring note in the very fantasy of escape. It may be no more than a ripple over the smooth waters, a vague disquiet or a distinct protest which they may or may not heed but which, nevertheless, will continue its whispering campaign against a life of sterility.

The fundamentals of the delusion are not difficult to assimilate. We begin life in pain and regret. Birth is a shock both physically and mentally; and it is also the beginning of dissociation. The prenatal mind is not prepared for dealing with the post-natal world; it is meant to sink out of evidence as soon as direct contact with the new world and, together with it, consciousness develops. By returning into the womb, we would escape from this dissociation. However, such return, such a-sociation obviously would have no integrating effect. Life progresses by complexity and diversity. Once we become dis-sociate by birth, we cannot—with impunity—become a-sociates of the womb.

The Fetal Man

A good deal is yet to be learned about the driving power which pre-natal nostalgia plays in our culture. From the omnific emotions of the unborn, fantasies of great historic mission or of demonic power may develop. They need not be on the negative side of life, but often are. Many adults live the life of a fetus in the womb of the world. In Hindu cosmogony the world is described as a lotus flower floating in a shallow vessel which rests on the back of an elephant, and the elephant on the back of a tortoise. The fetal man lives in a floating world. As a rule, he dislikes making efforts and considers himself the center of the universe. The neurotic desire to be carried, to lean on somebody and demand constant attention reveals such fetal character traits. The child who forgets to grow up and still has fantasies of being in the arms of his mother draws sustenance for this dream life from memories of being carried within the mother's body.

The same fetal tendency manifests itself in the life of ascetics who live in dried-up wells, deserted dens of wild beasts or among the tombs. Jeanne Le Ber, who built a chapel with her dowry and lived in a three-tiered stone tower behind the altar in a living tomb from which she only came forth at midnight for a half-hour's stroll in the church, shows fetal regression in its worst form.° The reason why religion permits the use of its protective cloak for such waste of human life is a mystical one. The return into the womb satisfies the yearning for the union with the divine. It is the place where we last saw God, where the Word became Flesh, and religion would not be true to its esoteric mission if it frowned on those who seek to find God by immuring themselves within the walls of the Holy Mother, the Church.†

Others, instead of shutting themselves within the womb, shut out the world by hysteric blindness in order to recapture the happiness of the pre-natal night, and to be fed and looked after by a wife as they were fed and provided for by the mother's body before birth. Still others behave like human kangaroos. A marsupial was defined by a school-boy as "an animal with a pouch in the middle of its stomach into which he can retire when hard pressed." Many neurotics retire into themselves in a similar psycho-physical way. Sometimes they hate their mothers and this forms an unconscious barrier for the normal form of pre-natal return. Instead of the

---

° Willa Cather, *Shadows on the Rock*, A. A. Knopf, New York, 1931.

† "The essential parts of a church are the house itself and the tower: but the tower is an age-old symbol of the man, just as the house is a symbol of the woman, and in accordance with this symbolism the church building represents the union of man and woman, an idea which seems to me to fit very well with the conception of the church as the bride of Christ, as also with that other that the church is the universal mother on whose bosom all men rest. Some church buildings follow the pattern of the Jewish Temple, in which there was the fore-court, the Holy Place, separated by a curtain from the Holy of Holies, in which only the High Priest might enter and where dwelt the Godhead. The resemblance between this and the mother's body can scarcely be mistaken." Georg Groddeck, *The Unknown Self*, C. W. Daniel Co., London, 1937, p. 161.

mother, they may imagine creeping into the father's or the lover's body, or, if nobody cares for them nor is willing to carry them, into their own body, which they equate with the maternal organism by unconscious mental acrobatics. One can carry oneself in a pendulous belly, which associates with pregnancy, in a blown-up stomach or in any other organ which is expendable. Self-love knows no end to monstrous manifestations. He who is not carried, must carry himself at all cost.*

Traumata of Pre-natal Return

The varieties of forms in which the desire to return is tied up with psychic problems will now be illustrated.

One case concerns a twenty-seven-year-old young man who blamed his mother for his failure in life. He had known love only in homosexual form and had no idea that he was escaping from incestuous fantasies and mother identification in veering towards his own sex. Yet instinctively he felt that his relationship with his mother was at the bottom of this unhappy emotional situation. The nature of this relationship was revealed in the following dream:

We were in a hotel, somewhere very high, and I was in a room with my mother. It was her room and I was conscious of having a room of my own in another part of the skyscraper. I looked out of the window and saw the most beautiful island I have ever seen in my life. It was rather curiously shaped, irregular and situated in the midst of a most beautiful sea. The water was green and luminous, as if phosphorescent. There were several islands, but I was struck with this one in particular. It was in twilight and in pale pastel. I said to mother, "Did you see the beautiful view from this window?" She replied: "Yes." Then I said, "Why didn't you tell me about it?"

Here is the note of blame. The mother had failed to enlighten him that he was haunted by a dream; that the mysterious tie to her was not a love fantasy which must needs find sexual terms for ex-

---

* This is not as bold and original as it may seem. Ferenczi stated it first in "Thalassa: A Theory of Genitality," *The Psychoanalytic Quarterly*, New York, 1938, p. 22, in these words: "Every human being, whether male or female, can and does enact with his own body the double role of the child and of the mother."

pression, but the memory of that island happiness which was his share in a remote past in the amniotic sea. The skyscraper is the mother's body, a link between heaven and earth, and his room is his own special place in the womb.

Not understanding the symbolism of the dream, the patient interpreted it as an anticipation of a golden future. It is easy to see that by such acceptance the dream fulfils a constructive purpose. The regression into the past is annulled by a projection into the future. Yet the constructive purpose cannot be accomplished without discovering the geographical location of the island beautiful. He had to be told of the spell which the memory of pre-natal bliss had cast upon his life, for only by so doing would he understand the conscious need of escape from the feminine sex and be able to yield to future pre-natal fantasies without paying a dreadful price. By so yielding he would be reconciled with his mother and re-accept her for all the beautiful things she had meant for him.

The problem of the future is a metaphysical one. All one can prove is that the dream looks back on the past. Nobody can prove that it does not look forward into the future as well. The unfolding of the future according to our dreams is largely conditioned by faith. The very dynamism of life makes it impossible that our dream life should be exclusively concerned with the past. The dream mind is not bounded by time. In helping us to solve problems, it is necessarily concerned with the future. If it is true that we cannot escape from our past, it is equally true that we cannot escape our future. Those who flee into dementia from the unbearable tension in their life do so because of the future which they dread. Thus an adumbration of the future is present even in a case of complete regression. The moment the dreamer projects his pre-natal fantasy into the future, by this very mental act he infuses it with that dynamic element to which visions owe their fulfilment.

Another man, in his early youth, was obsessed by cellar fantasies. He had a sense of exhilaration, security and protection in the cellar of his parents' house. Yet every time he yielded to his penchant for spending his time below, he was seized with an immediate desire to evacuate his bowels and had to rush upstairs to the toilet. Sometimes he would not go down again. If he did, the sensation of pressure in the bowels returned. The moment he mounted the stairs, the sensation was gone. Occasionally he evacuated right in the cellar on a piece of paper. It made no difference; presently he would become restless and have to go upstairs to gain relief. When his brother was sick and constipated, he seriously gave him the advice: "Go down to the cellar for a while, it will make your bowels move." He never understood the reason for his curious reactions. It seems that the fetal return desires awakened guilt feelings to life and he protested through his bowels against yielding to them.

The attempt to block himself from returning also manifested itself in recurrent dreams about swimming pools. In one dream, the swimming pool was in a park where he used to go. It was filled with people, but he was on the other side of a wall which separated him from the pool, and he kept on marching restlessly from one end of the wall to another, trying to look in and seeking a way to get in, without success. In another dream, he could not reach a certain part of the city because his car ran against a jetty. A sea appeared to occupy the middle of the city and people were swimming in the rough waves. At right angles, he ran into another jetty. He was puzzled; he did not know how to get across to the distant city blocks.

The protest emerges in a more dramatic and unmistakable form in the following instance:

I dreamed of a submarine which rammed into the trunk of a huge tree, then disappeared into it by becoming so small that it entered the atomic world. Then I remembered a passage in a cave. I wanted to go in and find out more about the submarine. Just as I was getting into the darker part, people called after me. Amongst them was Marie, my cousin. At first I hoped they would not see me in the partial darkness, and I did not answer. Then they saw me. I had to answer and return.

The submarine, resembling a fish, is a phallic symbol. Here it stands for the whole body. The huge tree is the Tree of Life, the mother. By entering into the atomic world in the form of a submarine, the patient returned into the pre-natal state. Then he varies the theme. The womb becomes a cave and he is in the uterine passage. He hears the Call of Life and has to return. Marie was his favorite cousin, regarding whom he had many erotic fantasies. She is the woman, distinct from the mother, who is the Way. The sexual fantasies that centered on her vaguely hint at a connection between sexual ecstasy and pre-natal bliss. He cannot yield to the regressive desire; reluctantly, he turns his back on pre-natal fantasies.

Happiness is composed of many hues. To some it means peace and security; to others ecstasy. Some find it in escaping from all problems; others in intense activity and in answering problems one by one. Some believe that happiness is achieved by being virtuous, others by satisfying lust. Some are satisfied with little; others reach towards the stars. Accordingly, we find fetal return fantasies that embrace a wide variety of human aspirations.

We may return into the womb to find the meaning of life or to be re-born for a new life. We may return in search of the mystery of ecstasy or to find the Beloved by re-establishing an archaic bisexuality. We may return for an answer to the riddle of our personality in order to better ourselves, and we may go back to satisfy criminal instincts by robbing our mother's womb.

In the following pages a detailed analysis will be attempted of a variety of motives of return.

21.

TO FIND THE MEANING OF LIFE

IN OUR restless search for the meaning of life we, run up against two formidable barriers. The one ahead of us is death; from its bourne no traveller is said to return to tell why we toil and suffer. The other, behind us, is birth, the ground of which feels more familiar. Were we able to retrace our steps to the very source of life, back to the mother's womb, we might find the answer to the mystery of our existence—at least we will not have this splendid illusion wrested away from us. It is right that we should not. Baffling as human destiny may be, we must not bow to its inscrutability. By so doing, we would deprive ourselves of the most exciting quest on earth.

The pursuit of life's Fata Morgana is shown in this picturesque recurrent dream:

I always dream about a cave. I see beautiful sand as I reach the mouth of the cave and I say to David (my son) or to my husband, "You cannot come in." I scrape away the sand and enter. Within I find a parchment, quarto in size, rolled up, yellow with age. I unroll it. The writing is in a foreign tongue. I ask David, "Can you read it? I cannot." Every time I get into the cave, the parchment becomes more brittle and harder to unroll. It is crumbling away. Every time I say, "I must find someone who understands this, it means a lot to me." I put it back, come out and fill in the hole. In the cave, a horrible smell of fungus assails me. I can still smell it when I wake up.

The cave is the womb. The parchment is inscribed with the meaning of life. She is unable to understand it. As the years pass, the problem loses much of its importance, and she spends less and less time in the cave. Her son cannot enter; yet she asks him if he can read the parchment. Dream work knows no contradiction. The statement that the son or husband cannot enter determines that the cave is private to her. Indeed, the womb is a place of solitude. Once this fact is clearly stated, the logistic objection can be ignored as the sudden presence of the son lends itself to symbolizing a mother and child relationship, alluding also to that fulfilment of life which every mother expects to find in her child. Thus the very contradiction is employed as a mysterious hint at the evolutionary purpose of life. The child may find out that which the parent cannot. The child may fulfil the destiny which the parent missed. A good measure of comfort could be derived from the acceptance of such orientation without the necessity of vicarious experience through the child.

The smell of fungus was an unusual element. The patient associated it with death and decay:

"Birth and death mean the same thing to me," she volunteered. "I seem to remember that I first smelt the fungus in some place where I had gone to sleep. It suggests to me everything nasty, damp and buried."

We need not be concerned with mystic interpretations. It is quite likely that the place where she had first gone to sleep stands for the reverse: the place where she first came to life. The function of the olfactory nerve begins with the first breath. It is by no means a far-fetched possibility that the smell represents the olfactory memory of the patient's own birth.

An approach to the meaning of life from the sexual angle is revealed by the following dream:

I went through a narrow tunnel, searching for an answer to an important question. I saw benches alongside. The end of the tunnel was blocked up. It looked like the tip of a phallus. I was gay and

228

untiring until I reached the end. There a voice said that I would have to go back.

The dream shows a combination of the male generative organ with the female one, the first being represented by the phallus, the other by the vaginal tract. The benches alongside carry the suggestion that the tunnel is a restful place and the dreamer's happy spirits reflect the care-free, blissful life of the unborn child within the womb. The tunnel is closed. Thus far and no farther can she go in her search. The answer to the important question is not found. The dreamer obeys the call of life and returns.

At a later stage, the same dreamer made another attempt to find the answer. This time, she summoned magic to her help:

Eliphas Levy came into the room. He had a beard and a moustache but only looked about thirty and resembled my husband. He said something which I cannot remember, and I answered that I was going to tell my husband to grow a moustache and a beard. Then I started walking and arrived in front of a huge wall which I saw from the distance. Behind it stretched a beautiful sky. It looked like the wall of Windsor Castle and was as thick as the wall of Jericho. It was of cork or honeycake, and I entered the wall by becoming small and green. I was like a dragonfly, a fairy dragonfly, and I understood the how, why and wherefore of life. I asked myself, "Am I dreaming this?" I answered, "No, I am not."

A miraculous transformation is hinted at in this fascinating dream. Eliphas Levy, the magician, is made to look like the patient's husband, a natural substitute for the father, the generator of life. Her mother was thirty years old when she was born, which explains the magician's age. He represents both the father and the mother. In real life the patient is a fairy-like creature and is often paid the compliment that in a previous life she must have been a fairy. She identified the dragonfly with a photograph of Pavlova and confessed as one of her greatest sorrows that her parents did not permit her to become a ballet dancer. It seems that she returns into the womb to find fulfilment of that which should have been. Windsor Castle is a reference to the royal estate of the unborn and gives a clue to the dreamer's abundant royalty fantasies. The honeycake and Jericho suggest the land flowing with milk and honey, the impregnable fortress of the womb.

The belief that the answer to the meaning of life is to be found in a definite plan, laid beforehand, is shown in the following dream:

I was going into the sea to swim alongside a dock with some other people. I swam under water into lots of beautiful places. It was like flying, not at all suffocating. It seemed as if I was flying from great heights. I had a definite feeling about what I was going to do as I approached the house into which I was going to enter. I felt that all my plans had been made.

The house she was going to enter is her mother's house. This may refer both to the actual house in which she was born and to her mother's body in which she was conceived. The swimming and flying delight is typically ante-natal and indicates that the dream deals with a return fantasy. We need not go beyond the pre-natal period. The definite feeling as to what she was going to do in life is quite consistent with the sensation of power which characterizes pre-natal dreams.

22.

TO FIND A NEW LIFE BY REBIRTH

IN THE legends that tell the story of the adventurous quest for the fountain of youth, the difficulties and hardships of the journey stand out conspicuously. The place of miraculous metamorphosis can only be reached by overcoming difficulties of an incredible character. It is guarded from the quest of the average mortal by the inaccessibility of the approach.

In Rider Haggard's *She* there is a stirring description of the ordeal of body and mind through which the adventurers must pass in order to reach a cave in the heart of the mountain, where the flame of life bursts forth from the ground in a stupendous rose-colored glow. In the glory of eternal youth, Ayesha steps into the fire from which she had emerged two thousand years before, and pays the awful price of death, aging and shriveling away in the matter of seconds, for she did not know that no man can bathe in the living fire more than once.

This romantic story is a beautiful allegory of the penalty attendant on our yearning to return into the womb. From that fountain of youth, from that living fire we had once emerged in the splendor of physical perfection. If we did find the way of return, our fate would be sealed by death. The quest, therefore, must be allegorical. Only by a spiritual journey can we reach the fountain of eternal youth.

The Christian religion expresses this truth by claiming that only through the water and the spirit can we reach the Kingdom of Heaven. That is the symbolic meaning of the baptismal ceremonies of the church, and we can dimly discern the presence of the same idea in the age-old claim of mythology that the dead, before they can reach the other side of life, have to pass through the river Lethe, Styx or Acheron. These gloomy journeys, however, are accomplished in the shadow of death and not in the glory of a new sunrise. The pagan world yearned for immortal life as much as the Christian yearns; however, in that age they knew but one instinctual way, through the mother's womb, and the pall of Hades was spread over their anticipations by the desperate nature of the undertaking.

The return into the womb may still spell death to the pagan layers of our archaic mind; on the more modern, more illuminated levels it may spell spiritual regeneration, a gathering of fresh energies from the deepest strata of unconscious life. In view of this conflict, we should expect a controversy over the meaning of return. Is it the fulfilment of *Thanatos,* Freud's death instinct, or is the "death instinct" rather a manifestation of the desire to return? We find lesser manifestations of the death instinct in self-mutilation, in addiction to operations, to accidents and disease; greater ones in suicide, especially by drowning or jumping out of the window, the symbolic suggestion of both of which appears to be particularly clear.

Death means a cessation of all activities, a complete release from struggle. The only state answering this description in organismic memory is the pre-natal state. If then death is not a quest for another life but an escape and a yearning for peace, the answer is in the womb. Oddly, the answer is equally there if the desire to return is motivated by a belief in a future life. Before the unborn spreads the promise of a life to come. The wish to be dead and live in another world has a close correspondence with our organismic pre-natal anticipations. Burial customs bear out this correspondence. Placing the dead in the crouching position of the embryo, as we find them in prehistoric graves, depositing the bodies in church vaults or caves, laying them out on islands or mountain tops or pushing them out to the sea in boats reveals the instinctual feeling that we pass away by the same road through which we came into life.

To Find a New Life by Rebirth

If Freud's death instinct is only an incentive for return into the womb, we might neutralize it by integrating the emotions, stored in the dim recesses of the human mind, that group around pre-natal experiences. To my view, the death instinct spells life, and I believe that by proper analytic technique this instinct may be harnessed for spiritual regeneration.

In the course of every analysis the stage is invariably reached when the birth of a new attitude, the desire for a higher state of life, or the determination to make a new start over the wreck of the old life manifests itself in dreams of re-birth, in a fantasied return into the womb, the purpose of which is to reveal a radical change in orientation.

The Serpent and the Lion

All initiation rites are ceremonies of re-birth. The deeper we descend on the scale of civilization, the more importance appears to be attached to an allegorical return into the womb as an assurance of the reality of a new life. The act of birth is imitated in the pubertal ceremonies of many savage tribes. Amongst the Kikuyus of East Africa a boy is not accepted as an adult unless, before his circumcision, he is born again. The mother stands up with the boy crouching at her feet and pretends to go through the pains of labor. The boy has to play his part by crying like a new-born child. Then he is washed and lives on milk for several days. The enforced seclusion before the puberty rites are performed is also reminiscent of the return into the womb. Some tribes enact a proper nightmare to represent birth. The novice is being swallowed and regorged by a monster.

It is very curious to notice how the psychic life of modern man reflects the same archaic imagery. Here is the dream of a post office clerk who was drafted about the time his analysis was concluded. The dream was sent from his camp:

I watch some miniature lions being placed in a small tank and I am surprised to see that a small fish gulps down the lions. I just catch the end, or the suggestion of the act, on noticing that the lions are gone. Then I realize that the fish is not as small as I thought. It

233

extends through a hole into an adjoining tank and it is long like an eel or serpent. The fish now lies asleep. A small fish enters its body through the rear and works its way up quickly under the skin to the brain. Then the large fish falls on its side. It is dead.

There is just one element missing from this dream to make it perfect: the absence of any indication as to what happened to the lions after the serpent was killed. It is by the emergence of the living from the dead body that the re-birth significance of the dream would unmistakably be demonstrated. However, there was no sequel to the lions. The dreamer shifted the importance of the scene to the tiny fish and stated, in a subsequent letter, that he was impressed by its stealthy approach and sensed its strong desire for retaliation in killing the great serpent by entering its body from the vulnerable rear. This impression increases the archaic appearance of the dream.

Almost all primitive tribes have legends that show a strong similarity to the journey of Jonah in the belly of the whale. The legends concern a hero who is swallowed by a fish, dragon or sea serpent and travels in its belly from East to West.° On reaching the Western shore, the hero kills the monster from inside and emerges victoriously, re-born, basking in the glory of immortal life.

Let us see how the dream of the post office clerk fits the pattern of the hero's rebirth. There are several small lions in a tank. The number may stand for emphasis by multiplication. When we say: I told you a thousand times, we mean a number of times; the figure only serves to stress the importance we attach to our statement. The lion is the strongest animal, a king of beasts, a fitting symbol for a hero. Brave men are lion-hearted and a young soldier, as the dreamer was, may conceivably be represented by a miniature lion. He is swallowed by the monster fish and travels from the lion's cage (the tank) into the adjoining greater tank in which the larger part of the

---

° "The heroes always resemble the wandering sun, which seems to justify the fact that the myth of the hero is a sun myth. But the myth of the hero, however, is, as it appears to me, the myth of our own suffering unconscious, which has an unquenchable longing for all the deepest sources of our own being; for the body of the mother, and through it for communion with infinite life in the countless forms of existence." C. G. Jung, *Psychology of the Unconscious*, Dodd Mead & Co., New York, 1946, p. 231.

serpent reposes. The hole through which the two tanks are connected suggests the uterus and permits us to assume that in being swallowed by the mythological resurrection animal, the hero passes from a smaller into a larger life. The monster is asleep, easy to kill; but sleep is also the intermediate state between life and death. We go to sleep at night and wake up the following day feeling new. Therefore, the very sleep of the monster is suggestive of the fetal night and heralds in a coming life. The hero kills the monster from within with his sword, which is a phallic symbol. So is a fish, a living sword for the purposes of the dream. It enters from the rear which is the past and therefore equates with East. It travels toward the head which equates with the West. The hero's legendary journey is from East to West and it is completed when he emerges on the Western shore. We do not hear further of the lions, but it is self-evident that the "sword-fish" is alive and is capable of emergence. The personification of the hero's sword was a common practice in the days of chivalry. The nobles of the land were expected to furnish so many swords to the king, meaning warriors. We may assume that the dream mind had no more use for the lions once the act of swallowing had been accomplished and the momentous under-water journey had begun. Hence a mechanism of adaptation comes into play and the land animal is transformed into an aquatic creature of the same size, stealth and courage. In birth we see the same adaptation reversed. The fetus, in a way, is an aquatic creature and emerges unto land after an ordeal which has some parallelism to the killing of the monster fish. From the point-of-view of the dream mind, the killing is the important element for once it is done the hero can no more be harmed. Hence the death of the monster is journey's end. It completes the drama of re-birth.

Jonah and the Whale

Escape from an unbearable past is sometimes the fundamental motive behind the re-birth fantasy. The following case expresses the thought: I wish I were born again, so that the past could not trouble me and I were completely free. It is also valuable because it encourages the view that the fantasy of return is a manifestation of a life instinct which no adversities, however inconceivable, can destroy.

The dream life of the twenty-five-year-old girl of this case was not too abundant but her powers of fantasy were phenomenal. In her 48th session she spoke of a dream in which she was in prison, but which she was unable to recall in detail. I asked her to relax, close her eyes and describe any pictures that might float into her mind. I have already pointed out that she was very voluble. True to form, a torrent of words broke from her lips and I had to make considerable effort to follow her in shorthand.

I am thinking of Jonah and the whale. I can see this big whale and a man is walking inside it. In other words, the man is alive, yet he is eaten. He ought to be dead, yet he is not, just trapped in there. He is trying to get out. There is no way out, except through the mouth of the whale. He cannot decide; he thinks of trying to go out at the back. The whale is so big that the back and front look like entrances to caves. Now he seems to be climbing out the back. There is a swinging ladder under the tail, and he is climbing down; but the whale is not in the water, it is in the air, and there is no place for him to step to, just space, so he climbs back into the whale.

Now he is sitting in the mouth of the whale, and the whale is so big that its teeth are like a front porch. He can see over the tops of the skyscrapers and aeroplanes that go by. Now an aeroplane is coming by, and he climbs from the whale's mouth onto the wing of the aeroplane. He knows that he will be safe because there is a motor in the aeroplane, while staying in the whale he would fall out and get killed.

Now the aeroplane lands and the man who gets out turns into my oldest brother John. I seem to be meeting him in the field. I am telling him I am in prison. He says he had come to get me out. Now we are driving in a big black car to some place. My brother and I are handcuffed together. I suddenly see the whale crashing down from the sky on top of a lot of houses, destroying everything. Now both John and myself are put into separate prison cells and the doors are locked on us.

To Find a New Life by Rebirth

I can see lots of people swimming away from a large ocean liner, and they all jumped off this liner. I am in the water, too. I have nothing on. I can see about ten little babies in long baby dresses in the water; they are all drowning. I can see them under the water. Now it is my oldest, my youngest brother and myself that are in baby clothes and we are all drowning in the water.

Now there is a very steep hill. It is in a city. There is a house on top but you cannot get up to it because the steep hill is of ice. It shines like glass. You can't get there even with a ladder. Which reminds me of a fairy tale about a hill of glass and somebody climbing up to win the King's daughter. A castle on top of a mountain of glass.

Now the ice is melted, and it is all slush, but the hill is still too steep to climb. People seem to be throwing a rope up like mountain climbers with stakes. They are climbing. Now I keep seeing No. 6. It seems to be written over the door of the house when we finally get to it.

Now I can see myself about the age of six. I am in the attic of the house. . . . Oh, my heavens. . . . I cannot tell you. It is awful. Why do I see such awful things? Oh, that's terrible. . . . My older brother seems to be in a kind of sailor suit. He seems to be about 8 and he is "going to the bathroom" on the attic floor. Now I can see on the floor this long thing, and he says that's his penis: No. 2. I had one when I did the same thing, but I wondered why do we lose it?

Now my grandmother is in the door of the attic. She looks tremendously large, she also seems to have red hair and I think she is going to attack me, spank me.

Now I can see a woman holding me. I seem to be about a month old. She is standing at the window, holding me and the wooden parts of the window form a cross. The baby that's me is trying to get away from this woman. She seems to be nursing me. I am kicking her stomach to get away. She is pressing me on the back of the head, pushing me to nurse and I am kicking her in the stomach.

Now I can see a big black spider on the ceiling of the room and I think of the arms of the spider as mother's arms. They suffocate.

Now I can see my father in uniform, coming up the stairs. He seems to have a policeman's club in his hand and he is smashing the baby with this club, beating it on the back of the head. He is also beating my mother with the club and she seems to be fighting him off.

I can see lots of underwater things now. All kinds of flowers, weeds and lily pads and one tremendous green flower. I am lying in the middle of that green flower, clinging to it, a little baby, about a week old, with nothing on. I am trying to hold on to it with my hands but I am afraid I shall fall off. Finally, I do fall into the water. Now I can see all kind of line-ups to attack this baby that's me. All kinds of fish and animals are rushing at this baby. Human beings, children and adults seem to be attacking this child; it is gasping, trying to keep its head above water and to get away from these people, but they seem to be circling all around.

Now I can see a snow hill with angels on top, and this little baby is running up the hill with nothing on but a little white sweater. It is a week old and is trying to get to the angels. Now it is up to the top and sees that the angels are only made of sugar, like those things that grandmother used to put on the cake.

Now I can see a man on a white road up in the sky, the child's idea of God, a man with a white beard, and the baby is trying to run to this man. Now the baby has wings on its back and is dressed. It is old now. It seems to be five or six years old and is in a sleeping garment with feet. It is flying in the sky, trying to get up to this God and now He has the Golden Book and has my name in it, with a question mark. The question mark refers to the future. The child is standing in front of the man, who is shaking his head, says no, and points back to the earth. The child is crying bitterly and starts flying back towards the earth. It is very peaceful in the sky but on the earth I can see volcanoes, earthquakes and tornadoes, people with hatchets like grandmother, all waiting for me, my mother half dressed looking drunk, my father with a tremendous penis, my stepfather looking very important but very stern and holding some kind of paddle, my two brothers with a train that they used to put in my hair where it would unwind and it would have to be cut out. They are all below waiting for me. I still look about six years old and keep on flying down because this God said I have to go back and I see this terrible thing waiting for me on earth. The only way of escape is the ocean, but I can see sharks there, so there is no escape. Now I am back on earth and these people are killing me. I am dying and the circles I used to see in my childhood nightmares are beginning to whirl and they are closing in on me. I lose consciousness. They are killing me.

I have quoted this extraordinary flow of fantasy in full because of its central motive: the wish for complete change of personality by re-birth holds the "dreamer" as fast, in spite of the skips and jumps of the narrative, as if she were held on a leash. The material is not a dream in the strict sense of the word, but it is better than an artificial dream, composed as it was at the request of the analyst in the waking state during the analytic session, as no attempt is made at impersonality and the patient is quite conscious of the emotional value of the material which she pours forth.

The impetus for the direction of the fantasy was given by the unremembered dream about being in jail. The patient was well able to interpret the meaning of this. Her stepfather used to act like the head of a penitentiary and they called him the warden. Just before her mother divorced him, he took an apartment in Ossining, near the penitentiary. The patient and her brothers used to joke, when they had to make a call, that they were going to visit the warden in the penitentiary.

The jail could thus well symbolize the confining effect of the home situation on the patient's personality. Indeed, this situation was so extraordinary that the wonder of it was that she succeeded in keeping her sanity. Her younger brother failed to bear up under the pressure, became demented, and was confined in a mental home. Her mother herself had to be institutionalized as a chronic alcoholic and sex pervert. Before, she lived openly with a notorious lesbian in her own home and was base enough to make occasional amorous approaches to her own daughter. John, the older brother, succeeded in breaking away from home as a youngster, earned his own living and settled down in marriage to a normal life. Because he had the courage to run away and stand on his own, he qualified for the patient as a hero ideal. She would have liked to do the same and she would have liked to be a man. As a man she could have been saved the agonies of feminine inferiority which was imputed by parental stupidity in much too open preference of the younger child for being a boy. The scene in the attic plainly reveals the "castration trauma" from which she suffered for reason of her birth. Fecal penis fantasies only served to make her more conscious of the anatomic loss. As she was made that way in her mother's womb, the only chance of undoing this grievous injustice lay in returning to the womb, in the hope that she would be made into a boy like John.

It is for this reason she puts herself, in the guise of John, into the belly of the whale. John was her hero and hence a *John* (an anagram on Jonah) goes through the ordeal of the hero's re-birth. All the traditional elements are present in the fantasy. The hero is swallowed by the monster which floats, instead of on the waters of the deep, in an ocean of air—itself a hint of sublimation. It is asleep, or apparently lifeless. The hero escapes and the monster dies. The aeroplane, to the archaic mind, is a perfect replica of the winged phallus. It is also a symbol of aspiration and emotional flight. By climbing on the wing of the aeroplane, the patient shows the wish fantasy to be re-born in the possession of a male organ. Once she emerges as a male, she has gained her new life and the whale can die. It is not even necessary for the aeroplane to rip the whale's body like a sword and it is probable that the death of the monster conceals more than an equation between birth and death, that similarly to the savage practice of eating the slain lion's heart to become imbued with the lion's courage, the whale dies because all its life has been transferred into the new-born.

The junction between the patient and John is not yet established. Hence the whale only crashes after they meet. The meeting shows the union of the male and the female, the repair of the injustice of birth. They are handcuffed together in a big black car and are heading towards the prison which instead of the womb of a new life, turns out to be the parental penitentiary. Being put in separate cells is the doleful recognition of the failure of the re-birth fantasy. The freedom for which the patient yearned cannot be accomplished by such fantasy means. Hence the attempt is given up and the patient is swept away by waves of self-pity in a succession of masochistic pictures which reveal remarkable glimpses of her home life and personality.

The hill of ice reveals that she is a frigid woman, or rather was. She could not reach a peak, she could not culminate because she failed to understand the inner protest against playing the feminine rôle. She did not want to be the King's daughter, but the King's son. The woman whom she kicks in the stomach is her mother. Her milk was bad and the patient had to be weaned too soon after birth. So she is a spider dispensing death instead of life. The grandmother, the father, the whole world is hostile, not a fit place for a child to live in, so she pleads with God to permit her to return to the place whence she came.

This is the most pathetic part of this extraordinary fantasy, and we cannot understand it without a deeper knowledge of the psychology of love starvation in the new-born child. I believe that the degree of love which the new-born child needs is in direct proportion to the intensity of the trauma of its birth. This particular patient happened to have an awful time of it. She was an unwanted child and was made aware of it too soon. Her mother neglected her completely and her care was entrusted to a grandmother hard as reinforced concrete. She was given no chance to recover from the shattering effects of the ordeal of birth. There was nobody to reassure her that all was well, that she was safe and that she was good. Not being loved by others, she failed to learn to love herself. Her ego feelings were at the lowest ebb when she came to analysis and she was haunted by the fear that she might commit suicide or go insane.

The fantasy shows that her life must have been exceedingly bitter after birth and between five and six years of age. She was deserted by men and God. A cruel fate compelled her to suffer the worst agonies of body and soul. She bows to her fate in a true Christian spirit. There is no sign of *Thanatos*, the death instinct, in the general acceptance of the term. She wants to live and not to die. Her meekness strangely parallels the passion of Jesus on the cross. At one moment the cry breaks from her lips: My God, my God, why hast Thou forsaken me? And the next moment she humbly repeats: Nevertheless, not my will, but Thy will be done.

23.

THE idea of re-entering the mother's body is frequently accompanied by sexual fantasies. This should cause no surprise, as birth cannot be divorced from its genital setting. In pictorial perception, birth is an incestuous event for men and a homosexual event for women, as the body of the infant is in a phallic relationship to the mother's genitalia. The re-enactment of birth by return can easily stir up repressed sexual ideas. Essentially, these ideas revolve around the mystery of sexual ecstasy. What is it and how can it be attained?

In infantile experience the answer is rarely found or remembered. Adult life, by reason of arrested emotional development or frigidity, may also fail to satisfy the early curiosity. In that case regression to the pre-natal state develops in the hope that the bliss of the unborn may reveal the precious secret of sexual ecstasy. The admixture of this motive mellows the nightmarish character of birth dreams. Fascination adulterates the fear and the return fantasy may become a mystic experience the effect of which may survive for a considerable time.

The following case has the unique feature that the monster of the deep refuses to swallow the candidate waiting for re-birth, that it has human and even god-like qualities and that it ignores the sensuous motives by which the dreamer is activated. The dreamer

243

is a widow, of scholarly attainments, and a student of Jungian psychology. She gave her dream the title "The Man-Lion," and this is how she worded it:

I dreamed that I was one of a group of eight people sitting on a platform, like a small grandstand, on the shores of a lake. It was a beautiful, large lake, surrounded by hills, and the time was just after sunset. Everything was perfectly still, and we sat in a kind of hypnotic trance waiting for something to happen. We knew in a vague way what it was and we were awestruck, but not frightened, and there was no thought of wanting to escape. We knew that some strange being, a sort of monster or god, lived there and would soon come to claim one of us as a victim.

While we waited, a great bird appeared in the sky, a sort of eagle, and made a great curving swoop down to the lake, diving beneath the water and emerging without having caught anything, diving again a second time and a third. The third time it emerged with a large fish in its beak. It carried the fish off into the sky and disappeared.

Then all was quiet again and we still waited. At last something appeared far down the lake, gliding on the surface of the water in graceful curves like a skater. At it drew nearer, we saw that it had the body of a man, dressed in a dark, one-piece garment, rather like a skating suit, the head of a great bushy lion, and webbed feet like a duck, which enabled it to glide on the surface of the water. It glided gracefully up to the platform and stopped. I suddenly wanted him very much to choose me for a victim, and he did. He held out his hand, and I took it and stepped down fearlessly on to the lake, and we glided off together, with our arms crossed like skaters.

It was a heavenly sensation gliding swiftly over the glassy surface of the lake and I was very happy. He said not a word, and we went on and on toward the far end of the lake. There he stopped, and embraced me, kissing me long and beautifully. I thought, "How funny, to be kissed by a big, furry lion," but it was rather nice, quite soft and warm. I thought, "Now he will eat me," but I was not afraid. Then he released me, and said in a quite matter-of-fact way, "I'd better be taking you back to your friends; they may be worried about you." I felt a sudden sense of a let-down and disappointment. Evidently I was not going to be eaten—or anything. We glided back in the deepening twilight without a word, and a great sense of joy and peace came over me. When we reached the platform, he helped me back silently, bowed gracefully like a dancer returning his partner to her place, and disappeared in the darkness.

Then I woke up, and lay for a long time in a sort of blissful trance, at peace with the universe. I felt that something wonderful had happened to me, which would somehow make life quite different, but I could not tell at all what it was. I just knew that everything would be all right.

A truly wonderful dream! The clue to its understanding was furnished by the patient's comment immediately after relating it. She had been analyzed by a Jungian, who searched restlessly for a father fixation, but found no trace of it. As a result, the dreamer concluded that she did not have one. Then something happened in England during a seminar of Jung's, who was visiting there. She heard him pronounce the word "development" with an emphasis on the first syllable. At that instant she uttered an exclamation of surprise. The memory of her grandfather came surging back. He used to pronounce that word in the same way. He died when she was six years old. That night a dream came to her in which she was on a bed with her grandfather in a tight embrace. Her grandmother came in and she thought of her as a nuisance, then consoled herself, "Well, she won't live long and then I can have my grandfather all to myself."

The dream reveals a grandfather fixation and the existence of death wishes against the grandmother. She accepted its evidence and inferred that the guilt feeling so incurred was responsible for the repression of her erotic memories about her grandfather. That, no doubt, was a true diagnosis. The repressed libido was not allowed to move forward. Moreover, the culmination towards which it could have moved was unattainable because of her age. Regressively, in the blissful memories of the uterine state, fulfilment might await her. Accordingly, in the man-lion dream, we see her in pursuit of a double objective: the recapture of fetal bliss and the finding of ecstasy.

The man-lion is a curious combination of the mythological dragon, to which virgins were offered as a tribute at stated periods, and of the monster of the hero's re-birth. The incestuous content of the dragon and virgin myth has been established by the researches of Dr. Otto Rank. The dragon is the father, and the weeping virgin is torn between desire and fear. The latter aspect stands out more clearly if we enlarge the concept of the dragon and consider it the fusion of both parental images. It is the mother who thwarts the incestuous aspirations of the girl child, and death wishes directed against her naturally result in the talionic fear of being swallowed or otherwise destroyed. Hence the dragon represents both the attainment of an emotional goal and the penalty for it, which is death.

Yet the eagle, which is a variation of the devouring monster, takes the fish heavenward. If we think of the fish as a representation of the child in the amniotic waters, the eagle's act may symbolize the merging of birth, death and resurrection. The lion is a pagan resurrection symbol and it also represents royal power. On an ancient Egyptian wall relief, Osiris is raised from the dead by the extended paw of a lion. In the dream, the man-lion appears in the twilight. If it swallowed the dreamer, the sun would set on her earthly life. But the setting sun is egg-shaped, it does not really set, it rises for another hemisphere and is re-born for our own in the morning. It becomes the flame of a flame, a new sun. The setting sun being swallowed by the womb of night fits the drama of uterine return and the drama of resurrection by re-birth.

The Christian element is supplied by the gliding over the water and by the plucking of the fish out of the lake. In Christianity, the fish is the sign of Jesus and the symbol of redemption. In mediaeval architecture we see the idea well preserved in the Vesica Piscis of the cathedral builders. It consists of two intersecting circles, concealing the shape of a fish, in the oval body of which the head of Jesus appears. But the dreamer uses the images of uterine resurrection for an ulterior purpose. She does not look for salvation through the water and the spirit; she is in search of sexual ecstasy. The lesson of the dream is driven home when the man-lion sends her back to life as if saying: there is no salvation through the uterus; it is not there that you should look for the riddle of life; it is not there that you should look for ecstasy. Nature decreed that the chasm between the pre-natal and post-natal life should not be bridged for the latter purpose.

The next case is the tragic history of a woman who thought she had known perfect love in marriage, but not ecstasy; who at the age of fifty-five did not what know what physical orgasm means; who lost her husband and her child because she fastened herself on them as an orchid fastens itself on a tree—until her husband broke away from her suffocating love and the son committed suicide; whose love was as possessive and all-inclusive as the love of the fetus must be for the maternal organism; whose ideals of perfection were formed by the unattainable ideals of the pre-natal state; whose consuming passion was a desire to regain this lost paradise through father, husband and lover; who hated her mother and replaced her image with the father's to such an extent that she dreamed of creeping into her father's body and living in it like a fetus or a sperm.

Love ecstasy, to this woman, was a tenderness reaction, a vision of gold-rimmed clouds and a sensation of deep contentment. She wanted a gentle embrace and sleep in her lover's arms. Physical love was only a means for the possession of a "living hot water bottle," her ideal of comfort and security. If something rendered her restless, she ate like a wolf. A man can resist incorporation, but food cannot. There is a cannibalistic element in love and never was a woman more conscious of it than this one. "I would love to be incorporated myself," she confessed. "I used to say to my husband, "I wish I could creep over your breasts and crawl inside. I would know all your thoughts; nothing would be kept secret from me!"

Too late, the patient recognized how terrible and monstrous her love aspirations were.

"I wanted to be everything to him. I was so immoral that I did not care if the whole world went to pieces as long as I had him. I feared that I might wish my father's death, so that I could give my inheritance to him. I wanted to give him everything in the world and be everything to him. If he looked at a cat and played with it, I was so insane I could almost imagine it was a woman. If his hand was around a pen, I wished I were the pen. If he looked at a sunset, I wished I were the sunset. I wanted to fill every need of his, so that he could not have anything else but me."

After their son's suicide, they adopted two boys.

"One of them was called Joseph. I loved him insanely as a substitute for John, my dead boy. Yet I used to have a terrible fantasy that I might drop him out of the front window."

The death wish against her father resulted in a strange fantasy. She refused to believe that he was dead. She would not touch the money which she had inherited. She fancied that her father would come back and would need it. Yet she was perfectly well aware that this strange hallucination had no foundation in fact, as she was present at her father's funeral. Inspired, no doubt, by her death wish guilt, she prayed, "Give me your spirit, Father, let the family have everything else." Then it seemed that her father rose over her like the Colossus of Rhodes and out of his flaccid penis poured a misty fluid which completely enveloped her. She interpreted the dream to mean that her prayer was answered; that her father would give her his spirit.

The fantasy shows much more than incestuous attachment to the father. To a small child, a grown-up man is a Colossus. Being enveloped by the misty fluid corresponds to her fantasy of creeping inside her husband. It is as if she wanted to be a seed within her father as she was before she had been conceived.

She had large breasts, and hated them. She had feet like her mother's and she could not bear to be reminded of them. She was short like her mother and her face was like her mother's. People told her of these resemblances, which annoyed her exceedingly. Her mother had spread herself over her body as she had spread herself over the people she loved. The womb is a place of re-birth. If she could creep into her father's "womb," she could be re-born into the shape of the father's body.

After her father's death, she was overwhelmed by guilt. The fantasy that the father was still alive was due to the desire to annul her death wishes. She could no longer creep into him and had to find a substitute. She chose Paul, her lover, but he became frightened of her possessive emotions and would again and again rudely rebuff her.

"Lying awake at night, I asked myself, 'Why do I yearn for this tenderness?' I thought of my mother and I thought of God. The Catholic writers picture God as a lover. Then something was drawing me up very tenderly, but I knew it was just an idea, not reality. I began to query, 'Why do I connect the sexual act with this tenderness? My experience should have taught me that it is not always there. Why is it of such importance to me when theoretically it is not important?' It occurred to me that the sexual act answered the demand for reality, the contact was a fact that could not be questioned and it made me feel more secure."

She was a great collector of bags and always refused to part with boxes. To her unconscious mind they stood for the womb to which she desired to remain attached. She liked confined spaces, particularly her own apartment, where she was haunted by a perfection complex. Everything had to be tip-top.

After her mother's death she dreamed that she was in a grotto with Paul. Through green arches she could see the river, and happy children and boats floating by. She was trying to lie very close to him and show him how beautiful everything was. She had a feeling of erotic excitement. Then suddenly he jumped up and left her. Her mother was dead; now she could creep back into Paul, the substitute father, without guilt, but Paul would have none of it. She rebelled, threw tantrums and made herself sick.

She dreamed again that she was talking to him about a letter. Then she went out into the street, where she saw a square wagon looking like a box. In narrating the dream, the box reminded her of the mail carriages they use in England. She entered the carriage to search for something. The door closed behind her and she found that this great big box, with a skylight on top and no window, was moving; looking up, she saw the clouds passing by.

Here the mail box (which is consonant with male box) is Paul's "womb." The skylight points to Heaven as a place of bliss. The movement is suggestive of the movement of the mother's body with the child within.

The first shift in this destructive fantasy life was indicated in the 132nd session by the following dream:

I was in a castle. It had high walls and lofty rooms, which were freshly painted. I thought my father and my mother had painted it, though the people in the dream did not look like my parents. The thought struck me: "The wallpaper changes the whole character of the castle. If we get our furniture in, it might look well." Then I went out of the castle with a girl down a road that reminded me of the highly built road on the Italian Riviera. I stopped to look at some tiny, fresh-looking baskets that I would have liked to have. Then I said, "It is just like me, I always want to buy these things." This time I did not buy, and told the girl I would like to show her my room in the castle. It seemed to be in the other wing, not where the painting and papering had been done, and it was kept more in the original style. Then I was back in this room. I saw big, turret-like apertures for windows and on looking out I saw the most heavenly landscape.

The castle suggested to her the Castle of Chillon where Byron was incarcerated. She had spent her "second" honeymoon (after a reconciliation with her husband) on the Riviera. It promised a regeneration of her happiness. In the dream she shows regeneration in terms of ante-natal integration. She is breaking with the past by refusing to buy new baskets. The Castle is being modernized and her old room looks like a fortress promising the same enchantment by the heavenly landscape (a symbol of pre-natal feeling) which it exercised over all her life.

The next development came after a visit to her brother. He had in his hallway a portrait of the patient's father. She looked at it very critically and wondered that anybody else looking at his face should like him as much as she used to. The picture was much less flattering than the face that lived in her memory. The lips were thin, the eyes sharp and it did not show a warmth of personality. It struck her that she always liked men with thin mouths, and that they were always cruel to her. She began to wonder if her father could have been cruel. The eyes did not look as kind as they lived in her memory.

That night she dreamed of seeing a person who she thought was her father becoming very little and shrinking. Her mother was somewhere in the background and she felt grieved in looking at her father.

The shrinking of the father image was an excellent indication that the spell in which her father had been holding her was at last breaking. The final dream that showed a complete reversal of the original unconscious attitude came a few weeks later in the form of a nightmare:

I dreamed that the telephone rang. A man's voice said something. It was not Paul's. I became terribly frightened that someone was in the house. I forced myself to get up and go through the rooms. Then I was spirited away somewhere, I don't know how. Somebody was carrying me. I had the feeling that something bad was going to be done to me, almost as if I was to be buried alive. I thought if I pretended to be dead perhaps I could escape. A lot of hiding and escaping took place and I was not always myself. Sometimes I was a little boy. I know I was scared and woke up, finding the room terribly hot and a lot of gas on my stomach.

The atmospheric pressure that night was exceptionally low. The patient said she was very sensitive to low atmospheric pressure as it produced a feeling of breathlessness. It is thus possible that the barometer had something to do with the nightmare of being buried alive.

When she denies that the voice was Paul's, she states a negative. There is no negative in dreams.* The voice stands for Paul's. It was

---

* Nandor Fodor, "The Negative in Dreams," *The Psychoanalytic Quarterly*, Vol. XIV, 1945, pp. 516-527.

unrecognizable because, against her amorous inclinations, it warned her of danger in the house. It was not easy to admit, even in a dream, that her love was destructive. The spiriting away and the burial alive suggest the devouring mother fantasy. It is enacted by the reverse. In the first part of the dream, a man is in her house; in the second part, she is in a man's body (spirited into it as one is spirited into the mother's womb). Whereas before the fantasy was pleasant, now it fills her with fear. She discovered something vulture-like about Paul, that he completely possessed her, almost in the way one possesses food without any feeling of responsibility and desire to give anything in return. She began to realize that the book which she was translating for him was a kind of psychic substitute for his body. She crept into it with all her creative gifts; she made the life of the hero her own. At last she was ready to turn away from him; at last she saw that all her life was spent in a world of illusion, that she played the part of the fetus in the womb of the world. Too late and with too much heartache; but she was getting ready to become the twice-born and cut the psychic umbilical tie that bound her to the pre-natal life.

24.

TO ROB THE MOTHER'S WOMB

ALL CHILDREN are afraid of losing their mother's love. It is their most precious possession, which they do not willingly share with another child. It is true that the prospect of a baby brother or sister arouses their curiosity and that they are often beguiled by the idea of gaining a playmate, but when they discover the sacrifices which a competitor imposes upon them, resentment and increasing hostility to further additions to the family will manifest themselves. Verbal or physical means of protest they have little or none, but the savage emotions that ruled the human race when it was young may well up in unsuspected abundance from the archaic levels of their minds. When we attempt to verbalize such emotions from the dreams of adults, we find ourselves confronted with this melodramatic representation: a small child re-enters its mother's womb for the purpose of destroying a sibling in order to eliminate a threat to its own security.

If this is a mere retrojection of emotions, there is no need to argue that only exceptionally do young children know enough of the facts of life to conceive of such hideous fantasies. The real query is why should such emotions be retrojected to the mother-body level? Is it because the dramatization satisfies the punitive designs of conscience or does it serve a therapeutic aim?

Let us first dispose of the hypothetical objection that children are ignorant or incapable of monstrous thoughts. The intellect of a child

253

develops much later than its emotions. The seat of the intellect is in the conscious mind. The seat of the emotions, for want of better localization, is in the unconscious, in the nightside of our life, from which primitive, racial instincts wage constant battle against social restraints. We feel a great deal more than finds expression in words or deeds, and we should feel horrified to see it so expressed. It seems that, whether we have expressed them or just felt them, intense emotions leave a definite pattern on our mind. Moral standards only arise at a later stage. To a new-born baby our concept of murder is alien, but leave that child hungry and in discomfort and its behavior will spell blue murder as eloquently as if verbal means had been put at its disposal. Nor are we grown-ups as far removed from this level as we pride ourselves on being. What is swearing if not wishing murder and sudden destruction on the heads of those who frustrate us in the attainment of our inmost desires? Only, being civilized, we know that words are just words and not deeds. Children do not know the difference between fantasy and reality, between feelings and deeds. Many of their fantasies are more real than actual experiences could be. They are angelic as long as they get what they want. When they don't get it, they are as savage and cruel at heart as any primitive man of the jungle could be. If they could, they would often murder those who resist them without the slightest compunction.

The objection that young children do not know the facts of life and therefore cannot conceive of entering their mother's body could also be disputed. We judge knowledge by what we consciously acquire and think of instinct as something haphazard, a guess that happens to come off, a very unreliable means of cognition. We don't like to admit the existence of instinctual awareness because the Board of Education has a monopoly over knowledge. Yet, while the majority of human beings have little knowledge of anatomy, the unconscious mind of each of us is in complete possession of all the data that concerns his body. How otherwise could the human machine be run to such perfection? Or how could it have been built without an organismic awareness of the part which the least component is destined to play? The more we learn consciously, the farther we seem to become removed from unconscious organismic awareness. The child lives more in its unconscious than adults. It has little knowledge of the facts of life as far as education and experience can impart them; yet it is aware of the shelter it had within the maternal body and of a passage that leads back to it, if dreams have any meaning at all.

It may also be argued that fantasies of fetal destruction are too absurd to have any significance. The answer is that we would not know about them if they had no significance. As long as we can discover the existence of such fantasies in the dreams of adults, they are psychological material of considerable value that, at the least, illustrate the mechanism of retrojection.

The most propitious period for the aggressive emotions that blossom out into fetal destruction fantasies is between the ages of two and five. The lack of conceptual formulation, together with the fear of the strong parent, help to bring about an almost instantaneous repression. As a result, these inchoate emotions remain locked up on the unconscious levels, where archaic mental deposits may add a racial quota to the later development of guilt. Judged by the dreams they inspire, the pressure of such fantasies is intense enough to provide a hotbed for neurosis or even psychosis.

Sometimes these destructive fantasies emerge explosively; at others they manifest themselves reluctantly and in a veiled form, according to neurotic character and strength of repression.

Way of an Epileptic

Very slow emergence is shown in the following story of a forty-eight-year-old man who lived with his widowed mother of seventy-five. Between a domineering mother and a brutal father he was completely crushed. Up to the time of his father's death, which occurred when he was thirteen, he slept in his parents' bedroom. After his father's death, his mother kept him in her own bed for a year. He suffered from epileptoid fits at moments of intense sexual excitement. His face would become contorted, he would utter a cry and lose consciousness for a split second. His life was mostly lived in fantasy. His parents brought him to America when he was two years old. He remembered nothing of his country of origin, yet he constantly yearned for the old country. Unknown to him, it stood for the pre-natal land of perfection. Into his childhood he could not escape, as it was too unhappy; so he escaped beyond it. It took him a long time to realize the nature of his nostalgia. In his sixtieth session, he stated spontaneously:

"When I was a child I used to stand at the docks near the river. I suppose the river always has an effect on a child. Things can be swallowed by it. It must have had an effect on me. Boys were diving and one of them dived far out. He stayed under for a long time and when I saw bubbles coming up, I was afraid he was drowned. I imagined that I was in his position, that something similar was happening to me. I am not sure what it was. I never learned to swim or to dive. Looking down from a bridge, I get a dizzy, nauseated feeling. I suppose there is something more in it than the height. I saw a notice in the newspapers about a woman who dived from a ship into the sea. There was no apparent reason. Some strange impulse made her do it. Do you think one wants to combine with Nature, with Earth or Water, to become one?"

The yearning for the pre-natal situation and the fear inspired by the trauma of birth are clearly recognizable in this confession. I explained both and he accepted the explanation. His dream life almost immediately showed a dynamic shift. He was a druggist by profession and in many of his dreams the drugstore stood for his personality in the same way as the house in which we live.

Now he dreamed that he was entering a drugstore on Canal Street. It was big and old-fashioned, with arched ceilings, and looked more like a laboratory than a drugstore. It was for sale. His mother was there, appearing and disappearing like a ghost, and in the street he had passed Uncle Joe, his mother's brother, who used to live on Canal Street and in the dream looked very much younger than he did in reality.

The dream mind often substitutes uncles for fathers. Canal Street was Uncle Joe's street. We like to speak in a proprietary way of the street on which we live. The canal which was his father's street (represented by Uncle Joe) is the vaginal passage of his mother. The womb is both a drugstore (a place of healing for all ills) and a laboratory (of life). The arch symbol is almost invariably present in the description of the pre-natal habitat. This habitat is now for sale. The mother's appearance and disappearance like a ghost is a subtle reference to two planes of existence. His father is only encountered in the street, outside. Inside, on the pre-natal level of existence, the father is an unknown quantity. The sale of the drugstore means that the patient is beginning to move towards reality. The size of the place suggested to him a big pharmaceutical store uptown. The movement, judging by this association, takes place in an uptown direction, towards adult existence.

A few days later he dreamed of large gun carriages, without guns, rolling fast down a slope towards the sea. Darkness was coming and the sea was flowing in. He turned back to avoid the water.

In this dream the absence of guns from the gun carriages suggested an easing of the conflict over the ante-natal situation. Battles cannot be fought without guns. The gun carriages were rolling down a slope towards the sea, i.e., the waters of life, the mother. The sea was coming in and he avoided it. It seemed that the dream indicated an important adjustment, as if the patient had decided to turn his back on desires of fetal return.

Yet, at the same time, the gun carriages suggested the presence of a hitherto undiscovered aggressive pressure in the patient's unconscious mind. During the same night, in another dream, he saw three chickens in a hencoop on the bar. He identified one with himself, the other with a girl friend and the third one with his mother. The third chicken looked very severely at the other two chickens, but they returned the look with complacency. As he thought that the severe look stood for reproof, the absence of disturbed reactions indicated that the sexual element in the mother situation was not as upsetting as it used to be. It remained to be seen why he should choose chickens to describe his new emotional situation. He suggested that his mother had "cooped him up"; in that case, with all his complacency, he was still in the coop and the reason for it was hidden behind the look of reproof.

The story broke in a subsequent dream. He was walking along a country road, looking for a restaurant, and found one in a private house. He was depressed and uneasy. He ordered scrambled eggs and then saw the face of an English woman, with a fresh complexion, flash by. He remembered no more.

In giving his associations, he mentioned that he never ate eggs in restaurants as he suspected their freshness. The country road looked like the road to Seagate, an exclusive community, and the English woman somehow suggested the home atmosphere he was missing.

England as an island country beyond the seas very frequently appears in the dreams of Americans as a symbol of the fetus floating like an island in the amniotic fluid. The home atmosphere he was missing seemed to hint at the patient's longing for the pre-natal home. The English woman, therefore, was his mother, and Seagate, meaning an entrance to the sea, pointed to the privacy of the uterus. Restaurant is another fitting reference, as the child in the womb is in a kind of private restaurant.

The significance of the hencoop dream now begins to emerge. If the mother was a hen, the eggs must refer to her eggs (ova), and as they are scrambled, the destruction of their life-bearing quality is indicated. In view of the fact that the patient's mother had given birth to another boy when the patient was two years old, the indication is that the patient had strong aggressive fantasies against this coming competitor and wanted to destroy it before birth; by eating scrambled eggs, he represented himself as a cannibal who devoured his own brother. Eggs that were not fresh had a history, so he became suspicious of them; he did not know that the history was of family concern.

Confirmation of this interpretation came in a later dream in which he saw a boy sitting at a table eating meat. He did the same, but at a different table, and felt sorry afterwards for having tasted it; for the boy was cutting out ovaries from the meat, and he woke up with a strong feeling of nausea.

In this dream he was apparently intent on dissociating himself from the boy criminal he felt himself to be. As in the epileptic syndrome repressed criminal instincts play considerable part, the query naturally arises whether fetus destruction fantasies may not contribute to the etiology of epilepsy. So far psychoanalytic claims have stopped short at pointing out the similarity between epileptic convulsions and labor in birth, and deduced that the fit represents an escape back into the womb from a criminal instinct. The present case suggests that the fit simply dramatizes the guilt which was generated by a fantasied attack against the mother's womb and that its purpose is not so much an escape as a punishment, a form of self-destruction by re-enactment of the trauma of birth.

Through the Anal Door

Another case shows a similarly veiled, yet more easily recognizable symbolism of fetal aggression. In the course of association the dreamer himself discovered the meaning of the symbols. The dream was:

In the desert somebody was raking up the wet mud of a dried-out spring and, with his hand, dug a deep hole which turned at an angle at the bottom. As if from a hiding place, he dragged out of this underground passage a pair of socks which belonged to my sister and some articles of clothing. This seemed to prove that the man was a thief. These were articles which he had stolen some time ago. Now he was bringing up the hidden loot. At this stage there was a feeling of identity between myself and the thief.

The wet mud in the dried-out spring reminded the dreamer of the film "Four Feathers," in which the hero of the story, disguised as a native, redeems a white feather—the stigma of cowardice—by acts of great daring. There was a scene in the film in which, almost dying from thirst, he was raking up the wet mud of what should have been a life-giving spring.

The angle at which the deep hole turned recalled to the dreamer a recent adventure in his landlady's bathroom. He threw into the toilet bowl a thick piece of cardboard, which went only half-way down and blocked the flusher. As a result, the bathroom was flooded. As he had just had an unpleasant talk with his landlady, he feared a scene, so he got down to the disagreeable task of removing the obstruction by rolling up his sleeves and diving for it with his hand. After some trouble, he succeeded in fishing out the obstruction and with that, to his relief, the water started flowing down. The angle which the thief's hand took in the dream was the same at which he had to bend his own to follow the curvature of the bowl. He was disgusted with the job because of its strong fecal associations.

Socks suggested a pun: sock's appeal—meaning sex appeal.

The picture which these associations formed in his mind was that the thieving of which his sister was a victim was of a sexual character. His sister was a serious threat to his infantile security. She was two years older, the only daughter in a chain of boys, and his mother's favorite. If another sister were to be added to the family, his own position would become hopeless. Actually, another girl came after him. The burglarious intent, he inferred, was directed against this coming sister. The toilet bowl, he thought, was the anal entrance to the womb, an inference drawn from the childish theory that babies are born through the rectum. By stealing his sister's socks (sex), he was defending himself against the birth of a baby sister, he was drying up his mother's fertility through the symbol of the spring in the desert; he was robbing his mother's body of the fetus, lest the coming child should turn out to be a girl.

The dreamer was two years old when this addition to the family occurred. He must have divined from carelessly dropped remarks that another child was expected and he remembered, from later years, his mother's statement that when she lost a girl child she would gladly have had another one the following day. This baby sister did die a few weeks, or months, after her birth. While her death removed the threat to his security, it must have increased the pressure of guilt. Unconsciously we believe in the omnipotence of thought. Death wishes always begin to weigh on our mind if the party at which they were directed happens to die. We feel as if we were responsible for the death. The Latin proverb: *de mortuis nihil nisi bene*—of the dead don't speak at all if you don't speak well—arises from the universal need to deny our evil intentions and thereby safeguard ourselves from remorse. The immature reasoning that the womb can be approached through the anus and the guilt feeling generated by the destructive fantasy did leave their impressions on the dreamer's character. While he could openly discourse on sexual problems, any discussion that concerned the anus elicited an unreasonable shyness and revulsion. There was evidence of a blind spot in his psychic development. His dreams showed a persistence of an infantile notion that the mother passed water through the anus. This identification between anus and vagina went so far that he never discovered the existence of an opening other than the anus in animals. At the same time he repressed all sexual ideas concerning the anus to such an extent that throughout a long period of association with a notorious homosexual who made a play for him, it never dawned on him that he meant "business" and was seriously suggesting anal intercourse. When, after the sudden death of this person, he accidentally found out about his homosexuality, he was almost petrified by the discovery and the implication of the many bantering talks which he had totally missed. Yet his dreams also showed a great deal of homosexual repression. The contradiction becomes intelligible on considering that, in the circumstances, a fancied anatomic similarity permitted an identification with the mother. Thus it was possible for him to translate on to his own body his incestuous desires. As the anus was already heavily associated with guilt, there had to develop a repression of unusual strength. To his good fortune, he never fell victim to an anal attack, or his repression might have failed, with disastrous consequences for his psychic health.

Flight from the Mother

This case is one of tremendous ramifications, productive of an abundance of neurotic symptoms and border-line psychosis. The dream occurred after 32 sessions and reads:

In the room where I used to sleep with Tom I saw ribs of beef fresh from the butcher, a whole rib cage. I dug into it and took out two little baby cows. They were very tiny, about two inches long, embryonic perhaps but ready to be born.

Then I was going along a dirt road. A woman with dark hair was going to have a baby. Two women were going to have two babies. We arrived at a farm house which looked like ours. It was time for the baby to be born. I told the farmer I would drive her to the doctor. The farmer was painting his car (a Chevrolet, I think) grey and black. He painted the windshield black. I offered to drive his wife in my car as I could not understand how he could drive with a black windshield.

Search for the Beloved

When we arrived at the doctor's, we found children there. I wanted to learn how to deliver babies. An older boy also wanted to learn. I saw a clothes line stretching quite a length. I grabbed hold of the pulley with both hands and he grabbed hold of another one behind me. We were supposed to lean with our whole weight on the pulley and bend our knees, so that we were hanging from the pulley alone and slowly slid forward and backward.

The baby was not born in the dream. I became confused and did not know whether I was the man with two wives or was myself merely. I recently saw a film, "The Fight for Life," in which a young doctor was learning to deliver babies under difficult conditions.

The dream leaves no doubt whatever that the two embryonic cows stand for children. The latter part of the dream contains ample explanatory references to childbirth. The purpose of the dream is also made clear when she wants to learn how to deliver babies. She did help the vet to deliver her Siamese kittens. The word "deliver," however, also means liberation. What she really wanted was release from a guilt situation concerning two unborn babies. The rib cage fresh from the butcher into which she digs clearly shows the nature of the guilt: destruction of the fetus within the body of the mother, of which the cow is an archaic symbol.

The two embryonic cows correspond to two boys, Tom and Bert, born after the patient, respectively two and seven years younger. The criminal fantasies which she had against them while they were on the way are well illustrated by the clothes line scene. The patient associated the clothes line with a Peter Pan act they had staged at home, which nearly ended with the strangling of Bert. With a boy behind her (which may mean something following her like a shadow) she is hanging from the clothes line, swinging back and forth, which indicates both a hanging fantasy and, by the drawn-up knees, the embryo's position and its relationship to the umbilical cord. One of the patient's governesses hanged herself when she was ten or eleven, but she did not remember whether she used the clothes line. This is the second association with death and clothes lines. The farmer's Chevrolet concealed another reference to criminal thoughts. The chauffeur of the patient's family had a Chevrolet. "He liked us tremendously; he delivered us from a lot of evil." The wording of the statement is significant. Both the farmer and the chauffeur (guide) are father symbols. The farmer blinds himself by painting the windshield black. He cannot be relied upon for help and the patient has to take matters into her own hands.

The father, indeed, counted very little in the patient's family. He was a naval man, spending but little time at home, weak and dependent on a very domineering and financially independent wife. All her life the patient felt a great need to develop her masculine side; hence her bitterness over the fact that she was a girl when her mother could have made her into a boy.

At the age of two, Bert nearly died from an attack of acidosis. For some time he was delirious. He recovered, but the attack must have mobilized the patient's buried destructive fantasies, for she developed a poison complex herself. At a Health Institute which she joined before her analysis, she regularly pumped out the food from her stomach after every meal with a stomach pump. She did this for a period of four months, also having an enema and a vaginal douche every morning. The radical treatment reduced her to skin and bones but did not deliver her from the fantasies of having poisoned her brother. In conformance with the *poena talionis*, she expected to go insane because Bert was out of his mind during his acidosis attack. Around the time when she decided to undergo psychoanalysis, she was beginning to hear distant mocking voices. They were the first heralds of insanity, but fortunately they could be suppressed before they became clear and intelligible.

Her unhappiness over her sexual situation and her uneasy conscience made her into a pathological liar and thief. All kleptomaniacs are love-thieves. They are trying to steal something that would compensate them for a very precious thing they have lost. This precious thing may be the mother's love, the maternal breast, the male organ, or the fetal kingdom. In her case it seemed to be a combination of all. She was hounded by her conscience, the fear of her mother and the fear of death throughout her life.

"I heard about the curse of the Pharaohs, that anybody who entered their tomb would die. I entered it in Egypt and thought I was going to die. Every night when I went to bed (I was only 11 at the time) I prepared myself to die. The agony was awful. I was terrified of ghosts, terrified of the supernatural, of cancer and of everything I heard or read. I refused to go to India for fear that I might get leprosy."

When she entered the tomb, it struck her how strangely the word mummy coincides with mother. But she could not relate her fears to birth or to memories of fetal aggression. She loved to climb mountains but when she saw the flaming sun over a white, mist-covered peak, she would be terrified and run home with a tight feeling in her throat. She was frightened on board ship that the boat might go down. She could not swim under the water because of the fear that something would pull her down and drown her. Slowly she realized that her mother stood in the center of all her fears; that "la mère," the French for mother, also means the sea; that she expected death by uterine destruction—to be sucked back into her mother's body to die as the talionic punishment for her own murderous fantasies.

25.

INCEST AND HOMOSEXUALITY

THE sexual fantasies which accompany the return into the mother's body may reveal a constructive purpose transcending in importance the search for ecstasy. In the memory of pre-natal life may be hidden the roots of the incestuous feelings of the male towards his own mother; and the lesbian emotions of the female (feminine homosexuality) may conceal an aspiration for the attainment of the same objective. The primary motive behind both drives appears to spring from a biological urge: the desire to re-attain the blissful existence of the unborn by union with the mother.*

The sexualization of this union is an inevitable concomitant of the desire. In man it becomes conspicuous because of the nature of his sexual organization. His rational thinking convinces him that the return cannot be accomplished in full. The conflict between fantasy and reality which is thus generated can be resolved by a partial return, in which the male organ plays the part of the child. Once upon a time (in birth) we have been in a genital relationship with the mother. Nature has placed the whole body of the child in the role of the male organ. The linguistic habit of calling the penis the little one, the child,

---

* In Sandor Ferenczi's words "The Oedipus wish is precisely the psychological expression of an extremely general biological tendency which lures the organism to a return to the state of rest enjoyed before birth." ("Thalassa: A Theory of Genitality," *The Psychoanalytic Quarterly*, New York, 1938, p. 19.)

rests on a biologic foundation. Nocturnal priapism (constant erection at night) might arise from an unconscious awareness of this penis-child relationship to the mother. In incestuous fantasies about the mother, the penis-child attempts to regain its lost kingdom. It was Sandor Ferenczi, the great Hungarian psychoanalyst and for a long time the chief disciple of Freud, who first discerned this motive in coitus fantasies. His claim that a man can always return into the womb because of his sexual organization is supported by the semblance of umbilical relationship which is actually accomplished when the penis takes on the role of the cord. One is tempted to add that the attempt is never a complete failure for the additional reason that the emotions accompanying such fantasies help to maintain the illusion that the fetal utopia is well worth striving for and is within our reach.

No such standby exists for the feminine sex. According to Ferenczi, women cannot maintain the illusion of a partial return unless first another fantasy, that of possessing a male organ, develops. Such fantasies create active feminine homosexuality. By its mechanism a woman, lying on top of a man in intercourse and fantasying that the man's organ is her own, may dream of an incestuous relationship with the mother in the same way as a man can. One is no more preposterous than the other. I believe, however, that the primary motive behind such fantasies is not the uterine return, but simply dissatisfaction with the feminine sexual organization and desire to play the masculine role in life.

Where masculine aspirations are absent, a woman still has two ways for the attainment of the uterine objective by partial return. In incestuous fantasies with the father the male organ may assume the role of the parental cord. Carried to its logical conclusion, the fantasy would amount to a situation in which the father takes the place of the mother. In a direct love fantasy with the mother, a homosexual factor appears. Carried to its logical conclusion, the fantasy would mean that the mother takes over the sexual role of the father. However, it is rare to find an actual sexual role assigned in such daughter-mother fantasies, and the term homosexual (or lesbian) is not really applicable; it is the only term we have to describe similar, though not umbilical, situations. It is true that the whole body, by reversing the process of birth, could play the part of the penis, but this fantasy is more operative for a mother than for a daughter. As long as the stigma of homosexuality can be attached to a love relationship between two women, a woman's desire for fetal union may produce homosexual guilt. It is for this reason that women as potential homosexuals far outnumber men. It is easier for a man to repress homosexual desires than for a woman. As a rule, men take to homosexuality to escape from the mother; women take to it to gain her.

A Kingdom for a Womb

The identification between incestuous emotions and pre-natal yearning is shown in a picturesque form:

Something like a catafalque was rising from a round hole in the earth. Fairy folks had something to do with it and one was powerless against them. It meant death to step on the catafalque, but one could not avoid doing so. However, I discovered at the last moment a military aspect to the situation in which the fairies did not figure. I forget what this was. On the catafalque was written in large letters: "King Oedipus IX."

On awaking the dreamer immediately remembered that he was the ninth child in his family. The epitaph was plainly his own, and it alluded to his incestuous relationship with his mother. He volunteered that the hole in the earth was the womb and that the Oedipus complex, in its basic aspect, means a return into the mother. The pre-natal state is another range of life; a fairy kingdom which can only be regained by passing through the portals of death.

It is interesting to note the helpless situation in which the dreamer finds himself. It is the fatalistic touch which characterizes birth dreams. "Military" suggests discipline, organization. The military aspect of the situation thus refers to analysis. It promises an escape from the Oedipal and pre-natal fantasies by awakening from them as one awakens from a dream.

A more dramatic and convincing case comes from a soldier who was not under psychoanalysis but was acquainted with the Freudian movement and its claims. While he was working on his M.A. thesis

and was momentarily awaiting a call to active military service, he had
a strange dream which repeated itself a second time with similar content. To quote from his written account:

*The first scene occurred in a bookstore of the customary second-
hand style where books are displayed on shelves all around the room
and also on tables. I was browsing in this store with Ruby B., a lady
who kept a salon for young people of intellectual tastes. She and I
found a copy of Karl Mannheim's* Ideology and Utopia *and determined to destroy it to save other young men from the contamina-
tion we seemed to recognize in the book. After making sure we were
not being watched, we proceeded to rend the book on the table. It is
possible that another book, George Sorel's* Reflections on Violence,
was also included in the destruction.

*The second scene took place further up on the other side of the
street in a large dormitory which I subsequently identified as the
Naval Armory where I attended a New Year's Eve dance shortly before the dream. On the lowest of the triple deck beds I went to bed
with my mother, apparently with incestuous intent. As far as the ex-
ecution of the act is concerned, my memory is hazy. Either the dream
itself lacked detail, or, more likely, there has been a later subconscious
repression of some of the original material.*

I shall now quote the original analysis which the patient had made
of the dream by his own unaided effort before I met him:

*The dream captured my interest immediately because it was, as far
as I can recall, the only incest dream I had ever had. When it was
repeated with similar scenario, I began examining it. The analysis I
came to was something like this:*

*Mannheim presents a frame of reference to sociological data which
had given me a more realistic interpretation of such gross social movements as wars, revolutions, etc. represent. This had completed my disbelief in the real efficacy of ideas, such as "making the world safe for
democracy," except as symbols which, if properly manipulated by
some realistic leader could inspire and direct social actions. The destruction seemed a wish not to know what I feel I "know" about the*

Incest and Homosexuality

bosses of social action, and thus to be able to accept simply a utopian standard as others do and go into war full of reckless enthusiasm, confident that I am working for a true cause. I did not want other young men to be disillusioned since they would have no choice whether or not they would fight, and if they did not read Mannheim and similar works, they might have a peace of mind while fighting.

The incestuous idea shocked me. This seemed very strange because I was familiar with Freud and had no difficulty in accepting rather casually all other dreams. The shock still surprises me and is not completely explainable. I had thought myself above any dramatics over the morals of such an issue.

After some thought on the subject, the content of the dream seemed to be logically stated like this:

War is a thing about which I have had illusions, but do not now have illusions. Others who must be in it are perhaps better off with some glib and self-ingratiating explanation. I must not let them become disillusioned. Incest is the most terrible thing which could occur. War is linked (temporally and spatially) with incest. Hence war is the most terrible thing which could occur and I want none of it.

The dreamer made a strong logical attempt to link incest with war. He would have been more successful had he stumbled to the symbolism of war for the unconscious mind; had he discovered that it stands for internal war; therefore the desire to redeem others covers the desire to release himself from the erotic bonds that have kept him tied to his mother from early childhood. The desire to return into the womb leads to incestuous fantasies and incestuous fantasies generate moral revulsion, conflict and fear. The tearing up of the book in the secondhand bookshop was an attempt to reorganize his deep-seated emotional drives.

Wishing to have a written record of the impression which my explanations made on the dreamer, I asked him to send me a summary of our analytic discussion with his critical remarks. This is what he wrote:

Although recognizing the general validity of the first analysis, Dr.

Fodor suggested an alternative interpretation of the incest sequence and of the ramifications of other parts of the dream content:

1. Mannheim=MannHeim, or "das Heim des Mannes." This would seem to refer to the uterine state and, coupled with "utopia," expresses a uterine wish.

2. The woman (Ruby B.) is a fertility or productivity symbol, both classically and because I had received much intellectual stimulation at gatherings in her apartment.

3. The destruction represents a turning back, or wish to turn back and the subsequent (or consequent) frustration.

4. The incestuous scene is actually an attempt, physically, at return to the pre-natal (uterine) state.

In general, I think this explanation has considerable weight in its favor over the previous one. One point, I believe, requires re-examination. I don't think that on the uterine theory the third finding is completely consistent. Rather do I think that since this destruction took place on a table and with the assistance of a woman, it actually represents birth itself, and the turning away from this physically to go to the dormitory is a way of saying, "Why was I ever born?"

In addition to this, other interpretations can be added if the situation is regarded from the uterine, rather than a sensually erotic point of view. The bed is a uterine symbol, as is perhaps the Navy. In general, the dream is not a mere statement of disapproval of war, as my original analysis indicated, but rather it is an expressed desire to escape from the crowded chaos of life (and probably the war in particular) and return to the uterine environment wherein all was pleasantly secure.

The summary is good, but weak in No. 3, which should have recognized the futility of regressive escape. The purpose of the dream is to teach this lesson, and the lesson culminates in the destruction of the Book of Life, as far as it represents the past. "Reflections on Violence" embrace the uterine state, the struggle of birth as an entrance into the post-natal life and the desire to return into the womb. This three-fold content might be discerned in the three tiers of beds in the dormitory. We need integration on the current, the historic and the pre-historic (uterine) levels of our mind and the dream seemed to indicate that the dreamer's future mental and spiritual progress hinged on such re-shaping of his fundamental instinctual drives. The New Year's dance with which the dormitory is associated contains allusions both to birth and re-birth:

Here are his final critical remarks:

I consider the re-evaluation of the latent meanings of the dream symbols advanced by Dr. Fodor to be of considerable theoretic and of perhaps even greater therapeutic value.

Such an explanation removes from the patient the felt necessity of self-accusation, such as would be indicated by a purely Freudian interpretation. This gives the patient an opportunity for optimism at the outset, which is conducive to integration, and a re-awakening of his confidence in his value as a member of society.

At the same time, although recognizably such a theory cannot be proven any more than any other competing or completing theory, it is more logically consistent and offers more meaningful interpretation of dreams or perhaps other subconscious data than previous theories.

Thus the interpretation advanced by Dr. Fodor is not only more pleasant to take and more flattering to the person's self-regard, but it is also more acceptable to the critical faculties of the patient, thereby probably avoiding the potential collapse and reversion of patients who came to believe (for intellectual reasons) in explanations they had once avidly seized when they were desperately floundering.

I consider Dr. Fodor's interpretation a much better therapeutic approach and probably a better theoretical foundation than any phase of psychoanalysis I have thus far encountered.

Should we discount the enthusiasm which the patient exhibits? Should we take it for a purely subjective manifestation, a sign of relief and objectively no proof of the correctness of my interpretation? That is what the scientific frame of mind would demand. But is healing always scientific? All miraculous recoveries take place in defiance of science as we know it. Should not the cure be more important than the proof of the manner in which it was produced? Every psychotherapist is confronted with this issue. In the present case it is a particularly weighty one because the interpretation of dream material in terms of incestuous and homosexual aspirations very often produces a deep shock in the patient's psyche. The patient may struggle against admitting these repressed emotions for weeks or months or may even run away from analysis because his courage fails him in facing it out. If we can avoid these shocks by a more penetrating concept which sums up the issue more in biological than in moral terms, we can do a tremendous service to the patient. We show reason why we can accept him as a normal human being; we gain his confidence and we considerably shorten the analytic period.

Umbilical Fantasies

The following excerpt is taken from the day dreams of the young girl whose fantasies of Jonah and the Whale were discussed earlier. It is introduced here as an example of umbilical visions, revealing an identification between the penis and the umbilical cord:

I can see a lake, the water making rings and whirling towards the middle where it is sucked down. There is a baby spitting blood into the pool, about six months old, blue in the face from violent rage.

Oh, my Heavens . . . that's it. The baby is lying on some canvas and the cord is coming around its stomach. The umbilical cord. It is very long, it stretches from the belly button up. The child is trying to break it off, cut it off or pull it off. Then this cord is full of something sour . . . Sour milk. . . .Oh, it is terrible. . . . This woman got the end of the cord in her mouth and seems to be spitting in it and the spittle is going down the tube into the baby's stomach. I see at the same time a field with burning red sky and sun. There are gravestones all over the field and vultures in the sky.

Now I think of a nanny goat. Something about a nanny goat and my grandmother. I think someone called her Nanny, or she called herself the Old Nanny Goat.

The sour milk in the tube is clotting. It looks like acidophilus milk. We used to get acidophilus milk for my mother in the t.b. sanitarium. . . . The spitting in the tube is as if she were syphoning, putting this sour business back into the baby's stomach. Then all kinds of bugs

would be crawling in the baby's stomach. I associate horrible bugs
with acidophilus milk. They grow out of it . . . Now the baby is vomit-
ing these bugs out of its mouth, and orange peels are in it. The bugs
as they come out of its mouth are as big as dogs and they rush. . . .

Now I think there is some confusion between this cord and the
penis. I think of my brother's penis. . . . There was an awful girl at
school who told us that orange is woman, banana is man. . . .

This is awful. I am cutting it off with a big butcher knife, the boy's
penis . . . my brother's, I guess. . . . I used to think that he was tied
to mother with the penis as with the cord. I thought his penis was
the cord and that I did not have one. He was tied to mother as a
baby by his penis.

The castration trauma of the Freudians carries back as far as circumcision. There it stops. Girls are not circumcised, but as they have
dreams which the Freudians interpret as similar to castration dreams
of boys, we are told that a girl is born castrated. The attempt to explain the trauma of birth in terms of castration is obviously futile. If
circumcision leaves a traumatic shock, there is no justification for ignoring the cutting of the umbilical cord. It often leads to more complications than circumcision. But admitting the trauma of the cutting
of the umbilical cord would be re-accepting the trauma of birth
through the back door, and the Freudian movement still shrinks from
it as if it would reflect on Freud that he had missed something so
important.

A comparison with this girl's fantasy of Jonah (or John) and the
Whale will reveal a transposition of the umbilical fantasy on to the
anus. The ribbon of fecal matter evacuated by the patient's brother
was evaluated as the missing organ. It seems thus as if the cutting of
the umbilical cord had been made responsible by the dreamer for her
anatomic insufficiency. Her life was poisoned by having been made
a girl. For this injustice, her mother was responsible. In the present
vision, the baby is desperately trying to tear itself free from the mother
and from uterine memories. She cannot and will not return to being
a sick woman. It would be her death. But her very struggle reveals
the existence of the urge—which we have seen so dramatically enacted

in the fantasy of John and the Whale. The struggle is motivated by her strong homosexual repressions. Her mother was a notorious lesbian and once in a drunken fit tried to make love to her own daughter. If the dreamer succeeded in tearing the cord-penis off, she would be safe from her own homosexual inclinations; she would be deprived of the means by which the return of the male into the womb is accomplished.

The Homosexual Way

The origin of homesexual emotions in an insomnia patient is revealed in the following dream:

There was a woman in my clothes in front of me. I was holding her breasts with both hands. We were in a cave and we were going towards some big light. She laid her head on my shoulder and spoke to me very reassuringly. I felt soothed.

The patient thought the dream concerned his femininity and his fondness of playing with breasts. It does, but it goes much deeper. The ultimate source of mother fixation is the memory of pre-natal union, of having been one flesh with the maternal organism. In the dream the incorporating medium is his clothes and the fetal situation is shown by reversal. It is he who holds his mother by the breast and it is his mother who lays her head on his shoulder. He is holding his mother in the same way that she held him in her arms when he was a baby and needed soothing and comforting, and he carries his mother in a way that can vaguely suggest the carrying of himself within his mother's body. The cave is the womb and the light is the light of illumination which he seeks, but also the light of life towards which he was progressing in his transition from the pre-natal to the post-natal life.

The dream explains in a very simple manner the genesis of the patient's repressed homosexual emotions. It shows his mother as part of his own body. Hence the woman in him is the mother. His femininity, therefore, is fed by memories of a pre-natal identification with the mother. Caves always had a tremendous fascination for him. In Hungary, his native country, he was the member of a cave exploration society and used to spend whole week-ends in caves searching for new formations of stalactites and stalagmites. In Hungarian both are described by the word "cseppkö" (drip stone), but "csepp" also happens to be the name applied to a very small child. Thus it seems that even in his early youth he was instinctively searching for the solution of the riddle of the womb. He could not find it. Both the incestuous and homosexual avenues proved to be blind alleys. Instead of happiness, they only yielded sickness and misery.

26.

THE incestuous and homosexual drive in man has another, more powerful determinant than the desire to recapture the static bliss of uterine existence. This motive is constructive and is furnished by man's never-ceasing quest to find the Beloved. The quest is rooted in the fundamental bi-sexual nature of humanity, which is revealed by vestigial sexual characteristics. Men have breasts, and women have a rudimentary male organ in the clitoris. The suggestion is that at some remote evolutionary epoch, the sexes were united in the proto-human body, as they still are in some lower forms of life. Theosophy pretends to possess a good deal of esoteric information on this androgynous state in which man was male-female; but we also find references to it in the religious myths of both cultured and primitive peoples. The Greeks erected a statue to the Divine Hermaphrodite. In the anthropomorphic concept of divinity, God had to possess dual sexual characteristics, or He could not be omnipotent. If man was created in the image of God, he too, had to be bi-sexual. In the Old Testament, we find a legendary account of how the separation of the sexes came about.

According to Genesis, God performed a surgical operation on Adam while he was asleep. He took out a rib and fashioned Eve. In modern psychological language, this means that Eve was split off from Adam. In this wording, the Biblical story conceals a profound evolutionary truth. Ever since the sexes have been separated, Man is restlessly searching for his Eve, the missing part of his self, and this view of the love-quest is confirmed by the marriage ceremony, which is supposed to make a woman one flesh and blood with a man and work the miracle of two souls in one body. The words "whom God hath joined together let not man put asunder," clearly suggest that the marriage ceremony is a restitution fantasy.

When a man falls in love with a woman, he is tricked by Nature into believing that he has found his Eve and that his personal part of the racial trauma of the separation of the sexes is about to be remedied. By the time he discovers that the woman is not his flesh and blood, it is too late; the continuation of the race is assured; and Nature has accomplished her purpose. Only rarely does it happen that Eve proves a soul-mate in the romantic sense. If and when she does not successfully objectify the missing sexual component, man's sexual restlessness remains unabated; and the archaic quest goes on. As for Eve, her disappointment and search parallel Adam's.

I believe this disappointment is the deepest determinant of the woman's masculine envy. It is said that a woman does not accept her femininity until she bears a son. The reason, on the foregoing theory, is that only in the male, arising from her womb, can she find an objectification of that for which she archaically yearns. It is still an illusion, but it comes as near as Nature permits to the fulfillment of an age-old dream.

It would seem to follow that the failure of the quest automatically assures mono-sexuality. So it would, but for a contradictory evolutionary event. The racial dream of sexual unification is actually on the point of realization when a new human being is conceived. The sperm buries itself in the ovum, the male has found the female. The great dream, however, meets with immediate or early frustration. The new human being, springing from the ovum and the sperm, cannot retain both sexual components. While it takes at least two months of embryonic development to find evidence, by autopsy, of the sex of the embryo, the biological view is that the die is cast at the time of conception, that the sexual future of the child is determined by the character of the male sperm that succeeds in uniting with the ovum.

Search for the Beloved

How the actual determination of sex takes place is a mystery. All we know is that the clash between the sexual nature of the ovum and the sperm is somehow resolved; and, whether this solution is instantaneous or not, a mono-sexual organic evolution begins.

Unquestionably, the speculative age in embryology has not yet been left behind. The speculations of a psychologist may prove to be a valuable addition to the body of data from which greater knowledge will arise. If a man is not an isolated individual but a product and representative of his race, it is conceivable that sexual determination leaves as profound an impression on his psyche as his original androgynous constitution has left on his body.

The psychological data which I have gathered from an intensive study of dreams in a pre-natal setting, indicate that sexual determination is achieved at the price of considerable struggle. Further, the appearance is as if the lost sexual potential had not been extinguished but had retired underground to haunt the winner for the rest of his life. To embryologists, this may sound absurd; but whether this is only a fantasy of humanity, which embryological data cannot yet support, this view has very great value from the therapeutic standpoint. It assures a simplicity of presentation of the facts of bi-sexuality and elicits gratifying response. Further, some of the deepest yearnings of the race can be traced to this concept of bi-sexuality.

It seems as if the poets, the greatest dreamers of the race, had always realized that the quest for Eve in the outside world is doomed to failure, because the real Eve only exists within.

Journey to Fairyland

For an enchanting illustration, I shall turn to *John, the Brave,* a famous Hungarian epic poem by Alexander Petöfy, one of the world's greatest lyricists. The poem is the apotheosis of the Hungarian *hussar,* or hero-ideal:

John, an illegitimate child, was found in a maize field. He became a shepherd and, after losing his flock, went to the wide world in search of adventure. He gained fame as a *hussar,* conquered human enemies and supernatural ones; but, throughout his heroic career, his heart was aching for Iluska, his sweetheart, whom he had to leave behind and who, unkown to him, had died at the hands of an evil stepmother. When he returned and learned the tragic news, he was broken-hearted; he plucked a rose from her grave and resumed his wanderings. Finally, he reached the end of the world, the "*operencia,*" the fabulous sea which stretches into Infinity. Somewhere far out in that sea is fairyland, and John determined to reach it. He blew his whistle and the giant, whom he had conquered in his earlier adventures and who had sworn fealty to him, appeared. John commanded the giant to take him to fairyland. He traveled on the back of the giant for three weeks; and when he reached the island kingdom, he found three gates guarded in succession by three bears, three lions and three fire-spitting dragons. He killed them all and entered fairyland. Though he had reached the end of his quest, his heart was still full of unhappiness. In despair, he threw the rose which he had plucked from the grave of Iluska into the blue waters of the fairy lake. A miracle happened! The lake contained the Waters of Life, and the flower changed back into his beloved. John dove into the water and rescued her. The fairies elected them for their king and queen and they lived happily forever thereafter.

It does not take much imagination to discover the fetal elements in this delightful fantasy. Fairyland is the kingdom of the unborn; and the fabulous sea is the impenetrable barrier between the prenatal and the post-natal world. It can be surmounted only by supernatural force. It takes a giant to conquer it. To the giant's huge size, John is as diminutive as the fetus to the adult. The nine guardians of the gates speak of the nine months of gestation; and the fire-spitting dragons represent the cannibalistic concept of birth and uterine return. We have been disgorged in pain and fear from the belly of the maternal giant in birth, and we are afraid of returning to the pre-natal Elysian fields because we would have to pass through the jaws of monstrous death. John, being a hero, succeeded in killing the guardians of the gate with his sword; and the portals of Utopia sprang open before him. But he cannot be happy in the womb as a lonely male. Far back, at a remote evolutionary period, he was complete, male and female. In Iluska, he had found his female self but had lost her. Now, in the amniotic waters of fairyland, he finds himself united with her. He is male and female, a real king in the Unborn's universe.

A story by H. G. Wells, *Mr. Skelmersdale in Fairyland* gives a delightful description of the adventures of a keeper of a small shop who went to sleep on Aldington Knoll and woke up, reduced in size, in fairyland. The fairy queen wished to keep him there; but he had Millie, his fiancée, in the world; and the illusion that Millie could not be his Eve had not yet been shattered. So the fairy queen let him go. But no sooner did he return than his former sweetheart vanished from his mind, and the image of the fairy lady became triumphant. He tried to sleep on the Knoll again, hoping to be taken underground, but it was of no avail. The longing for fairyland and for the union with the true beloved could be fulfilled no more.

Pierre Benoit's *Atlantide* plays on the same motif; but there the mysterious African queen ruling over the Tuaregs is a vampire-like creature, who destroys her lovers, until the real Beloved comes and causes her destruction. For the hero who finds the fabulous queen finally flees from his love—and his hate of her.

Let us now see what happens in the dream life of those who seek for the Beloved but suffer from similar mental confusion.

Giving Birth to One's Self

A woman of twenty-six, who is married and is the mother of a three-and-one-half-year-old boy, dreams of seeing a girl dressing a wooden doll, putting wadding on the chest and binding it with strings. It is the figure of a boy, and she has a feeling of frustration at the sight.

The immediate query which the dream prompts is: Was she sorry that she was not born as a boy? She was. Her mother wanted a boy; the girl always played with boys and to this day likes heavy work and masculine jobs. Six months ago, through stillbirth, she lost a boy-child. She still had milk, had had too much with her first boy; and her breasts are of fair proportion. By the wadding, the dream girl (who was herself) was making a bi-sexual figure out of the boy doll. "Bi" means two. She always wanted to have two children, and in her dreams, people who had twins or two children figured abundantly. She was an only child and had suffered in infancy from love-starvation. Was her twin-fantasy an attempt to give a loving companion to the child in herself? Or was the fantasy only due to the male-female preoccupation?

She dreamed of going up hill, seeing water or a dam. Then, in a bright room, she opened a very large book about two worlds and something between them. She was thinking of an atlas and of separating. She seemed to be a boy, ten years old; and she explained to "another" ten-year-old boy that she was accomplished in love because she had a nursemaid who was left unsatisfied with her lover; and she took his place. The book was filled with holly, the sharp edges of which fitted together. The pattern suggested drawings of spermatozoa.

Here we have proof of masculine regret and also of a split. She is two boys; the book speaks of two worlds; separation and a fitting together are mentioned with references to spermatozoa; a double number (10) is given which, from the phallic viewpoint, hints at the male and female shapes. Going up hill may indicate progress; and, from the book, she apparently wishes to learn something; perhaps separation and fitting together are not antithetic terms; perhaps her integration is dependent on the clarification of her male and female status in life. She admitted frigidity and general restlessness and dissatisfaction without knowing why. But women did not attract her, and she had no sexual interest in them.

Her son had an attack of convulsions, and she took him to the hospital in the middle of the night.

When I came home, it was early morning. It was misty. Steam came up from the manholes in the street and I experienced a wonderful feeling of elation as if walking into the complete unknown, as if I were going out of this world. It reminded me of Dante's "Inferno." I have seen such misty mornings on Long Island, when the contours are lost; you are alone and, in the distance, faint lights twinkle in big buildings. At the head of the Eighth Avenue subway, the feeling of hurtling down into a tunnel of flickering lights gave

281

*me a similar sensation. I also experience it sometimes in the morn-
ing on Washington Square and on ferryboats to Long Island.*

The description fits the vague feelings which well up occasionally
from the pre-natal levels of our minds.

*I dreamed of being in the house of an unpleasant neighbor wom-
an who is always getting involved with everybody. My husband had
a mink coat on and looked fine in it. I thought I could cut it down
to fit me. I tried it on, but as I kept arranging my bag and coat, the
fur was gone, the coat was threadbare, a wreck.*

Men do not wear mink coats. It is a mistake to wrap her own
femininity around her husband. He is not the lost Adam; he must be
permitted to be himself. As long as she keeps on objectifying her
masculinity in him, her marriage will be a wreck.

The same night she dreamed:

*We made our double bed into a single bed by pushing it together.
I thought I could pull it apart again if I wanted to. Then I looked
under the bed and saw that I wouldn't be able to reach the gas hole
for light.*

Here is proof that she is attempting to fuse the male and female
but that she is doubtful of its practicability. The gas in her apartment is not for light, but for heat. She is confused about both—the
heat of passion and the light of understanding.

But she was progressing fast, and her relationship to her husband
underwent a wholesome change.

*I am riding in the prow of a boat and see Archie, my boss, swim-
ming in the water. He is carrying my son and a little girl on his
back. My son fell off but was all right.*

This completes beautifully the pre-natal bi-sexual picture. Her
masculinity is now represented by her son. It fell off in the waters of
birth. Her femininity stands out as conspicuously as the little girl on
the back of Archie. His name contains an allusion to the pubic arch,
and, as he is her boss, he represents in himself both parents fused.
As she had heard some gossip regarding his homosexuality, no

doubts can be entertained about the correctness of this interpretation. The dream continues:

Upstairs, in a closed-in sun porch, tomatoes are growing, in large sand-boxes. It is bright and sunny and I have a vision of water. Then comes the feeling of uselessness: the New York soil is bad; you cannot raise plants in it.

When the patient was pregnant with her son, the only thing she could keep on her stomach was tomatoes. This association and the vision of water confirm that the closed-in sun-porch is her own womb. She is striving for bi-sexual balance, but is still skeptical.

A few days later, she dreamed of being in a hospital with her husband and her son, who was in the baby carriage. Then her son ceased to be a baby. In his place, there was garden soil in the baby carriage and she was stirring it up, being conscious that she had to finish something. The hospital was a composite picture of hospital, art gallery and a bank.

Stirring up the soil hints at some basic biological adjustment. The bank is another womb symbol, a place for valuables and the most valuable thing is the seed locked up in the vault of the womb. Proof of the symbolism came the same night in this dream:

I heard a siren. It suggested a combination of fire, air raid and earthquake. I fell down and got my hands dirty in a mixture of sand and oil, such as you find on garage floors. Then I got up to put my son to sleep in another room. It turned out that they had put him to sleep in the bank vault. They had to open it to get him out. I was told I should get a letter, in order that he should be able to get a job when he grows up.

Not only is the patient putting her masculinity in another room after it is brought to the light of the day, but she is setting out to prepare an outlet for it in adult life. The repressed male, represented by her son, is given birth, and the time is envisioned when he will have an equal place in the sun. Then, alone, will her sexual balance be complete, and she will rise up and forget about the cosmic catastrophe which knocked her down at the very beginning of life.

Search for the Beloved

The Secret Rebellion

No repression is ever complete. Occasionally, a dream of defiance will point to the lost self as having a dream life of its own, in which fantasies of liberation, tragic resignation, or revenge are the dominant motives. Perhaps the reason why men are essentially afraid of women, and women of men, is the crime of repression against part of ourselves, an abuse of the anatomic privilege, in much the same manner as a first-born son usurps an entailed estate to the exclusion of his brothers and sisters. The law is on his side, which does not prevent rebellious unconscious reactions against him in the psyches of the others. Here is an illustrative dream:

A guest singer was to appear at the Opera. She objected to the emphasis on "guest," she wanted to monopolize the operatic stage. For that reason, the regular singer was kidnaped and was threatened with death unless she resigned. I felt identified with her but figured out that the threat could not be carried out and refused to resign. Whereupon, she was carried away and kept in Denmark up the "furze" in an isolated building in a gorge, from where she was not permitted to have any communication with the world. Whenever she tried, the messengers were interrupted, so it seemed inevitable that she should be absent, and the reason of her absence would be a mystery.

Half-waking and half-sleeping it occurred to the dreamer that his daughter, who was a member of the opera company, could carry the message which would finally lead to "her" release.

Thus the daughter, on a kind of second thought, receives a key position in the dream. We see the statement of a feminine problem of the dreamer's masculine make-up right at the beginning when he identifies himself with the regular singer. Considering the dreamer's personality, this identification was amusingly absurd. Obviously, it was not the rôle of the singer but the feminine guise that mattered. As one's own child in a dream often stands for one's own childhood, the reference to the daughter, the only child the dreamer had, would not in itself refer to the matter of femininity. It is a common belief that we re-live our childhoods in our children; and it is also true that neurotic persons re-create their childhood traumata by treating their children in the same way that they were treated. But, by putting himself on the operatic stage, the dreamer stepped into his daughter's shoes, as if to change his sex. Hence the feminine problem, which he wishes to present, must go beyond the realities of his childhood; it may stretch back to the biological stage. As the most common man's problem of this sort is the problem of his missing femininity, perhaps the message of the dream is carried by the daughter—because by this construction, the meaning of the dream is presented simply and effectively. No watchful censor could deny the entrance of a daughter into the dream of a father. This daughter happens to fulfil an interpretative rôle on the stage, and the stage is often associated with our fantasy life. Thus it is quite possible that this is a dream of make-believe, in which the repressed feminine self (the guest singer) succeeds in monopolizing the stage of life and pushes the regular singer (the male self) back into the limbo where the feminine self was kept locked up.

Behind the fear of kidnaping, claustrophobia is often hidden. He who is kidnaped is locked up. What the victim of morbid kidnaping-fears really dreads is this locking up. But claustrophobia, in its turn, often reaches back to birth and the compression experienced in the process of delivery. The isolated building up the "furze" (fur— genital hair) in the gorge thus seems to be the womb. There were many reasons why this building should be associated with Denmark, into which we need not go. (The simplest was the association: something stinks in Denmark.) The dream shows the victorious feminine self locking up the male self in the same prison in which the feminine self was condemned to lead an underground existence after sexual determination. It is a retaliation fantasy; and it fails, but not completely, as it leaves the object-lesson behind that the repressed femininity of a father has a wonderful chance of being relived in a daughter. The essential message of the dream emerges when the regular singer is liberated through the daughter. It is through her that the repressed femininity should find a sublimatory outlet on the stage of life.

285

The dream thus not only presents the feminine problem but also its solution. The same solution was tendered in the case of the woman who delivered her son from the vaults of the bank and was told to get a certificate by which he would find work when he grew up. The person who has children of an opposite sex has a natural evolutionary way of finding employment for the repressed sexual component. In a way it might be found perfectly true that not only does a woman fail to accept her femininity until a son is born to her, but that a man's masculinity will also suffer from internal pressure and limitation until the birth of a daughter permits a sublimation of his bi-sexual repression. We should not, however, be satisfied with such natural sublimation, as life does not always oblige us with children appropriately sexed. Further, no sublimation is ever complete. Integration by psychological education is indispensable.

Death in the Pool

Let us see now the tragic note which the bi-sexual repression assumes in the case of a young girl.

I was swimming in a pool. The stage director was in charge of everything. The boys were in Faust costumes, but they were wearing red, old-fashioned doublet and hose with a Jack Horner hat. We seemed to be rehearsing. The girls were there, too. An accident happened beforehand but I did not know what it was. Suddenly, I and another girl looked down into the water at the edge of the pool and we saw, under the water, a boy in a blond wig at the edge of the pool, apparently dead from drowning. The other girl said, "Don't say anything to anybody; just pretend that we did not see it; we must not be the ones to announce it." I protested that it was impossible to leave a dead body like that, floating around in the water. It was too horrible. Then apparently the body was discovered by others and they pulled him out. He turned into a girl but had the same costume on, and she opened her eyes and began to move her lips; but no sound came from her mouth, as if the water had choked everything off.

The dream was nightmarish and left a bad, depressing effect behind. The dreamer could not imagine what it meant and greeted the solution with great enthusiasm and relief. The solution appeared to be that the lost male self was playing dramatics. It was drowned out of post-natal life by the accident beforehand, sexual determination. It existed underground, repressed; and it changes into herself out of the pool because in post-natal life only a female self exists. It could not speak because no analytic understanding had yet given it a chance of self-expression.

God and the Rabbi

A rabbi of forty-three has been struggling with this same problem, through the torments of neurosis, the greater part of his life. Twenty years before he came to me, he underwent psychoanalysis for six months. It failed, and he thought he was incurable. He suffered from constant pains in the left side, which made him gasp and caused an ache in the left eye; from chronic constipation; from loss of appetite and from attacks of nausea, which were particularly in evidence on Saturdays, when he had religious services to conduct.

His conflict with God was immediately revealed by the dream he chose as typical of his dream life:

I am in the Synagogue. It is Saturday. I am wearing a fountain pen and pencil in my left breast pocket. They say, "Du trogst on Sabbath?" (Do you carry on the Sabbath?) I seize the tools with my right hand and throw them high on top of the Holy Ark. This puts me in an embarrassing position. I fear I shall be publicly disgraced.

A terrible dream for a rabbi. He is defying the laws of his religion, and he is committing sacrilege against the Holy Ark.

"I noticed twice that instead of the Torah Scroll, I kissed the robe of the man who carried it. Does that reveal a homosexual tendency?"

Such questions usually are very significant, but not in the case of those who have had analytic experience. I soon discovered that the unsuccessful analysis was more responsible for his preoccupation with homosexual thoughts than his instinctual drives. I answered him by saying that kissing the robe of the man who carried the scroll might have stood as well as homosexuality for an escape from God. His aggression against the Holy Ark sufficiently explains the escape. Our job is to find out the meaning of his aggression. Would he tell me what was kept within the Ark?

He replied that a scroll with the Ten Commandments, Aaron's rod and a pot of manna were supposed to be kept in it. I asked him if he ever tried to figure out the symbolism of the content of the Ark. He had not. A great light broke on him when I suggested that Aaron's rod and the pot of manna might represent male and female symbols which, together with the Law of Life, represent human generation. The Ark is the Holy of Holies, the womb of the Mother. His conflict with God is rooted in a feeling of guilt about the womb. The fountain pen and the pencil are phallic instruments. The pen (which was red) squirts black ink (black semen) and defiles the Ark.

The answer was an immediate protest:

"I never had any unsociable, evil or sexual thought toward my mother; but I always felt cold to her, and it made me uncomfortable if I had to kiss her . . . I am a cold type, incapable of losing myself in affection. I was born alone and will die alone . . . I burst out crying when my last brother was born. It happened just when I was *barmitzvaed.** I suspected nothing. I was so blind! I went home and found out I had a baby brother. I took it as an act of disloyalty on the part of my mother toward me. I always hated my father, perhaps I hated her, too."

The statement which began as a denial turned into a confession. He was aggressive toward his mother because a new brother came out of her "Ark" just when he was admitted into manhood before the Ark. On a deeper level, this aggression went back to the suffering imposed upon him by his own birth.

"When I was seven years old, I had a vivid dream I was unable to forget. I saw my uncle Louis in the middle of the yard, holding in his hand a pair of tongs which ice-men use and lifting with them a cake of ice; but this block of ice was red hot."

The meaning of this dream began to emerge with the revelation that Uncle Louis looked very much like the patient's mother. It oc-

---

* The nearest Christian ceremony is "confirmed." The *barmitzva* is an initiation into manhood.

curred to me that the pair of tongs might represent the forceps used in his delivery, in which case the block would refer to blocking; ice to fear, and the red-hot condition to the bruising of his body in the course of delivery. I did not communicate these thoughts to the patient. I also kept the idea to myself that by changing his mother into Uncle Louis he might have revealed a tendency to escape from incest to homosexuality. The pair of tongs recalled the unexplained element of the attack against the Torah. Why should he have thrown a pair of tools (pen and pencil) on top of the Ark?

No explanation came forth until the patient volunteered that he always dreamed of pairs. The fountain pen was longer than the pencil. In the pairs in his dreams, one was always bigger than the other. Then, by a startling mental acrobatic, he suggested: pair is *père* in French: "father." Was he aggressive against the Ark because he resented his father, or because he could not copy his father?

More light came in the next dream:

The congregation has bought a new Frigidaire. My wife and I were trying to get into it. It was locked but the walls seemed to be made of paper. My wife said, "Push your hand through it." I did, and felt very guilty. The congregation discovered that it had been broken into, and the burglary was traced to me because I had left my keys in the lock. I determined to make a clean breast of it all.

The Ark is now replaced by a Frigidaire. It is a symbol which we find in the dream of every frigid woman. It has a genital significance—a cold woman is called an "ice-box." The maternal element is represented by the man's wife. The collusion probably stands for temptation. Instead of throwing writing tools at the Ark, he is aggressive with the hand that wields the tools. He leaves the key in the lock; and this is contradictory. It is a psychic key. His dream mind is out to solve his religious conflict. He is guilty of incest, of partial return to his pre-natal home. He suffers from confusion between the instinctual desire to return to the womb and the sexual act. The inability to solve a conflict of this character usually leads to a homosexual compromise.

Search for the Beloved

The same day that this dream was discussed, this patient recalled a dream that had occurred over twenty years previously:

I was standing on the steps of my Hebrew high school. Two men were below. One pushed a piece of ice into my left breast.

The ice again, the third time. It recalled an accident he had had as a youngster. He fell over some steps and impaled himself on the spikes of a fence. But it also recalled something else, which was much more revealing:

"During my first analysis, a tooth fell out of my mouth in a dream. The analyst remarked, 'Like a woman, dreaming of having a baby.' I used to have such fantasies, lying on my back and thinking that a large slice was missing from my side—that it was cut out.

"About a year afterwards, I described this fantasy as a Caesarian delivery . . . I am very much interested in what you told me about birth. Adam was born on a Friday night, before the commencement of the Sabbath. My nausea would begin at 3 or 4 P.M. on Friday and last until Sunday morning . . . In the dream about the Ark, they asked me, 'Are you carrying?' That may refer to bearing.

"Last night I dreamed of a mountain. The crater on top of it was frozen and Americans were skating over it. I saw a woman and a child. She was embarrassed because the child moved its bowels and she had to clean up the mess."

The Ark, after the Frigidaire, turns into a volcano. The crater is frozen. The combination of heat and cold (red hot block of ice) re-appears and the desire to re-enter the womb is blocked.

"I did think of the mountain as a pregnancy symbol when I woke up. 'Hara' in Hebrew means mountain and also pregnant. Life was always full of difficulties for me. I made a mountain of little things. In certain situations I would feel frozen and could not move. If I feared an attack, I never could run. I remained fixed and immobile. I used to ask myself, 'Is this a memory of the time when I was a child in the womb?' I also had many dreams of frustrated return. I used to have a recurrent dream of getting to a train, and the gate would shut in my face every time."

In the following session he added an important supplement:

290

"I forgot to tell you, the woman did not clean the child of feces but of something that covered its body all over. It was pink, like the stuff which would cover the body of a child in birth."

Here was evidence that the volcano dream was indeed a uterine fantasy and that when the patient spoke of feces he fused with them the idea of anal birth.

I returned to his Caesarian birth fantasy, and he suddenly asked: "Why shouldn't we think of ourselves as being born from men? According to the Bible, woman came from a man's rib."

Glimpses of the stupendous vistas embraced by the patient's fantasy-life now began to appear. He was not a woman, nor a passive homosexual, playing with pregnancy fantasies. He was a man, Adam, from whose body Eve was born. He was androgynous, both male and female, and incest or homosexuality represented blind instinctual strivings toward achieving the apparent perfection of androgynous life which the race had left behind millions of years ago.

The maternal rôle which he played in his Adamite fantasy first began to confuse him at the age of sixteen, when he attended the *Yeshiva* to become a rabbi. His left eye began to hurt. He always wanted to wipe away something from it.

I could not help thinking of the mucosa covering the child's body in reference to the volcano dream. Could it be possible that it got into this patient's eye, or that the silver nitrate dropped into his eye after birth had left a traumatic effect? The query did not strike the patient as strange.

"I kept on giving myself affirmations as far back as fifteen years ago: 'My left eye is not a vagina.'"

It appeared that the identification between eye and vagina was a remnant of his previous, abortive analytic education. It was coupled with another formulation: "I am not my mother." After repetition, both affirmations lost their affect.

The affirmation implied that he had taken his mother's body unto himself like a mantle, but he had failed to understand this. If he had understood it, he might have grasped the meaning of the homosexual identification with his mother and sister, of which his previous analyst had spoken.

What he should have done by way of auto-suggestion was to word the affirmation this way: "I am not the child being born through my own eye as through the mother's vagina." He had missed the most important fact, that in identifying himself with his mother, he was giving birth to himself.

Preposterous as this fantasy is, it pales in significance compared to his Adamite fantasy. The latter helps us to a complete understanding of the deeper motives behind his attack against the Holy Ark. The pen and pencil, as a pair, represent the male and female. Within the Ark, these two principles correspond to the pot of manna and Aaron's rod, and establish an androgynous unification. In this patient's Caesarian birth fantasy, Eve was cut out of his body. By his attack against the Ark he was returning Eve, the missing half of the pair, into the womb of creation, an act which would help him re-emerge, androgynous, like God whom the Greeks worshipped as "The Divine Hermaphrodite." The aggression against the Ark thus was essentially a fantasy of union with the Divine. Here is how the patient reacted to this final explanation:

"I have often affirmed I am God, wondering what it would do for me. I often queried why God has to create. I also believed that there is no evil. Evil is Eve. You mentioned the crater of the volcano. It struck me that crater is also Creator, and that I am lost in myself until my creative activity is inspired with the idea of returning into Divinity. But it was all too confusing. I just could not make head or tail of it."

I suggested that his attack against the Ark could also be construed as a quarrel with God over His creation. He admitted it:

"For weeks I denied all creation, I said there was no such thing. Why in hell did God create the universe? Why did He go to all that trouble if He was so perfect, so wonderful?"

"I had a nightmare during the week. Somebody was pursuing me. It may have been a Chinaman. Then I seemed to get into a house or group which was sympathetic to me. Two small Chinese children, or devils, were pursuing me. A woman had control over them. In

China, the mother controls the children. Somebody said: 'Let her drive them away.' She caught the two pursuing devils, knocked their heads together and told them: 'Begone.' . . . and they were gone. At some part of the dream, my left palm was pierced by a curved Chinese dagger."

The dream seems to the writer to be a wonderful confirmation of what has developed before. The patient's first association with Chinamen was birth "because all children look like Chinamen at birth." He appreciated the curved dagger as a phallic symbol, the left as the female, the weaker, the smaller side. In the light of these associations, the two devils may stand for the masculine and feminine, representing the androgynous conflict, which his previous analyst coarsely described (in my personal opinion) as a homosexual conflict. In uniting the male (dagger) with the female (palm), he uses sexual aggression as a symbol of integration. It is a form of androgynous integration that he needs, an acceptance of the feminine within.

Anima and Animus

Having traced the sexual conflict to the drama of sex determination, we may now raise another important query. What if the conflict is merely psychic, what if man has a composite male-female soul, and sexual determination becomes a traumatic event because the primary sexual organization exacts a corresponding psychic unbalance?

The query leads us to the Jungian postulate of "Anima," the female soul in man, and "Animus," the male soul in women. If we are not afraid of embarking upon an investigation that borders perilously on metaphysics, we shall find ourselves confronted with the question: is there a definite point at which the male and female soul are split apart? Is it with a finality at birth, or is it much earlier, at conception?

In investigations of this sort one always meets with the objection that thoughts and theories of the analyst are responsible for the emergence of certain types of dreams, i.e., the patient dreams to oblige the analyst. Fortunately, the problem to be discussed here was presented to me by a man whom I have met only twice in my life and with whom my conversation was restricted to matters pertaining to psychical research.

He sent me a long dream by mail and said it was that of a friend; would I oblige him by a professional interpretation? He had his own explanation but preferred to withhold it, since he did not wish me to be influenced by it. He gave but one piece of information relevant to the dream material: on waking from the dream and reviewing it, the dreamer suddenly had the feeling that his companion was not his wife but his mother. I quote from the dream:

My wife and I stood alone facing a small house. To our right, the land sloped away into a beautiful valley. Here and there, the landscape was dotted with individual or small clusters of trees, merging on the far side of the valley into mountains and forests. The sky was blue and studded with clouds, and all was visible in a mysterious half-light, as of late afternoon. Small groups of people were seen here and there, members of which appeared to be busily engaged in conversation among themselves.

We knew that we were there for some serious purpose, and were properly imbued with the solemnity of the occasion. Presently we were joined by two or more people whom we seemed to recognize as friends, though I did not specifically identify them. They were to give us our instructions.

We were going on a journey, they said, in order, through this experience, to solve some great psychic mystery, and we would begin this journey by entering the little house before us. This we did by going in the front door, which led into an ante-room, seemingly much more spacious than would appear from the external view of the house. The light was dim and yet we could see a number of people loitering about, evidently conversing about matters of concern to them.

Our mentors again joined us, and again told us of the seriousness of the journey we were now about to undertake. They explained, and we knew, that, in seeking to solve these great psychic mysteries, we would encounter great perils and dangers. I clasped the hand of my companion and could feel the warmth and affection which existed between us, and also felt the fear which began at this moment to steal into both our hearts. Our guides reminded us, too, of a friend who had gone this way before us and, in his attempt to understand the great mystery, had been the victim of a great tragedy. We seemed to know who this friend was, and that some dreadful fate had overtaken him.

In all of this, no word was spoken by our guides or by my wife or by me. The communication seemed to be mental.

By now it was nearly dark. Our friends left us, and we started forward alone into the darkness ahead. As we progressed I was increasingly conscious of the warmth of affection which seemed to flow from the hand clasped in mine, and also of the fear which filled her heart, all of which emotions found their counterpart in me.

Soon the darkness was complete, but somehow we knew that a corner had been reached. We turned to the left, and again to the left, so that now we were progressing back toward the direction from which we came through another part of the same building. I was conscious only of our journey and the increasing intensity of fear and affection which possessed us.

At length we came to a large door, which opened on to a small courtyard or patio. Across it we saw another doorway to a room beyond. The courtyard seemed impassable, filled with water, mud and trash. The only way to reach this room safely seemed to be by way of a timber or "waling" fastened to the wall of the building, on the left side of the yard. Turning loose the hand of my companion, I sought to reach the distant doorway by walking along this narrow beam, supporting myself as best as I could by my hand against the wall. I came to a hole in this wall but I would not grasp its edges because I knew some frightful danger was concealed on the other side. My hand or arm might be crushed, just as certainly as my body would be mangled if I attempted to pass to the other side of this wall. Coming to the end of the wall, I leapt through to the doorway, only to find my companion in the room there before me.

It then seemed that we were at the end of our journey and could go no farther. Again I held her hand, to share an abounding love *and a great terror, as we stood in the impenetrable gloom. We knew that whatever fate was to overtake us would now be upon us, and as the oppression and fear turned to horror beyond endurance, I heard these words explosively whispered in my left ear: "Go out! Go out!"*

I struggled to go back to the doorway to jump out, but, in spite of all my struggles, I could not move. I knew we could never escape that which was about to destroy us both. Consciousness was the only refuge and I awoke.

In my answer, I expressed the opinion that the dream is a birth dream. The small courtyard or patio, filled with water, mud and trash and negotiated with considerable difficulty, is the uterine passage. The hole in the wall is the gate to life. The frightful danger concealed on the other side is a dramatization of the ordeal of birth. The anxiety of the dreamer that his arm might be crushed or his body might be mangled reveals precisely the affliction which we face in being born.

The small house, I continued, is a symbol of the mother's body. The darkness is the night of the fetus. The friend who "had gone this way before us" suggests the loss of a brother or sister before the dreamer was born. So far, the analysis of the dream is on fairly safe ground. For the rest, I said, I would throw scientific caution to the four winds and say that the dream deals only incidentally with birth; that it may equally well be described as a conception fantasy, may even be a pre-maternal one.*

"You seem to fear," I said, "that somewhere you have missed an important turning in life, that you are not doing exactly that which you came here to do. The dream appears to answer this deeper anxiety. It is telling you that you have a mission; it is an admonition in no uncertain terms that you have undertaken something definite in another state of existence. No indication is given as to what your precise undertaking is. If there is a pre-maternal state, probably this

---

* By the latter term I meant to cover the shadowy realm of pre-existence. I had a strong suspicion that the dream was dreamed by my correspondent and not by any friend of his. As I knew of my correspondent's interest in Spiritualism, I had to extend the reach of his fantasies beyond the bounds normally encountered.

is as far as any dream could go. The essential part of any such undertaking might be that you will not be reminded of it again.

"My impression is that the journey in order to solve some great psychic mystery is voluntary, but that you had already forgotten what you intended to do. That might be expected. We do not carry over a continuity of consciousness from the pre-maternal state. Yet, the forgetting of the mission, from the pre-maternal point of view, might be called a tragedy.

"The identification of your wife with your mother may serve the purpose of a uterine reference. This, however, leaves the greater question of her joint descent unanswered. It is not enough to assume that the wife-mother is the feminine self which stays behind, imprisoned in the womb, as it were, because of the primary sexual organization. It is not enough, because the wife-mother is present, apart from yourself, before you enter the maternal home. The speculation which this permits is that we may have to postulate more than an androgynous body; that we may have to think of an androgynous soul." (This is where the "Anima" of Jung enters into the picture.)

My correspondent complimented me on the "noteworthy success" which I attained with the interpretation. The dreamer was the writer himself; and he sent me a copy of his own original interpretation, in which he was assisted by no psychoanalytic knowledge.

From his earliest childhood, the dreamer had suffered from a dysfunctioning of his autonomic nervous system, which found expression chiefly in digestive upsets. The dream came to him in answer to a mental request which he addressed to his unconscious before he fell asleep. When it dawned on him that the hand which he held in his in the last room was not that of his wife but that of his mother, he was filled with amazement, because he then realized that the dream "is of the child in its mother's womb before and at the moment of birth." He learned from an aunt that he was not the first child in his family. His mother had had a miscarriage before his birth.

"The friend, then, who in the dream had gone that way before us and who had been overcome by some great tragedy was the representation of this stillborn child . . .

297

"I have never before attempted to analyze one of my dreams, much less those of others, and do not consider myself competent to do so. Nevertheless, I am certain that my interpretation of this dream is correct . . . The answer to my question is: 'The disturbances in your autonomic nervous system are due to psychic trauma at birth.'

"The question now arises: 'Is this dream telling the truth?' My answer is, of course, that I do not know and any judgment on the matter must be conjecture . . . My mother's first pregnancy resulted in a miscarriage with the loss of her child and no doubt a danger to her own life. It could hardly be otherwise than that the development of her second pregnancy was a time of increasing fear and love for her child, culminating at delivery. It is not 'cricket' in medical circles to suppose that a child should acquire traits or dispositions due to pre-natal states of the mother. Perhaps they are right, but it is still my thought that continued telepathic impressions may have passed from mother to child, to remain imbedded in some manner in the developing subconsciousness of the latter; to reveal its presence throughout life in the personality of the man. So far as I know, this idea has never before been expressed, and I know of nothing in the literature of psychic phenomena to support it.

"It may be of interest also to note that in the flash of enlightenment as to the meaning of the dream there was an accompanying feeling of familiarity, that I should have known, or did know once, that it was all true . . . that it was somehow part of myself."

Unaided, without any knowledge of pre-natal problems, the dreamer did remarkably well. His interpretation illustrates one fundamental truth: The dreamer always knows the meaning of his dream, but he is seldom able to bring this knowledge up into his conscious mind. This dreamer succeeded remarkably well, though he failed to solve the meaning of the feminine element.

I doubt if anyone could give him a really authoritative answer. The best we can do is to note the tremendous speculative problem which it raises and to hope for future data that will better enable us to retrace our journey into this life from the point of birth to conception—and perhaps beyond.

To Find the Beloved

Acceptance of the ideas advanced in this long study would lay the foundations of a pre-natal psychology as a counterpart to embryology, which bases its conclusions on the animal nature of man. The only concession which the science of embryology is willing to make to psychology is thus summed up by George W. Corner, of the Department of Embryology at the Carnegie Institution of Washington, in *Ourselves Unborn.*

"Humbly employing such visions as may be granted to an embryologist, I declare my conviction that the spirit of man—all that makes him more than a beast and carries him onward with hope and sacrifice—comes not as a highborn tenant from afar but as a latent potentiality of the body. It too is received as a germ, an opportunity, something to develop. The spirit, with the body, must grow and differentiate, organizing its inner self as it grows, strengthening itself by contact with the world, winning its title to glory by struggle and achievement." *

---

* George W. Corner, *Ourselves Unborn,* Yale University Press, New Haven, 1944, p. 121.

BOOK III.

Traumata of the Unborn

27.

SORROWS OF THE UNBORN

PRE-NATAL dreams do not always reflect a state of rapture. The life of the unborn is not necessarily one of unbroken bliss. Events may occur that cast gloom over the life of the fetus during gestation.

The unborn child is dependent on the mother's blood-stream for oxygen, for food and for the elimination of its waste products. Before "the cry of wrath at the catastrophe of birth" (Kant) is uttered, the child is exposed to various types of asphyxia or apnea, mainly from the faulty or excessive use of narcotics and hypnotics to ease the pain of labor; but the troubles of the unborn may begin well before this stage. If the mother becomes seriously ill, the child within her may also suffer.* Fever may cause an uncomfortable rise in pre-natal temperature. Poison and microbes may attack the child through the mother's blood stream. The mother's asthmatic attacks or an accidental loss of blood in advanced pregnancy or anemia may curtail the supply of oxygen to the child in the womb. Conditions akin to air-hunger and water-starvation may arise in the system of

---

* Intra-uterine pneumonia may result from the aspiration by the unborn of the amniotic fluid which has become contaminated. Smallpox can be transmitted through the placenta to the child. The mother's rubella (German measles) during the first and second month of pregnancy produces congenital abnormalities in the eyes and other organs of the fetus. (George W. Corner, *Ourselves Unborn*, Yale University Press, New Haven, 1944, p. 110.)

303

the unborn. The nutrition of the fetus may be impaired. The antibodies of an Rh-negative mother's blood may attack the red blood cells of the Rh-positive fetus. The elimination of the child's waste products may become sluggish.

Accidents suffered by the mother may expose the unborn to physical shocks through the protective amniotic cushion or cause premature birth. We cannot tell the extent to which such occurrences weaken the child, causing it to succumb to the ordeal of birth or even die before its term. We do know, however, that many children seem to start post-natal life with a handicap. A careful record of the period of gestation could give psychoanalysts valuable light on the factual basis of fantasies which appear to deal with the pre-natal state.

The word "fantasy" implies the absence of reality. We have to use the word for want of criteria by which memories of the actual conditions within the womb imprinted on the organismic mind could be clearly recognized. We cannot approach the psyche of the unborn except through the study of post-natal dreams with a pre-natal setting. To distinguish between fact and fantasy is admittedly difficult. Yet fears and anxieties may point as clearly to an actual pre-natal happening as ordinary nightmares in describing an infantile traumatic event. The real difficulty is in deciding whether the fear is retrojected from the higher levels of the mind to the pre-natal foundations, or whether high level fear experiences have actually mobilized deeply buried, organismic memories and, having associated with them regressively, succeeded in forming a constellation of great disturbing potentiality.

A clear case of retrojection of unhappiness to the pre-natal level is shown in the story of an epileptic, who dreamed of "a faraway world, a bleak landscape, dark mountains, with no growth, something unearthly, weird, an empty place, perhaps a mirage of something existing elsewhere, gigantic noises, thunder and lightning." The details were none too fixed. Their fluid character was revealed as soon as the patient was pressed for more information. "Maybe a little light was shining, maybe these noises were just within my brain." This patient was guilty of a fetal destruction fantasy, from which he was trying to escape all his life. Owing to the fact that his little brother was born ailing and died very soon, his guilt was exceptionally heavy. He was only two years old when this brother was born, and the difference between fantasy and reality was not yet known to him; so when the hated competitor died, he automatically accepted responsibility for his death. It was as if his savage resentment had killed his brother. His retrojected guilt blighted the fetal land, and the thunder and lightning stood for the wrath of God ready to strike him down if he entered the gate.

Love Starved in the Womb

In some instances, pre-natal unhappiness can be due to love starvation. This emerges from the following dream:

Evelyn, my sister-in-law, is expecting a baby (as she really is), but I am also pregnant (which is not the case). We are somewhere in the country. She is supposed to go to the hospital but cannot. So the doctor comes and delivers the baby at the house. It is quite a big girl, with a nice, round face, blue eyes, very pretty, looking eight or nine months old. I say to Evelyn, I will take the baby and watch it tonight; you'd better get a good night's rest.

I take the baby to bed. Downstairs the dog's breakfast was prepared in a little bowl with Gro-Pup dog biscuits and chopped meat. During the night the baby crept out of bed, went downstairs and ate up all the dog food. I saw her while she was eating it and became alarmed. I immediately called in Dr. R. (who had attended me when my daughter was born). He said the baby must have been very hungry because she stayed in Mrs. A. too long. Nothing a child would eat when hungry would hurt, so I should not worry. I took the baby upstairs and deliberated whether I should tell Evelyn what happened. In the morning, the baby seemed to be all right, so I told her. She called in her doctor, who said the same thing.

In the dream my pregnancy seemed to be quite advanced, but I did not feel life and was worried. I should mention it as an odd coincidence that Evelyn's baby was born during the night I had this dream. I used to call her up every day and teased her that the baby should have come four weeks ago.

305

Here is the thought on which the doctor's statement is based that the baby stayed too long in her mother and was starved as a result. The whole dream is built on this idea. Physically, a baby cannot be starved within the mother. Through the blood stream it will get all the food it needs at the expense of the maternal organism. No appreciable loss of weight has been noticed in the babies of starving mothers. In dreams, food starvation is often used to symbolize love starvation. Being fed is evidence of being cared for, being loved. The baby that has to sneak down in the night to eat dog food is starved of love. The dream mind treats it like a dog. As in dreams we are concerned with our personal history, the suggestion is that the dreamer was an unwanted child and that she suffered from the absence of the mother's tender thoughts even before she was born.*

To support this conclusion, Evelyn's pregnancy must be her own, and her own pregnancy must display the maternal body within which her deprivation occurred. Her married name, indeed, is the same as Evelyn's; she is pregnant like Evelyn; they stay in the same house; she takes the baby to bed herself; and she calls in the doctor who delivered her own child. Further, her own pregnancy is as advanced as the apparent age of the dream baby. Counting from conception, a baby is nine months old at birth. The dream baby's age thus conceals a reference to gestation. But the dream baby is very agile, while her own shows no signs of quickening. This apparent contradiction is resolved if we think of the baby's hunger as proof of love starvation, a condition which could also be represented by the absence of liveliness, by the deadening effect of untendered love.

The next vital question is whether the absence of life alludes to death wishes of the mother felt through a telepathic rapport, or

---

* "I believe first of all that which all my patients assert, that the embryo already feels plainly whether its mother loves it or not, whether she gives it much love, little love, or none at all, in many instances in fact in place of love, sheer hate." (Dr. J. Sadger, "Preliminary Study of the Psychic Life of the Fetus and the Primary Germ," *The Psychoanalytic Review*, July, 1941.) As an opposite to this extreme statement, the query could be raised: why should not the mother be equally affected by the unborn's mental state? It is tempting to speculate whether such thoughts could lead to a better understanding of certain queer symptoms that occur in pregnancy.

whether the feeling is due to retrojection from a later level of experience. The latter is supported by the fact that the patient did feel unwanted and had an unhappy childhood, but this alone, or a single dream, is not sufficient to determine such a weighty issue one way or another.

In a supplement, the patient added to the dream that while she was alarmed at the sight of the baby eating dog food, she was also amused by the situation. This indicates that the tension is not too dynamic, that she can release herself from it, provided she can bring it up into her conscious mind. She accomplishes this by calling in the doctor who delivered her own child and by receiving from him the assurance that love-starved though she was within the womb, nothing is wrong with her. The assurance is re-affirmed when Evelyn consults her own doctor and receives the same statement.

There are other more objective foundations for sorrows of the unborn. The next two chapters will deal with the psychological reactions of the unborn in the face of deliberate aggression from outside its universe.

28.

RAIDS AGAINST THE UNBORN

ONE of the main contentions of the preceding chapters is that the fear of death originates in the fear of birth; that the panicky journey through the uterine passage is an experience in dying; and that we are haunted more by the projected memory of this trial of body and soul than by the dread of future extinction.

The argument, based on an intensive study of nightmares of birth, is empirical, but it suffers from one logistic weakness. Physically, the child is carefully prepared for birth; at the end of nine months, it is ready to face a change of life. Why should this readiness be solely physical? Why should not the intelligence that builds the body and the brain also prepare the child mentally and thus safeguard it from the worst of its agony?

The question is legitimate. It cannot be ruled out of court by the rejoinder that fitness for survival is better tested by the joint agony of body and mind. If a predisposition to neurosis is its least result, the trauma of birth is more likely to disqualify than qualify for life. While it is true that in primitive communities, at times of war or in struggles against hazards of Nature it is the fittest that survive, in our civilized society the unfit often lingers after the fit dies. Further, birth is not a competitive affair. Social or economic exigencies have nothing to do with it. Birth is only rendered imperative by the physiological insufficiency of the maternal organism to provide continued and adequate maintenance.

Raids Against the Unborn

On the other hand, we must not be too hasty in deciding that the unborn is not prepared mentally for birth. It is possible that the unborn child may have a premonition of the transition it has to face. Such foreshadowing of the future may become a source of anxiety in itself. Moreover, while the physical environment within the womb is perfect and impacts of discomfort are generally of minor character, we have not yet dwelt on external shocks against which embryonic development provides no more defense than the gravitational balance of our solar system does against the intrusion of a comet from the void. It may well be that shocks from an external source are responsible for the upsetting of the equilibrium between mental and physical preparedness for birth.

The dreams to be discussed are tendered as psychological evidence that such shocks do occur in pre-natal life. They permit the inference that the severity of the trauma of birth may be determined by panicky experiences antedating delivery, and that the fear of death may also originate in traumata suffered previous to birth.

Crucifixion Fantasies

In the animal kingdom, sexual activity is seasonal. The female loses her sexual desire after impregnation and is left alone by the male, whose sexual appetite can well be satisfied by the plurality of females. On the animal scale this design of Nature works well. On the human scale it does not. Few husbands and wives will practice abstention after impregnation; the best that can be expected of them is restraint in the last few weeks prior to birth. In not placing seasonal limitation on man's sexual activity, Nature left the unborn child unprotected against the violence of parental intercourse in the advanced stages of gestation, and thus exposed it to an ordeal the traumatic nature of which is clearly traceable in dreams throughout our lives.

A dream of my own was the starting point of my investigation of pre-natal traumata. The second part of the dream I remembered first.

I saw a tiny beetle, about the size of the head of a pin. It opened its wings and now it was a butterfly, about an inch-and-a-half long and of a very nice pattern. I was preoccupied with how I could preserve this beetle with outspread wings. I fantasied, half-awake, that somebody invented a method of killing it at the moment the wings opened.

Then the memory of the earlier part of the dream came back with a rush. I was swimming happily in an underground grotto. I had a vivid recollection of the stone vault, and the clearness and the depth of the water. The swimming could be better described as a darting, like a fish. The speed was extraordinary and exhilarating. I had no hands, or did not use them. A young boy, fast as lightning, was always just ahead of me. We both came from somewhere else, waters outside. Then the raiding party came. I vaguely thought they were Russians. The entrance to the grotto was sealed. On the bare, rocky wall no opening could be seen from outside. My daughter was with me now and she talked so loud that the raiders heard her and found the entrance. I was fearful they would put me to death. For this my daughter was to blame, and I wondered how she would feel on knowing what she had done.

The meaning of the second part of the dream is transparent. The grotto is the womb and the darting about, as if driven by a tail, is a reference to pre-natal development by allusion to the tadpole stage. The grotto is sealed because the womb is sealed during pregnancy, and as I associate Russians with the Russian colossus, the raiding party could only stand for the father's penis that threatens to break into the womb and inflict death. My daughter stands for myself as a child, illustrating the mother and child relationship and the innocence with which the unborn faces the fear of death. The purpose of the dream is to reveal that the unborn child is capable of experiencing traumatic shocks before birth.

Thoughts about the younger boy ahead of me yielded the immediate association of two childhood friends. One was a hunchback, a small, misshapen human being, the other a live wire with a flaming sexual imagination, always full of stories about a gigantic penis or an immense vagina. I could not tell what made me think of these two boys, but I could readily see that the hunchback was a good association with the embryo, the other with the invader.

The meaning of the beetle dream was now beginning to unfold. I collected beetles when I was a child, sticking pins through my prizes. Sometimes they wiggled on the pin for days; and it never struck me that the act was cruel or that it was a kind of crucifixion. The dream beetle was too small for a pin. I think it stands for the embryo and the butterfly for the embryo transformed into a human child. The killing of the beetle for purposes of preservation at the moment when the wings opened suggests a reference to the agony caused by parental intercourse in the human stage of gestation. Birth is crucifixion, an experience equivalent to death; but the fear of death, as indicated by this dream, does not originate in birth alone, it antedates it and is caused by coitus shocks to which the unborn child is exposed.

Victim or Murderer

The time element enters into pre-natal dreams in many interesting forms. Sometimes the dream mind appears to make an attempt to set the approximate date at which the shock of parental intercourse was experienced during gestation.* Here are, for instance, two dreams recalled by a married woman during the same session:

I was underground in a very dark place where many prisoners were kept. I had to hide because someone was after me. A little child was there. When the guard looked into the prison through the bars, I grabbed this child and pushed the nipple of a bottle into her mouth to make the guard believe that I belonged to the child, lest he might say that I was not a prisoner. The child looked about two or two-and-one-half years old. She was horrified. There was another little girl there, Sidy, an idiot whom I had known in my childhood. She hid in a closet.

---

* Regarding my claim that every dream has a hidden date, see Nandor Fodor, "The Psychology of Numbers," *Journal of Clinical Psychopathology*, July-October, 1947.

311

This is the first dream. The imbecile girl hiding in the closet suggests an insane fear. The dungeon is symbolic of the womb and the fear of the prison guard hints at a pre-natal attack against the unborn through the bars. The dreamer makes an unsuccessful attempt to dissociate herself from this fear by pretending to be a mother or a nurse of the child. She does not really want to leave the dungeon because it is within it that the horror of the pre-natal night must be faced. If she succeeds in facing it, she will no longer be haunted by it. The suckling on the bottle indicates that the human stage of embryonic development has been reached. The human stage begins at seven months. It is not impossible that the estimated age of the child is a reference to the last two months of gestation. Every dream has a hidden date. It is in numbers that the date can be most simply concealed. But activities that in themselves contain a time determinant may also be used for such an allusion. The second dream is an excellent illustration:

A funny cave. I am packing. Irene K. is with me. I always dream of her when something big happens. Then somebody said we could not go. We were all packed. They said they were looking for a murderer, and it was one of us. I felt the terror of being caught.

Murder is a symbol for something terrible. The patient's psyche was burdened by guilt over a fetal destruction fantasy directed against a sister born after her. As she had fantasied about her destruction, she can consider herself a murderer. The funny cave, as a symbol of the womb, fits into this setting. Being all packed suggests that she was ready to be born. The presence of Irene K., as a second person (just as the presence of the imbecile girl as a second) may allude to a double situation. It is quite possible that the foundation for fetal destruction fantasies is the attack to which we were exposed before birth. It furnishes a pattern which might readily lend itself for use against a competing sibling. Being attacked within the womb is equivalent to being murdered. Thus, both victim and murderer may describe the dreamer. In the dungeon she was punished for a fantasied crime and, at the same time, was the innocent victim of an apparent crime. She was not allowed to leave the funny cave because she was psychically arrested by the shock of parental intercourse as she was about to be born. As Irene K. seemed to represent her traumatic self in many previous dreams, it is possible also that the pre-natal shock caused a degree of dissociation; therefore, her integration cannot be completed until the pre-natal levels of her mind have been fully explored.

When Parents Are Gentle

Another case illustrates the same time problem in parental intercourse during gestation, but its chief revelation is the striking difference in impact on the unborn child of a gentle parental contact: The patient is a masseuse by profession, and this is her dream:

I am in a hotel. It looks very comfortable, it has nice rugs, it gives the impression of a home. Friends of my father are present, playing cards with him. I recognize one, Mr. Kronheimer. I do not want to play. It is boring.

Then I go to the toilet, which was in a funny place. I have to duck under a wooden bar to get in. At the back of the toilet, a window opens on a church. On the window sill I see some glassy brown paper which had the tendency to curl up. The window pane is missing. I wonder if the paper is meant to take the place of the glass. Then the door of the toilet opens and the son of Kronheimer comes in. I remember saying: "Just . . ." I wanted to say, "Just a minute, you cannot come in." He said immediately, "That's all right," and went out. As if he had used the wrong door, he goes over to the church to attend the service. I see him there through the window. I pass water. Then I wake up with a strong bladder pressure and have to go to the toilet.

The suspicion that the dream deals with a pre-natal situation is first aroused by the wooden bar under which the dreamer has to duck in order to enter the lavatory. Such bars often symbolize the pubic arch. If that assumption is valid in this dream, the lavatory must stand, as bathrooms usually do, for the womb. Confirmation might be found in the adjoining church. A church is a universal symbol of the womb, the Holy of Holies of human generation. The unobstructed window between the lavatory and the church establishes a close association between the two places. The hotel is another reference to the pre-natal home. The mother's body is a hotel for the unborn child. The very name of Kronheimer contains the word "home" (Heim) and "crown" (Krone), a royalty reference, so commonly associated with the uterine state. Kronheimer, the son (of whom the patient had no erotic memories) may stand for the penis, the father's little one entering. He enters through the wrong door. The wrong door is the anus, the lavatory door. Yet, as far as the lavatory is concerned, it is the front door as well. The two aspects can be reconciled on the supposition that the entrance refers to intercourse from the hind position. Kronheimer apologizes; he just pushes himself in and goes out. Does this refer to very gentle intercourse, just between the labia, yet sufficiently powerful to produce a bursting of the waters, which the release of the bladder pressure indicates? Does the glassy brown paper that curls up so easily refer to the amniotic sac?

On this basis we can understand the card-play. The intercourse spoken of is more or less a play. She objects to it because it is too boring. The word has an ambivalent meaning. It may refer to the sexual act. As far as the patient's imagination stretched, her father was the type of man whom she could imagine to have intercourse with his wife up to the last moment. He was sensuous, not a waster of opportunities.

At this point, the patient narrated her second dream, which brings confirmation of the pre-natal solution just discussed.

I am on the main floor, massaging. Then I go next door. It is a ladies' lingerie shop. I remember touching a blue nightgown. It was hanging down by the head, the lower part being on top of the counter. Then I go downstairs into the basement. The room at the back of the house opens into the country. It is Harry's office. He had told me he had two offices. I want to be nice to him and I lie down on the floor with him to have intercourse. We are side by side. I want to say, please be careful, I don't want any trouble, when I no-

*tice that my mother is sitting across the room watching me. I
thought I better not say anything or she will be worried.*

Here is the reverse of the usual Freudian situation: the child returning into the womb in fantasy to watch the parents in intercourse. It is the mother who is watching her. She uses two mechanisms: the opposite and substitution. Harry, her one-time lover,
substitutes for the father, and she is afraid of getting hurt by his
penis. She never had intercourse with Harry on the floor. We may assume that the floor stands for the ground level, the pre-natal. It is not
the mother who is watching her but it is she who is preoccupied
with the meaning of the contact between the parents. The side by
side position suggests the hind contact previously indicated by the
wrong door. The basement is the womb and the back view is the
pre-natal landscape. Confirmation is furnished by the position of
the nightgown. It is head downward, like the child within the womb.

The dream contains the hint that the choice of her profession as
a masseuse may have been determined by erotic motives; further
that the patient's prevailing fear of strangers may have originated in
pre-natal fear impacts. To the unborn child, the invasion by the
father's organ, manifesting itself in upsetting shocks and a great in-
flow of blood, is something unknown, mysterious, out of the orderly
course of its universe. It is quite possible that the fear of the unknown is later projected into the world, imbuing it with an unintended hostility. In other words, the dream suggests the query
whether strangers in whose presence the patient always felt oddly
embarrassed, did not represent her father's penis?

The formulation of this query was a shock to the patient. Her
immediate answer was the admission that her fear of strangers is
far more pronounced regarding men than women. As subsequent
dreams showed an easing of this psychological situation, it is quite
possible that the interpretation had hit home.

Fear of Rape

The fear of rape may originate in the fear of birth by a translation

315

of the crushing experienced in the mother's genitalia onto a woman's own genital tract. It is possible now to go a step further and investigate the possibility whether the fear of rape may not originate in parental intercourse traumata of the unborn child.

A woman patient reads Pearl Buck's *Dragon Seed* before going to sleep. The book describes the rape of Chinese women by the Japanese. They knock at the door of a place of refuge and ask for five or six women to go with them, in which case they promise to leave the rest in peace. A few women sacrifice themselves and depart with the Japanese.

After going to sleep, the patient wakes up at 2 A.M. with an urge to go to the bathroom and urinate. There she feels a sudden sharp pain in her vagina. Immediately, Pearl Buck's book comes to her mind with the memory of a "ridiculous dream." It was this:

I am taking part in a play, accompanied by music which I had to introduce. I am supposed to do something like Desdemona or Ophelia, recite a little piece of poetry in a sing-song fashion and accompany it on the piano. It all takes place in the bathroom. I look out and see a tremendous audience. Somehow or other the play is a flop. I turn around and say to the director, "We did not have a piano, I could not sing the way I should have, that's why the show was a flop."

The dreamer was not quite sure of the part, but when she added that "it was a play in which the heroine goes crazy," she pointed to Ophelia. She woke from the dream very suddenly, as if the censor had stepped in, and the sharp genital pain which she experienced indicated that part of the dream content was repressed. Immediate associations or symptoms on awakening belong to the dream that preceded them. Though the dream visibly did not upset her, she was unable to fall asleep again and had to take a sleeping pill. This, too, points to considerable concealed affect.

Ophelia's background of insanity offers a good starting point for our investigation. Insanity and insane fear are very close equations in dreams. The patient began her analysis by narrating a year old nightmare which almost drove her out of her mind. She was in the war and a Japanese had stabbed her in the heart with a golden dagger. She cried in her sleep and her tears felt like blood on her arms. She woke up with violent palpitation, ran into the bathroom and looked at her face in the mirror:

My eyes had deep circles underneath, I was yellow and I had a terrible sensation of ringing in the ears. My stomach started rumbling, I belched and hiccoughed, my strength was drained, my breath was failing and I thought the hour of my death had come. I went to say goodbye to my children, kissed them, then I wakened my husband and told him I was dying. He called the doctor, who found me suffering from shock and kept me in bed for a week.

Judging by the effect of this nightmare, the patient suffered from an overwhelming fear of death. One of its manifestations was a morbid fear of rape. As she was reading of rape by the Japanese before going to sleep, we may safely assume that the sharp genital pain felt on awakening stands for assault. We do not know how the assault was dramatized in her forgotten dream, but as she did not wake up in panic, we may infer that the antecedent analytic labor had considerably reduced the pressure, and that in the Ophelia dream she was trying to act out the traumatic situation in which the nightmare originated. The confusion between Ophelia and Desdemona must have some significance to which her associations may give a clue. She said:

"Desdemona is the wife of Othello, young and beautiful. He is very jealous of her, kills her and then kills himself. Desdemona sings something, too. She is isolated."

Death and isolation are the outstanding ideas in this explanation. In the dream, we find no trace of death, but the isolation is evident. The bathroom reveals it to be the isolation of the womb. Death is repressed, but behind the role which she plays in the bathroom, as on the stage, we find a vague allusion to an insane fear. That fear appears to have been at the root of the earlier Japanese nightmare. In the role of Desdemona or Ophelia, she is taking part in the drama of parental aggression against the unborn child, herself, trying to show through the combined symbolism of bathroom, Japanese dream antecedents and genital after-pain that her death and rape fears arose from a translation of the invasion of her mother's uterine passage by the father during gestation on to her own genitalia in post-natal life. The golden dagger is her father's penis, and the stabbing in the heart is a displacement of the fear from the heart of the unborn to that of the adult.

The show is a flop because of the absence of the piano. Sexual feelings are frequently expressed in dreams by play on musical instruments. If we substitute intercourse for the rhythm of the piano, we can understand why she cannot sing. She was too frightened to share in the pleasure of the parents. She only received an impact of fear.

The date of the Ophelia dream coincided with the date of her original menstrual cycle. Sometime previous to the dream she departed from it and her menstrual periods became very disorderly and painful. She was ill the greater part of the month and could not stand the sight and smell of blood. Her last period was three weeks delayed. I found reason to think that the fear of bleeding to death was behind the delay and that this fear, in its turn, arose from the fear of rape.

The drama which she tried to enact in the bathroom failed because her repressions were still too strong to permit her free self-expression on the stage of life. Yet the dream was a success inasmuch as it called attention to fundamental features of her neurotic life.

Mother's Penis

An interesting query now suggests itself. Does the well-known dream fantasy that the mother has a penis originate in memories of ante-natal aggression, in which the invading organ is conceived of as part of the maternal environment? In great fear and with a wildly beating heart, a woman woke from the following dream:

A huge ape, of which people were afraid, was at large and I undertook to lead it back into the cage. As I stepped within, the door shut and I found myself locked in. I did not have the key, so I could not get out. I tried to distract the monkey's attention until the key could be brought, and I was very frightened.

Raids Against the Unborn

Later, she added a supplement to the dream about thumbing somebody with both thumbs. She suggested that the thumb looked like a penis and that the embryo holds its hands in that position in the womb.

The thumb-penis identification struck me as a routine Freudian association, but the embryonic reference surprised me. Monkey and embryo are not far apart. The human child looks like a monkey at a certain stage of its pre-natal development. As the cage can well symbolize the womb, it was possible that the dream presented an antenatal setting for the explanation of an overwhelming fear. The key for which she is waiting to effect her deliverance is strangely consonant with monkey (mon-key). Was the key to the nature of her fear hidden in the size?

The monkey or rather ape was big and dangerous. If it had not been, there would have been no need to lead it back to the cage. By leading it back, the dreamer is tracing the fear to its source. Into her mind floated the story of King Kong, Edgar Wallace's last motion picture. It is about an immense ape captured in a pre-historic jungle, and a beautiful woman who, in comparison, is so small that the ape can shelter her in its palm.

As king stand for the father and the ape is said to be the ancestral father of the human race, it appears as if the pre-historic setting described the fear of the father within the womb. In being locked in with the ape, the latter is made an organic part of the pre-natal environment. Instead of the usual mechanism of *pars pro toto* (part for the whole), we are facing here a *totum per parte* (the whole for the part) situation. The ape is the father's penis, part of the maternal body, and as such the source of wild fears. Occasionally, these fears are clothed in a dream in which the mother has a male organ, a discovery which usually has a very upsetting influence on the dreamer.

The thumb describes the specific function of this substitute organ by illustrating intercourse. An understanding of the pre-natal attack will open the cage in which part of the patient's personality is still confined.

319

Search for the Beloved

The pre-natal attack apparently generates an aggressive reaction. The manner of its objectification in the father, together with the guilt reaction that necessarily develops from this situation, is illustrated in the following dream:

I was in a large room in front of the fireplace in which fire was burning. One of the soft cushions was trussed up against the fireplace and part of its covering was burnt off. I called my wife's attention to it, regretting the incident. Then the doorbell rang, and Ellen M. said she would come with me to the door. There was a short-circuit and the room went dark. I called out through the door: who is it? Somebody said he had brought the pictures. Now I remembered that I had sent some pictures to be framed and I decided to let the man in. At the same time I thought that he could attack me in the dark, but felt no particular anxiety.

In the next scene I was pursued by the police. I ran into a yard, leaving my coat somewhere in the front, and tried to hide behind piles of staves. The hiding places seemed to be too obvious; experienced searchers would find me immediately; I had no chance of escaping them. I was feeling cold, which was another reason why I would not run away into the open. Then I heard two people talking. One of them was outside a window trying to climb in from above. He did not notice me. I wanted to stop him. I bobbed up suddenly and began to hurl things through the window. The man ducked his head a few times, then he was hit fully in the face. I smashed at his hands holding the window frame, and he collapsed. Then the thought came: if I take his coat off, the pursuers will find my coat and believe it belongs to him; they won't search for me and I shall be safe.

The first part of the dream helps in understanding the second. The warmth within the apartment, together with the burnt-off cover of the seating cushion, is placed in vivid contrast to the cold and the discarded coat of the second part. Both the fire and the cold are represented as injurious. It is tempting to assume that the fire represents injury by passion, and the cold injury by fear. In that sense, both are enemies. It happens that Ellen, in the dreamer's native tongue, means enemy. The short-circuit and the darkness create conditions that are conducive to an attack and the attack would materialize through the door. He who falls a helpless victim to an attack is often described as framed. The dreamer thought that the frame-up must concern the maternal situation, as suddenly he recalled that there were peasant rug runners on the floor as in the home of his parents. He added further that the seating cushion in his own living room is covered with satin. As satin is often used to describe the feel of the skin (satiny skin), the burn injury must relate to his seat.

The second part of the dream permits the conclusion that the seat (anus) is a translation symbol for the mother's womb and that the dreamer is intent on explaining the origin of his aggressiveness against his father by an attack against himself before he was born. There were piles of staves in his parents' yard. Sometimes they were grouped in such a manner that a free square place was left in between which was easy to build over on top and then could be called a house. He vividly recalled a gap at the bottom between two piles which he enlarged by hammering a number of staves apart to make an entrance into the "house." He used to spend pleasant hours in this hiding place, feeling secure and certain that nobody would find him. While in his childhood the desire to return resulted in pleasurable fantasies, now he finds the place unsafe. The police (a symbol of the pursuing father) would find him. In admitting he has no chance of escaping, he gives the dream that fatalistic touch which we always find in birth dreams. Nevertheless, he also gives evidence of strong hostile emotions. These are directed at the penis which is about to invade the womb. The *totum per parte* (the whole instead of the part) principle is shown in operation in a curious form. There are two people outside. One of them, about to climb in, is the penis, often described as the little one, the child. If so, the other one is the owner, the father—split up—not so astonishing as it first appears as the penis has qualities of life and lends itself to personification. Hitting the man fully in the face is a fantasied smash back at the glans penis. The collapse of the intruder represents the success of the dreamer's cas-

321

tration fantasy. The fight has gone out of the invader; it is no more erect and by skinning it (taking off the coat), he will retaliate for the burned seat and keep himself warm and safe within the womb.*

Decapitation Fantasies

Here is the nightmare of a man of thirty-six, recurrent since early childhood:

A herd of cows surges forward from grazing pastures and chases me downstairs. I find shelter between wooden fences that protect me in front and in the back, but I am afraid the cows will crash through the fence. Then the scene changes into an underground tunnel. I am in the train and see cows rushing towards me and dashing head first into the train, bruising themselves. Then the whole scene becomes ridiculous. One of the cows turns into a woman dressed in cowhide. She tries to reach a switch before a villain gets there. The villain is dressed in a big ape skin and looks like a Frankenstein. The woman tries to kill him but he escapes. Then there is a duel in a swimming pool. The woman throws a cake of soap at the villain. He wards off the soap with a sharp knife, hurls the knife at the woman and kills her. I take the knife and throw it back with such a force that it decapitates the villain. His body sinks down in the water, with the head swimming above. I swim quietly down the pool, away from the corpse.

This case objectifies the aggressive reactions of the unborn against both assaulting parents. Not until both are destroyed is his pre-natal security complete. That the cow stood for the dangerous mother was revealed in the analytic material collected before this dream. Now we see the cow actually changing into a woman. The wooden fence recalled an interesting memory. The patient recognized it as the railing of his crib through which he witnessed the "primal scene." As usual with small children, he mistook it for a deadly fight between his father and mother.

---

* Popular acceptance of the existence of such aggressive fantasies is shown by the following story: Two embryos talk about the future. "What do you want to be?" asks one. "I shall be a lawyer because lawyers can always defend themselves. What will you be?" "I shall be a prize fighter," answers the other. "Why?" "Because I want to take a smack at the guy who comes in every night and spits in my eye!"

Raids Against the Unborn

Once his father had become a villain, regressively he would also become the chief actor in the pre-natal drama of aggression. The tunnel is a reference to the uterus. The cow dashing head first into the train is a coitus shock, its repetitious character being represented by the herd. As it arises within the maternal environment, it is first ascribed to the mother. The switch to the father occurs at a later date. The villain is not immediately there. The discovery of the villain makes him side with his mother. For reason of the primal scene, he wanted to kill his father, so he decapitates him. For reason of the pre-natal scene, he wanted to kill his mother, so he permits her to be killed. The pool is the amniotic lake, and the decapitated head swimming above is the invading penis, the mother's (the head of the cow), and the father's, at last out of the way.

A dream displaces the decapitation fantasy on the ancient phallic symbol of the snake:

I am about to walk down a wooded lane that looks like a tunnel. I may encounter a snake on the way, so I pick up a couple of stones. Then I find a long, thick stick which I can use. Yes, very soon I see a large snake lying on the right side of the road where I am to pass. It narrows down in one part like a bloodworm used for bait when it is no longer fresh. I decide to jab "him" with the stick and pin him to the ground. I had better strike him near the head where the neck should be, that would give a better hold. I must have socked him a few times with a stone, or hacked away with a knife or something, then I flung him away. Possibly he had been impaled on the stick, and I flung him off the stick. He landed on a slanting shelf along the wall, such as you find in a store-room, right in the open mouth of a manila bag. The bag was not a new one; the paper at the mouth was worn and crinkled. I could see that the snake was badly damaged, mushy in fact, but I thought that his head inside the bag might still be alive and dangerous. I could picture the fangs, so I pulled the snake out of the bag and laid it on the ground. The only way to make sure the snake was properly despatched was to cut off his head. I made some progress, but before I completed the amputation, the dream was over.

The patient's own interpretation of the dream was that he was destroying fear. That is quite true, but the dream makes the fear specific. The snake is a "he" and it is found in a tunnel, i.e., in the uterus. After his murderous attack, the snake is half in and half out of a manila bag. He saw manila bags the day before in his landlady's larder. The landlady's bag is the mother's womb, worn and wrinkled at the mouth by the many deliveries and intercourse. The thinning of the snake's body recalled to the patient the head of the circumcised penis. He is bent on cutting off this head (glans) from the beginning of the dream, but his purpose is not made clear until he pictures it within the womb, out of sight but still dangerous. There can be no doubt that the snake stands for his father. The impersonal representation has the advantage that it evokes no fear and guilt reactions. The dream censor passes it, up to the moment of complete amputation when misgivings arose and the dream suddenly broke.

It may be objected that the dream is a simple castration fantasy with the usual background of incestuous jealousy; that the walk within the tunnel may stand for the retrojection into the uterus of the young son's hostility over the primal scene.

The answer is that taken out of the context of a long series of extremely complicated dreams (all pointing to a more involved story than an incestuous fantasy) the corroborative material is indeed wanting. However, the objection itself is based on an assumption,—which is that castration fantasies of this type are rooted in the jealousy of the son because the father possesses the mother. Freudian psychology was unable to carry its research beyond this point. I tried to carry it back to birth in the chapter on *Birth and Castration*. I see no reason why the inquiry should stop at this point. We may well find yet that father castration fantasies arise from pre-natal motivation.

29.

ATTEMPTS AT ABORTING THE UNBORN

PRE-NATAL problems so far discussed have made it abundantly clear that, filed away in the mysterious recesses of the human organism, there must be a record of the master plan on which the human body is built, just as there is a record of the impacts which hit the unborn within the womb and a record of the adaptation to those impacts.

We know of no extraneous overseer whose care would account for the perfection with which our body functions and regenerates itself. The least we are forced to postulate is the existence of an organismic memory in which this blueprint is preserved and in which it can be consulted. It is certain that the design is not stored in the memory cells of the brain because the body develops before the brain, the full growth of the latter occurring in a belated stage of embryonic history. It is equally obvious that the intelligence to which we owe the perfection of our bodily functions cannot be called an automaton, a mechanical principle that cannot help working out what it does and has no conception of the end in view. If anything is clear about embryonic development, it is its purposiveness. At the end of gestation, we find a human being ready for birth and completely equipped with mental faculties and complicated biological devices for post-natal life.*

---

* Prof. Hans Spemann postulates a growth directing monitor which he calls "the organizer." Paul Weiss, a German biologist, calls the mysterious architect "the biological field."

Search for the Beloved

At this point our mental agony begins. For once we admit the purposiveness of embryonic development, we are forced to broaden the concept of organismic memory, which we have postulated as a minimum concession, and give consideration to the existence of an organismic mind or organismic consciousness which controls the relationship of the growing human being to the maternal environment within the womb. It is easy to draw the line between this organismic consciousness and that of the ego-consciousness built on the feelings and sense impressions that flood us from within our body and from without, through the sensory organs. The relationship between the unconscious mind and this organismic consciousness is none too clear. Structurally the organismic consciousness is a deeper stratum, perhaps the very bedrock of the unconscious mind, ordinarily beyond our psychological reach, yet an ever-present fundus without which no human edifice can be built.

Faculties of the Organismic Mind

In the Freudian concept, which is purely mechanistic, the unconscious mind cannot reason; it can only wish. It is quite true that reasoning is the supreme function of the conscious mind. As, however, the unconscious mind shares all the knowledge and experience which the conscious mind acquires, it would be less misleading to claim that we reason because the unconscious mind helps us to develop this faculty for the purpose of securing its grasp on the material world.

Such a construction would make it clear that we do not dominate the unconscious mind by our reasoning faculty; that we are not rendered superior to it, but are only part of it. The unconscious mind "reasons" through the conscious mind.

Having enthroned reason, Freud was bound to think of the unconscious mind as a lumber room in which instinctual drives run around like rats and mice in a cage and in which nothing else lives. This is a serious limitation of Freudian psychology. Groddeck and Jung have tried to free us from it, Groddeck by his concept of the "It," which embraces both the conscious and the unconscious mind, investing it with almost godlike power,* Jung by giving us the impersonal (racial

---
* Georg Groddeck, *The Unknown Self*, C. W. Daniel Co., London, 1937, pp. 40-43.

or collective) unconscious mind, and thus opening up vistas of which Freud could not dream because of his personal quarrel with God.

Both Groddeck and Jung took a leap into the spiritual, but missed, more or less, an important stepping stone: the embryonic stage. They ignored the psychic life of the unborn. While Jung is willing to postulate the influence of the racial mind on the individual psyche, he fails to give consideration to the influence of the maternal psyche and of the maternal organism.

It stands to reason that the organismic consciousness of the unborn must needs be aware of endocrine disturbances in the maternal body through the channel of blood. The colloquialism that our blood turns cold under the effect of fear or hot under the effect of rage or passion plainly hints at the appreciation of psychic upheavals through the bloodstream. Yet it takes courage to affirm the existence or determine the scope of such appreciation by the unborn child, for of the function and powers of the unconscious mind we know little, of the organismic mind nothing.* Nevertheless, we have by now progressed beyond the stage of pure speculation. Experimental findings in telepathy now form a sufficiently impressive body of facts to show that the unconscious mind has its own channels of awareness. Telepathy might be but one, and the precise nature of even this one is totally incomprehensible to the conscious mind.

No two human beings are closer to each other than the mother and the unborn child. If telepathy is at all operative between human beings, it should be operative between the mother and her child. It may fulfil very important functions. It may, for instance, act as a shock absorber for the weaning of the child from the mother's body in birth. The mother's fond expectations and reassuring thoughts may have a very salutary influence on the psyche of the unborn child. But if so,

---

* The organismic mind, as I conceive it, is less than Groddeck's "It." It does not embrace post-natal consciousness and is not endowed with the mystic powers which Groddeck ascribes to the "It."
  "There are in the fetus frequent and violent movements which have as their purpose the avoidance of painful feelings; moreover there exists certainly a memory, although an unconscious one, of embryonic days, which persists throughout life and may continuously determine an action." (Dr. J. Sadger; "Preliminary Study of the Psychic Life of the Fetus and the Primary Germ," *The Psychoanalytic Review*, July, 1941, p. 333.)

the reverse would be equally true. The loneliness of the unwanted child may be more than a post-natal psychic structure, it may reach back to its psychic isolation within the womb.

D. H. Lawrence voices this idea in his *Sons and Lovers*. Describing the mother with an unwanted child in her arms, he says: "Its clear, knowing eyes gave her pain and fear. Did it know all about her? When it lay under her heart, had it been listening then? Was there reproach in the look? She felt the marrow melt in her bones, with pain and fear." * As D. H. Lawrence was speaking of his own mother in the book, the queries represent an intuitive analytic exploration of the pre-natal levels of his own mind.

We have no knowledge as to how and when a telepathic faculty comes into being in an adult.† It may not be a new faculty at all but an archaic method of communication antedating the development of speech. In that case the possibility of its existence in the pre-natal state (which corresponds to the prehistoric era of the race) may well demand consideration. This very possibility is bound to exercise a

---

* D. H. Lawrence, *Sons and Lovers*, Kennerly, London, 1935.

† Geza Roheim, "Telepathy in a Dream," *The Psychoanalytic Quarterly,* Vol. I, 1932, pp. 277-291.

Sigmund Freud, "Dreams and the Occult," *New Introductory Lectures on Psychoanalysis*, W. W. Norton & Co., New York, 1933.

Leon J. Saul, "Telepathic Sensitiveness as a Neurotic Symptom," *The Psychoanalytic Quarterly*, Vol. VII, 1938, pp. 329-335.

Hans J. Ehrenwald, "Telepathy in Dreams," *British Journal of Medical Psychology*, Vol. XI, 1942, pp. 313-323.

Hans J. Ehrenwald, "Telepathy in the Psychoanalytic Situation," *British Journal of Medical Psychology*, Vol. XX-1, 1944, pp. 51-62.

Nandor Fodor, "Telepathic Dreams," *American Imago*, August, 1942, pp. 61-87.

Nandor Fodor, "Telepathy in Analysis," *The Psychiatric Quarterly*, Vol. XXI, 1947, pp. 171-189.

Jule Eisenbud, "Telepathy and Problems of Psychoanalysis," *The Psychoanalytic Quarterly*, Vol. XV, 1946, pp. 32-87.

Jule Eisenbud, "The Dreams of Two Patients in Analysis Interpreted as a Telepathic Rève á Deux," *The Psychoanalytic Quarterly*, Vol. XVI, 1947, pp. 39-60.

Jule Eisenbud, "Analysis of a Presumptively Telepathic Dream," *The Psychiatric Quarterly*, January, 1948.

Geraldine Pederson-Krag, "Telepathy and Repression," *The Psychoanalytic Quarterly*, Vol. XVI, 1947, pp. 61-68.

Albert Ellis, "Telepathy and Psychoanalysis: A Critique of Recent 'Findings,'" *The Psychiatric Quarterly*, Vol. XXI, 1947, pp. 607-659.

profoundly disturbing influence over present-day psychology. If telepathy can be proven to be an organismic function, the organismic consciousness of the unborn child may be as exposed to shocks, fears and surging joyful emotions as is the post-natal mind.

We have no accessible records of such impacts because of complete pre-natal amnesia. Perhaps it is the shock of birth or the sudden flooding of our new senses with vivid and startling impressions that produces this amnesia; perhaps other more mysterious factors are involved. We have a parallel for pre-natal amnesia in post-natal repressions and in infantile amnesia, which covers the period from birth until about five years of age. The fragmentary recollections which occasionally occur in the latter are totally missing regarding the pre-natal record of life. Nevertheless, we appear to have access to it in our dream life. Just as the post-natal unconscious mind can be stimulated by current events to disclose in dreams the existence of subterranean areas of pressure, so can something rise from the organismic levels of the mind to indicate pre-natal traumata and demand their release. No psychoanalytic integration of a personality can be completed until it reaches the fetal levels of the mind because it is before birth that the psychic foundation of our being is laid.

Birth-marks

The thought that telepathy might be a function of the organismic mind first occurred to me during a discussion of birth-marks. Numerous stories are told of pregnant mothers who, frightened by a mouse or insect, clasp their bodies nervously, and find on the new-born child's skin a mark "exactly" corresponding to the shape of the mouse, insect, etc. at the "exact" spot. Science tells us that such stories have no factual foundation; birth-marks show few variations; only a vivid imagination can find in them a correspondence in shape to something that had frightened the expectant mother; there is no nervous connection between the mother and the child; therefore the fetus cannot suffer from the shock which the mother experiences.*

---

* "Nothing gets through the placenta from mother to child unless it is capable of being carried in solution by the blood, and of passing through the walls of the villi and of their blood capillaries, which together constitute an exceedingly fine-meshed semipermeable membrane. There is no other means of communica-

329

The trouble with this scientific attitude is that it is based solely on materialistic considerations. Prove the existence of telepathy, and you have proven that shock effects can be transmitted from one mind to another without nervous connection.

I hold it very probable that any resemblance between the birth-mark and the visual object to which the mother was exposed is purely accidental. The nervous seizure of the body is more likely to be the focal center of the shock than the mental impression. The emphasis in most of the birth-mark stories is not on the shape but on the spot. Is it so absurd to think that the body of the unborn may react as a tuning fork to a localized nervous shock?

The popular belief in the origin of birth-marks may be labelled as mere superstition. Nevertheless, again and again we find that such beliefs represent the intuitive knowledge of the race with which science belatedly catches up. Some birth-mark stories are so startling that any imperious rule against them savors of an intolerance which has no place in science.

To present the problem practically, here is an instance:

A mother burns herself accidentally with hot cigarette ash over the right eyelid in the eighth month of her pregnancy. She gets a shock, and the thought comes to her immediately: will the child within her be affected by it? The child is born with a red mark over the right eyelid. Five years pass. The mark is still visible, sometimes fading, at other times brighter. It is not due to injury during delivery. What then has caused it? Is or is not its existence purely coincidental with the mother's story?

The cases in which the shock of the mother is not followed by a marking of the child's body furnish no contrary argument. Negatives never prove anything. The problem of birth-marks only arises because positive correspondences have been noticed throughout the ages.

One case began by a discussion of birth-marks, of the splash type,

---

tion between mother and child. In particular it should be emphasized in capital letters that there is no connection between their nervous system. Not a single nerve fiber crosses the placental barrier; there is no channel for the transmission of feelings or intentions, moods, memories or ideas." (George W. Corner, *Ourselves Unborn*, Yale University Press, 1944, p. 53.)

which are usually accompanied by the story that the mother had burned herself accidentally with some hot liquid. The case was illustrated by the coffee-colored splash on the neck of a beautiful woman whose mother had spilt hot coffee over herself while carrying the child. The unusual part of the story is that the mother had twins, two girls, and the birth-mark was only found on one. This seems incongruous with the theory that such marks are due to the shock coming from the maternal body. Yet it is not necessarily an argument as we know nothing about the relative sensitivity of twins and of the conditions in which the hypothetical transmission from the mother to the child can take place.

The important result of the discussion, which settled nothing, was the dream which it induced in an eighteen-year-old girl, the niece of the woman with the splash-like birth-mark. She saw herself in a rocky pool, shallow at one end, deep at another. Her mother was trying to kill her by various means. One after another was postponed. At first she was terrified, then became resigned, impersonal. At the end, she went upstairs and told a boy about nine that she had escaped.

The rocky pool is an obvious womb symbol. The graduated depth may refer to the progressive development of the child, using spatial symbolism for this purpose. If this is correct, her awareness of the mother's murderous attempts against her must refer to abortion. As no actual attack is depicted in the dream, the threat is purely mental. The dream seems to reflect the mother's death wishes, and not her acts, against the child during gestation. This is what puts the dream in a special category. It appears as if the conversation on birth-marks had stirred up the young girl's memories of pre-natal shocks telepathically imparted by her mother's mind. The alternative is that the dream is a fantasy of an unwanted child, in which release of her unhappiness is sought by weaving the mother's hostility into a pre-natal drama.

The answer to this alternative is that the dreamer was not an unwanted baby and had a fine upbringing with abundant love. Her childhood was unquestionably happy. However, after conception, she was considered as coming too soon and attempts were made by the mother to re-establish the menstrual flow. These attempts were given up at an early stage, and the child was expected with joy.

331

Search for the Beloved

The dreamer, according to her mother's assurance, could have gained no knowledge of this phase of her earliest history. If we accept this assurance, telepathic registration, at an early stage of embryonic development, of the mother's destructive intent appears to be the only solution of the dream. The destructive intent need not be restricted to actual steps to producing an abortion. Nor need the transmission be considered instantaneous; it may be delayed and cumulative. Most pregnant mothers have death wishes against the coming child at one time or another during pregnancy. They are seized with periodic doubts: would it not be better not to have a child, than go through the agony of carrying, labor and sacrifice? Such thoughts may not find utterance; they may be pushed back into the unconscious mind from the moment they arise. Telepathically they may become accessible to the organismic mind of the unborn child, create a fear reaction and the type of tension which the dream indicates.

The fatalistic touch of resignation in face of the mother's murderous attacks is a typical characteristic of birth dreams. By reversal, going upstairs may indicate descending in birth. No attempt is made at running away. From the dreamer's attitude it appears that birth is the only escape. The hope of the parents was that she would be a boy. This was no secret to the dreamer. The age of the boy whom she informs of her escape probably refers to the months of gestation.

The dream mind makes no half statements. This is an important principle in dream interpretation. I do not recall that this has been stated in psychoanalytic literature. It means that if one dreams of an escape, the nature of the danger from which one is escaping will also be present concealed in the same dream. The forces of repression, of course, come into play against it and the recollection of the explanatory part of the dream may be vague and confused; nevertheless, as an addendum, it usually emerges during the discussion of the dream. In this particular case, the danger from which the dreamer escaped lay in the death wishes of the mother against the unborn.

Blaming the Father

In this remarkable case, the meaning of the dream was revealed

by a slip of the tongue right within the dream. The dreamer is a man
of thirty-two, who hated his father virulently and had terrible conflicts with him all his life.

As if I was reading a story: father and son are flying in a plane.
Something goes wrong; they are about to crash. The father says: let
us commit suicide, let us get it over. The son objects: while there is
life there is hope; it is a crime against God to commit abortion. He
meant suicide but said abortion. With a white handkerchief he tied
himself to the cockpit, and they were both saved.

The dream is so clear that it hardly requires an explanation. The
story is presented in the form of fiction, which makes it far removed,
impersonal—an excellent means to beguile the censor. There is no
crash; it is only a threat. It stands for the fear of death through abortion. Flying fantasies are typical of the pre-natal setting. The white
scarf shows the tenacity of the child to hang on. The only question
which the dream leaves is: why is it the father who urges the son to
suicide? It is the mother whom one would naturally expect to find in
this role.

Before we attempt to answer this question, we should read the
continuation of the dream, which removes any lingering doubt that
attempts to abort the unborn is its basic thought:

I am sitting in the lobby of a movie. A man on the stage tells of a dis-
covery by which grown-up people can be reduced to tiny, miniature
creatures. The audience jeers at him, but unexpectedly one of his lilli-
putians walks out on the stage and talks. He is only a few inches high.
The audience is still sceptical and accuses the man of ventriloquism.

Two men in the front row want to shoot him. They take a long ob-
ject, about a foot in measure, and sharpen it as a pencil, then they
load it into the rifle. I am on the stage watching the scene and feel
outraged. The lecturer speaks the truth; the audience is making fun
of him and now these people try to shoot him. The two men now de-
cide to shoot hot water at his legs and cripple him by scalding. Dr.
Ferries is one of them and he will aim at his left leg. (My left leg went
numb in the movie again.) I see my superior officer sitting in the front

row and grinning. I spit in his face. The lecturer is also a doctor, but does not know of the hot water plot until he touches the index finger of Dr. Ferries and feels it is hot. He pulls a slip of paper from his pocket and reads out noble thoughts: never despair, hope is never far behind. (It amounted to the same thing which the son said to the father in the aeroplane). I cannot stand it any longer. I give Dr. Ferries a piece of my mind and walk away. Dr. Ferries follows me. I turn around and point a gun at him. He also pulls one and points it. It is a stalemate. Then he tells me how his ancestor made his fortune.

An embryonic stage-setting is revealed in this fascinating dream by the reduction of adults to the size of lilliputians and in the accusation of ventriloquism, which conceals a reference to maternal anatomy. Further, two attempts at abortion are indicated, one with a pointed object, the other with hot water, suggesting a vaginal douche. Both attempts are directed at the doctor-lecturer, who represents the analyst. By transference to him (while the patient himself is on the stage and sides with him) they are objectified and easier to face than if they were represented as matters of direct personal concern. At the same time, the patient makes it plain that he considers the pre-natal ideas of the analyst fantastic and is in conflict regarding their acceptance. Yet his inner self approves and he is outraged at the Doubting Thomas in him. This outrage is a good cover for his hostility towards his father. As in the previous dream, it is the father who is behind the pre-natal murder. He spits in the face of one father authority and tries to shoot the other. The second father authority is Dr. Ferries. He speaks of the fortune made by an ancestor, which is a reference to a previous and luxurious life.

Not one woman appears in the dream. All the dramatic personae are men. The reason for this concentration on the male emerged when the patient stated:

"I don't think my mother wanted me; she hated my father."

It must be a terrible psychological situation for a woman to have a child from a man whom she hates. Not only would it lead to very strong death wishes against the child and to actual attempts at abortion, but if telepathic transmission from the mother to the child is to be admitted, the hatred of the father would also be communicated by the maternal emotions. Such assumptions would help to understand the reason why this patient bore an undying hatred to his father and why he wrecked his own life by punitive reactions for his vindictiveness.*

The next case illustrates the difficulty in distinguishing between abortion nightmares by retrojection of father fears from the post-natal levels of the mind and genuine pre-natal impacts. If the child knows that he was not wanted, if he is afraid of his father, if he is not spared the excitement caused by the mother's recurring pregnancies, it is likely that his abortion nightmares are due to retrojection or at least reveal a mixture of confused impressions and fantasies.

The dream comes from the same patient who was chased by cows in the dream discussed in the previous chapter. It also shows how close is the link between a raid against the unborn and fantasied or real attempts at abortion:

I was in a large, rambling house, part of which was cut off and rarely used. I wanted to find someone or something that was lost in this disused part of the house. I turned on the switch which lighted up the place. With a brown cocker spaniel by my side, I opened the door and entered. Having progressed along the passage, the door behind me closed. Continuing further, I was horrified to find long straight cracks appear in the floor ahead. I looked back and there the same thing was happening. I was cut off. Long partitions descended from the ceiling. I found myself enclosed in a small chamber, about six feet square. I was trapped in a prison.

After a few seconds, the partitions lifted. Now the room was differently arranged. In front of me was a glass screen. I saw two men ahead of me and a third behind me. I gathered that the one behind me had manipulated the shutters. He was furious that I should have dared to enter into this part of the building and said that I was a nuisance

---

* Dr. J. Sadger goes even deeper: "Inasmuch as each ovum is part of the mother, every sperm cell a part of the father, without doubt the resistance of the parents to each other is transferred likewise to the fission of the cell from which the future human being develops." ("Preliminary Study of the Psychic Life of the Fetus and the Primary Germ," *The Psychoanalytic Review*, July, 1941, p. 339.)

who ought to be put out of the way. One of the other two men, who had a moustache and a quiet voice, proposed to put me in a poison bath. The poison was DIAN AMERICILL. I awoke moaning.

In this astonishing dream the dreamer enters his unconscious mind, a large, rambling house in the disused part of which he seeks for a lost part of his personality by the light which analysis provides. To the question why he should enter with a cocker spaniel, he answered:

"To protect myself. As a faithful friend and a retriever, the cocker spaniel is a good symbol of you, the analyst. Brown to me is the color of trust and confidence."

The analyst does help to retrieve lost memories. These memories, as the trapping in a small, prison-like chamber suggests, concern the pre-natal life. The cracks in the floor stand for the fear of falling through and being crushed in the course of birth. Six, describing the size of the room, is consonant with sex, a probable reference to the genital character of birth.

The second part of the dream reads like a chapter from embryonic history. The scene changes and the dreamer is no more conscious of the limitations of space. The wording "I saw two men ahead of me and a third one behind me" may bring in a time element: two months have passed, the third is not yet completed, therefore not seen, not known. It is during the second and third months that parents face the critical question of permitting a child to be born or deciding against it. The patient knows that his father violently objected to his coming. He was the seventh child, so he was a nuisance. He remembered violent scenes between his parents because his mother became pregnant again and again. The man who manipulates the shutters must be his father. It depends on the father whether the child is to be shut out of life or not—and in the dream the father decides against him.

The poison bath, the patient suggested, must refer to something his mother was supposed to take to bring about an abortion. This bath links up with his previous dream of murder in the pool, and the screen suggests the railing of the crib, from behind which he witnessed stormy scenes between his parents. He thought DIAN AMERICILL garbled three words: die or dying, America and kill or ill. As the patient was born in Europe, to him America is the new world, a symbol of birth. Birth is a dying for the pre-natal state. The new life, after birth, had new terrors. He was afraid his father would kill him.

A new-born infant, however, is not likely to be exposed to such intense hostility on the part of a father as the dream portrays; at least it is not likely that the child should become so keenly aware of it. If the last word in AMERICILL refers, indeed, to a danger to life, the probability is that we have in it a three-fold condensation: a telepathic transmission from his mother blaming his father, the memory of being attacked within the womb in parental intercourse and the retrojected fear of the father as the murderer of unborn children. Whether this reasoning is entirely or only partly correct, the abortion drama itself is clearly revealed by the dream and was spontaneously appreciated as such by the patient himself.

30.

THE LOVE LIFE OF THE UNBORN

T HE influence of parental intercourse on the unborn child has always exercised popular imagination. Some believe that it is harmful for the child and that the parents should abstain from it after pregnancy has progressed beyond the first few months. This attitude might be called instinctual; its factual basis we have already discussed. Others think that parental passion helps to mould the psychic life of the child—at the price of sexual precocity. It is commonly believed that "love children" are more beautiful because forbidden love between unmarried people is more intense than between married ones. The latter idea carries the influence of parental attitude way back to conception. The belief that alcohol weakens the germ plasm and drunken parents produce imbecile children is a similar illustration that the popular psyche is not afraid of tracing the psychic formation of the child to the beginnings of pre-natal life.

To forbid intercourse from the moment of impregnation would be as extreme as it is to practice it to the last stages of gestation. The sexual activity of man is not seasonal as in the animal kingdom. As Nature imposes no restriction, the reasonable attitude is the avoidance of extremes and wise moderation in indulgence. Pregnancy may quicken a woman's sexual passion, and for men the period of gestation is too long for continence. An alarming increase in adultery would follow if stringent restrictions were imposed. Further, sexual life is more normal during gestation as the necessity of taking precautions against impregnation no longer harasses the parental mind. Frigidity often evaporates when the fear of pregnancy is banished; with the acceptance of this condition sexual pleasure may reach heights previously unattained.

The medical attitude is that in the last few weeks of pregnancy intercourse should not be indulged in. In this consideration the care for the mother outweighs the care for the child. Too much excitement is not good for the expectant mother; the violence of sexual contact may burst the amniotic waters too soon and produce premature birth. Of the shock which the child may suffer from premature birth, or of the possible psychic effect of intercourse on the unborn too little is known for the formulation of a definite scientific attitude. It is the job of psychoanalysis to prove that such shock effects exist and that it is incumbent on the parents to establish a closed period.

Basing an opinion on the study of pre-natal nightmares, this closed period should cover at least the last two months of gestation. The human child is completely developed at seven months, only requiring growth. It stands to reason that from the seventh month on, the organism of the unborn is more wide awake than during its formative development, and that it may react turbulently to such sudden changes in the environment as intercourse creates.

The nightmares discussed in Chapter 28 exemplified the fear reactions of the unborn. The intensity of the fear is apparently dependent on the violence and frequency of intercourse. Where the violence is less, signs of a pleasure reaction begin to emerge. While this reaction is more difficult to trace, it is sufficiently outstanding to justify the query: is there a love life of the unborn? In support of this query we may quote Wilhelm Preyer's statement in his *Special Physiology of the Embryo* that "the ability to distinguish pleasure and pain is pre-natal and inherited and in the true sense congenital."

The problem can be approached from two angles. One is the investigation of the physical effect of parental intercourse on the child, the other is the psychic effect by the hypothetical but by no means impossible telepathic interaction between mother and child.

On the mother the primary physical effect of intercourse is a state of excitation, tense anticipation and quickening of metabolic functions. The heat of the body and the rate of breathing rises and the genitalia become gorged with blood. We know the effect of an overdose of oxygen on our own system; it causes intoxication and it could cause death by burning up the lungs. The state of glow, the exhilaration which we experience in swallowing great drafts of fresh mountain air, comes from the greater oxygen content of this air. The unborn receives its life-sustaining oxygen from the mother's blood. A speeding up of the mother's circulation, under the effect of sexual excitement, will drive more blood and more oxygen through the fetal system than it ordinarily receives. The result will be a state of intoxication. This intoxication is not of a sexual character but as a derivative of intercourse it may play an unsuspected part in sexual precocity. Nymphomania and satyriasis may yet be found to originate in this condition. The yearning which intercourse cannot satisfy is comprehensible once it is carried back to the pre-natal levels of the mind.

The psychic transmission of pleasure from the mother to the child might be questioned on this ground: the desire is so intense that it should cancel the panic of the child which the physical act causes; if no such cancellation takes place, there is no telepathic transmission. The argument is fallacious. It ignores one important fact: the magnitude of the physical shock. The sense of proportion of the parents is not adjusted to the pre-natal level of life. Between an emotional and a real tidal wave the difference is great. The mother experiences the first, the unborn may only experience the second. Even if the child were able to rise to the mother's thrilling expectations, it would fall victim to panic unless the parental contact remains very gentle on each and every occasion.

The reason why the problem of pre-natal pleasure cannot be left out of analytic consideration is that we find it admixed with the fear reactions of the unborn. It should be emphasized that these pleasure reactions differ from the sexual fantasies that accompany the return into the mother's body; but they may play some part in the genitalization of birth and in the search for ecstasy within the womb.

The Love Life of the Unborn

Pleasure of Being Eaten by a Shark

The case concerns the adolescent girl who dreamed of her mother's attempts to murder her in a rocky pool.

On Waikiki, Tahiti or Hawaii Beach. Beautiful scenery. Pools of water left in the sand. The air is translucent and warm. I am walking with Mummy and Daddy. Suddenly, I see a huge shark cutting ahead of us. We cannot all escape. I have to sacrifice myself for Mummy and Daddy. I wrestle with the shark on the ground. It changes into a very good looking colored boy, then it becomes a shark again. I tell the others: now is the time to knife it.

The dreamer confessed that the wrestling with the shark gave her very pleasurable sensations. She was ashamed to mention them in her narrative. The "colored" boy represents the shame, while the change of the huge shark into a male of the human species plainly reveals the sexual character of the struggle. The sacrifice shows her as the victim of parental sexual pleasures in a pre-natal setting. The hot, tropical beach is a symbol of the womb, life emerging from the warm waters of the sea. The shark is the father's invading organ. Significantly, the wrestling does not take place in the waters, but on the ground which permits closer bodily contact in rolling around, thereby reproducing a more rhythmic movement than the waves would permit.

It should also be noted that the fear which one would expect to find in a dream of this type is absent. The pleasure of the wrestling acts as a tempering and balancing influence. The reason why this tempering was successful lies in the thoughtfulness of the father. He stated that his sexual behavior was very gentle when his wife was big with child.

Witness in the Bathtub

The dream to be considered here is instructive for students of incestuous fantasies. Ever since the Oedipus complex was postulated by Freud, dreams have been placed on record in which the dreamer was spying on parental intercourse from within the womb. Such dreams were considered the products of over-heated sexual imagina-

341

tion. It did not dawn on the early analysts that the retrojection might originate in pre-natal pleasure memories which were mobilized by too much exposure to sexual emotions at a tender age. Here is a dream of a twenty-four-year-old girl whose early childhood was characterized by a sexual curiosity of almost obsessive dimensions:

I was in the bathtub at your house, with a quilt on my lap. I don't remember seeing water. The bathroom opened into the hall and it was different from yours. A design on the quilt showed the path of sexual intercourse. I was studying it. You and your wife were having intercourse on the floor. I was very embarrassed and looked occasionally over the side of the tub. I don't think you saw me. The path was traced on the quilt by a sort of remote control. You were talking all the time, explaining things. Once your wife jumped up frightened, and you said she should not be silly, you would not hurt her and if she shrieked the whole world would be in there. You were very annoyed.

This curious dream is an excellent illustration of transference between the analyst and patient. By shifting her past emotional fixations to the analyst, the patient objectifies them as though they were current events, which permits the discussion and release of her repressions. The analyst and his wife appear in the rôle of the patient's own parents at the time when she was within the womb. Being in the bathtub is a typical representation of the pre-natal position. She is not seen because she is within, and she is trying to figure out the meaning of the rhythmic shocks which she experienced in the pre-natal state. On higher levels of her unconscious mind she knows the solution of the mystery, but this knowledge can only reach the deeper levels via the conscious mind; hence the dream of intercourse on the floor, the bottom level or beginning of life, alludes to the need of working through by the help of the analyst. The remote control and the path of sexual intercourse on the quilt is a highly original presentation of ante-natal seclusion. The quilt, as a cover, is a hint at something hidden behind the apparent drama of intercourse. The bathroom door opens into the hall, which is the hall of life, and the door is the vaginal door. My explanations are the analytic ones which she hopes to receive. The sudden fright of my wife is the fright which she had experienced when the parental intercourse shocks became violent; my annoyance similarly reflects her own emotions.

"I felt like an intruder in the dream," she added.

In reality, it was her father's penis that intruded. The dream fantasy encourages the assumption that the dreamer's tremendous sexual curiosity in early childhood had rested on the pleasure reactions which she had experienced from the conjugal act in the pre-natal state.

The Devil and the Incubus

That insomnia, fear of the dark, and the fear and fascination of the supernormal, may be rooted in pre-natal fear and pleasure experiences, are the inferences offered by the next case. The patient, a very active and ambitious married women of twenty-eight, with a pronounced gift of clairvoyance, finds it hard to go to sleep if alone, and ever since she can remember, she was afraid of the dark. She began in her first session:

"I think my father frightened me. I used to hear him talk of the Devil and of evil spirits. I feel people in the dark, hear sounds, and my imagination builds on them. I never let my hand come out from under the bed covers. I imagine it will be grasped by an evil spirit.

"When I was seven or eight, we moved to a new town and lived in a railroad flat. My father sent me one night to the back porch for something. I told him I was afraid to go, but he insisted. I started walking through the dining room, the bedroom, then another bedroom and got as far as the kitchen. A big cupboard was there. As I came near to that cupboard, I felt a hot breath on my neck. I don't remember whether I was grabbed or not, but I screamed. It seemed as if I was transported clear back to my folks. I don't remember touching the floor. I was feverish all that night. My mother left the light on and stayed with me. I was in a delirium.

"My father used to say, if anyone should knock at the door, we must never call out 'Come in,' for the devil might come in; we should just go to the door and open it. Once I was in the room alone and I thought the Devil was in it with me. The thought just paralyzed me, I could not speak, move or breathe. I thought I would die."

"How do you picture the Devil?" I asked.

"In my dreams it was like my father. Sometimes I could not tell which was my father and which was the Devil."

"Did your father look like the Devil?"

"No, he looked like Abraham Lincoln."

"Was he cruel and bad to you?"

"No, I just worshipped my father. He was always generous and good. He was very religious, but in my dreams he was evil. I used to fall through floor after floor to escape him. Then I would put on an apron, wash the dishes in the Devil's kitchen and pretend that I had been there all the time, so that the Devil should not know I was the person who had just escaped from him. He would come in and look so much like my father that I would run to him, thinking he was my father, and tell him that I was frightened. A cunning smile would come over his face, and then I would know he was not my father, because my father would not look at me like that. Then another devil would come in, again looking like my father. I would think he was the real father and would ask his help against the other. Then he would turn into the devil that he was. There would be any number of them."

Then followed a statement which was little short of sensational:

"I think the Devil was my first lover. He would lock me in a closet and I would have waves of emotion or desire come over me. It was a mad, happy darkness. I did not know what was happening, but now I know that I was having intercourse with my father in the shape of the Devil."

I believe that the solution of this extraordinary identification of the Devil with the father lies on the pre-natal levels of the patient's mind. In intercourse with the mother while the patient was within the womb (kitchen), the father was an invisible enemy, a fiend. He both frightened her and aroused in her waves of hot desire. The closet into which she was locked, the mad, happy darkness, and the cupboard at which the ghost seized her, suggest experiences in the womb. Her fear of the dark may originate in the fear of pre-natal aggression, the darkness representing the darkness of the fetal night. It should be a protective darkness, but it proved destructive to her. The floor upon floor through which she sank until she reached the Devil's kitchen was a good representation of levels of the mind, until the bottom level, the womb was reached. The apron which she puts on is an excellent cover reference to the genital situation. The multiplication of the father-devils probably refers to the multiplicity of intercourse or is simply used for emphasis. The patient's father was a very big man, with a healthy sexual appetite. Instead of a God he became her Devil. The fantasy is of considerable interest because it suggests that the origin of incestuous emotions (or, for that matter, homosexual ones) may have to be traced back to parental intercourse memories.

From the devil there is but a short step to the incubus, the demon lover of witchcraft days. But in the shape of the incubus the sexual experience through which this patient twice passed was infinitely more horrifying.

"I hardly know how to describe it. It was a sexual encounter with something nameless, impersonal, elemental. It had no male organ but lip or mouth both below and above. I fought against it madly and desperately because I desired it but dared not yield to it. I finally succeeded in waking myself. My heart was pounding like a steel hammer, I could hardly breathe and was shaking all over. For many nights, I could not bear to go home if the lights were not on. I even hated the idea of taking a bath because if I relaxed I would lay myself open to this terrible thing. The experience occurred again, but in a minor form. The attack was similar, but I fought it off. When it was leaving me, I thought the thing looked like a dog."

The patient was quite positive that she never had any sexual experience with dogs. The idea was too repulsive to her. It is possible that the dog (the shape of which the mediaeval incubus so often assumed) is a rejection symbol, and the incubus experience fits in the same class as the sexual encounter with the devil-father. The pre-natal aggressor is formless, ghostlike. The incubus probably represents both the fear and pleasure element of pre-natal aggression. The pleasure element drives her to yield; the fear element makes her panicky.

The reference to relaxation and bath, in connection with the dream, also explains the patient's restlessness in everyday life; she was driven by an unceasing ambition, without ever achieving much. If she relaxed, she would be overwhelmed by the pre-natal pressure, and she achieved little because her energies were used up in fighting this memory. It anchored her to an other-worldliness, the half-world of the unborn in which psychic influences, not of the material plane, might play on the child. The pre-natal trauma suggests the basis on which the patient developed her psychic character and clairvoyant powers of perception.

Sexual Cannibalism

Let us now take an example from Dr. Wilhelm Stekel. He tells of a man who dreams he is in a circus which looks like a ball or crystal. There is a kind of reddish illumination. The dreamer sits in a small loge and looks through a small window into the circus, which is as yet unlit. Suddenly some men stuck a long bar of sugar right through the window into his mouth. He bit a piece off . . . and awoke with a great erection. Stekel calls this a typical maternal womb dream. The dreamer, who was treated for apron fetishism, is within his mother's body, peeps out of a small opening: his father appears and he bites his father's penis off. He later remembered several dreams in which he was buried alive. In many instances, he was of diminutive size. It seemed as if he wanted to crawl back into his mother's womb. He then recognized that the apron represented his mother's skin. With this realization the apron fetishism came to an end, but not yet the maternal fantasy life. Stekel continues that he then became interested in cannibalism and revelled in the thought that the fetus exists on the blood and tissue of the mother. Suckling is a substitute for such blood sucking.*

In spite of the plain language of these fantasies, the suspicion of pre-natal traumata completely escapes Stekel's attention. He criticizes Freud for his constitutional component theory. According to this the traumatic experience acts as a shock only in persons who are constitutionally predisposed to neurosis. What this constitutional predisposition is, Freud does not explain. But significantly, he

---

* Wilhelm Stekel, *Sexual Aberrations*, Liveright Publishing Co., New York, 1940, Vol. II, pp. 58-60.

formed this theory when he found several neurotics who experienced no trauma. Stekel remarks: "Of course, the whole psychogenetic conception of neurosis is shattered with this contention, if it be true." He says further that "the neurotic predisposition seems to me to be a glandular disorder involving the sexual chemism of the endocrines."

The necessity for theorizing vanishes the moment we consider pre-natal fantasies as not due to retrojection but to memory traces of actual experiences. The severe neurotics who experienced no trauma in post-natal life may have experienced them pre-natally. The fact that the pre-natal dreams came from an adult does not dispose of their factual basis. In the instances quoted from Stekel their purpose was to shed light on the origin of the patient's fetishism and cannibalistic tendencies. The dreams and fantasies show a pre-natal love fixation, bearing out the central idea of this chapter that parental intercourse also produces pleasure reactions in the unborn.

Such pleasure reactions as we have just discussed might be responsible for resistance to integration. We want to get rid of pain but we are very reluctant to give up that which we treasure. In the following instance the cover symbol for the treasure is an apron, as in Stekel's case, and the cannibalistic element is also represented in similar terms of food pleasure. This is the dream:

I am coming down some steps. I come upon an apron on the stairway. It had been torn up for dust cloths by the maintenance men of the office. It was a favorite apron of mine, with red and white stripes, and was not even worn. I am very upset and am trying to find out who tore it. The maintenance men acknowledged that they had done it; they did not realize it was a good apron until it was torn. I want to make somebody pay for it. I go to see the principal of my school about it. He is putting me off. His wife is butting in, which annoys me even more. Sometime in between this, I am eating stalks of celery. I can hear myself crunching on them. I ask the principal, "Could this be some compensation for the destruction of a perfectly good apron?" He says I am crazy to think about the apron.

The lady of this dream was in the final stages of her analysis. I entitled the dream "The Revolt of the Fetus," because it alluded to her refusal to give up her pre-natal pleasure fantasies. The apron is a cover symbol for the womb. It was torn because analysis (represented by the maintenance men) destroyed her pre-natal dreams. She was mad and vindictive about it. She felt robbed of something precious and delectable. The stalks of celery suggest the nature of the delight, and closely correspond to the long bar of sugar of Stekel's patient, but there is no aggression motive shown against the father. The emphasis is not on revenge but on pleasure. She is seeking compensation for what she is losing by analysis, and then answers herself, through the principal, that the quest for such compensation is nonsensical.

Confirmation of the womb symbolism of the apron came in a supplementary recollection:

"There was a large canvas bag somewhere, of the type used in the office to hold waste paper or old clothes. At one time the apron was in that bag."

The bag is a universal symbol of the feminine organ. The torn apron in the bag clearly indicates that something on the pre-natal level has been destroyed. The meaning of the stalks of celery was further elucidated by the recall of a previous dream in which she was eating long stalks of rhubarb. When the rhubarb sticks were handed to her, she was sitting at the feet of a man called Adam, with her elbow on his knee and her head resting on it. The position brought her into close proximity with the man's genitalia. The inevitable Garden of Eden association with Adam justifies a lining up of this dream with the pre-natal fantasies that concerned the apron and the stalks of celery.

The possibility deserves notice and investigation that the sexual practice called fellatio may originate in dream fantasies of the character just described.

The Desire for Rape

There are some indications that the fear of infection (syphilophobia) may also be traceable to pre-natal love sensations. Essentially, the fear of infection is the fear of penetration of the organism by an alien, poisonous substance. By its psychic effect on the organism of the unborn child, the invasion of the mother's genitalia in coitus may fit this definition. That the fear is fed by a repressed desire, is revealed in this dream:

> *I am going into the bathroom. A colored man follows me. He likes me. I do not want my fiancé to see me with him. I am in the bathroom over the toilet in a standing position as usual, as I never sit down in a public toilet. I am about to let go when the colored man opens the door. I had a Kotex on which I had pushed aside. He must have seen it. "Are you diseased?" he asks me. I am very frightened and answer, "Of course not." He is very passionate and is about to attack me. Then two men come in and pull him off. I wake up and have to go to the toilet badly.*
>
> *Later I am looking for a toilet. I find a public one with lots of individual compartments, all open. I walk in. People are in them. I think I will wait until they get out. I wake up just in time. I am about to pass water.*

The dream should be studied as a sequel to Chapter 11 on *Birth and Rape.* It will be recalled that the subject of the case was frightened by her mother in her impressionable years with the possibility of catching a sexual disease from contact with public toilet seats. As an adolescent girl she barely escaped violation in a taxi in a dark garage way. She saved herself by saying that she had her menstruation and besides suffered from syphilis. Thus menstruation and infection had become closely associated in her mind. As menstruation is popularly called a "curse," the association is not too incongruous.

We see the association at work in the dream. The Kotex suggests that she is menstruating and the Negro queries: "Are you diseased?" As menstruation is not a disease, the Kotex is a substitute for infection. She associated Negroes with rape. No attempt is made in the dream to disguise this meaning. Rape is the manifest content of the dream. The latent emphasis is not on assault but on infection. To the dreamer, the color of the Negro suggested something unclean and hidden, a "nigger in the woodpile." The toilet and the desire to pass water (the latter being a wish of somatic origin) are symbolic of release. It is tempting to assume that the deeper, analytic wish behind the relief of bladder pressure is the revelation of the origin of the patient's infection fears for the purpose of ridding her psyche of this burden. In the last part of the dream this desire is strongly in evidence. The toilet is public and all its compartments are open. Nothing secret can take place in such toilets, but people can find in them relief.

Let us now discuss the hidden pleasure elements of the dream. The wording gives us the first clue: "A colored man follows me. He likes me. I do not want my fiancé to see me with him." These are not the words in which a woman who is frightened of rape would describe pursuit by a colored man. She is pleased at being liked by the colored man. She does not so much mean being followed by him as being with him, and it is this that she wants to keep secret from her fiancé. In other words, she desires rape. In evidence of this desire, she fails to lock the bathroom door, surely an elementary precaution for one who does not wish to be surprised in the act of self-exposure. She wanted to be attacked because of a repressed pleasure urge, yet she contrived to save herself by the timely appearance of two men. It follows that she is in need of release both from the fear and from the desire of rape, and that a clue to her syphilophobia will be discovered in the desire.

Actually, the clue is a double one. If we entitled the dream "The Negro in the Bathroom" we would vividly represent both.

The Negro not only symbolizes rape but also the unknown, the darkness and the alien race or alien world. Every man is a "nigger" in the dark, so the "nigger" is the unknown assailant. It would require, however, an almost unbelievable combination of circumstances for a woman to fall victim to rape without being able to identify the assailant. Who then is this man of mystery who can follow the patient into the intimacy of the bathroom where she is in danger of infection?

If we return to our definition that the fear of infection is the fear of penetration of the organism by an alien, poisonous substance and if we recall the discussions we had on the symbolic use of the bathroom for the mother's womb, we shall find the answer readily.

The dream enacts a pre-natal drama, and the unknown attacker, both feared and desired, is the father in intercourse with the mother

. during advanced pregnancy. The door of the bathroom is open because it is not within the power of the unborn to shut the vaginal door. The poisonous substance which threatens with infection is the father's seminal fluid and the water which she wants to pass aims at releasing this fluid by setting it in reverse gear. Alone she cannot accomplish this release. She needs help. Only from two men could such help be forthcoming: her analyst and her fiancé. The latter was also an analyst but their intimate relationship deterred her from making the disclosures to him that could be made to another analyst. Ultimately, for the purpose of accomplishing her analytic integration, it was not sufficient to deliver her from the fear of rape; she had to be delivered also from the desire for rape. Her infection fears were a mask for this desire. Ante-natal traumata cannot be clothed in sexual language until education in sexual matters places the necessary pictorial and verbal means at our disposal. The structural pattern has been provided by the mother's exaggerated warnings against the use of public toilets. From then on the disturbing pleasure memories of the parental attacks against the unborn manifested themselves in an abnormal fear of infection.

The understanding of this residual element of the fear of rape had a beneficial effect.

31.

INTEGRATION OF PRE-NATAL TRAUMATA

STRONG grounds were advanced in the preceding chapters for the belief that the trauma of birth is not the bottom-most determinant of neurotic predisposition for later life. Parental intercourse which impresses the unborn as a murderous attack or the mother's attempts to break up pregnancy, may produce almost all the shock effects in which the trauma of birth manifests itself. It follows that the fear of death is not necessarily only a projection of the fear of birth; it may also be a projection of the pre-natal fear of extinction caused by the invading father when he is making love to the mother or by the measures which the mother employs in trying to produce an abortion.

The threat of being thrown out of the womb by the father or the mother involves death by falling, by being crushed or by being burnt up in the fever heat of sexual passion. The foundation of nightmares of the supernormal, cannibalism and murder may also be laid prior to birth on remoter strata of the organismic mind. The root of criminal instincts may hide in retaliation fantasies for pre-natal aggression or in morbid pre-natal nostalgia. The latter may furnish the motive for the tortures of ascesis, fantasies of royal blood, of historic mission, of demonic power, of astral projection and of reincarnation. Overwhelming sexual curiosity may develop from the instinctual search for the meaning of life, for the secret of ecstasy, for utopian bliss.

Integration of Pre-Natal Traumata

Umbilical fantasies may explain the genesis of incest and homosexuality. The death instinct as conceived by Freud may express a yearning for pre-natal life, which may instead be harnessed for spiritual regeneration. We have seen a fascinating field of research opening up in the study of telepathic interaction between the mother and the child. It appears possible that crucifixion fantasies, rape fears, syphilophobia, paranoid homosexual obsessions, fantasies about the mother's penis, about castrating and decapitating the father, and determinants of a schizophrenic dissociation may result in part from the violence of parental intercourse during gestation, while the devastating effect of maternal death wishes against the child in the womb loomed up strongly in aggressive dreams against the father and the mother on the pre-natal score.

The release of the trauma of birth is the introductory phase of prenatal integration. The more vital phase concerns the shocks suffered prior to birth. In order to release these shocks, the conscious mind must take cognizance of their existence and nature. As no verbal mechanism was available at the time of their occurrence, an intellectual grasp of the nature of these deep, subterranean upheavals is the prerequisite of their catharsis. By the power of understanding, a mental valve is turned, through which these primitive fear reactions find an outlet into the conscious mind and gradually cease their pressure. If, for lack of knowledge, the individual is unable to recognize that his traumata are of pre-natal origin, or if, for intellectual bias, he is incapable of accepting the facts, no pre-natal integration will follow. A period of waiting for mental growth will ensue during which these vital issues will remain in abeyance. He will not be set free until his mind matures and understands.

I learned this lesson from an odd and complicated dream of my own five years after I had dreamed it. Only then did I discover that a message was concealed in the dream: you will not understand this just yet; nevertheless, struggle with it as best you can; the real meaning will dawn on you in time.

Prelude to Pre-natal Understanding

Dreams that teach lessons are not a novelty to me. For some strange

353

reason the deeper self within us cannot reach our understanding di-rectly. One of the many ways in which it tries to convey a message is through dreams. At the time when the dream to be discussed oc-curred, my mind was side-tracked. I was aware of the terror of the unborn caused by the invasion of the father's organ, but I did not know enough of the symbolic means by which the inner desire for the cancellation of such traumata and for the unification of the pre-natal and post-natal levels of the mind can be expressed. This was the dream:

I was to give a lecture on Sir Rider Haggard. I remembered that he was afraid of Poles, and this seemed to have been generally known. But I discovered that he was also afraid of Sundays and of the num-ber 7.

I saw a scrapbook which somebody had picked up in a book store. It contained a lot of information about Sir Rider Haggard and I was sorry that I had not bought it. Pasted in the back of the book was a letter written in Hungarian and signed by the fantastic name of Habarék. It was a friendly letter and it surprised me. It implied that Sir Rider Haggard knew Hungarian. On rereading the letter, the sig-nature changed. It was signed Georginu—as best I can remember it.

The book, as I turned its pages, contained a number of maps of Europe. There was one of France but Lombardy was printed across it. Bound in the front part of the book, as a pamphlet might be, was a lecture by Chibbett and somebody asked me if that was the lecture I was going to deliver. I answered very definitely: no.

As I was waiting to be called for the lecture, two parcels arrived from Budapest from my brother Henry. I think they were for Sir Rider Haggard. One of them contained, amongst other things, a New York telephone book. The paper of this parcel was torn. I took the parcels into the lecture room and found, to my surprise, that proceedings had started and people were sitting in a semi-circle before a cathedra.

Somebody stood up and said that the lecturer had arrived, intimat-ing that through my fault they had been kept waiting. It was now 9 P.M. and the lecture should have begun an hour earlier. I answered that I was in the room all the time, waiting to be called. Then some-

body said that the attendance was too small, and they had decided not to give the lecture. I remembered having seen quite a number of people in the audience, but I was told they did not come to stay and were now gone. Indeed, I saw only a few scattered people in the lecture hall.

Then my daughter came in to tell me that Charlotte S. wanted me to give her the check which I received for the lecture. She was broke. I went to see her and, as I received no check for the lecture, looked into my wallet to see if I had a dollar bill or two to give her, but I had absolutely no money, not even a penny.

Sometime later I saw girls appearing on the top of a slanting roof at the Marble Arch, London. They came out of arched roof windows and jumped off. I was scared until I realized that they had jumped into a pool. The pool was not in sight as houses between me and the roof concealed it, but it appeared to be an intermediate pool at a certain height because now from the top of the house where they landed the girls were jumping down straight into our pool on Edgeware Road, near the Marble Arch. The higher pool must have been somewhere on the top of the Regal cinema and the house from which the girls jumped in the first place was opposite to it. The jumps were very fast. No time was given for hesitation. It seemed to be a matter-of-fact procedure.

Just before I woke I had a fantasy about a girl who wanted to force marriage on Sir Rider Haggard. Instead of submitting, he drew a gun and shot her and himself.

The original notes on my associations with the dream reveal the manner in which Sir Rider Haggard came to preoccupy my mind.

The day before the dream, I was reading the case history of a patient of mine who had been intrigued from early youth by the problem of Atlantis. From Atlantis, my thoughts wandered to Pierre Benoit's book *Atlantide* and to the charges of plagiarism that had been levelled against him because his mysterious desert queen resembled "She," the central figure of Sir Rider Haggard's famous story. Then I thought of Jung, who had analyzed the character of *She* and described it as a representation of the feminine archetype, the Anima.

These associations linked up Sir Rider Haggard and psychoanalysis, as far as my mind processes were concerned.

A second train of thought, from the day before the dream, concerned Poles. Poland, Polish cities and Poles used to occur frequently in my old anxiety dreams. Reviewing these dreams, I had found them intelligible on discarding the capital letter and on attaching a phallic value to the word "pole." It appeared that the fear of poles represented the pre-natal fear of the father's phallus.

Applying this idea to Sir Rider Haggard's fear of poles, it seemed apparent that he stood for myself and that as a lecturer he was about to reveal something concerning me. Indeed, he is credited in the dream with a knowledge of my native Hungarian, and he is linked with my family through the two parcels which my brother sends him from Budapest. Further, "rider" means horseman and dreams about riding and horses had a special significance for me. In one, which was very vivid, I was standing before the gate of a field into which I was not permitted to enter, and on looking up saw a man riding a horse high in the air. I experienced some anxiety, as his only support was a long pole which reached from his right-hand side to the ground. Thus I had dreamed of rider and pole before Sir Rider Haggard appeared on the scene. Fear makes one haggard. Very possibly, Sir Rider Haggard stands for the Frightened Horseman, and that horseman apparently is myself. The fear, if I think of the dream about the horse in the air as a clue, is plainly that of being unseated by the horse and falling. The horse, therefore, is dangerous. It could cause death.

I also recalled that the day before the dream I debated in my mind whether I should write an essay on my horse dreams. Writing is not too far removed from lecturing. As I was to give a lecture on Sir Rider Haggard, I assume I was to speak on my horse fears. In children's nightmares a wild, stampeding horse usually stands for the father. I had such dreams myself and, occasionally, the infantile perspective was indicated by the enormous size of the horse.

So far the threads of my dream were wound up satisfactorily. Presently I went off on the wrong track. From the absence of interest in my lecture I concluded that it was superfluous because the horse and pole problem had been disposed of by understanding. It did not occur to me that in that case it would be unnecessary to dream about lecturing, or that, if I still did, the fear of poles and horses might need further investigation. It was the scrapbook which was responsible for this hiatus in my reasoning. I took it as a symbol of scrapping which I had accomplished, instead of the scrapping that was waiting to be done. As it contained a lot of information about Sir Rider Haggard, I argued—quite logically—that the scrapping must refer to infantile ideas. The name "Habarék" seemed to fit in with that. It is a more or less artificial Hungarian word, meaning potpourri, mush or nonsense, something not worth worrying about.

Then, by a magnificent sweep of imagination, I carried the idea of cancellation to a transcendental scale. In those days I used to move amongst people who were ardent believers in reincarnation. When they asked for my opinion, I answered, "I don't believe in it"—for an ulterior reason: I did not want to come back. As these discussions had been in the forefront of my mind at the time, I argued that the dream may have come to me in support of this wish. This is how I figured it out:

Sunday is the day of rest. The seventh day (represented by the number 7) closes the week and opens a new one. The fear of Sunday could stand for the fear of a new week, a new life, reincarnation. As parcels usually represent burdens in dreams, the two parcels might be symbolic of two lives: past and present. Chibbett was Research Officer of an organization called "The Link," so he was an excellent symbol of linking past and present. The number 8 (the hour at which my lecture should have started) is composed of two intertwined circles, serving a similar symbolic purpose (it looks like two links in a chain), while the number 9 (the hour at which I present myself for the lecture) is not only the number of gestation but, as the highest individual number of the decimal system, it is also the number of completion. The cancellation of my lecture at 9 P.M. thus could stand, I reasoned, for a cancellation of incarnations—in answer to a wish or fear. Support seemed to be lent to this view by the two pools—with their patent amniotic references. Marble Arch and the arched window on the roof twice determined the pubic arch, and the higher pool contrasted with the lower one suggested the descent of the spirit into life through conception and birth.

A good deal was left unexplained by this reasoning, and I was aware of it. It failed to cover numerous references to duality, such as two additions to the scrapbook at the back and front, two signatures to the letter in the back, two lectures, two hours for lecturing, one or two dollar bills and two murders in the end. Further, there was the name Georginu, the map of Lombardy over France, Charlotte, the New York telephone book and the forcing of marriage. I was unable to connect them into a single picture, thus leaving the dream unsolved which, if I took the lecture as a symbol for self-instruction, was foreseen in its very cancellation.

Yet, I believe that every interpretation of a dream by the dreamer himself has a subjective value, even if it does not hit the mark, even if it tails off into pure metaphysics as mine did. It is at least an addition to the dream, concealing some other truth which is obscured by intellectual bias. In this instance, it seems that the main message of the dream did get through. It was a dream of cancellation, but on a more modest scale than I assumed it to be. The fear of poles should have kept me on the right track. If this fear, as inferred from my previous dreams, was indeed the fear of father's phallus raiding the child within the womb in the last stages of pre-natal development, the cancellation must concern the pressure arising from the pre-natal levels of my mind. Sunday is the day of the sun. If the Sun is the Father, and the number 7 is associated with it in fear, it is permissible to assume that the seventh month of pre-natal development is referred to, that the successive numbers of 8 and 9 complete the cycle before birth and the frequent references to the number 2 may also serve as a measure of the interval from 7 to 9, or refer to the duality of pre-natal and post-natal life.

Let us recall that Sir Rider Haggard's name was conjured up through associations during the previous day with Atlantis, the sunken continent, a pre-eminent symbol of the pre-natal environment, and that over Pierre Benoit's *Atlantide* and over Sir Rider Haggard's mysterious African country a god-like creature ruled who, according to my Jungian associations, was the archetype of the Anima. Let us next examine the geographical setting of the dream. Change-overs from one country to another occur three times: twice with hidden symbolism, once openly. The first change-over is concealed by the name Georginu. It has a Rumanian ending, it sounds Rumanian. At the beginning, the name was Habarék. Why should a Hungarian name be changed into a Rumanian? I could answer this question immediately: many such changes were effected through political compulsion when Transylvania, a Hungarian province, was ceded to Rumania in 1918 after the first World War. Transylvania means "Beyond the Wooded Land." If Hungary as my native country is the maternal environment, Transylvania could well stand for the unknown, the unremembered, the pre-natal one. The change of name thus would be a substitute for the compulsive change of country through birth.

The second change of environment is hidden in the symbolism of the New York telephone book, which is one of the two parcels my brother sent from Budapest. The parcel with the telephone book was torn open. Tear and scrap are synonymous terms. The telephone book is sent to Sir Rider Haggard and the scrapbook contains a lot of information about the same man. Further, the scrapbook had two special inserts: a letter at the end and a pamphlet in the front. Here was the first hint, redetermined later by the doubling of the parcels, that something at the beginning and at the end should be brought together. Lest the hint should be missed, as I missed it in my first interpretation, the book in the parcel is a telephone book, speaking eloquently of connecting and of integrating by linking Budapest with the United States. As the greater part of the dream plays in London, I assume that the United States refer to a uniting of psychological states. It is by uniting the historic and pre-historic levels of the human personality that we banish fears and reach complete integration.

The third and open change is from Italy to France; maps are discovered in the scrapbook and the name Lombardy, an alien (Italian) province is set in the body of La Belle France.

A fourth fundamental shift, expressed in different terms, confronts us in the change from one pool to another. Marble Arch, where the scene is laid, outside the obvious pubic arch reference, contains the syllable of "Ma," an abbreviation of Mamma, the name of the mother all over the world. In the reference to the Regal cinema, regal means royal. The unconscious mind is fond of using extravagant terms in describing the pre-natal state. But I overreached myself; by thinking of conception and birth, I missed the message of the dream. I refused to accept Chibbett's lecture on "The Link" and contrived to miss my own. Having missed on two scores, I displayed an insufficiency of understanding and as a result the audience, which I saw sitting in a semi-circle (another reference to the arch) deserted me. I was left with the problem of the check (inhibition), which I had to settle with Charlotte, a name by which my mother was sometimes referred to. I learned nothing and because of it I had nothing to give, not even a penny. I failed to get the dream gold and remained a beggar.

Many details are yet to be filled in. Regarding Lombardy, I gathered in a crop of curious linguistic associations. It makes difficult reading. Be it sufficient that the picture emerging from an etymological discussion of Lombardy, Habarék and Georginu is one of violence. That this violence is of conjugal character, is indicated when marriage is being forced on Sir Rider Haggard. He is myself, not as an adult, but as the unborn, the victim of parental intercourse. The double shooting is a defense reaction. Suicide often results from repressed aggressiveness coming home to roost, turning against the self. As in the person of Charlotte the mother appears in the dream and, under a carefully prepared alibi, all help is denied to her, it seems as if the rage of the unborn infant against the pre-natal aggressor were venting itself on the maternal environment. On the pre-natal level it is impossible to direct the hostility to other quarters. If this is true, the girl who is shot is the mother and the suicide that follows grimly demonstrates the self-destructive character of repressed aggressiveness. The lesson of the dream is that not until this aggressiveness is released can a union between the prehistoric and historic levels of the mind be established.

The dream is long, complicated and rambling, yet its essential uterine setting is clear. Sir Rider Haggard meant to me a great deal in my youth. It was through his books that I learned English. His African romances had a tremendous fascination for me. Nearly all of them describe journeys of discovery into a mysterious inland country of tropical temperature, isolated from the outside world and never before reached by white men, a country in which the explorers were considered gods and were eventually accepted as rulers. I have no doubt that the appeal of these books was due to my pre-natal nostalgia. Hence it was appropriate that I should endeavour to work out my pre-natal problems through an identification with the author of these strange return journeys into the womb.

Beginning of Pre-natal Integration

Integration begins when the ground has been cleared by preliminary spade work. I date the beginning of my own pre-natal integration from the period when the nature of pre-natal traumata and the need of integrating the pre-natal levels of my mind with the post-natal personality had dawned on me. The symbols I used are rather picturesque and include some astonishing mental acrobatics. However extreme or far-fetched they may appear to be, they nevertheless had their effect in increasing mental health and developing a more mature orientation to life, which is, of course, the prime criterion. The first and third part of the dream in which I noticed the beginning of pre-natal integration, is a Hop o' My Thumb fantasy, and it calls attention to matters which I have neglected. The second part digs deeper into the life of the unborn and uses prehistoric images of the race to illustrate problems of fetal psychology.

In my native tongue, Hop o' My Thumb is called Matthias Thumb (Hüvelyk Matyi), and a diminutive variation of Matthias is Matyi or Mityu. The latter is the pet name of the first son of my oldest brother. This Mityu had played no part in my life. In the dream I seem to use him for myself because his name, actual stature and family status permit a play of opposites, which is a favorite device of the dream mind. My oldest brother is old enough to be my father and I am my father's last living son, the sixteenth child. First and last is often associated with size. Our methodical mind finds pleasure in scaling members of the family as if they were organ pipes. As will be seen, I am exceedingly small at the end of the dream and describe myself as Hop o' My Thumb. Presently, the scaling is reversed. On the pre-natal level, the place of embryonic Hop o' My Thumb is taken by a prehistoric monster. But let the dream tell its own story:

I receive a letter from Mityu in which he explains his financial situation and sends me a book showing it. His financial situation is good. He mentions how much he earned and how much he needed. He needed over nine . . . daily, and I figured that his monthly income would be over 400. The first, incompletely remembered, figure mattered more than the second. I answer him inside the book, on the back of the front cover, writing in pencil. I notice that the cover page is torn and that it looks like a book on psychoanalysis which I recently bought. Then I discover I have no time to mail the book because I am overdue at school and I have been missing school for a long time. This causes a slight anxiety. I look at my watch. Instead of 3:45 which I expected, it is now 4:30 P.M. and I have to rush.

In Mityu's letter there is a statement which makes me remark, "That's odd because I dreamed of the same thing." The "same thing" is a very fascinating dream. Excavation was being done under the foundation of my parents' house (the house standing), and they dug up a prehistoric auroch, a huge bull, dead, petrified but with the flesh intact. The neck had been severed but the head had been replaced, though the cut was visible. Somebody, perhaps my father, came in riding the auroch. It did not seem strange that a dead bull could move. I said, "This is a splendid archaeological specimen; let us have it in the house as an exhibit." Vaguely I recalled that a huge pre-historic bird, perhaps a pterodactyl, was also dug up.

Then I am going somewhere, high up, on a narrow soil ledge, over deep diggings. Towards the end of the path, the soil crumbles; I fall or sink and am swept away somewhere underground. A maid called Anna is present. I call to her in a tiny voice. Now she is a giant and she either dives in or puts a hand into the tunnel, saying jovially, "I suppose I've got to do another bit of work!"—and pulls me out into safety. I am only the size of Hop o' My Thumb.

It is this last part of the dream which unmistakably speaks of birth. It combines a typical falling and drowning dream with the uterine symbol of the tunnel, and the rescue is accomplished by a mother substitute, a maid. The day before the dream a patient mentioned Anna as her mother's name and called my attention to its reversibility. It reads the same backwards as forwards. This reversal seems to be present in the construction of the dream itself. First I fall back into the uterus, then I am brought out. The oscillation is not dissimilar to the play between Mityu, Hop o' My Thumb and the auroch. Maid is also a play on "made," which relates to conception and security as mother represents it, and may explain the jovial tone of "another bit of work," the sixteenth in a long series of child-births.

With the help of this part of the dream, it is not difficult to understand the first. The balance sheet gives a picture of the state of integration. The figures sum up my psychological progress. Altogether four figures are mentioned, two of them (9 and 400) dealing with sums, the other two (3:45 and 4:30) dealing with time. In my inability to recollect the first figure completely I see an overshadowing from the dream work. Immediate associations on awakening are recognized as belonging to the dream. I believe that an immediate inhibition of association or recollection is similarly part of the dream process, as resistance is not an exclusively conscious manifestation. It can be a dream mechanism by which, in this case, emphasis is laid on the first digit at the expense of the others, to which no latent significance is attached but which serve as camouflage to avoid interference by the censor. Therefore, I should not worry over the unremembered figures. "He needed over nine daily" means that I daily need (i.e., I cannot afford to neglect) the information concealed in the number nine. The answer which I write in the book concerns this information. It is the answer to the tear in the cover page: a hidden (cover) psychic injury which the dream narrative localizes inside at the back of the front. The answer is written in pencil. The choice must be deliberate as it is not good form to write letters in pencil. I derive the word pencil from the Latin penecillus. In my native country, this is also the word for jack-knife and penis. There is another sexual reference in the failure to "mail" the book. The unconscious mind equates the word with "male." Mail-box, for instance, usually describes the female genitalia (a box for the male). The word sex actually figures in the title of the book of which I am reminded in the dream. The tear (trauma), therefore, must be of sexual character. It must be vitally important as I am stated to be overdue at school. Schooling stands for education. The anxiety is due to my neglect to acquire an important piece of information.

What is this missing information?

The usual anxiety dream in connection with schools concerns examinations. These dream examinations, in Freud's view, reflect the fear that the dreamer might not be able to pass an impending sexual test, that he might not be able to penetrate. Let us recall that in writing an answer to Mityu's letter, I place the pencil inside at the back of the front. If the pencil is a phallic symbol, this is a form of penetration. It is not impossible to look upon the book as a container, a feminine symbol. I have read somewhere that the bushmen of Australia describe a book as a clam because it opens and shuts. There is, therefore, an equation in my mind between book and clam, and the feminine significance of the latter cannot be disputed. Nevertheless, I do not refer the slight dream anxiety to penetration but to its reverse. The rescue of Hop o' My Thumb speaks of issuance from the womb, deliverance from the pre-natal conditions, and the tear (trauma) is indicated to have taken place within, prior to birth.

The second part of the dream plainly aims at giving information regarding this vital matter by a redetermination of the tear in the form of the decapitation of the auroch. This part of the dream is an inset, a dream within a dream. I have many instances on my files in which the inner dream, as a remoter psychic state, symbolizes the fetal night. A similar use of the inner dream is shown in the present instance by the excavation under the foundation of my parents' house. As the house is a widely used symbol for the personality, the foundation well describes the line of demarcation between the conscious and the unconscious mind. An excavation under the foundation refers to the exploration of the unconscious mind. However, instead of the foundation of my personal home, the dream speaks of my parental foundations. The wording—which I consider as part of the dream— takes us back to the genetic stage. The house stands, meaning that the genetic influence persists and the exploration exposes the skeleton in the family closet, the womb.

Integration of Pre-Natal Traumata

Of a wide variety of prehistoric monsters, the choice falls on an auroch, the ancestor of the bull. I can see a fascinating reason for this choice. My first name is Nandor, but many of my friends call me Nandi, an abbreviation with a decided East Indian ring. A slight variation leads to Nanda which, as I had read in Lewis Spence's *Encyclopaedia of Occultism*, is the sacred bull of a sect of Siva worshippers. Sacred animals are sacred because they represent the divinity. In my philosophy, our last contact with God was within the womb, at the time of conception. In the moment of the creation of human life, the spirit loses whatever supernal estate it had enjoyed before. The prehistoric auroch of the dream thus dramatizes the Fall of Man as my personal tragedy. It is the petrified remnant of fetal omnipotence. For the unborn is an unchallenged ruler of its own universe until its feeling of power is shattered by birth or, prior to it, by the panic which the earthquake of parental intercourse may impart. Beheading is an ancient symbol of complete domination, of the power over life. In more merciful ages, the victor satisfied himself by placing his foot on the neck of the fallen enemy. Big game hunters who have themselves photographed with the beast they have slain, yield to the same urge of showing their mastery. When, therefore, my father comes in riding the auroch—whose head is now replaced—the thought seems to be that the auroch had been killed by the father, but that he also had brought it back to life. In other words, in the prehistoric nightmare land of my mind, a reconciliation is taking place with the father. By describing the auroch as a splendid archaeological specimen, an educational interest is shown as replacing the terror of death.

The vague vision of the pterodactyl fits into this picture well. It recalls to my mind a scene from Conan Doyle's *Lost World*, in which Professor Challenger's party is attacked by a pterodactyl. In the last pages of the book, an attempt is made to exhibit a captive pterodactyl before a gathering of scientists in London, but the huge bird gets free and, before the startled scientists recover from the shock of its appearance over their heads, it wings its way out of the open window to freedom. The Lost World is, of course, the fetal kingdom, and the huge predatory bird is a symbolic challenger of the spectres of the fetal night.

Search for the Beloved

It is not possible to foretell just how long it takes until pre-natal integration is accomplished from the time the first signs of the process appear. A lot depends on the extent to which the unconscious process is paralleled by a conscious appreciation. If the interchange between the two minds is quick (which is hardly possible without expert analytic guidance), the process is fast, if not it lingers.

As I dwelt at considerable length on the symbolism of pre-natal integration in my own case, it may be well to quote some further dreams of mine to illustrate subsequent developments.

I was on the seashore with my wife. As I undressed, I noticed that I had left my swimming suit at home. My wife said, "Use my own." Her swimming suit was old-fashioned, one-piece, of the balloon type and very big, far too big for her delicate frame. I said, "No, I can't put that on, it would be ridiculous." Though it required a great deal of effort, I decided to go home and get my trunks.

The outstanding element in this dream is my refusal to get into a balloon-type swimming suit which was too big for my wife but would have just suited my mother, whom I remember having seen in such a garment. I would have floated in it in the sea as a child floats within the mother. Instead of the womb, I chose my own trunk, my own body. I will not be carried by my mother but, even though it entails considerable effort, will carry myself. The dream shows separation from the pre-natal state in unmistakable language. In another dream:

A mole was attacking a rabbit. The rabbit tried to shake off the mole but could not. The mole kept on harassing it until the rabbit was roused and killed the mole.

Then I was mounting a ladder which was leaning against a wall or window. My daughter was climbing after me and I cried out warningly, as I noticed that the ladder began to sag and the top was slipping towards a point where the wall fell away. It was too late. The ladder slipped but instead of falling straight down, it fell at a lower angle against another wall further back. I saw a tiger pacing below ready to devour me. I could escape it by climbing up a pole that led to a hole or window. It was a difficult climb, beyond my strength, but it could be done if it had to be done. I had the feeling that I had done this climb before when I had more strength.

Finally, I was floating in a street of my native town, taking long jumps and demonstrating how slowly I was coming down and what distance my jumps covered.

Neither of these dreams is too complicated. The mole, tearing up the garden soil, is a destructive rodent. It is blind, very small and wild. The rabbit is a domestic pet, the nursery's delight. It does not kill. As rabbits are mostly associated with children, who undergo a somewhat similar process of domestication, we may safely assume that the rabbit represents the child in the post-natal state, while the mole stands for the unborn and the nuisance of pre-natal traumata.

Two of my associations bear out this interpretation. One is the name of Lady Moles, who was involved in a spiritualistic case in England which revolved around alleged messages from the dead, on the strength of which a considerable sum of money changed hands. The pre-natal state can be likened to a state in another world. The second association concerns the ambivalent meaning of mole. It also means a birth-mark, and marks usually postulate a previous injury. It seemed, therefore, that the killing of the mole by the rabbit symbolized the elimination of personality disturbances arising from the pre-natal levels of my mind.

The continuation of the dream is picturesque and dramatic. The difference in size between the rabbit and the mole is paralleled by the difference between myself and my daughter. One's child, in dreams, usually represents the infantile self, here the pre-natal one. It carries sufficient weight to make the ladder sag. It is by no means a negligible quantity. Further reference to the pre-natal state can be seen in the symbolism of the two walls. The first wall, when the ladder slipped, seemed to be cut off in mid-air, and the second one appeared under it a little further back. Two levels are thus indicated and they are linked by the fear of falling and the fear of the devouring tiger. Falling in dreams is always reminiscent of birth, the first fall of the child.

Search for the Beloved

Falling into the tiger's jaws strongly suggests the ordeal of birth, whether the tiger is considered as a death symbol or as a symbol of the devouring mother (cat), who destroys the child by uterine absorption, which is a typical infantile nightmare. Climbing up a pole into a hole or window re-enacts birth by reversal. The pole can be described as an inverted tube and as such well symbolizes the uterine passage. It leads from the womb into the post-natal world. The window above is the door to life. The climb is difficult, beyond my strength, but we all have done it before. When first I did it, I had more strength, for then I was being born. Now, with lesser strength, I am indicating the possibility and difficulty of its re-enactment for the purpose of delivering myself from disturbing ante-natal memories. Floating in my native town in the street is a typical uterine dream, confirming that the drama which we just reviewed is played within the womb.

Fear is not the only element that determines the need for pre-natal integration. Enjoyment of the intra-uterine situation creates another pre-natal bond resulting in a tendency to regression which is not compatible with the evolutionary urge. The yearning for the womb for reason of libidinal memories must also be cancelled. Here is a final dream of mine which illustrates this phase of pre-natal integration:

I dreamed of the arrival of a box or glass container shaped like an oblong cube. It was addressed to me in the hand-writing of Mrs. L., a dermatologist. It contained a large number of sample cordials of odd names, which I cannot remember. A big square box within the outer box was crushed in shipping. A lot of glass came out. I cut my finger slightly on a glass splinter and I saw some dry green stuff looking like pine needles but softer, which I knew was poison. Part of this green poison got on the edge of our big blue casserole. The casserole was full of remnants of burnt food and though I carefully wiped off the poison from the edge, I suggested to my wife that we had better wash the casserole completely. She said, however, that she had some seedlings in it. Indeed, now the space seemed to be very big and I saw asparagus or an oil plant growing in it, or perhaps oil was applied to make it grow.

Integration of Pre-Natal Traumata

My first comment on this dream is that I do not know Mrs. L. She was a temporary connection of my wife. However, her name, by its sound, reminded me of a lady I do know, whose husband collects sample cordials. Apparently, I merged the two ladies for the purpose of describing a "stimulating woman," and of indicating, at the same time, the need of curing myself of the effects of such stimuli. As the dermatologist is a kind healer, she can symbolize the analytic effort to cure a skin-erotic condition. Both women stand for my mother: the lady friend (who comes from my native country) as a type, the dermatologist as a link to my wife, who is a natural mother substitute. The unconscious mind is capable of the most atrocious puns, mine certainly is. "Derma" strikes me as a good approximation of "dear Ma." Moreover, the word, meaning skin, may also describe the membranes of the womb which provide the unborn with a tactile stimulus, the degree of which may considerably increase during parental intercourse. As the cordials are within the box, the dream speaks of internal stimuli that must be eradicated because they are poisonous. I often use the simile of a box within a box to describe pre-natal and post-natal relationship. The breaking of the big inner square box thus represents the smashing of an enchantment. When the box changes into a casserole, an equation is set up between womb and alimentation. The remnants of burnt food hint at the injurious character of this conversion of love into food—injurious because it often results in a variety of digestive afflictions. The cutting of my finger with a glass splinter, the careful wiping of the poison from the edge of the casserole and the suggestion to wash it completely, all speak of damage and repair, while the seedlings reveal new growth in the old soil. A curious parallelism is set up between the dry green pine needles and the asparagus or oil plant. Asparagus has a coniferous appearance, it looks like a miniature pine cone. Pine needles should be evergreen. In the dream they had a dried appearance. It seems as if the dead green were being replaced by a new, life-giving green, a symbol of onward-striving, of never-dying life. The oil plant probably describes an olive plant, which is also green and symbolizes both peace and healing.

To sum it all up, the dream reveals a breaking away from pre-natal bondage and indicates a new unfolding on the deepest levels of my mind.

Reclaiming the Fetal Sea

The pre-natal and post-natal levels of the mind represent a duality. Not infrequently, this dual relationship takes the form of a twin fantasy. The dreamer has another self, a non-existent sister or brother, usually of dark coloring, who stands for the pre-natal part of the personality. It is through injuries which this twin-self suffers in dreams that the need of pre-natal integration is indicated.

Miss B., a young girl of twenty-four, dreams of a Nineteenth Century manor house, big and lavishly decorated. She goes swimming in a lovely pool. After that her dark sister sets out on horseback in the direction of the pool. In a little while she follows her. Now I quote:

To my unbearable horror, I found her awfully mangled, stuck between two rocks, the horse nowhere to be seen. She looked nearly all eaten. The left side of her face below the eye, including the mouth down to the base of the chin, was chewed away. From the top of her left shoulder to the middle of her right heel, her body was eaten off. Her left leg was entirely missing. She had no skin, just muscles. She was a reeking, raw mass of flesh, like entrails spread on the ground. She had long, beautiful black hair and two black eyes. They were still there. She tried to move when she saw me, letting out despairing cries from what ought to have been her mouth. Her pleading moan was heart-rending. She tried to rise on one arm. She had nothing else. She fainted and slipped from the rock. After a while they brought her back to the house. Amazingly enough, she got well but mentally she was crippled. Her only physical trouble was a black eye. She looked very tragic. She said she had a poisoned life, poisoned by her mother's breast. She would make her baby drink from a cow.

It is interesting to record the patient's own interpretation of this dream. She said she felt very "twinnish," as if she had been deprived of a playmate. She thought that her mother might have had a dead twin at the time of her own birth.

The symbolism of the pool is self-evident. But the horror packed in the dream is too much for personal acceptance; so the dreamer protects herself by projecting it onto a non-existent sister. She was not born as one of twins, and the best answer to the fantasy of a dead sister is that at the beginning of the dream the dark girl is alive. After the ride, she is found stuck between two rocks and is, at first, unable to move. Such situations in dreams are typical illustrations of birth: the child, bruised and hurt, being held in an iron grip by the contracting uterine muscles and pressed against the pubic arch. The description of the horror of mutilation in terms of chewing and eating is rather suggestive of infantile nightmares in which the strong parent devours the helpless child. It is the horse which is apparently responsible for the dark girl's terrible plight. Though it is not suggested that the horse had eaten her, the construction of the dream leaves us to infer that she was thrown by the horse into the cleft of the rock. In infantile nightmares, the horse is frequently used as a symbol for the father. At the house, i.e., after birth, she recovers but mentally she remains scarred. The consolation of the sweetness of the mother's milk is denied to her. It did not agree with her and she had to "drink from a cow" from the very start.

In other dreams during the same night, the patient showed murderous retaliation against Conrad Veidt (the analyst-father, by a fancied resemblance), and she was his daughter in the dream. As the father is not responsible for birth, we may rightly assume that the mutilation story stretches further back and that it represents a fusion of the trauma of birth with the traumata suffered through parental intercourse while within the womb.

Subsequently, but before the first dream had been analyzed, the patient dreamed of being in the office of the chiropractor from whom both she and her mother were having treatments. In the dream her mother was in a slip, being treated, and she was waiting for her turn. There were electrical machines in the place and a sort of tunnel through which her mother was supposed to crawl.

I happened to look behind the sofa and saw maps of the Mediter-ranean sea at various ages. I remember looking at one from 1860. On this Italy seemed to cover everything, it flowed right into Africa. I said to myself: I wonder if the world was really like that in 1860, or didn't these people know what the world was like?

The first dream took place in a Nineteenth Century house. If we take this life as the present century, the previous century can well symbolize life before birth. The map of Italy is dated from 1860. As the dreams were reported in 1940, the territorial growth of Italy at the expense of the Mediterranean takes us back eighty years of which forty belong to the present, forty to the past century. As the number eighty had no application to the patient's own age (which is twenty-four), the division suggests an equality of importance, from the dream mind's point-of-view, of post-natal and pre-natal life. The mother is a symbol of the maternal condition. The reference to the tunnel through which the mother has to crawl suggests the necessity of returning into the pre-natal state for the purpose of integration which the chiropractic adjustment symbolizes. The importance of the map of Italy now appears in proper light. The purpose of analysis is to enlarge the conscious mind at the expense of the unconscious. If the unconscious mind is symbolized by the waters, the conscious mind is the land sticking out of the waters. Italy is the only part of the European continent that reaches deep into the Mediterranean, which has been the cradle of European nations, the fetal sea of great empires. When, therefore, Italy "overflows" the Mediterranean, a tremendous gain is indicated at the expense of the dormant pre-natal part of the dreamer's personality. A reclamation of the fetal waters is shown not so much as an accomplished fact but as a program, a task set before the conscious self, the achieving of which depends on the understanding of the mysterious significances that the dream reveals.

The next case is interlinked with the reclamation of the Mediterranean. Mrs. G., who brought me the dream, uses strikingly similar symbolism to Miss B.'s, the patient of the previous case. Miss B. did not know that Mrs. G. was being analyzed by me at the same time that she was. Socially, they were in contact; in fact, a kind of mother and daughter relationship existed between them. Mrs. G.

was of great help to Miss B. at a critical period of her life, and gave her the love which she always hoped to get from her own mother. At the time of the dream, they were apart and neither of them knew of the dream of the other. The coincidence between their dreams and the strange fact that they occurred during the same night was discovered by myself and was only known to me. What makes the situation still more odd, Mrs. G.'s dream begins with a journey the purpose of which was to visit Miss B.'s mother, and then it continues:

Someone directed us wrongly. I said, "Stop, I can see it; the place is on the top of that mountain to the left." We got out of the car. Two men and a girl came along the road. The girl said, "I can guide you to it if you want me to." I answered, "That would be lovely because it is a pretty stiff way straight up." We went up some steps that were exceedingly steep. The girl was leading, holding a man's hand, then I came and my hand was held below by the second man. I said, "We are making a fuss about going up a few steps," but the fuss did not seem to be important. As we came up, there was a tremendous sheet of water. It was like a sheet of glass. I said, "Good Lord, that's going to be slippery." When I stepped on it, it was not water but ordinary land. Mysteriously, there was a house to the right. It perched on the mountain side like Lama castles in Tibet. They said, "You have to go through this house to get there." Someone pressed a button and a mysterious, great window opened. A funny woman who looked like my maid began to bully me about something. I went up to her and said, "If you say that I will slap your face." She looked at me and said it again. I hit out with my hand but it became arrested before it reached her face. I woke up fighting mad.

The dream raised many interesting questions. To begin with, Miss B.'s mother does not live on a mountain. In the dream she does and to the left; further, the dreamer is directed wrongly. As left usually means the wrong side in dreams and represents problems that await solution by analysis, the dreamer's relationship to Miss B.'s mother needs elucidation. This came forth instantly:

"She is a symbol of the domineering woman. She never asks me to dinner, she tells me that I am going to have dinner with her. I was too great a coward to resist her."

Judging by this information, Miss B.'s mother exemplifies the dreamer's weakness in resisting feminine aggression—which, indeed, she acknowledged to be one of her outstanding characteristics. She associated the mountain with rising towards freedom, so we may assume that the dream aims at achieving self-domination instead of domination by others. This is borne out by the aggressive tone which she uses at the house perched on the mountain. She reaches the house after an ascent of steep steps by the help of a human chain—a symbol of social co-operation, and after passing across a sheet of water, which turns to dry land as soon as she steps on it.

The sheet of water and the steep mountain side did not seem an incongruous combination in the dream. She associated the water with the passing of the Red Sea, and thought that the change from water to dry land was a wonderful symbol of liberation. In view of the fact that she was a singer by profession, particularly fond of arias from Tannhaeuser, the mountain also had a feminine significance. When the waters change into dry land, she seems to be reclaiming the fetal sea in the same way that Miss B. reclaimed the Mediterranean. Coinciding with Miss B.'s choice of Italy, the land of operas, Mrs. G. chooses a mountain that associates with Tannhaeuser. Venusberg is as eloquent a symbol of maternal conditions as the fetal waters are. Mrs. G. was an illegitimate child. As such, she was literally born on Venusberg. Mysterious castles and houses usually symbolize the womb. She is told that she has to go through a house, which suggested to her Tibet, the land of religious mysteries. The big window which opens on pressing a button is the vaginal door. She has to re-enter the womb in order to attain a new life, of which we always talk in terms of re-birth. It is noteworthy that no fear is connected with the undertaking; rather the opposite, a heroic attitude is expressed. The maid who bullies her in the dream was her nurse in childhood and was still exercising her early authority, behaving more like a mother than a maid. It is against this maternal domination that, at first sight, the dream encourages her to rise. There must be, however, a good reason why her hand becomes arrested in trying to slap the maid's face. I thought the reason was this: her mother's body had to be her own house (in passing through it); by hurting her mother she would hurt herself, and this must stop as it leads to self-destruction.

"This is rather wonderful," the patient answered, "because it recalls the fight which I had with my mother over a friend eight years ago. She boxed my ears. I said, "Mum, I have stood a great deal from you, we are no longer mother and daughter, don't do it again." With that I hit her back, and we had a splendid fight. She put my shoulder out and I hurt her thumb. Ever since, my thumb has been giving me pain. I always had a sense of guilt about it, but I did not know why, as I forgot the fight with my mother. Now I realize it was her thumb. I hurt it and it hurts me."

This is a striking exemplification of the Law of the Talion, an eye for an eye, a tooth for a tooth. The dream ended before the dreamer passed through the house, but her problem has been stated by her recollection. Her meekness and submission to women in life was the retribution for her repressed aggression against the mother, the motives of which included her illegitimate birth. In going through the mysterious house, she would be born again, become legitimate and free. This is why the fetal sea has to be reclaimed. The dream envisages the end of the quest by arresting (i.e. stopping) her vindictive designs against her mother.

A Modern Wedding of Cana

One case sheds light on important practical aspects of pre-natal integration. The dreamer was a completely frigid woman who had a strong fixation on her brother and, on a remoter level, on her father. The desire to escape from identifying the men that came into her life with these two love images led to a development of lesbian tendencies, from the repression of which further conflicts arose. An understanding of these principal motivations put an end to her sexual anaesthesia. The dream which follows traces the origin of both emotional drives to the umbilical relationship to her mother and indicates, by striking unification and liberation symbols, that henceforward her freedom will be complete:

I was in bed and there were two men in my room. My boy friend was one, and he was lying fully dressed on my bed on top of the cover. The other man, whom I do not recognize, was about to leave. I did not want him to go, so he decided to stay. I felt happy that I succeeded in keeping him. After a while my boy friend was no longer there. I had bright red pajamas on and was admiring them, lying on my elbow. They were trimmed with gold. I have never seen anything so beautiful. I don't wear pajamas because I don't like anything around my waist when I am in bed. I sleep in a nightgown. But I liked these.

Then I was on a rocky mountain. I had to struggle to reach the top. There was no path or road and I was very tired when I reached it. There were no trees, but the rocks were covered with laurels. It was beautiful. There were two houses on this mountain top. I lived in the smaller one, while my step-grandfather and my step-grandmother inhabited the other. My step-grandfather died and left me alone on this terrible mountain with his wife. It was a very disagreeable situation. Then from nowhere another house appeared. It belonged to the people who lived next door to my mother and dad. When they cooked something special, they used to send a plateful over to my mother to taste. They were very good things. The wife was cooking again and the yard of their house was full of tables. I never saw so much food and of such variety in all my life. It seemed that they were having some sort of celebration. They made punch in an old, discarded bathtub. People were going with their cups to the tub and were drinking. It was strange, but with those people everything used to go.

The analysis of a dream may begin at any point. Sometimes the most promising approach is made through the oddest element. Punch-making in an old, discarded bathtub is rather unusual. The patient herself found it strange in the dream. Meditating over it, she was inclined to take it as something constructive. No one would discard an old bathtub unless first she had acquired a new one. She argued that not only was an ancient piece of equipment discarded and, by inference, replaced with a modern one, but that a new utility had been discovered for the old tub; instead of water it was now holding punch.

I observed that punch is a kind of wine. In a flash, she answered that the water was changed into wine, which suggests the wedding of Cana; and that wedding stands for unification, integration. The celebration, therefore, must have been a wedding celebration.

"Those people celebrated weddings in a big way, just like that. They must have been preparing for a wedding feast."

The laurels and her success in reaching the top of the mountain fit in with the idea of celebration. She suggested that laurels stand for victory.

"The orgies which they used to have in the days of Rome come to my mind."

She pronounced "orgies" as the "g" is pronounced in "good." When I called attention to it, she further associated: organ, origin, orgasm. Indeed, orgasm is almost inseparable from orgies. The victory, thus, is won over frigidity. That is why the water, a cold liquid is replaced by punch, a hot stimulant. In this connection, the mention of "organ" is most appropriate. As to "origin," the old bathtub eloquently speaks of it. One floats in a tub as a child floats in the amniotic fluid within its mother's womb. The tub, therefore, is an excellent symbol for a woman's genitalia. This symbol, in the present instance, seems to have a double application. It represents the patient's own vagina, in which coldness is replaced by passion, but it also stands for her mother's womb to which, by the change of water into wine, the origin of her frigidity is traced. If the principal aspiration of her libidinal life was the re-establishment of the umbilical relationship between herself and her mother, it stands to reason that she had no use for men. The mother's place could only be taken by other women. With men the illusion of accomplishing a return into the pre-natal state could not have been maintained. A man has no womb. The fantasy necessitated the development of lesbian tendencies. The distortion in her love life was due to an in-

377

tense pre-natal fixation on her mother. If she discarded the old tub, she would be free from this distortion.

It seems that this freedom also covers the incestuous tie to her father. The step-grandparents are parental substitutes. She shows alienation from both: from the father by letting her step-grandfather die, from the mother by resenting being left with her step-grandmother, and from both by living in a house of her own. The symbol of alienation is further determined by the sudden appearance of the Hungarian family. Hungarians are aliens and the patient knew that her analyst was of Hungarian extraction. It is the analyst who alienates her from her parents and helps her to her freedom. The celebration is justified both by the victory over frigidity and by the success of this alienation. The patient, after a hard struggle, reached the mountain top. The struggle is over, she wins the laurel crown of victory. She can have punch. The word, as a verb, is a symbol for intercourse; as a noun, with a capital P, it stands for the little man, the phallus.

In the first part of the dream, the red pajamas trimmed with gold stand out because, contrary to her conscious reactions, she was pleased with having them. She likes red, and red is frequently used in dreams in reference to passion. Pajamas are in two pieces. We speak of them as a pair. That, in itself, hints at unification, and the trimming in gold is a further allusion to a precious attainment. Pajamas are kept in place around the waist line by an elastic band. That is a tie. The lower, rejected self (sexual life) is tied up with the higher, spiritual one. The bed symbolizes the love situation. Two men are involved. It is tempting to assume that they represent the double aspect of the boy friend: father-brother and man. When he is above the cover, not only is a cover situation suggested but the barrier which kept the patient from him is also shown. If the brother and the father aspect disappears, as indeed the boy friend does in the dream, the male aspect can be accepted. Hence the patient's elation over her success in persuading the second man, the stranger, to stay. He is a stranger because the awakening of passion is a new phenomenon in her life.

The interpretation was enthusiastically accepted. In confirmation, the patient told the story of a vision which she had during the day after the dream. An old ship blew up. It was like a boat on the Mississippi. A famous literary man, after whom the patient's father was named, died in such an accident. She felt an urge to look up the story of this accident as she would learn something from it.

The dream had already shown what she could learn. The old boat is the old tub. Boats are frequently called tubs. By being blown up, it is eliminated as the old tub is by discarding. It is a father-mother symbol. She is becoming free of both the incestuous and lesbian tie. The origin of the lesbian tie we had explained. The incestuous tie appeared to have blossomed out of the same root. If the ultimate goal of a woman's libidinal aspirations is to re-establish the umbilical relationship with the mother, it is conceivable that the penis of the male would be discovered as a substitute for the umbilical cord, and that it is unconsciously accepted as such at that early age in which the father fixation first appears and in which the influence of the unconscious mind on fantasy life is almost totally unrestrained.

Summary

32.

SUMMARY

BOOK I—THE TRAUMA OF BIRTH

BIRTH and death are interchangeable terms. Of life after death we cannot be certain, but we know that we lived before birth in the pre-natal state. The change-over from pre-natal to post-natal life involves an ordeal as severe as dying. Hence the fear of death begins at birth and is based on a maelstrom of bewildering experiences that are covered by infantile amnesia but break through in nightmares or become converted into symptoms. Many of the symbols that represent birth are so clear and universal that they can be recognized immediately, but the effect of the trauma of birth is not always so apparent. The fear of rape or childbearing, for instance, seems to have little in common with birth because the mechanism of "translation" (my own term to describe the shifting of affect from another person to one's own body, in this case from mother's genitalia to the woman's own) has not been recognized.

The child's reactions to birth are always catastrophic. The later genitalization of the event increases the psychological complications with which the experience abounds. For this reason any event that threatens the self or the organs of procreation with destruction may mobilize the trauma of birth and cohere with it by a process of regressive associations. One can recognize birth dreams by a touch of fatality which accompanies them. This is an important diagnostic

383

feature. The dreamer cannot escape or bear the pressure except by waking up.

The breaking of the amniotic waters, the process of labor, injuries in actual birth, immediate post-natal impacts from the environment, the bewildering function of the sensorium and other physiological shocks provide a hotbed on which neurosis may build. Sleep-walking is a primitive attempt to solve the conflict by returning into the womb. An intelligent recreation of the conditions of birth and a re-living of the ordeal by simulation are techniques which the growing generation desperately needs.

Morbid suffocation fears and the air-hunger of fresh air fiends may originate in birth or in antecedent fetal distress due to the fact that the maternal body was no longer capable of providing fully for the needs of the unborn child. The sensation of a sudden loss of breath and the subsequent panic is one of the chief symptoms of claustrophobia, a widespread and serious incapacitation, producing acute physical and mental distress, which often combines with chronic insomnia and the fear of insanity. The orthodox analytic technique is too slow in alleviating this condition. To Birth Therapy both the primary suffocation fear and the secondary fear of being crushed yield in a dramatic manner.

The most common recurrent nightmare is that of falling through space. The old Freudian sexual explanation is insufficient. The fear of death is the most likely determinant. To primitive man meeting death by falling into an abyss must have been one of the first experiences of the race. The behaviorists claim that the fear of falling or loss of position is one of the original, unconditioned fears with which the child is born. Why should it be unconditioned when birth is a falling away from the mother's body and is equated, in the unconscious mind, with death? Here again is a challenge for Birth Therapy. Can it cure falling nightmares? My answer is an unhesitating yes.

Another common recurrent nightmare concerns water. In such dreams, the water is often identified with the amniotic fluid. Treatment of these nightmares on the uterine level delivered a woman from an allergy to fish from which she began to suffer after a miscarriage many years ago. The fear of floods and drowning or the fear of crossing bridges may develop in self-protection against the recurrence of an event that proved fatal to pre-natal security. Time stands still for the unborn child. We all carry an awareness of our fetal existence and birth locked up in the depths of our unconscious mind. Water is the symbol of life but also of death. A symbolic death in water may be the price we have to pay for a new life or rebirth, and we are as afraid of paying it as we were at the time of our first arrival into this world.

There is good reason to assume that the fear or fascination of another world arises from the basic biological experience of having lived in another world. All utopian visions reveal a nostalgia for the bliss which we lost on leaving the maternal womb. The intensity of the ordeal of birth may have a determining influence in our other-worldliness. It happens but very seldom that a patient is able to re-live emotionally the cataclysmic event of birth on the analytic couch as Yvette did. The factual value of such an experience is less important than the therapeutic result it may bring.

Morbid reactions to fire are very common. Alexander the Great was believed to have been conceived by a thunderbolt that fell on the belly of his mother. In the dreams of modern women we still meet with fire as a symbol of conception or birth. Sometimes it is replaced by hot water and steam. Sometimes it speaks of frigidity as a displaced genital resistance to the over-all bruising which the child's body receives in birth. In one instance, we see it combined with a terrible windstorm from which the dreamer always succeeded in escaping in the past until in reality a tornado caught her and hurled her car upside down into the flooded waters of a ravine with herself locked inside. Finally, we see the legendary Phoenix consumed in a blaze in the dream of a G.I. Joe (who had a policy with the Phoenix Life Insurance Company), representing the surrender of security of his old life and the acceptance of a new one.

Some gods of Hindu mythology are credited with the amazing feat of giving birth to themselves. Stranger than this is the story of the man who, symptomatically, gave birth to himself through his own anus. In Freudian terminology, the case falls under the heading of anal castration. But the term castration is used very loosely in psychoanalytic literature. Chapter 10, illustrating varieties of castration, clears up some of the confusion that surrounds this fascinating subject.

In discussing the role of the mother in the fear of rape we learn of the trauma of being born asleep, as revealed in the dream of a twice unhappily married woman. Subsequent inquiry proved that the reconstruction of her own birth was accurate; further that her rape fears were a cover memory for the greater fear of birth by a displacement of the all-over pressure on her body into pressure within her own genitalia.

Does sex shame originate in birth fantasies? Do recurrent examination dreams refer to a successful passing of the greatest test of fitness for life, that of passing from the pre-natal to the post-natal state? Should we look to the genital character of birth as the origin of incestuous emotions in our children? These are the questions on which the chapter on *Superstructures on Birth* dwells.

Varieties of Birth treats on the fantastic theories that survive on the unconscious level of our minds about the coming of babies in the absence of proper enlightenment in childhood. Thrombotic haemorrhoids may be the price that adults pay for buried anal birth fantasies. Clinical experience shows that all abdominal swellings are instinctively and immediately associated with pregnancy, and fantasies of self-impregnation by gases or by swallowing air may result from a translation of the mother's condition on to our own body irrespective of sex. Similarly, oral birth fantasies may lead to globus hystericus, tonsil, adenoid and thyroid swellings or tooth-extraction fantasies.

An understanding of the trauma of bearing is of great importance for public health. It is my contention that bearing a child becomes traumatic whenever the similarity between giving birth to a child and the experience of having been born approaches close to our threshold of awareness. The number of women who become panic-stricken at the prospect of bearing a child is larger than it is generally believed. Miscarriage or abortion often results from a protective mechanism set up unconsciously. The mother may pay a price for her panic even after confinement. Where the delivery was dreaded, after-pains of bearing are more likely to develop than in a case where the mother was comparatively fearless. Little do these mothers suspect that the morbid fear of bearing arose from the mother's identification of herself with the child in her womb, and that unconsciously the mother was expecting to give birth to herself. It is as if the mother had lost the distinction between being a mother and an unborn child. The miscarriage or abortion which may result from this confusion has dire consequences. An unconscious tribunal of justice converts the guilt into sickness. The dead child may be replaced by a cyst or tumor in the ovaries, the uterus or the breasts. In one clinical instance a painful verruca was produced on the patient's right foot just under the arch. In a dream it was spontaneously connected with an abortion. The extent of self-destruction by successive operations to which miscarriage and abortion guilt may lead knows almost no limit. It seems as if the woman who loses a child through her own fault would sin against the race, as if the retribution which follows would be an archaic evolutionary safeguard. Yet too much importance should not be attached to this appearance in view of the relative ease with which the guilt is resolved. Basically it seems to originate in the trauma of one's own birth.

The trauma of illegitimate birth raises a fascinating problem, the psychoanalytic angles of which have not yet been well explored. The imputation of illegitimacy alone is sufficient to produce severe psychic scarring. The voices which a schizophrenic patient heard in his head had a most spirited debate on the analytic couch about the merits and demerits of killing father who, for some time in the past, had refused to acknowledge the patient as legitimate.

The hunger for the breast in children who were weaned in pain and against strong resistance may lead to strange fantasies and afflictions in mature age. There is a fascinating story about a New York chemist who thought he discovered, in recurrent dreams, a cure for cancer in the sap of milkweed. There is another of a millionaire's daughter who became a jewel thief because of fantasies that she was born with a pearl in her navel. Love and food are synonymous and interchangeable terms for the unconscious mind. The breast-starved child can be recognized late in life by the tremendous food fantasies that fill his dreams. An overabundance of such dreams unfortunately sets up a corresponding physiological mechanism; an overflow of digestive juices will occur to dispose of the fantasy food with the result that the surplus acid will attack the walls of the stomach of the duodenum, producing serious gastric disturbances and eventual ulcers.

The mother's after-pains of bearing, as far as her body is concerned, are medically acknowledged and properly treated. No recognized therapy exists for the treatment of the after-pains of birth of the child. The most common after-pain is a compressive headache, usually described as steel bands around the skull. It is often possible to trace such headaches to the pressure of the pubic arch or of the instruments of delivery on the head in the course of birth. In other instances, severe pains in the navel may arise as an organismic reminder of the cutting of the umbilical cord and loss of the maternal body. I believe that epileptoid fainting spells may echo the trauma of birth, the catatonic phenomena being a re-enactment of the child's ordeal during the mother's labor. Easy bruising, a morbid fear of being touched, oversensitivity to bloodletting, to the smell of blood, to anaesthetics, to colds and to fever may also fall under the heading of after-pains of birth. Every traumatic birth dream is an after-pain. Originally the word nightmare was reserved for an oppressive dream in which pressure on the chest threatened the dreamer with suffocation. We may look for the genesis of such dreams in the atmospheric pressure on the uninflated chest of the new-born child. Menstrual disturbances frequently represent a complaint against the trauma of birth, the pain and disorder standing for an unconscious attempt to release the pressure through the corresponding part of feminine anatomy. Expose the hidden birth fear, and the menstrual distress disappears. In the male sex, the re-enactment of birth is more complicated than in the female. Some men are seized with anxieties during and after intercourse because their unconscious mind equates the penetration of a woman's genitalia with their own passing through the mother's uterus. If the anxiety is too severe, impotency or *ejaculatio praecox* develops. In other instances nocturnal priapism may manifest itself. The prevailing opinion that unconscious sexual fantasies are responsible for constant and painful night erections or that pressure of water in the bladder causes it appears not to be adequate. Sexual fantasies would come to light in the patient's dreams, the emptying of the bladder would stop the erection for the rest of the night, or pressure of water would provoke it in the daytime as well. None of these factors accounts for this disturbance. The absence of erotic dreams and the persistence of erection, even though the sexual appetite has been satisfied, suggest that the penis stands for the child stiff with fear because of memories of birth. Finally, two cases are adduced to illustrate air-hunger and water-hunger of the unborn as causing after-pains of birth.

We all suffer from dissociation, beginning from our birth. Our mind splits when we arrive into this world. This was confirmed by Harry Stack Sullivan in these words: "Man's first experience, birth, is schizophrenic." At a considerable cost, we adapt ourselves to this baffling world. Whether or not we pay with neurosis for this adaptation depends on our ability to withstand shocks before the crust between the conscious and unconscious mind becomes sufficiently hard to keep the stormy emotions of birth out of echoing range.

The corner-stone of Freudian psychology is catharsis (abreaction). It is said that unless the patient recovers the memory of the repressed and, in recovering it, re-lives the original event, he cannot become free. However, Freud conceded later that early memories may appear only in the form of fantasies from which the original situation can be reconstructed. Mental registration is not an exclusive attribute of the conscious mind. The unconscious mind records many impressions which the conscious mind is not able or too preoccupied to notice. Further, all repetitive acts give evidence of memory. The very function of our vegetative system is inconceivable without postulating an organismic memory and a registration not only of the process of growth but also of the reaction to dangers that threaten the whole of the organism with destruction. If the dream is an urgent message about pressure in the unconscious mind which demands release, there must be a way of releasing that which the conscious mind never experienced, or dreams cannot possibly serve a psychological purpose.

The way, as I practice it, is through building up in the conscious mind the knowledge that corresponds to the consciously never appreciated and never verbalized experiences of the pre-lingual period of our life. If truth makes us free, knowledge is just as likely to bring about emotional release as emotional release is likely to bring back forgotten knowledge. By the power of his intuition or by the evidence he has gathered, the analyst may present the truth to the patient with the effect of a shock, producing instantaneous catharsis and the cessation of annoying symptoms. This is the essence of the technique of releasing the trauma of birth.

Book II—RETURN INTO THE WOMB

Belief in a future life may spring from the certainty of a past existence the haunting glamor of which forever escapes clear recollection. Some project this certainty backwards and become firm believers in reincarnation; others project it forward and become spiritualists or theosophists. The instinctual acceptance of either direction rests on the simple foundation of having lived before birth within the mother's womb. Unexpected landscapes sometimes inspire a strange familiarity. The observer suffers from a curious depersonalization; reality becomes vague and undefined and a feeling of historicity, of living somewhere else, in a past and distant epoch takes its place. This is the mystery of the *déjà vue*. Pre-natal emotions, which the unconscious mind often clothes in scenic pictures of a fairy land, play an important part in the genesis of such sensations. Poets have always known how to translate into words and pictures these strange yearnings of the heart. In children and in eternally young seekers of adventure we find them manifesting themselves in a love of mysteries, in a fascination for secret doors, caves, treasure hunts, royalty and jungle fantasies. The appeal and success of Tarzan novels is chiefly due to a response from the pre-natal levels of our mind. Remotely, we feel identified with Tarzan because we all had jungle dreams when we were young and may still have them. That is, in some measure we still suffer from fetal nostalgia, and deep down we are as surly about our expulsion from Paradise as Adam and Eve were in Biblical days.

The search for pre-natal happiness emerges in many floating fantasies. Those that have a uterine setting are marked by curious exhilaration. The Bird Gods of Egypt probably owe their origin to such fantasies. The medicine men of ancient Mexico wore bird masks and used whistles in bird shape because the bird was a symbol of power; some birds, like the eagle, of supernatural power. Prophets of the Bible were caught up by the Lord. In Scotland, fairies were responsible for mysterious aerial transportations. The witches of the Middle Ages were carried to the Sabbath by the Devil, spiritualist mediums who figure in vanishing mysteries ascribe the feat to the spirits of the dead, while lesser miracle worshippers report experiences in astral projection. Modern man satisfies his hunger for uterine bliss by flying in planes, an example of how the desire to return into the womb can be harnessed constructively for the good of mankind.

The outstanding motive behind the desire to return into the womb is the attainment of happiness in the only perfect form we have known it. It is from this inner assurance that the Biblical concept of Heaven arose, and the measure of organismically remembered perfection is the very drive behind our ceaseless struggle for betterment. In normal circumstances, the memory of this happiness is an ideal and inspiration. For the neurotic, it is a promise of easy escape from unhappiness. The simplest of such escape fantasies manifests itself by retirement into bed. As a faithful friend, Brother Bed has few rivals. Closest is the home itself. Neurotics who closet themselves in their houses and deny entrance to others attempt to lock out the world in the manner of the unborn, whose happiness depended on complete isolation. If birth creates a dissociation, by returning into the womb we would escape from a sort of schizophrenia. This, however, is an idle dream. Life progresses by complexity and diversity. Schizophrenia has its redeeming features. We cannot, with impunity, become a-sociates of the womb.

A good deal is yet to be learned about the driving power which pre-natal nostalgia plays in our culture. From the omnific emotions of the unborn, fantasies of great historical mission or of demonic power may develop. Many adults live the life of a fetus in the womb of the world. Most of them are eternal children, always leaning on somebody else, never making an effort except in demanding unceasing attention for themselves. Some clothe their fetal drives in a religious garb and become ascetics, living in dried-out wells, deserted dens of wild beasts or among the tombs. Others shut out the world by hysteric blindness in order to recapture the happiness of the prenatal night, to be fed and looked after as they were by the mother's body before birth. Still others are human kangaroos, returning into their own pouches in a psycho-physical manner. One can carry oneself in a pendulous belly, a blown up stomach or in any organ which is expendable. Self-love knows no end to monstrous manifestations. He who is not carried, must carry himself at all cost.

There are, however, respectable aspirations also behind fetal return fantasies. To find out the meaning of life is one. Death is an unknown quantity. Birth is more familiar ground. If we were able to retrace our steps to the very source of life, back to the mother's womb, we might find the answer to the mystery of our existence. At least, we will not have this splendid illusion wrested away from us.

To find a new life by re-birth is the best known quest, well represented in the myths of the race all over the world. The place of miraculous metamorphosis can only be reached by overcoming difficulties of an incredible character. It is guarded from the quest of the average mortal by the inaccessibility of the approach. In Ayesha's sudden death on re-entering the living fire from which she had emerged two thousand years before in the glory of eternal youth, Sir Rider Haggard presents us with a beautiful allegory of the penalty attendant on our yearning to return into the womb. From that fountain of youth, from that living fire we once emerged in the splendor of physical perfection. If we did find the way of return, our fate would be sealed by death. The quest, therefore, must be allegorical. Only by a spiritual journey can we reach the fountain of eternal youth. On the modern, illuminated levels of our mind the return into the womb may spell spiritual regeneration, a gathering

392

of fresh energies from the deepest strata of unconscious life. Hence the query arises: is the desire to return a fulfilment of *Thanatos*, Freud's death instinct, or is the death instinct rather a manifestation of the desire to return? If death is not a quest for another life but an escape and a yearning for peace, the answer is in the womb. But if Freud's death instinct is only an incentive for return into the womb, we might neutralize it by integrating the emotions, stored in the dim recesses of the human mind, that group around pre-natal experiences. To my view, the death instinct spells life, and I believe that by proper analytic technique this instinct may be harnessed for spiritual regeneration.

The psychic life of modern man reflects the same archaic imagery that, as witnessed by our legends, our forefathers possessed. A hero is swallowed by a fish, dragon or sea serpent and travels in its belly from East to West. On reaching the Western shore, the hero kills the monster from inside and emerges victoriously, re-born, basking in the glory of immortal life. The dream of a post office clerk and the Jonah and the Whale fantasy of a twenty-five-year-old girl reveal the agelessness of the human spirit. There is no sign of *Thanatos* in either. They both want to live and not to die. The desire to die is not human.

The idea of re-entering the mother's body is frequently accompanied by sexual fantasies, as birth cannot be divorced from its genital setting. In pictorial perception, birth is an incestuous event for men and a homosexual event for women, as the body of the infant is in a phallic relationship to the mother's genitalia. This is the explanation why the re-enactment of birth by a return fantasy stirs up repressed sexual ideas. Essentially, these ideas revolve around the mystery of sexual ecstasy. A regression to the pre-natal levels may develop in the hope that the bliss of the unborn would reveal, for the emotionally arrested and frigid adult, the precious secret of sexual ecstasy. The admixture of this motive mellows the nightmarish character of birth dreams and the return fantasy may become a mystic experience the effect of which may survive for a considerable time.

The savage emotions that ruled the human race when it was

young may well up in unsuspected abundance from the archaic levels of children's minds. When we attempt to verbalize such emotions from the dreams of adults, we find ourselves confronted with this melodramatic representation: a small child re-enters its mother's womb for the purpose of destroying a sibling in order to eliminate a threat to its own security. Such fantasies of fetal destruction may appear too absurd but they are psychological material of considerable value. Judged by the dreams they inspire, the pressure of such fantasies is intense enough to provide a hotbed for neurosis or even psychosis. Sometimes they emerge explosively, sometimes reluctantly and in a veiled form, but whichever is the case an understanding of their infantile nature brings the dreamer considerable relief, and the guilt feeling to which they give rise fades away to the degree that such nightmares peter out.

Sandor Ferenczi, the great Hungarian psychoanalyst, for a long time the chief disciple of Freud, was the first to claim that behind a man's coitus fantasies the desire to return into the womb may be concealed. This means that in the memory of pre-natal life may be hidden the roots of the incestuous feelings of the male towards his own mother and of the lesbian emotions of the female. They both spring from a biological urge to re-establish the union with the mother, which inevitably becomes sexualized. It is easier for a man to repress homosexual desires than for a woman. As a rule, men take to homosexuality to escape from the mother; women take to it to gain her. The ordinary interpretation of dream material in terms of homosexual and incestuous aspirations very often produces a deep shock in the patient's psyche. Summing up the issue more in biological than in moral terms relieves the patient because he sees himself accepted as a normal human being. Many sexual fantasies are purely of an umbilical character, the penis taking on the role of the cord. Castration traumata, in Freudian psychology, carry back as far as circumcision. There they stop. Girls are not circumcised and when they have dreams like boys, we are told that a girl is born castrated. If circumcision leaves a traumatic shock, there is no justification for ignoring the cutting of the umbilical cord. It often leads to more complications than circumcision. But admitting the trauma of the cutting of the umbilical cord would be equivalent to accepting the trauma of birth through the back door, and the Freudian movement still shrinks from it as a supreme sacrifice because it vaguely threatens the Oedipus situation as the core around which the life of the neurotic must revolve.

The incestuous and homosexual drive in man has another more powerful determinant than the desire to recapture the static bliss of uterine existence. This motive is constructive and is furnished by man's never-ceasing quest to find the Beloved. The quest is rooted in the fundamental bi-sexual nature of humanity. At some remote evolutionary epoch, the sexes were united in the proto-human body, as they still are in some lower forms of life. The religious myths of both civilized and primitive peoples have ample references to this androgynous state. The rib from which Eve was fashioned means, in psychological language, that Eve was split off from Adam. In this wording, the Biblical story conceals a profound evolutionary truth. Ever since the sexes have been separated, man is restlessly searching for his Eve, the missing part of himself. "Whom God hath joined together let no man put asunder" clearly suggests that the marriage ceremony is a restitution fantasy—doomed, for that very reason, to disappointment both for the male and the female. This disappointment is the deepest determinant of a woman's masculine envy. It is said that a woman does not accept her femininity until she bears a son. The reason, on the foregoing theory, is that only in the male, arising from her womb, can she find an objectification of that for which she archaically yearns. It is still an illusion, but it comes as near as Nature permits to the fulfilment of an age-old dream. The psychological data gathered from an intensive study of dreams in a pre-natal setting indicate that sexual determination is achieved at the price of considerable struggle. Further, the appearance is as if the lost sexual potential had not been extinguished but had retired underground to haunt the winner for the rest of his life. To embryologists this may sound absurd, but whether this is only a fantasy of humanity or not, there is great virtue in it for therapy. It assures a simplicity of presentation of the facts of bi-sexuality and elicits gratifying response. Further, it can be demonstrated that some of the deepest yearnings of the race are traceable to this concept of bi-sexuality. It seems as if the poets, the greatest dreamers of the race, had always realized that the quest for Eve in the outside world is doomed to failure, because the real Eve only exists within. In neurotics, some of the strangest dreams revolve around this problem of unification, and the final problem to which they lead is: can the conflict be merely psychic; may not man have a composite male-female soul; may not sexual determination become a traumatic event because the primary sexual organization exacts a corresponding psychic unbalance?

Book III—TRAUMATA OF THE UNBORN

We have now progressively advanced to the point where the fly in the ointment is discovered. Pre-natal dreams do not always reflect a state of rapture. The life of the unborn is not necessarily one of unbroken bliss. The unborn child is dependent on the mother's blood-stream for oxygen, for food and for the elimination of its waste products. There are many maternal afflictions that affect and perhaps weaken the child before birth. Many children seem to start post-natal life with a handicap. A careful record of the period of gestation could give psychoanalysts valuable light on the factual basis of fantasies which later appear concerning the pre-natal state. We cannot approach the psyche of the unborn except through the study of post-natal dreams with a pre-natal setting. It is not easy to decide whether a fear in a dream is retrojected from the higher levels of the mind to the pre-natal foundations, or whether there was an actual mobilization of deeply buried, organismic memories. The story of the baby that crept out of bed during the night, went downstairs and ate up all the dog food is entertaining and instructive as it points to love starvation as the cause of pre-natal unhappiness. Dr. Sadger's extreme statement that "the embryo already feels plainly whether its mother loves it or not" could be countered by the query: why should not the mother be equally affected by the unborn's mental state? It is tempting to speculate whether such thoughts could lead to a better understanding of certain queer symptoms that occur in pregnancy.

Summary

It has been stated throughout the preceding pages that the fear of death originates in birth. The objection that might be raised against this statement is: how is it that the intelligence that builds the body and the brain does not prepare the child mentally for birth and thus safeguard it from the worst of its agony? We do not know why, and we cannot even be too hasty in deciding that the unborn is not prepared mentally for birth. It is possible that the unborn child may have a premonition of the transition it has to face, but such foreshadowing of the future might become a source of anxiety in itself. Furthermore, we have not yet exhausted the sorrows of the unborn, to say nothing of external shocks against which embryonic development provides no more defense than the gravitational balance of our solar system does against the intrusion of a comet from the void. It may well be that shocks from an external source are responsible for the upsetting of the equilibrium between mental and physical preparedness for birth. Thus it follows that the fear of death may have a remoter source than birth, which may appear independently or telescoped into the trauma of birth itself.

The first of such external shocks arises from the fact that Nature places no seasonal limitation on man's sexual activity; the unborn child is not protected against the violence of parental intercourse in the advanced stages of gestation, and thus it is exposed to an ordeal the traumatic nature of which is clearly traceable in dreams throughout our lives. It is possible that the dissociation caused by birth is antedated by such shocks because there are dreams that indicate a striking difference in impact on the unborn child of a gentle parental contact. In the case in question, the patient's painful and disorderly menstrual periods suggested that she suffered from the fear of bleeding to death. This, in turn, arose from the fear of rape, the ultimate source of which led back beyond birth to parental intercourse traumata. All fears tend to projection. The fear of the unknown, when projected into the world, imbues it with an unintended hostility. This resulted in a fear of strangers, which was the prevailing affliction of this patient's life. Other dreams of a definite pre-natal character suggest that the well-known fantasy that the mother has a penis may also originate in memories of ante-natal aggression, in

397

which the invading organ is taken as part of the maternal environment. A further important point is that the pre-natal attack apparently generates an aggressive reaction which may find objectification in the father or in both parents. The thought which some dreams display is that not until both are destroyed is the pre-natal security complete. Decapitation dreams with a pre-natal background permit the assumption that father-castration fantasies may stretch beyond the Oedipal and birth situation and originate in the fetal period of one's life.

Filed away in the mysterious recesses of the human organism, there must be a record of the master plan on which the human body is built, just as there is a record of the impacts which hit the unborn within the womb and a record of the adaptation to those impacts. An organismic memory in which this blueprint is preserved and in which it can be consulted is a minimum postulate. But how can any adaptation take place without an organismic mind or organismic consciousness which controls the relationship of the growing human being to the maternal environment within the womb? "The organizer" of Prof. Hans Spemann, which is a growth directing monitor, or "the biological field" of Paul Weiss admits the same necessity of assumption. The relationship between the unconscious mind and this organismic consciousness is none too clear. Structurally, the organismic consciousness is a deeper stratum, perhaps the very bedrock of the unconscious mind, ordinarily beyond our psychological reach, yet an ever-present fundus without which no human edifice can be built. Groddeck and Jung tried to free us from the limitations of the Freudian concept of unconscious mind by taking a leap into the spiritual, Groddeck by his concept of the "It," Jung by his idea of the impersonal unconscious. They both missed an important stepping stone: the embryonic stage. They ignored the psychic life of the unborn. The concept of the organismic mind helps to bridge this gap. It is less than Groddeck's "It." It does not embrace post-natal consciousness and is not endowed with the mystic powers which Groddeck ascribes to the "It." Experimental findings in telepathy at Duke University and elsewhere now form a sufficiently impressive body of facts to show that the unconscious mind has its own chan-

Summary

nels of awareness. Telepathy might be one, and the precise nature of even this one is totally incomprehensible to the conscious mind. However, no two human beings are closer to each other than the mother and the unborn child. Hence telepathy, if at all operative between human beings, should be operative between the mother and her child. It may fulfil very important functions. It may act as a shock absorber for the weaning of the child from the mother's body in birth. The mother's fond expectations and reassuring thoughts may have a very salutary influence on the psyche of the unborn. But if so, the reverse would be equally true. The loneliness of the unwanted child may be more than a post-natal psychic structure, it may reach back to its psychic isolation within the womb. Telepathy as a function of the organismic mind may be a profoundly disturbing assumption for present-day psychology, yet it may not be anything new; for all we know, telepathy may be an archaic method of communication antedating the development of speech, hence the faculty that comes automatically into play when the embryo re-enacts in nine months the whole evolution of the race. Present-day scientific arguments do not admit the possibility of the fetus being affected by a shock which the mother suffers because there is no nervous connection between the mother and the child. But prove the existence of telepathy, and you have proven that shock effects can be transmitted from one mind to another without nervous connection. This gives a new lease of life to the discredited belief in birth-marks, but worse than that, it opens up new avenues of shocks for the unborn in death wishes of the mother against the coming child and in attempts at producing abortion.

On the pleasanter side of the ledger another popular superstition raises its head: that parental passion helps to mould the psychic life of the child. So much is clear that the intensity of pre-natal fears is apparently dependent on the violence and frequency of parental intercourse; and that where the violence is less, signs of pleasure reaction begin to emerge. While this reaction is more difficult to trace, it is sufficiently outstanding to justify the query: is there a love life of the unborn? The query is supported by Wilhelm Preyer's statement in his *Special Physiology of the Embryo* that "the ability to distinguish pleasure and pain is pre-natal and inherited and in the true sense congenital." It is easy to admit that the fetus must be physically affected by the state of glow of the maternal body. As a derivative of intercourse, the metabolic stimulation of the fetal body may play an unsuspected part in post-natal sexual precocity, nymphomania and satyriasis. The psychic transmission of pleasure from the mother to the child is much more questionable. But we are interested in dreams and we must follow them to whatever pastures they lead. The dream is stranger than truth, and stranger than fiction.

The release of the trauma of birth is the introductory phase of the integration of pre-natal traumata. The more vital phase concerns the shocks suffered prior to birth. In order to release these shocks, the conscious mind must take cognizance of their existence and nature. As no verbal mechanism was available at the time of their occurrence, an intellectual grasp of the nature of these deep, subterranean upheavals is the pre-requisite of their catharsis. If, for temporary intellectual bias, the facts cannot be accepted, a period of mental growth will ensue during which these vital issues will remain in abeyance. I learned this lesson from an odd and complicated dream of my own five years after I had dreamed it. Only then did I discover that a message was hidden in the dream: you will not understand this just yet; nevertheless, struggle with it as best as you can; the real meaning will dawn on you in time.

It did.

CPSIA information can be obtained at www.ICGtesting.com
Printed in the USA
BVOW05s2153130715

408661BV00019B/238/P